A SILENT SUCCESS

A Silent Success

Master's Education in the United States

CLIFTON F. CONRAD

JENNIFER GRANT HAWORTH

SUSAN BOLYARD MILLAR

The Johns Hopkins University Press

Baltimore and London

This book was prepared under the auspices of the Council of Graduate Schools with the support of a grant from The Pew Charitable Trusts. Any opinions, findings, conclusions, or recommendations expressed herein are those of the individual authors and do not necessarily reflect the views of the Council of Graduate Schools or the supporting foundation.

The Johns Hopkins University Press
2715 North Charles Street
Baltimore, Maryland 21218-4319
The Johns Hopkins Press Ltd., London

Library of Congress Cataloging-in-Publication Data

Conrad, Clifton.
    A silent success : master's education in the United States / Clifton F. Conrad, Jennifer Grant Haworth, Susan Bolyard Millar.
        p. cm.
    Includes bibliographical references and index.
    ISBN 0-8018-4508-4
    1. Master of Arts degree. 2. Universities and colleges—United States—Graduate work. I. Haworth, Jennifer Grant. II. Millar, Susan Bolyard. III. Title.
LB2385.C66   1993
378.2'4—dc20   92-1612

A catalog record for this book is available from the British Library.

Dedications

Pam, Erin, and Abigail Conrad
John Conrad and Virginia Margaret Angell Conrad (1923–69)

Steven Haworth and Dorothy Lewis Sanville

In memory of Ruth Bleier

Contents

viii   **Contents**

Tables

Foreword

This book describes the past, present, and perhaps future of the master's degree in the United States. The authors, who examined a wide variety of programs and institutions, present a unique and comprehensive view of this most protean degree, a view that derives from their interactions with hundreds of people directly involved in master's education. This book is about master's education: live, in real time, the way it is.

What emerges will surprise some people, confirm the long-held beliefs of others, and even shock a few. But, above all, this book provides, for the first time, a way to think about master's education on its own terms, independent of field of study, type of institution, or other academic degrees that precede or follow it. This runs counter to a more traditional view of the master's degree, which holds that there is no way to understand master's education except at the individual program level, that it is impossible to generalize about the nature and quality of these programs, and that the value of master's education is related to its use as preparation for other advanced degrees, particularly the doctorate.

Most people who pursue master's degrees do so by intent, not default. They are seeking a kind of advanced education designed to expand their understanding and improve their skills so that they can be more effective in their careers. For the most part, they believe that they are well served by the education they receive. But they also believe that they are more than just recipients; they are participants, along with faculty, administrators, and employers, in what is probably the most direct link between society and higher education: the master's degree.

It is the voices of these participants which you will hear as you read this book. We urge you to listen.

Nils Hasselmo
President, University of Minnesota
Chair, National Advisory Board, National Study of Master's Degrees

Barbara J. Solomon
Vice Provost for Graduate and Professional Studies and Dean,
 Graduate Studies, University of Southern California
Chair, Steering Committee of Graduate Deans, National Study
 of Master's Degrees

Jules B. LaPidus
President, Council of Graduate Schools

Preface

During the last several decades, as colleges and universities in the United States responded vigorously to complex demands and opportunities fueled by the larger society, considerable national attention has focused on bachelor's and doctoral education. Meanwhile, relatively little attention has been given to master's education, which has experienced unprecedented expansion and diversification throughout this period. From 1970 to 1990, there was a 48 percent increase in the number of master's degrees annually awarded, and more than one-half of all master's degrees earned in the history of American higher education were conferred. Since 1987, about 300,000 master's degrees—nearly one of every four degrees earned at the bachelor's level and above—have been granted each year.

As master's education increasingly came to be viewed as an important means for enriching the knowledge and skills of professionals in an information-centered society, much of the expansion and diversification of master's education occurred in professional programs. Since the early 1980s, well over four-fifths of all master's degrees have been awarded in professional fields such as engineering, education, nursing, and business. Many new fields of study aimed at preparing individuals for the emerging professions also were introduced, including discipline-based and interdisciplinary programs in the liberal arts and sciences such as applied anthropology and environmental studies. Paralleling these developments, many institutions developed innovative approaches to master's education, including external degree programs, new instructional technology, and alternative delivery systems.

Perhaps most compelling, significant changes in master's education have taken place in terms of clientele. Of the people earning master's degrees since the early 1980s, about 90 percent earned degrees in professional fields outside the traditional liberal arts and sciences. Over 50 percent of degree recipients were women, and more than 12 percent were members of ethnic minority groups. About one-half of all master's students were thirty years of age or older, and two-thirds were enrolled part-time. For the most part, this is not the population that graduate education in the United States has served historically. Yet it is increasingly the population upon which business, industry, education, government, and our health care systems depend for expertise and leadership.

Aware of these developments, and concerned about the lack of attention given to master's education, in the mid-1980s the Council of Graduate Schools (CGS), a comprehensive organization comprising all aspects of graduate education, appointed a task force to develop plans for a national study. With support from The Pew Charitable Trusts CGS—under the leadership of its president, Jules LaPidus—asked Clifton Conrad to serve as principal investigator for the study. In 1989 he invited Jennifer Grant Haworth, Susan Millar, and Karen Prager to work collaboratively with him in conducting a two-year study of master's programs in the United States. To oversee the study CGS appointed a thirteen-member National Advisory Board chaired by Nils Hasselmo, president of the University of Minnesota, which included representation from colleges and universities, federal and state government, professional associations, foundations, and business and industry. In addition, CGS appointed a seven-member Steering Committee of Graduate Deans chaired by Barbara Solomon, dean of graduate studies at the University of Southern California, whose membership represented a wide range of colleges and universities offering master's degrees.

The researchers, in concert with the advisory board and steering committee, agreed that the overarching purpose of the study was to investigate, interpret, and generalize about master's programs in ways that would benefit individuals involved in the development, planning, evaluation, and study of master's programs. Our intended audience included not only administrators (including graduate deans) and faculty in higher education but also other groups both within and without higher education who have an interest in master's programs: state and federal policymakers; people from professional associations; employers in business and industry and across the professions; and current students, prospective master's students, and graduates of master's programs.

To serve these multiple audiences we formulated three questions to guide the study. First, how do people directly and indirectly involved in master's education interpret and evaluate their master's experiences? Second, to the extent there are differences in the experiences of people involved in master's education, how best can we interpret these differences? Third, what characteristics, or "attributes," of master's programs do people involved (directly and indirectly) believe contribute most to enhancing the "quality" of master's experiences?

In addressing these questions we used an open-ended, multicase study design that was grounded in the perspectives of 781 interviewees representing forty-seven master's programs in eleven different fields of study. Inasmuch as we learned in our review of the literature that the "voices" of many groups involved in master's education—notably students, alumni, and employers of graduates of master's programs—had not been included in the published discourse, we interviewed a broad range of people involved in master's education. Specifically, we interviewed people from six different groups who, from our perspective, had a vital stake in master's education. These six "stakeholder" groups included institutional and program administrators, faculty, students, program alumni, and employers of program graduates.

Our interviewees—the people we interviewed between 1989 and 1991—provided us with a vast amount of information and a wide variety of perspectives. After many months of analyzing this interview material, we came to interpret master's education in three major ways. First, we began to understand stakeholder experiences, and variations among them across the forty-seven programs in our sample, in relation to choices made mostly by administrators and faculty in five "decision-situations," that is, particular types of circumstances in which stakeholders make decisions that influence how they and others experience their master's programs. These decision-situations, in order of their relative importance, are: approach to teaching and learning, program orientation, departmental support, institutional support, and student culture.

Second, using the choices that stakeholders made in the first three decision-situations as a tool for helping us differentiate among programs, we developed a typology that partitioned the forty-seven cases into four clusters. This typology, based on what interviewees communicated to us about their overall master's experiences, is comprised of four "idealized" program types: ancillary, career advancement, apprenticeship, and community-centered.

Third, and also on the basis of what we learned from interviewees, we sought to describe those attributes of master's programs which contributed to the quality of stakeholders' master's experiences. These attributes represent program characteristics and conditions that substantially strengthened stakeholders' master's experiences and often had positive, long-term effects on participants in master's education. We defined four clusters of attributes: culture, planned learning experiences, resources, and leadership and the human dimension.

Organized around these three broad sets of findings, which are based on three different analytical approaches to our interview material, this book is divided into four parts. In part 1 we provide the setting for the study, including a review of the literature and a discussion of our approach to inquiry. In part 2 we analyze what we learned from our interviewees by organizing our interview material around choices stakeholders made in the five key decision-situations. In part 3 we devote a chapter to each of the four idealized program types. Finally, in part 4 we extend our cross-case analysis by generalizing across all forty-seven cases in our sample, organizing our interview material around those program attributes that most contributed to high-quality master's experiences. We also present our conclusions and raise some considerations aimed at reinforcing the vitality of master's education. Introductions to each of these four parts provide an overview of the chapters and discuss the analytical approaches we used to weave our way through our interview material. These introductions elaborate on our analytical approaches and assumptions, some of which are not addressed within chapters, and, thus, are important.

Throughout the book, we continuously seek to make explicit our role, as researchers, in relation to the people who we interviewed and the book that we wrote. Our role, as we defined it, was to listen to and learn from interviewees and, based on what they told us, to interpret the character of their master's experiences in ways that would be useful to people involved in the planning, evaluation, and study of master's programs.

In closing, we emphasize two points. First, in collaborating on the writing of this book, we sought to write in a single voice, as a collective "we." Just as we interacted with one another throughout the duration of our research, we constantly engaged one another—through questioning, challenging, persuading, negotiating—during the writing and editing process. This book is the result of our joint understandings and efforts, and authorship of the book is shared equally among us.

Second, this book is animated, for the most part, by the voices of the people we interviewed. To distinguish our voices from the voices of interviewees, we rely extensively on quotations from interviewees throughout the book. We invite readers, through these quotations and our more mediated interpretations of stakeholder perspectives, to join us in an ongoing conversation aimed at understanding the experiences of those who participate in master's education.

Acknowledgments

While we assume full responsibility for the contents, this book is grounded in the efforts of many people, beginning with the 781 individuals we interviewed and the liaisons in each of forty-seven master's programs who helped us identify and arrange meetings with interviewees. These people generously gave us their time and candidly shared with us their perspectives on master's education. We would like to acknowledge others as well.

First, we wish to thank three organizations upon whose support the study depended: the Council of Graduate Schools (CGS), for initiating and generously supporting the research and for allowing us to pursue our work free of constraint; The Pew Charitable Trusts, for providing a grant of $400,000 which financed the study; the Wisconsin Center for Education Research (WCER) at the University of Wisconsin–Madison, for providing space, technical support, and an enriching environment.

Second, we wish to thank the following individuals and institutions: The individual we feel most gratitude to is Karen Prager, our other colleague on the project. For a year and a half, she committed fully to the study then took a position with the Center on Organization and Restructuring of Schools just as we commenced writing the book. She was a perceptive interviewer and analyst, who continuously brought fresh insights throughout the interview phase of the study. In addition, Karen produced many well-crafted summaries that were essential to us in writing this book, and she made many helpful editorial suggestions on drafts of the book.

As president of the Council of Graduate Schools, it was Jules LaPidus who first recognized the need for a national study of master's education. His stewardship was vital to us throughout the study. Jules was actively involved in every phase of our work: providing encouragement, raising questions about our research design and analysis of interview material, responding in detail to each draft of the book, and arranging meetings of the National Advisory Board and Steering Committee of Graduate Deans.

Although he made many suggestions, not once did he try to impose his own views. For his generosity, and for his steadfast leadership and commitment to enhancing the experiences of people involved in master's education, we are most grateful. Moreover, we greatly appreciate the contributions of Thomas Linney and Peter Syverson of the Council of Graduate Schools, both of whom contributed technical expertise and helpful suggestions throughout the study.

Under the thoughtful and dedicated leadership of Nils Hasselmo, president of the University of Minnesota, the National Advisory Board provided instructive advice in various ways and reminded us that this book should be useful to a range of audiences. Besides Nils Hasselmo, the members of the board included: Robert Armstrong, John Corbally, Edmund Cranch, Gordon Davies, Emerson Elliot, Judith Glazer, Kay Kohl, Shirley Malcolm, James Mingle, Allan Ostar, Ted Settle, and Jules LaPidus.

Under the adept leadership of Barbara Solomon, dean of graduate studies at the University of Southern California, the Steering Committee of Graduate Deans was made up of the following graduate deans: Jim Anker, Hazel Garrison, Robert Holt, Judith Liebman, Henry Solomon, and Vivian Vidoli. This group was actively involved throughout the study, providing us with insights into the kinds of questions that would help to make the study useful to administrators and faculty and giving us extended feedback on our research design, analytic procedures, and findings.

Andrew Porter, director of the Wisconsin Center for Education Research, is not only a fine scholar but also a talented administrator, who knows how to provide the kind of supportive environment which nourishes scholarly inquiry. His interest in the study was much appreciated. We are grateful to him and to the helpful support of many others at WCER, including Sandy Treptow and Jerry Grossman.

We are grateful to Jacqueline Wehmueller, acquisitions editor at the Johns Hopkins University Press, for her immediate, enthusiastic, and unflagging support for the study. In the many months during which we had the pleasure of working with her Jackie provided invaluable substantive and editorial advice. Her acumen, catholicity of mind and style, and commitment to what we sought to accomplish far exceeded our expectations.

Robert Holt, professor and former dean of the Graduate School at the University of Minnesota, who chaired the CGS task force that developed plans for the national study, was involved in every phase. We greatly appreciate his scholarly insights, discerning observations, and strong support.

Jim Anker, Jon Barwise, Estela Bensimon, Colleen Capper, Edmund Cranch, Patricia Gumport, Bob Holt, Joseph Kauffman, Judith Liebman, Terry Millar, Maureen Noonan, Gary Rhoades, Patricia Scott, Ted Settle, Peter Syverson, and William Tierney carefully read and provided many useful suggestions on drafts of this book. We are grateful for their friendship and colleagueship as well as their generosity.

Lois Turner typed many drafts of the manuscript and supported our work in myriad ways. We are grateful for her expertise, patience, good humor, and extraordinary support throughout the study. Rose Byrd arranged our extensive travel plans and provided logistical support during our field visits.

Last, each of us wishes to thank our families and friends: Clif Conrad expresses deep appreciation to Pam Conrad, whose own commitments to education and children he has always admired, for her enduring support. He also thanks their two daughters, Abigail and Erin, for their patience and understanding and for the joy and meaning they have brought to his life. In addition, he wishes to thank many friends and colleagues he has worked with over the last two decades who have contributed to his understanding of higher education: Robert Blackburn, David Eagan, Judy Diane Grace, Martine Hammond, Larry Leslie, Ann Morey, Anne Pratt, Gary Rhoades, Paul Schrode, Patricia Scott, Ted Settle, Sheila Slaughter, Mary Talbott, David Webster, Richard Wilson, and Jean Conover Wyer. Last, he wishes to acknowledge his parents for their formative influences on his life and work: his father, John, for his example of a lifetime commitment to education and public service; and the memory of his mother, Virginia Margaret Angell Conrad, for her passionate commitment to learning and to serving others.

Jennifer Grant Haworth expresses her heartfelt thanks to Steve Haworth, her husband, and Dorothy Lewis Sanville, her mother, for their cheerful endurance and loving support as she wrote, worried, dreamt, and, for the most part, lived this book for the past year. In addition, since much of this book addresses issues related to teaching and learning, she would like to thank the many teachers who inspired and nurtured her interests in social science and education, including: Terry Astuto, David Buckholdt, Howard Dorholt, Ann Egan, James Holstein, Mary Ladish, Ellen Condliffe Lagemann, Dale Mann, and Sister Judith Schmitt. Finally, Jennifer wishes to acknowledge that without the strength, hope, joy, and comfort she experiences from her faith, family, and friends, completing this book would have been far more difficult and markedly less fulfilling.

Susan Bolyard Millar voices thanks for the support Ruth Bleier gave her. She thanks Baine Alexander for sharing her journey and Jon Barwise for the role he played in her understanding of the nature of meaning. Other enduring friends whom she thanks are Albert Beaver, Elwin Cammack, Jim McGloin, Naomi McGloin, Alice Robbin, and Ruth Robertson. She is grateful to her new colleagues—Estela Bensimon, James Fairweather, Linda LaSalle, Karen Paulson, James Ratcliff, Patrick Terenzini,

William Tierney, and Maryellen Weimer—for support during the completion of this book. For the confidence and love that lie at the center of her work, she acknowledges her parents, Kirk Bolyard and Celia Wicks Bolyard. She greatly appreciates the support of her children, Jessica Millar and Matthew Millar. Her deepest gratitude goes to Terry Millar, who sustains her in all ways.

A SILENT SUCCESS

PART ONE

THE SETTING

In most books reporting the findings of a major study, the first several chapters include a review of the literature and a discussion of the method of inquiry to provide readers with a context. We adopt this conventional approach on the grounds that our review and critique of the literature greatly informed our study and because familiarity with our approach is essential to understanding our analysis and presentation of the material upon which our findings and conclusions are based.

In chapter 1 we explore the published literature on master's education in the United States. We identify those who participated in the published conversation and consider their findings, observations, and perspectives. In so doing, we organize the literature into four periods: 1859–1900, 1900–1945, 1945–70, and 1970–91. We conclude the chapter by suggesting two major limitations of the literature. First, we observe that there has been little scholarship on the experiences of those directly involved in master's education. Second, we note that the published discourse presents the perspectives of people holding a limited range of positions relative to master's programs—mostly administrators and faculty—and leaves silent those in other important positions: students, alumni, and employers.

In chapter 2 we present our approach, which was organized around a multicase study design grounded in the perspectives of 781 interviewees ("positioned subjects"), who represented 47 master's programs throughout the United States. These interviewees included institutional and program administrators, faculty, students, alumni, and employers. We begin the chapter with a brief discussion of our positioned subject approach to inquiry. We then describe our multicase study design, including our selection of cases (programs) and interviewees, and develop the implications that this positioned subject approach had for our fieldwork procedures, analysis, and the writing of this book.

Historic and Contemporary
Perspectives on Master's Education

Following a cue from Kenneth Burke (1957, 95–96), we view our inquiry into master's education as part of an ongoing conversation that predates us and which will continue long after our work has been considered by others. To understand and appreciate what has been said before, in this chapter we explore the published literature on master's education in the United States. In the process of identifying those who have participated in the conversation and considering their perspectives on master's education, we highlight the developments, trends, and issues that have attracted attention. We organize the literature around four periods: 1859–1900, 1900–1945, 1945–70, and 1970–91.[1] We conclude the chapter by noting two major limitations of the literature and indicating how these limitations influenced the direction of our study.

Graduate Education and the Master's as a Scholarly Degree for College Teachers (1859–1900)

In their writings on the master's degree, Hastings Rashdall (1895) and R. Freeman Butts (1939) underscored that the word *master* comes from the Latin term *magister*, meaning "teacher." Along with other historians writing late in the nineteenth and early in the twentieth centuries, Rashdall and Butts suggested that the master's degree had been associated with pedagogy since the degree was first offered at the University of Paris in the twelfth century. From their vantage point, the master's of arts degree enjoyed considerable status throughout the Middle Ages; many would-be professors obtained their master's degree by studying the liberal arts for up to three years after finishing their baccalaureate degree and defending a thesis. Their writings also suggest that the master's degree eventually lost status to the doctorate in continental Europe but continued to prosper in England as the highest earned degree.

Many historians (Brubacher and Rudy 1976; Rudolph 1962) emphasized that it was the English universities, notably Oxford and Cambridge, that had the greatest impact on higher education during the colonial period in the United States. The nation's first college, Harvard, began awarding master's degrees in the mid-seventeenth century, and, as other colleges were established, many followed suit. Following the Oxbridge model, these colleges granted the master's degree to alumni who studied on campus for one to three years following completion of their undergraduate programs. Many graduates assumed teaching positions after completing their studies, and, according to some historical accounts, the master's degree enjoyed considerable public respect as the highest degree throughout the colonial period. Michael Pelczar, for example, suggested that during the colonial period the master's signified "rigorous academic achievement" (1979, 117).

William Mayville (1972) and Richard Storr (1953) indicated that the master's degree gradually ceased to be a symbol of significant academic accomplishment by the end of the eighteenth century. As their writings suggest, by the early 1800s many colleges granted the master of arts "in course" to virtually any baccalaureate graduate who was willing to wait several years and pay a diploma fee. According to various historians, however, there were several notable attempts to restore the master's as an earned degree during the antebellum period. The University of Virginia (1831), Harvard University (1831), the University of the City of New York (1835), and the University of North Carolina (1856) tried—apparently with little success—to establish earned master's degrees (Rudolph 1962, 126–30; Spurr 1970, 64; Storr 1953). Not until 1859, when the University of Michigan awarded its first earned master's degree, did the master's, in Walter Eell's view (1963), again begin to enjoy a measure of public respectability.

Laurence Veysey and other historians closely linked the resurrection of the master's as an earned degree to the rise of the university in general and graduate education in particular during the last half of the nineteenth century. As Veysey (1965) chronicled in *The Emergence of the American University,* the period from 1865 to 1910 witnessed the gradual development of a new institution, the university, which challenged the hegemony of the oldtime liberal arts college. Veysey suggested that widespread dissatisfaction with the classical curriculum, the growing need for trained individuals to support the nascent industrial revolution in the United States, increased state and federal support for higher education, and the attractions of the German universities and advanced study were factors that contributed to the growth of universities in the United States.

Between the mid-nineteenth century and the turn of the century, several highly visible university presidents—Henry Tappan and William Angell at Michigan, Daniel Coit Gilman at Johns Hopkins, Charles Eliot at Harvard, and Andrew White at Cornell—staked their careers on advancing their visions of American universities. They paved the way for far-reaching reforms throughout higher education, including the all-purpose curriculum (including subjects such as economics, engineering, and agriculture), advanced graduate study, and an emphasis on research. As Veysey and other historians of the period—such as Frederick Rudolph (1962) and Richard Storr (1973)—suggested, the oldtime college did not go gently into the dark night; the late nineteenth century was punctuated throughout by vigorous debate about the ends and means of higher learning. As Bernard Berelson interpreted these historical changes, however, there was "no stopping" the university movement and, along with it, the rise of graduate education (1960, 9).

Richard Storr, among other historians of higher education in the United States, emphasized that the "early reformers had not agreed to make the Ph.D. degree the chief reward for graduate study" (1953, 134). Yale awarded the first Ph.D. degree in this country in 1861, but it was not until 1876—when the new university in Baltimore, Johns Hopkins, established the doctorate as the centerpiece of its mission—that academicians began to view the Ph.D. as the major reward for advanced study. Historians (Brubacher and Rudy 1976) of this era suggested that, despite the emergence of the Ph.D., the graduate degree structure remained unsettled, and for a time the master's degree had its own identity, separate from the doctorate.

The historian John Snell (1965) advanced two major explanations for the growing status of the earned master's degree from 1870 to 1890. First, the increasing popularity of the Ph.D. degree stimulated some universities to offer the master of arts (M.A.) and master of science (M.S.) degrees along with the Ph.D. Second, since the supply of those having earned doctorates did not approach the demand for college and university faculty, there were many teaching positions in higher education for individuals who had secured their master's degree in the liberal arts and sciences. Snell (1965, 75), for example, noted that, in 1884, only 19 of the 189 members of the Harvard faculty and only 6 of the 88 Michigan faculty held the doctorate.

As graduate education steadily expanded during the late nineteenth century, then, colleges and universities introduced new "earned" master's degrees and transformed unearned master's degrees to earned degrees. In most cases, these earned master's degrees included at least one year of advanced study and completion of a thesis (Brubacher and Rudy 1976, 194). By 1872 Harvard had granted its last M.A. "in course" (Morrison

1930, 452), and, four years later, Yale offered its first earned M.A. degree. Other institutions (such as the University of California and Columbia University and later Stanford University and the University of Chicago) followed suit. Whereas 879 master's degrees were awarded in the United States in 1880, this number had increased to 1,500 by 1900 (AAU 1945, 112; Snell 1965, 176). The majority of master's degrees were given by no more than fifteen or twenty "leading" universities, such as Columbia and the University of Wisconsin. In short, during the last quarter of the nineteenth century, the earned master's—described by historians primarily as a scholarly degree in the liberal arts and sciences intended for prospective college teachers—gained a foothold in the emerging scheme of graduate education.

Multipurpose Master's Education: Ph.D. Steppingstone, Professional Degree, and Terminal Degree (1900–1945)

Shifting Purposes and Expansion

According to historians of the period, the major developments in master's education during the first half of the twentieth century concerned the advancement of new and shifting purposes for the degree and its rapid expansion. Perhaps most significant, the original intent of the earned master's in the liberal arts and sciences as the entry-level degree for college teachers gradually diminished as college and university administrators increasingly expressed a strong preference for the Ph.D. degree as a basic requirement for college and university faculty. To be sure, there were several attempts to maintain the master's as a degree for college teachers. John Brubacher and Willis Rudy (1976), for example, wrote that in the early 1900s Johns Hopkins and Yale advocated the idea of a two-year master's degree for college teachers, with the Ph.D. reserved for researchers. But the attraction of the Ph.D. degree, as Berelson suggested (1960, 21), thwarted these and later attempts to maintain fidelity to the original intent of the earned master's degree.

As two historians put it, the Ph.D. degree did not "supplant" the master's degree; it was "merely superimposed on it" (Brubacher and Rudy 1976, 195). From their perspective the master's degree in the arts and sciences was viewed by administrators and faculty at doctoral-granting universities as a steppingstone, or way station—and an appendage—to the doctorate. This view, according to many historians, was maintained throughout the twentieth century as the great majority of students in the arts and sciences discontinued their graduate work (voluntarily or otherwise) after completing their master's degree. Referring to the role of the master's in the arts and sciences throughout this period, Donald Spencer, a contemporary scholar as well as a graduate dean, articulated what was a prevailing perspective among faculty and administrators at Ph.D.-granting institutions at this time: "At its best . . . the master's represented little more than a waystation on the road to the doctorate; at its worst, it became a consolation prize for those who could not compete successfully at the more advanced level" (1986, 2).

Beginning in the late nineteenth century, another major purpose was incorporated into master's education: providing postbaccalaureate education for an increasing number of professions. Owing to the growing emphasis across the country on the professionalization of primary and secondary teachers, education was the first major professional field aside from college and university teaching to emphasize the master's degree. According to Brubacher and Rudy, the "master's degree had practically become standardized in America as the badge of the secondary school teacher" by the 1920s (1976, 194). Following the establishment of other professional schools in colleges and universities, postbaccalaureate study leading to a master's degree was increasingly offered in agriculture, art, business, city planning, engineering, forestry, music, pharmacy, public health, and social work (Geiger 1986, 15; Walters 1965, 21). In addition, a number of institutions began to introduce terminal master's degrees in avocational fields such as liberal studies.

Throughout the first four decades of this century, the expansion of master's education mirrored the overall growth of higher education. According to historical accounts, a number of factors fueled this expansion. Indirectly, the growth of doctoral education, both in the liberal arts and sciences and in the professions, contributed to this growth, since students usually were expected to complete their master's degrees before entering a doctoral program. More directly, factors such as the continuing demand for college faculty; the growing demand for the degree from high school teachers; the rise of coeducation and growing numbers of women seeking postbaccalaureate education; and the development of summer schools, which enabled high school teachers to pursue graduate work without interrupting their professional careers, also contributed to the expansion of master's education during the first half of the twentieth century (Snell 1965, 75–76).

Reports published by the Association of American Universities (AAU) chronicled a burgeoning in master's enrollments and sharp increases in the number and diversity of institutions offering the degree over this period. Whereas a small number of highly visible universities conferred approximately 1,500 master's degrees in 1900, about 300 institutions (including four-year public colleges, liberal arts colleges, and universities) granted some 27,000 master's degrees in 1940, an eighteenfold increase over this forty-year period. Of the 27,000 master's degrees awarded in 1940, approximately 15,000 were in professional fields, and 12,000 were in the liberal arts and sciences. Slightly less than two-thirds of the professional degrees conferred were in education (9,500), followed by engineering (1,350), commerce (650), and agriculture (600) (AAU 1945, 112).

Based on estimates that about 75 percent of the master's degrees in the liberal arts granted at this time were earned by public school personnel, Conrad and Eagan (1990) calculated that roughly three-fifths of all master's degrees awarded in 1940 were awarded to individuals employed in elementary and secondary schools. Assuming that most of these individuals, along with most master's graduates in other professional fields (as well as some master's graduates in the liberal arts and sciences, many of whom secured college teaching positions with their master's degree), did not go on for a doctorate, we infer that a relatively small proportion—probably no more than 10 percent—of all master's degrees granted in 1940 served as "steppingstone" degrees for those individuals who chose to pursue the doctorate. As Clifton Conrad and David Eagan (1990) pointed out, by 1940 the master's degree increasingly had become a professional, and terminal, degree for teachers and school administrators as well as individuals in a variety of other professional fields.

Mounting Criticism: Three AAU Reports

Paralleling the growth of graduate education during the first half of the twentieth century was the rise of the Association of American Universities, which had been established in 1900. According to historians of this period, this organization provided the focal point for much of the national discourse on master's education from 1900 to 1945. As the historian Everett Walters put it, the discussions and publications of the AAU became "required reading for graduate deans in and out of the AAU" (1965, 17). Originally made up of fourteen highly regarded universities (such as Chicago, Cornell, Michigan, Princeton, and Yale), the AAU early became a major public forum for member institutions—each represented by both president and graduate dean—to examine mutual concerns regarding the consolidation and standardization of graduate education. From 1900 to 1945, AAU proceedings were punctuated with statements indicating that many AAU graduate deans and university presidents held serious concerns regarding the purpose, meaning, and "quality" of the master's degree. In 1927, for example, the graduate dean at the University of Wisconsin, Charles Slichter, sharply criticized the master's degree in a paper he presented at an AAU annual meeting entitled " 'Debunking' the Master's Degree." Dean Slichter (1927, 107) especially criticized the "tendency" of many master's students to short-circuit full-time study by taking correspondence courses, extension work, and summer school. These and other concerns were further reflected in three AAU studies—published in 1910, 1935, and 1945—that, according to historians of the era, represented the major public statements regarding master's education during this period.

In 1909 the AAU commissioned the first major study of the master's degree, a survey of graduate deans at member institutions conducted by a committee chaired by Calvin Thomas, dean of the graduate school at Columbia University. In presenting the findings at the 1910 annual meeting, Dean Thomas expressed the committee's concern about the diverse aims of the degree. While reporting that most AAU universities regarded the master's as largely a "scholar's (or investigator's) degree, to be awarded for work similar in kind to that required for the Ph.D.," Thomas suggested that the degree had become partly a certification degree for secondary school teachers, partly a "culture" degree, and partly a terminal degree for many students in the arts and sciences who did not pursue the doctorate (1910, 37). He emphasized that "the time has come to recognize the fact that the master's is now a vocational degree" (43).

The committee chaired by Dean Thomas conveyed especially strong reservations about the lack of uniformity, both within and across institutions, in requirements for the master's degree. Speaking for the committee, he indicated that "graduates and undergraduates [were] nearly everywhere instructed together to some extent" (39), that there was little standardization in either admission or graduation requirements (such as examination and thesis requirements), that there was disparity in residence requirements, and that there was little standardization of degree titles. In addition, Dean Thomas opined that "the master's degree is not conferred exclusively by universities that are worthy of the name and can be trusted to maintain a high standard under a regime of perfect liberty. . . . If, then, in the country at large, we are to have no standard at all for the master's degree; if it is to betoken nothing more than a year's study following a bachelor's degree, there is reason to fear that the second [master's] degree may gradually lose such prestige as it has now acquired at the better institutions, and become a sort of academic joke" (42). Notwithstanding such concerns, the 1910 AAU committee made no recommendations for standardizing the degree save that a bachelor's degree (or equivalent) be required for admission and that the degree include intensive work in a single subject.

A quarter of a century later, in 1935, the AAU Committee on Problems Relating to the Master's Degree issued a report on the purposes, standards, and nomenclature of the master's degree (AAU 1935). After describing the master's as a "research degree, a professional degree, a teacher's degree, and a cultural degree," the committee stated that "attempts to characterize the work for the master's degree exclusively on the basis of one or the other of [these objectives] is [*sic*] likely to prove artificial and futile" (32). Accordingly, the committee accepted these multiple purposes and made several recommendations for strengthening the degree: a one-year residency requirement, a "unified" program of graduate courses, a final examination (written, oral, or both), and a thesis. In addition, the committee expressed concern about the "multiplication of degrees" and affirmed the M.A. and M.S. degree designations, supplemented (if necessary) by a qualifying phrase to limit the growth of professional degrees (AAU 1935, 33). The committee's report was accepted by the AAU, but its recommendations were nonbinding on member institutions, and, like other AAU studies and reports, the 1935 report apparently had little or no impact on master's education.

In 1945 the Committee on Graduate Work issued the hardest hitting of the AAU reports on the master's degree, as reflected in the introduction to its final report: "That we return again and again to the study of the [master's] problem is indicative of general dissatisfaction with the degree in question. And the causes of this dissatisfaction are not far to seek" (112). The committee articulated in considerable detail a range of concerns that often had been expressed in the annual proceedings of the AAU since the turn of the century. To begin with, the committee bemoaned the diverse nomenclature of the degree, noting that there were sixty-five different designations of the master's degree in AAU institutions. They also sharply criticized the diversity of standards for the master's degree:

> Recipients of a master's degree from some institutions could hardly qualify for the baccalaureate in others, while even in one and the same institution the multiplicity of objectives gives rise to divergent requirements and procedures. The degree is awarded on such different bases as: research in some specialized body of knowledge, programs of courses oriented towards exclusively vocational ends, a period of time spent in college beyond the baccalaureate and determined by thirty hours of course credits, perhaps even mere pertinacity on the part of the candidate and conscientious but ineffective effort to make the grade of the doctorate. (AAU 1945, 113)

In particular, the committee inveighed against the lack of uniformity in admissions requirements, the tendency in many universities to give degree credit for courses associated with undergraduate instruction, insufficient subject matter content in programs for secondary school teachers, and undue emphasis on student acquisition of factual knowledge.

To "bring some element of uniformity into the chaos" (113), the 1945 AAU committee made a series of recommendations for standardizing master's degrees and degree requirements. It proposed that different types of programs be distinguished by degree designations, as follows: the M.A.

and M.S. would be primarily research degrees, the M.A.T. (master of arts in teaching) and M.Ed. (master of education) would be primarily teaching degrees, and "technical" subjects (such as engineering) would be identified by the M.A. or M.S. degree and a professional modifier. In terms of degree requirements, the committee recommended that no graduate credit be allowed for correspondence or extension work, that one year of full-time residence be required, and that each student successfully complete a comprehensive examination and a thesis.

In summary, during the first half of the twentieth century, numerous senior administrators at major universities voiced their concerns about master's education and repeatedly called for standardization in the degree (as represented in three AAU studies of the master's degree). These concerns—about purpose, meaning, quality, and standards—were expressed mostly by graduate deans who had backgrounds in the liberal arts and sciences and who were employed in the nation's most highly regarded universities. Despite their concerns, however, master's education continued to expand and shift purposes.

Expansion, Professionalization, and Diversification (1945–1970): Post–World War II Developments

Following steep declines in enrollment during World War II, enrollment in master's education grew rapidly in the postwar years, as master's programs expanded and diversified. Historians suggested that this expansion was rooted in certification and promotion policies in the elementary and secondary schools, which encouraged teachers and administrators to pursue graduate work; the growing demand from business and government for master's graduates who had advanced specialized training; the needs of universities to maintain large numbers of students as research and teaching assistants; and the aspirations of colleges and universities to enhance their reputations by introducing or expanding graduate-level offerings (Berelson 1960, 35; Conrad and Eagan 1990, 110–11).

By the early 1960s the number of master's degrees awarded annually had risen to about 80,000, almost three times as many as in the early 1940s. Over this twenty-year period, the number of institutions granting master's degrees more than doubled, from about 300 to 621 (Snell 1965, 83). A substantial number of liberal arts colleges and many four-year public colleges, including former teacher's colleges, introduced master's programs. By 1962 public institutions awarded 60 percent of all master's degrees, up sharply from 42 percent fifteen years earlier (Snell 1965, 77–79). The number of students in master's programs in the liberal arts and sciences grew steadily after World War II, partly because the majority of the nation's doctoral programs required a master's degree for entry. Yet, owing to even greater enrollment increases in professional fields, the percentage of master's degrees in the liberal arts and sciences declined during this period; by 1957–58 they accounted for no more than 29 percent of the master's degrees awarded, down markedly from two decades earlier, when they accounted for roughly 44 percent of all master's degrees conferred (Berelson 1960, 187).

As these data indicate, the "professionalization" of the master's degree was a pronounced trend during this period as the degree increasingly became associated with preparing individuals for advanced professional practice. In 1961–62 almost thirty-six thousand, or 42 percent, of all master's degree recipients earned their degrees in education, up significantly from 35 percent two decades earlier; about nine thousand degrees were conferred in business, over five thousand in business and commerce, and over one thousand in agriculture (Snell 1965, 83). Many new fields and subfields, the clear majority of these in professional disciplines, also were established, as reflected in an outpouring of new degree titles. In 1960 Walter Eells and Harold Haswell identified 121 varieties of the master of arts degree and 272 varieties of the master of science degree as well as professional degrees such as master of education, master of fine arts (M.F.A.), and master of religious education (M.R.E.). Accompanying this proliferation of new degree programs, overall participation in master's programs grew dramatically during the 1960s, from an annual output of about 80,000 master's graduates at the beginning of the decade to over 208,000 in 1970 (NCES 1991).[2]

The Old Refrain: Criticism and Calls for Reform

Beginning in the late 1950s, a new set of published studies, reports, and essays emerged criticizing the purpose, meaning, quality, and standards of master's programs. As in the previous half-century, the authors of this literature were mainly administrators (graduate deans and presidents), most of whom were trained in the liberal arts and sciences and employed in the nation's most visible public and private universities. In contrast to analyses made earlier in the century, however, this criticism was more severe and widespread, and the proposals for reform more strident.

Critics attacked master's programs in the liberal arts and sciences as well as those in the professions. Social critic Howard Mumford Jones declared, for example, that the master's degree started as a "social distinction, became a post-graduate degree . . . and today is alternately a consolation prize, an insurance policy, or a sop to public education" (1959, 211). The graduate dean of arts and sciences at Harvard University, J. P. Elder, caustically accused the master's degree of being all things to all people (1959, 133), and, at the 1959 annual meeting of the American Council on Education said of master's programs in the arts and sciences: "We

might just as well say openly—I point a finger at some areas in my own
Cantabrigian backyard—that universities should either improve their
weak or easy or consolatory master's programs or should stop awarding
that degree in those fields. Gresham's Law works too surely" (Berelson
1960, 188).

Two national studies conducted during this period provided some
support for those dissatisfied with master's education. The first, sponsored by the Association of American Colleges, examined several aspects
of master's programs in the nation's liberal arts colleges, including standards, program requirements, faculty, and students. The authors of a report drawing on both survey and interview data presented a hard-hitting
conclusion about the weaknesses of master's programs in liberal arts colleges: "In short, the [master's] programs tend to be oriented not so much
for the graduate student but for the benefit of the college itself. Thus many
of the programs lack a distinctive identity. They tend to be utilitarian and
technical rather than to place emphasis upon the acquisition or advancement of knowledge for its own sake (an all too common fault in many of the
larger graduate schools as well)" (Ness and James 1962, 125). In addition,
Frederic Ness and Benjamin James sharply criticized curricula that provided little more than an extension of undergraduate work and noted a
"strong tendency 'to slump to undergraduate standards' " (125).

The second study was conducted in the late 1950s by Bernard Berelson
(1960), a professor of behavioral science at the University of Chicago. His
multifaceted investigation of graduate study in the United States was perhaps the most comprehensive ever conducted of graduate education in
this country. Tellingly, however, the investigator placed most of his emphasis on doctoral rather than master's education. In brief, Berelson identified two major "problems" with master's education: growing diversity and
declining quality (1960, 185–90). Regarding diversity, he wrote that the
master's degree

> is given for a wide range of work: another year of coursework with no
> general examination, no thesis or "essay" and no foreign language; a two-
> year professional program as in business; even a three-year program in the
> history of fine arts, where it is a strong degree and recognized as such. In
> several universities, standards for the degree vary within a single depart-
> ment, as with the many optional plans for the master's (usually with or
> without thesis); some have varied for decades, as at Minnesota. The very
> proliferation of titles for the degree indicates how varied it is. . . . In many
> professional fields, or parts of them, the master's is, or may be on the way
> to becoming, the first professional degree, e.g., in engineering, business,
> education, social work, library science. In such fields it is the capstone to
> the final year of what is essentially a five-year program of study. In many

academic fields, it is the terminal degree mainly in cases of discouragement and consolation; in most professional fields it is terminal by design.

Berelson concluded that, in terms of quality and prestige, the master's degree had slipped considerably in the post–World War II period. He attributed this change to two major developments: the degree had become increasingly associated with professional practice rather than academic training, and it had been "weakened" in the nation's "better institutions" (187). Expressing little hope that the degree could ever be "prestigious," Berelson concluded that the master's was "flourishing" because it was needed "for certifying, for testing, for consoling" (189).

In the wake of these and other like-minded judgments that university administrators and historians made from the late 1950s through the early 1970s came various calls for reforming the degree (Leys 1956). In 1957–58 a committee of the Association of Graduate Schools (AGS), an organization of graduate deans formed in 1948 under the AAU, advanced the first of several reform proposals that focused on revitalizing the master's degree for both secondary school and college teachers.[3] This committee proposed that the master's degree be redefined and oriented toward secondary school teachers, suggesting, in the words of Stephen Spurr, that an "affirmative" M.A. was preferable to a "negative A.B.D. ["all but dissertation"] (1970, 69).

Concerned about the current and impending shortage of college faculty, Harvard's Dean Elder in 1959 proposed "reviving" the master's degree as an entry-level credential for college teachers. He recommended that, rather than attaching master's programs "like a poor cousin to the Ph.D.," they be given wholly separate standing. This would eliminate the master's as a consolation prize for "the Ph.D. candidate who has done his best (which was not good enough) and whose feelings mustn't be hurt (though, of course, they always are)" (1959, 135). Ironically, in the same issue of the *Journal of Higher Education* in which Elder made his proposal, Theodore Blegen argued contrariwise that it was "absurd to suppose that the multiform and multipurpose master's degree can or should be replaced by some new and rehabilitated master's degree" (1959, 131).

A year after Elder's proposal, Oliver Carmichael (1960, 1961), a former university and foundation president, proposed rehabilitating the master's as a qualification for teaching in junior colleges or the first two years of four-year colleges. He recommended a three-year master's education, beginning with a student's junior year in college and ending with the awarding of a master of philosophy (M.Phil.) degree. With Ford Foundation support several universities launched three-year pilot programs, but these were discontinued when funding expired. In the mid-1960s the dean of the graduate school at Yale announced that his institution had established the degree of master of philosophy. According to John Miller, the M.Phil. was to be awarded to individuals who completed all Ph.D. requirements except for the dissertation and was introduced in part to help meet the demand for college teachers without "debasing the Ph.D." (1966, 377). By 1972, however, the Yale faculty had essentially abandoned the M.Phil. degree and voted for reinstatement of the traditional master's degree (CGS 1977, 147). As Stephen Spurr had observed several years earlier, college and university faculty strongly preferred to hire faculty members holding a doctorate (1970, 72).

Several other proposals were made for reviving the master's degree in the 1960s and early 1970s. In 1963, at a meeting of the Council of Graduate Schools (CGS)—the national organization of graduate deans established in 1960, independent of the AAU—there was widespread agreement that the M.A. was losing prestige to the M.B.A. (master of business administration) and M.F.A. and that remediation of undergraduate education was a reasonable purpose of master's education (Glazer 1986, 12; Spencer 1986, 2). Three years later a CGS committee on the master's degree proposed that the degree embrace three interrelated purposes: the first year of graduate study, a terminal professional degree, and a transitional year for students to make up deficiencies (CGS 1966).

In 1970 Stephen Spurr, dean of the graduate school at the University of Michigan, published a major report on academic degree structures for the Carnegie Commission on Higher Education. Anchoring his recommendations in the assumption that the master's degree in the liberal arts and sciences had been "relegated to second class or consolation prize status," he proposed that all students be admitted directly to a master's program before pursuing doctoral study and that there be a reduction in the number of master's degree titles (1970, 80). Several years later a professor of higher education at Pennsylvania State University called for "radical surgery" on the master's degree and recommended that master's programs be completely separated from doctoral programs (Toombs 1973, 153). These proposals, however, along with virtually all other proposals advanced over the previous two decades, apparently had little impact on master's education. As Gordon Whaley observed, this reluctance to reform master's education, in spite of continuing criticism, reflected widespread ambivalence within academe about the degree (Whaley 1966).

Transformation of Master's Education: Challenges to Traditional Beliefs (1970–1991)

In the late 1980s two independent observers of master's education reached a similar conclusion: there had been a transformation in master's education, both across and within master's programs, during the last several decades. Both defined and explained the transformation in much the same way, suggesting that recent developments challenged traditional beliefs about master's education. We draw on these writers to introduce contemporary trends in master's education, change and innovation within master's programs, and recent concerns about quality and quality assessment at the master's level.

In 1986 Judith Glazer, a dean at St. John's University (New York), published an extensive review of the literature on master's degrees. She concluded that over the previous two decades there had been a "paradigmatic shift from the arts and sciences model to manifold professional degrees." As she put it: "The dominant paradigm is practitioner oriented, emphasizing training in skills, career development, and pragmatic goals. It is linked to the needs of the student and the demands of the marketplace and driven by externally imposed standards, and it emphasizes practice rather than theory, skills rather than research, training rather than scholarship. . . . The master's degree is overwhelmingly professional, it is largely terminal, and it is practice oriented" (1986, 83–85).

In advancing her thesis that a paradigmatic shift had occurred, Glazer proposed that by the early 1970s the traditional liberal arts master's degree had become—partly as a result of the expansion of doctoral education—little more than a credential, introduction to a field of study (steppingstone), or consolation prize. At the same time, she argued that the model of the master's-as-a-professional degree had become dominant because of the societal shift to a knowledge-based economy, a demand from individuals for both advanced training and a credential for job advancement and mobility, a demand from employers for more highly trained practitioners, and an eagerness in many professions to enhance their statuses by upgrading the degree requirement for entry to the occupation (1986, 21–25). Throughout her monograph, Glazer explicitly and implicitly suggested that the new paradigm of the master's degree challenged traditional beliefs about master's education held by many people in the arts and sciences, among them that master's programs should be primarily for full-time students and should emphasize a theory-based curriculum rather than an experiential and "practice-oriented one."

In an essay addressed to graduate deans entitled "The Master's Degree in Transition," Donald Spencer, a graduate dean at the University of Montana, traced the "checkered reputation" of the "traditional master's degree" in the liberal arts and sciences (1986, 1). The bulk of his essay, however, was devoted to elaborating the "new face of the master's degree," which he explained this way:

Unburdened by the imperatives of any tradition to which the academic community was passionately attached and lacking any but the most elemental and mechanical guidelines for structuring the degree, those faculties and administrators responsible for designing master's programs have enjoyed a measure of discretionary authority essentially unique in modern American education. Thus, as tidal changes have swept across American civilization since World War II, the academic community has proven willing, on a campus-by-campus and largely *ad hoc* basis, to adapt the master's degree more readily than any other level of education. (2)

Spencer's "new face of the master's"—which encompassed trends in master's education writ large as well as within master's programs—included five basic dimensions: "specialization" (proliferation of highly specialized programs), "professionalization" (proliferation of programs for practitioners), "application" (integration of practical experience), and "decentralization" and "depersonalization" (meaning no universal standards of residency and mentorship). Each of these dimensions, according to Spencer, represented a significant departure from traditional academic canons. In discussing the trend toward application, for example, he emphasized that the rise in internships and experiential learning (as well as the widespread practice of using nonacademic professionals to supervise such experiences) was almost unprecedented in the history of graduate education. He concluded his essay by emphasizing that the new face of the master's not only challenged the traditional master's degree but was contradictory to it as well:

> At stake in the continuing redefinition of the master's degree is nothing less than the meaning of graduate education. Integrating prospective academicians into "the life of the mind"—the aim of almost all graduate study prior to World War II—presupposes full-time, sustained examination of an academic discipline, unlimited access to mentors and research facilities, mastery of broad academic skills in research methodology and foreign languages, and an explicit expectation that the novitiate would produce new knowledge in the form of a monographic thesis. Implicit in the new face of the master's degree is an entirely contradictory set of assumptions: that students should be encouraged, through evening and external programs, to consider graduate study as an adjunct to the other priorities in their lives; that they are expected to master specific, rather than general, techniques and bodies of knowledge; and that they are being trained to become, however tired the cliché, consumers rather than producers, of scholarly research. . . . Every indication is that existing trends will continue to aggravate the conflicts inherent between the traditional and the modern master's degree. (3)

Expansion, Diversification, Interdisciplinarity, and Professionalization

According to figures compiled by the U.S. Department of Education, there was substantial growth in master's education during the 1970s and 1980s: 208,291 master's degrees were awarded in 1969–70 in contrast to 309,762 in 1989–90, a 48 percent increase. Following dramatic growth in the early and mid-1970s, the number of master's degrees annually awarded declined somewhat until 1984 but then increased each of the next five years. In the late 1980s and early 1990s nearly one-fourth of all academic degrees awarded each year were master's degrees. A recent National Center for Education Statistics report predicted that, while overall enrollments in higher education will remain relatively constant throughout the 1990s, the annual output of master's degrees will increase gradually (NCES 1991).

Jules LaPidus (1987) observed that a sharp increase in the number of institutions awarding master's degrees paralleled the substantial increase in the number of degrees awarded. Since the 1960s many liberal arts colleges and four-year public institutions added master's programs. Whereas 621 colleges and universities granted master's degrees in 1961, almost twice as many (1,192) did so in 1985. Among these institutions were 473 doctorate-granting institutions (which had long awarded the majority of master's degrees) and 719 master's-level institutions (Grant and Snyder 1983, 105; LaPidus 1987, 4). In addition, Nancy Nash and Elizabeth Hawthorne highlighted the establishment of about ten "corporate colleges" that offered master's degrees (Nash and Hawthorne 1987).

Conrad and Eagan proposed that the most striking trends in master's education over the last two decades were diversification and professionalization and a proliferation of new fields and subfields, which included many new interdisciplinary academic areas (1990, 122–24). Among others, the newly established interdisciplinary programs included liberal arts and sciences programs in fields such as liberal studies and women's studies. Commenting on this development, Donald Spencer suggested that a national trend toward such interdisciplinary programs, "especially in the humanities, represents a startling new departure from the historical definition of graduate study as being rooted in the methodologies and content of specific academic disciplines" (1986, 10). This view was supported by the national visibility that some of these programs gained (such as the master's in liberal arts at Johns Hopkins University). Most of the proliferation of new and interdisciplinary master's programs, however, was in programs oriented toward the professions, both within the liberal arts and sciences and in specialized fields.

In the 1970s and 1980s many colleges and universities introduced new terminal degrees for "practitioners." These included new discipline-based programs in fields such as applied anthropology, applied history, and applied philosophy and new interdisciplinary programs in areas such as environmental studies, urban problems, health care for the aged, and genetic counseling (Hatala 1982; Mayhew and Ford 1974).

Within fields traditionally referred to as "professional," there was a similar explosion of new fields and subfields. Many colleges and universities introduced new master's programs in areas as diverse as aviary medicine, film education, international marketing, dental hygiene, physical therapy, building construction, and advertising management. As Spencer put it, "almost no American profession lacks an appropriate master's degree program" (1986, 2). In addition, as Conrad and Eagan observed (1990), many institutions introduced joint or dual master's programs that combined course work from two or more professional fields, such as social work and public health or business and engineering.

The professionalization of master's education, not only in the professions but also in the liberal arts and sciences, was reflected in the most recent NCES figures (1989) concerning earned degrees at the master's level. (As we understand it, these figures understate the extent of "professionalization," since there are no published data available concerning degrees awarded in professional programs in the liberal arts and sciences.) These data show that 84 percent of master's graduates received their degrees in a professional field in 1988–89, with the remainder earning their degrees in the liberal arts and sciences (see table 1.1). Fully one-half of all degrees awarded were in the fields of education and business, with engineering, health sciences (including allied health), and public affairs accounting for another one-fifth. In the 1980s the most rapidly growing fields at the master's level were business, health sciences, engineering, and computer science. Meanwhile, education, library sciences, foreign languages, and letters sustained relative declines (NCES 1991).[4]

From our perspective, it is also important to mention significant changes that occurred between 1970 and 1990 in the demographic characteristics of master's students. Over this period there was a sharp increase in the relative proportion of female students receiving master's degrees: in 1970–71 women received 40 percent of these degrees, whereas in 1988–89 they received 52 percent. Meanwhile, although there was a marked increase in the relative proportion of people identified as ethnic minorities receiving master's degrees during the 1970s, only a slight overall increase took place during the following decade (from 11 to 12 percent). As many higher education scholars have noted, these composite data mask trends within minority group subpopulations: the proportion of African Americans receiving master's degrees declined during the 1980s, whereas Hispanic and Asian/Pacific Islander proportions increased correspondingly. While no comparative data are available, one of the more notable demo-

Table 1.1. **Master's Degrees Conferred, by Field (1988–89)**

	Number of Degrees	Percent of Total Degrees
Professional		
Agriculture and natural resources	3,245	1.0
Architecture and environmental design	3,378	1.1
Business and management	73,154	23.6
Communications	4,233	1.4
Computer and information sciences	9,392	3.0
Education	82,238	26.5
Engineering	24,541	7.9
Health sciences / allied health	19,255	6.2
Home economics	2,174	0.7
Law	2,098	0.7
Library/archival sciences	3,940	1.3
Parks and recreation	460	0.1
Protective services	1,046	0.3
Public affairs and social work	17,928	5.8
Theology	4,625	1.5
Visual and performing arts	8,234	2.7
Total	259,941	83.9
Liberal arts and sciences		
Area and ethnic studies	978	0.3
Foreign languages	1,911	0.6
Letters	6,608	2.1
Liberal and general studies	1,408	0.5
Life sciences	4,933	1.6
Mathematics	3,424	1.1
Multi-/interdisciplinary studies	3,225	1.0
Philosophy and religion	1,274	0.4
Physical sciences	5,737	1.9
Psychology	8,579	2.8
Social sciences	10,854	3.5
Total	48,931	15.8
Grand total	309,762	

Source: National Center for Education Statistics, *Earned Degree Surveys* (Washington, D.C.: Center for Education Statistics, Office of Educational Research and Improvement, U.S. Department of Education, 1991).
Note: In 1988–89 890 conferred master's degrees (0.3%) were not classified by field of study.

graphic trends during the 1980s was the substantial increase in the proportion of master's degrees earned by international students; by 1988–89 international students earned 11 percent of master's degrees awarded. Finally,
there was a sharp increase in the proportion of part-time and older master's
students during this period; by the late 1980s approximately two-thirds of

master's students enrolled part-time and about one-half of master's students were thirty years of age or older (NCES 1991).

Change and Innovation within Master's Programs

Glazer (1986) as well as Conrad and Eagan (1990) suggested that widespread change and innovation within master's programs, in terms of both delivery and content, amounted to a transformation of master's education during the 1970s and 1980s. From their perspective, these developments supplemented and, in some cases, replaced traditional approaches (especially in professional fields), thereby challenging traditional beliefs about master's education. These authors summarized a substantial, albeit diffuse, body of literature, written primarily by individual scholars representing a wide range of fields (especially professional fields) and consisting mostly of field-specific essays and descriptive studies (Conrad and Eagan 1990, 114–38; Glazer 1986, 37–82).[5] Here we briefly highlight four of the major changes and innovations identified by Conrad and Eagan (1990) and given considerable attention in this literature: new instructional technology, external degrees, experiential and applied learning, and a trend away from a thesis requirement.

Developments in instructional technology, especially in information access and delivery, resulted in a variety of innovations in master's-level instruction during the 1970s and 1980s. Many programs, particularly in professional fields, began delivering graduate courses to both on-campus and remote sites via telephone networks, public radio, recorded or live videotape, public and cable television, satellite transmission, and interactive computer.

As reported by Conrad and Eagan (1990), scholars have described the implementation of new instructional technologies in professional fields such as engineering, education, nursing, and business. In engineering, considered by many higher education scholars as the leader in the use of innovative master's-level instructional technology, numerous publications described the delivery of off-campus courses. Morris Nicholson (1982), for example, reported on the efforts of the Association for Media-Based Continuing Education for Engineers (AMCEE), whose member universities televised live and videotaped courses to engineers at their workplace. Among many others, Nell Eurich (1985, 85–87) described the National Technological University (NTU), a national university that delivered off-campus master's programs in engineering-related fields through advanced telecommunications technology (live and videotaped courses) transmitted directly to industrial and corporate sites across the nation.[6]

In seeking to accommodate those working and place-bound students unable to enroll in traditional on-campus programs on a full-time basis, many colleges and universities developed external degree programs at the master's level which did not require traditional patterns of graduate study, such as off-campus programs offered in the evenings, on weekends, and in other nontraditional formats. Scholars writing on master's education, including Bruce Broderius and Mary Carder (1983) and W. H. Matchett (1980), indicated that external degree programs were offered in fields ranging from education and social work to business and computer science. At some institutions external master's degree programs were the rule rather than the exception. Richard Doyle (1979) reported, for example, that the Institute for Personal and Career Development—the external degree-granting arm of Central Michigan University—had centers located throughout the country offering master's programs in fields such as management and community leadership.[7]

One of the most significant developments within master's programs, according to Conrad and Eagan (1990), was a trend toward applied and experiential learning. According to Lewis Mayhew and Patrick Ford, a growing focus in master's programs on knowledge that emphasizes the "practical aspects of emerging problem-areas" coincided with the rise of the professions in the 1960s and 1970s (1974, 133). Many scholars of master's education emphasized that learning through practical experience (via internships, practica, workshops, field studies, clinicals, internships, apprenticeships, and cooperative education) was not "new" in what were traditionally viewed as professional fields; rather, it was the introduction of experiential learning in such liberal arts and sciences fields as biology, English, speech, and history (Carroll 1982)—and the expansion of experiential learning approaches in professional fields—which was new. The overall growth of practice-oriented master's programs was well-documented in the literature (Glazer 1980; LaPidus 1987; Pelczar and Frances 1984; Zumeta and Solmon 1982).[8]

The fourth major change in master's education which Conrad and Eagan (1990) featured in their review of the literature on master's education was the movement away from a thesis requirement in master's programs. As the master's became less a traditional research degree, especially in the arts and sciences but also in some professional fields, many master's programs either dropped the thesis requirement altogether or introduced a "nonthesis" option (Boddy 1970). Jules LaPidus estimated in 1987 that close to 70 percent of all earned master's degrees were nonthesis degrees.

In summary, our review of the literature on trends and innovations supports the views of Glazer and Spencer that a transformation within master's education occurred in the 1970s and 1980s. As Spencer suggested, many developments in master's education contradicted traditional beliefs. Such developments as professionalization, external degrees, innovative instructional technologies, applied and experiential learning, and the introduction of the nonthesis option also raise fundamentally new conceptions of the who, what, why, when, and where of master's education. In this context we turn to issues raised in other recent publications on master's education.

Concerns about Quality and the Assessment Movement

Coinciding with the writings published by Spencer, Glazer, and Conrad and Eagan was yet another set of documents, many developed by policy-making bodies. These latter publications conveyed a continuing concern about the quality of master's programs. In the early 1970s, for example, a study by the New York State Department of Education found that "many master's—especially at public colleges—were ill-conceived and loosely administered and served no clear end," which led William Mayville to conclude that "it would seem that an attitude of collusive mediocrity has been adopted among students, faculty, and administrators at the master's level" (1972, 1). Fifteen years later, in a monograph entitled "The Master's Degree: Jack of All Trades" (Green 1987), several state higher education officers, the president of the national association of graduate deans (CGS), a professor, and a university administrator raised hard-hitting questions about the quality of the master's degree. Robert Barak, for example, a senior academic officer at the Iowa Board of Regents, argued that the "master's degree remains the weakest collegiate degree in America. . . . If there is a skeleton in higher education's closet, surely it is the poor quality of master's degrees that have been consistently neglected over the years" (1987, 32). Referring to several statewide studies of master's programs, he stated that these studies indicate that many master's programs "lack meaningful admission standards; clear and appropriate purpose; rigor appropriate to the graduate level; course standards appropriate to graduate work; and faculty dedicated to the needs of master's students" (34).

Other individuals, from graduate deans to professors to state higher education officials, raised similar concerns about the quality of master's education. In our analysis many of these concerns were associated, either directly or indirectly, with the changes and innovations introduced in master's programs during the 1970s and 1980s. The president of the Council of Graduate Schools and his co-author gave voice to a similar analysis in 1984: "A major issue associated with master's programs is that of assessing their quality. . . . This is an issue that needs more attention by the graduate community, particularly since programs with an applied, career-oriented focus are on the increase" (Pelczar and Frances 1984, 5). The same year, the dean of the Claremont Graduate School opined that "education for practicing professionals is often given only reluctant commitment. As a result, most educational institutions significantly underestimate its complexity and difficulty, do minor adaptation of their standard approach, and deliver a product of indifferent quality" (Albrecht 1984, 15). Several years later, in her review of the literature on master's education, Glazer concluded that "quality control is problematic" and that "diversity and proliferation have engendered ambiguity in the meaning of the master's degree" (1986, 84–85). And David Stewart and Henry Spille, in a book targeted at "diploma mills" in higher education (including master's education), criticized non-traditional degree programs in which students were given credit for "life experiences" without adequately documenting or assessing the kind of learning that had taken place (1988, 47).

While concerns about the quality of master's programs were omnipresent during the 1970s and 1980s and bore much in common with concerns expressed before 1970, they did not lead to any national studies of the quality of the master's degree, much less to proposed reforms for reviving the degree. Instead, the major by-product of these concerns, as we understand it, was a growing concern with "quality assessment," a movement focused on developing assessment criteria and indicators in order to "strengthen" master's programs. Indeed, between 1970 and 1990 a major national task force and numerous individual scholars proposed various approaches to quality assessment, including assessment criteria and indicators.

In 1978 the Council of Graduate Schools established the Task Force on the Assessment of Master's Level Programs to address the issue of quality control in master's programs. The task force identified six assessment criteria (faculty, students, resources, learning environment, curriculum, and placement of alumni) along with indicators for each criterion. The task force then conducted a nationwide survey, asking about 200 graduate deans to evaluate the relative importance of these criteria and the availability of indicators (Downey 1979, 90–91). The survey found the following criteria to be most highly valued (Ames 1979, 40):

1. Quality of faculty, including instructional, scholarly, and artistic contributions, commitment to program, training, and experience.
2. Quality of incoming students, including academic ability, commitment, and motivation.
3. Resources, including faculty, facilities, services, and administrative support.
4. Learning environment, including the competitiveness and rigor of the intellectual environment.
5. Curricula, including academic offerings and degree requirements.
6. Characteristics of recent alumni, including satisfaction with education.

The task force later worked with the Educational Testing Service (ETS) to design and field-test questionnaires for graduate departments to use in self-assessments of master's programs, which eventually led to the establishment of the Graduate Program Self-Assessment Service (GPSA).

Most scholars of quality assessment at the master's level echoed the assessment approach developed by the task force. As Conrad and Eagan pointed out (1990, 139), these scholars developed criteria and indicators that traditionally were used to evaluate program quality at the doctoral level, such as the research quality of the faculty and the adequacy of resources, and placed little emphasis on such considerations as student outcomes. James Fisher (1979), for example, proposed five criteria and related indicators for evaluating master's programs, only one of which—"strength of program graduates"—addressed student outcomes.

Scholars who looked at nontraditional master's programs frequently suggested that traditional quality criteria and indicators should be the same for both traditional and nontraditional programs (Carr 1979). Donald McCarty, for example, claimed that traditional quality standards in graduate education, such as faculty research and scholarship, are "few but powerful" and that nontraditional programs should adhere to these general standards, except for residency requirements (1979, 69). Similarly, Grover Andrews endorsed traditional criteria and indicators of program quality and, further, argued that the "establishment of different sets of standards for different types of master's programs will create an unacceptable situation for the degree recipient through a devaluation of the credential" (1979, 63).

Most contributions, in our reading of this literature, reaffirmed traditional approaches, although a few individuals suggested that quality assessments of master's programs should place at least as much emphasis on student outcomes as on traditional criteria and indicators such as faculty and student quality. In a sharp critique of traditional approaches, Kenneth Clark (1979), suggested that new standards and criteria be introduced for master's programs and that the major criterion for judging the quality of master's programs should be the impact of the program on students. Similarly, Robert Kirkwood (1985) decried the neglect of "outcomes studies" at the graduate level, and Richard Millard (1984) suggested that the assessment of the quality of innovative graduate programs should place special emphasis on how well students are able to realize program objectives.

Reflections on the Literature: Gateway to the Study

In this chapter we have sought to tell the story of master's education as chronicled in the published literature, thereby providing context both for our readers and for our own efforts to understand master's education. As we have seen, the changes in master's education—from the appearance of the master's as a degree for college teachers to its emergence as a multipurpose degree that, in recent years, challenged traditional beliefs—led to the development of a considerable body of literature. This literature includes reports, studies, and essays that not only portray developments in master's education but also, in quite a few instances, are sharply critical of it. In some cases reforms, recommendations, and proposals for strengthening master's programs were suggested and advanced.

Without in any way diminishing the contributions of those who have gone before us, we make two major observations about the extant literature and indicate how these observations influenced our approach to this study. First, we were surprised by the dearth of serious scholarly study of how individuals involved in master's education experienced the overall character—and effects—of their master's programs. Put simply, the literature gave us very little information and understanding about what is inside the "black box" of master's education. Moreover, we noticed few instances in the literature where master's education was defined as a separate and legitimate degree activity in higher education in the United States. Most published accounts of graduate education define master's education as either a "postbaccalaureate" or a "predoctoral" degree activity. To be sure, the literature includes studies of specific changes and innovations in master's programs and studies of program requirements as well as scores of essays and reports that pronounce judgments about the condition of master's education. From our perspective, however, narrowly conceived studies and conjecture and opinion are inadequate substitutes for systematic inquiry that examines master's education on its own terms.

Second, in reviewing the literature on master's education, we observed that the published discourse presents the perspectives of a limited number of stakeholders in master's education, where *stakeholders* is defined to mean those people who have a vital stake in master's education. With few exceptions the published conversation about master's education has been shaped by a small group of stakeholders who have held administrative and faculty positions in academe: presidents, graduate deans, scholars, and officers of professional associations, most of whom enjoyed primary associations with highly visible universities. For the most part the voices—we use *voice* to refer to a speaking subject's perspective, conceptual horizon, intention, and worldview (Wertsch 1991, 51)—of administrators and faculty at less prestigious universities and of students, alumni, and employers across all types of institutions have not been represented in the literature.

These two limitations were critical to the design of our study. In light of the need for research focusing on the character of master's experiences on their own terms, we chose to use an open-ended case-study approach that would concentrate on the experiences of people in a diverse set of master's programs. Moreover, having learned that many voices were missing from the discourse, we chose to include a broad range of stakeholders—including students, alumni, and employers as well as faculty and administrators associated with master's programs at a variety of institutions—so that we could more fully understand their perspectives and, in so doing, further contribute to understanding of master's education in the United States.

2

A Positioned Subject Approach
to Inquiry

We learned from our review of the literature that few studies have examined master's education on its own terms and that the range of voices represented in the published conversation has been limited. On the basis of these understandings, we decided to conduct a broad-based study of master's education in the United States. In brief, we used an open-ended, multicase study design in which the perspectives of diverse stakeholders—people who have a vital stake in master's education, whom we variously refer to as "positioned subjects," stakeholders, and interviewees—animated our inquiry throughout. Altogether we interviewed nearly eight hundred people associated with forty-seven master's programs in thirty-one colleges and universities, including institutional and program administrators, faculty, students, alumni, and employers of program graduates.

Since the study was informed throughout by our understanding of interviewees, ourselves, and our readers as positioned subjects, we begin the chapter by briefly describing our positioned subject approach. We then describe our multicase study design (including our selection of cases and interviewees) and, in turn, discuss our fieldwork procedures, analytic processes, and the textual approach we used in writing this book.[1]

Positioned Subjects as an Approach to Research

From the beginning of the study, we wanted our research to focus on how diverse stakeholders interpreted their master's experiences within their own particular settings. At the same time, we wanted our research to allow us to generalize about master's education on a national level. By studying master's education at the individual program level and then generalizing

28

across programs, we would be in a position to interpret stakeholder experiences in master's education.

To these ends, we chose a positioned subject approach to inquiry, one that assumes that people, as positioned subjects (where *subjects* refers to people with particular needs, perceptions, and capabilities for action, and *position* refers to the environment in which they are located), actively interpret and make sense of their everyday worlds.[2] In brief, this approach provided us with a strategy for research and analysis: we would focus on how people understood and interpreted master's experiences within programs—including how they made sense of them and what they valued in them—always from their own standpoints, or perspectives. In so doing, we viewed each program in terms of this positioned subject approach, namely, that each program was located, or positioned, within a particular setting and that, by understanding various patterns across these programs, we could develop a broad-based understanding of master's education in the United States. Moreover, like the stakeholders we interviewed, we also viewed ourselves, and our readers, as positioned subjects who interpret and make meaning based on our experiences and perspectives.

Multicase Study Design

Consonant with our positioned subject approach, we used a multicase study design that placed the perspectives of the individuals we interviewed at the center of our research.[3] We first developed a representative sample of 47 case studies and then selected a representative sample of 781 interviewees. To flesh out our design, we discuss our overall sampling strategy then turn to our selection of cases and interviewees.

Sampling Strategy

Our sampling strategy, including our selection of case studies as well as interviewees within cases, was based on a major premise in multicase study design: if a credible claim is to be made that our findings can be generalized from individual interviewees to each case study as a whole, and from a group of cases to master's education in this country, then the sample must be *substantively* representative of the population it claims to represent. To provide for substantive representativeness, contextual characteristics of the population which may be theoretically relevant must be represented in the sample. There is no need, however, as Greene and David emphasized, to "require adequate representation on every conceivable variable, parameter, or factor that one might think of. In particular, there is no reason to prefer—let alone require—a sample that includes all the principal selection factors in every combination with each other (i.e., a 'fully-crossed' design). If there is a substantive reason for a particular combination of factors to be included in the sample, that is sufficient; otherwise, no particular combination of factors is more essential than any other" (1981, 30).[4]

Following this reasoning, we used a sampling strategy in which we intentionally selected cases across the nation, and interviewees within each case (program), which represented those program and interviewee characteristics we believed might be theoretically relevant. Hence, at the national level, we selected cases that varied in terms of characteristics such as field of study, institutional type, and type of control, along with other characteristics such as geographic location, instructional delivery system, and program prestige.[5] At the program level, we selected individuals representing six different stakeholder groups, including institutional administrators, program administrators, faculty, students, alumni, and employers of alumni. Below we discuss how we chose our sample of forty-seven cases and our within-case interviewees.

Selection of Case Studies   To provide for heterogeneity (substantive representativeness) in terms of discipline, we selected eleven fields of study which represented diverse professional and liberal arts and sciences fields and which, among other considerations, varied in terms of their annual production of master's degrees. We selected five programs in each of nine fields along with one program in two fields (sociology and computer science), for a total sample of forty-seven programs.[6]

Our forty-seven-case sample was distributed across the eleven fields of study as follows: five established professional fields, four emerging professional fields in the liberal arts and sciences (including one interdisciplinary field), and two traditional fields in the liberal arts and sciences. From established professional fields, we selected business, education, engineering, nursing, and theater. We chose business, education, and engineering because, in recent years, over one-half of all master's degrees awarded annually were in these three fields. Given the range of specializations offered by most of the programs in these three disciplines, we chose subfields that recently granted the largest number of master's degrees within their respective fields: in business, business administration; in engineering, electrical engineering; and in education, teacher education. We selected nursing because it grants the largest percentage of master's degrees in the health sciences and chose theater as a representative field in the performing arts.

In terms of emerging professional fields, we chose applied anthropology, computer science, environmental studies, and microbiology as representative fields in the traditional liberal arts and sciences in which, in recent years, a nonuniversity job market has developed for master's-educated people. (Environmental studies also was chosen because it is an interdisciplinary field in which a growing share of master's degrees have been awarded in recent years.) In the traditional liberal arts and sciences, we selected English and sociology as core disciplines representing the humanities and social sciences, respectively. (Applied anthropology and microbiology also are representative fields in the social and biological sciences.)

Further, to represent the range of institutions offering master's programs in the United States, we selected cases on the basis of differences in terms of institutional type and type of control (i.e., public or private). In terms of institutional type, we chose our forty-seven cases from among four types of institutions which we identified for purposes of this study: national universities, regional colleges and universities, liberal arts colleges, and specialty institutions.[7] The forty-seven case studies, chosen to reflect national data on master's degrees awarded, were distributed as follows: national universities, eighteen programs; regional colleges and universities, twenty-one programs; liberal arts colleges, five programs; and specialty institutions, three programs.[8] The thirty-one institutions represented in the sample include seven national universities, sixteen regional colleges and universities, five liberal arts colleges, and three speciality institutions.[9] With respect to type of control, nearly two-thirds of the forty-seven programs in our sample (that is, thirty-one programs) were located in public institutions, with the remainder (sixteen programs) being located in private (independent) institutions.[10] (Table 2.1 shows the distribution of cases by field of study and by institutional type. Table 2.2 shows the distribution of case studies by institutional type and by type of control.)

Since master's programs in this country vary in other ways that might be theoretically relevant, we also chose programs that differed in terms of the following characteristics: geographic location (East, West, South, or Midwest), levels of degree offerings in departments (master's-only, bachelor's and master's, bachelor's, master's, and doctorate), student attendance patterns (full-time, part-time, mix), type of delivery system (traditional day/evening, nontraditional weekend/summer, nontraditional satellite), percentage of students who are minorities (high or low), and program prestige ("prestigious" or "nonprestigious"). In addition, we included four programs located in four predominantly black institutions and one program at a predominantly women's institution. Table 2.3 shows the distribution of the forty-seven cases across these six characteristics as well as by field of study, institutional type, and type of control.[11]

Selection of Interviewees   Consonant with our positioned subject approach, we chose to interview individuals who represented various stakeholder positions within the forty-seven master's programs in our

Table 2.1. **Distribution of Case Studies, by Field of Study and Institutional Type**

	Institutional Type			
Field of Study	National	Regional	Lib. Arts	Specialty
Established professional				
Business	2	2	1	
Education	1	3	1	
Engineering	2	2		1
Nursing	2	2		1
Theater	2	2		1
Emerging professional (Arts and sciences)				
Applied anthropology	2	3		
Computer science	1			
Environmental studies	2	1	2	
Microbiology	1	4		
Traditional arts and sciences				
English	2	2	1	
Sociology	1			
Total	18	21	5	3

Note: Four predominantly black institutions and one predominantly women's college were represented in the sample. A total of thirty-one institutions were included in the sample.

Table 2.2. **Distribution of Case Studies, by Institutional Type and Type of Control**

	Type of Control		
Institutional Type	Public	Private	Total
National universities	14	4	18
Regional colleges and universities	15	6	21
Liberal arts colleges	1	4	5
Specialty institutions	1	2	3
Total	31	16	47

sample, including institutional administrators, program administrators, faculty, students, alumni, and employers. We selected these specific stakeholder groups on the grounds that each had a major stake in master's education.[12] In addition, we strove to diversify our sample by interviewing people who differed in terms of personal characteristics such as minority status and gender, among others. Table 2.4 shows the distribution of people interviewed by stakeholder group, minority group status, sex, field of study, and institutional type.

To identify people to interview we relied on a program liaison from each of the forty-seven cases included in the study.[13] These individuals chose interviewees[14] on the basis of written criteria we had outlined in our formal request for their assistance.[15] For the most part, program liaisons were able to select interviewees according to these criteria, though sometimes practical considerations limited their ability to comply fully with our request.

We acknowledge that our interview selection method has a positive, or at least a systematic non-negative, bias that is linked to our procedure of asking program liaisons to select interviewees.[16] Although we ran the risk that program liaisons might select individuals who would describe their programs in a highly favorable light, we used this procedure for two reasons. The first is that selecting interviewees ourselves would have been impossible given our time constraints; we were unable to spend more than three days visiting each program, and we did not wish to spend our time selecting interviewees then scheduling interviews. The second reason is that we suspected, on the grounds that this would have been intrusive, many programs would have declined to participate if we had insisted that we choose interviewees.

We have often been asked why we did not interview at least a few stakeholders who were not selected by the program liaison. We decided against this in order to avoid undermining our efforts to establish trusting relationships with program liaisons. While cognizant of the trade-offs involved, we believed that the congenial relationships we developed with program liaisons, many of whom became key interviewees, encouraged both them and the people whom they selected as interviewees to be more open in their interviews. Our retrospective judgment is that we learned more this way than we might have by insisting that we interview people whom the program liaison did not choose.[17]

Interview Process: Dialogue between Positioned Subjects

In keeping with our positioned subject approach, we viewed our interviews as "dialogues between positioned subjects."[18] As such, we presented ourselves not as "invisible" observers but as participants in a conversation.[19] Our conversations were not balanced exchanges, however, as we encouraged interviewees to do most of the talking. Except when interviewing current students, we met one-on-one with each interviewee to allow both parties to concentrate on a single, sustained dialogue.[20] We arranged group interviews with students, one of us meeting with three or four students, because we thought students were most comfortable with this arrangement. We taped almost all of our interviews (with the permission of each interviewee) and took notes.[21]

In terms of our interview protocol, we developed a broad set of topics that we sought to address in each interview. In general, these topics were

Table 2.3. **Characteristics of Case Study Sample**

Pseudonym institution	Field of study	Type (1=National, 2=Regional, 3=Liberal Arts, 4=Specialty)	Control (1=Public, 2=Private)	Location (1=East, 2=West, 3=South, 4=Midwest)	Degree Levels[a] (1=M only, 2=B+M, 3=B+M+D)	Student Attendance (1=Full-time, 2=Part-time, 3=Mix)	Delivery System (1=Traditional Day/Eve, 2=Nontrad. Wknd/Sum, 3=Nontrad. Satellite)	Percentage of Minority Students (1=High, 2=Low)	Program Prestige (1=Prestigious, 2=Non-prestigious)
Pierpont University	Business	1	2	1	1	1	1	2	1
Major State University		1	1	4	3	1	1	2	2
Parks-Beecher University[b]		2	2	3	2	1	1	1	2
Peterson University		2	2	1	2	2	2	2	2
St. Joan's College		3	2	2	2	2	2	2	2
Major State University	Education	1	1	4	3	3	1	2	1
Laramie University		2	2	2	1	2	2	2	2
Chester College		2	2	1	3	2	1	2	2
Southwest State University		2	1	2	3	2	2	2	2
Lake College		3	2	4	2	2	2	2	2
Major State University	Engineering	1	1	4	3	3	1	2	2
Prestige State University		1	1	2	3	1	1 and 3	2	1
Middle State University		2	1	3	3	3	1	2	2
Moore A&T University[b]		2	1	3	2	1	1	1	2
United Technological University		4	2	2	1	2	3	2	2
Major State University	Nursing	1	1	4	3	2	1	2	2
Barrett State Medical Center		1	1	2	3	2	1	2	1
Peterson University		2	2	1	2	2	1	2	2
Southern State University		2	1	3	3	2	1	2	2
Western State Medical Center		4	1	2	3	2	1	2	2
Major State University	Theater	1	1	4	3	1	1	2	2
Phelps University		1	2	1	1	1	1	2	1
Helena State University[c]		2	1	3	2	1	1	2	2
Trafalgar College		2	2	1	2	3	1	2	2
National Conservatory College		4	2	2	1	1	1	2	1

Discipline	Institution							
Applied anthropology	Land-Grant University	1	2	2	2	1	2	2
	Atlantic State University	1	1	2	1	1	2	2
	City-State University	2	3	2	2	1	2	2
	Southwest State University	2	2	2	1	1	2	2
	Southeast State University	2	3	3	2	1	2	1
English	Major State University	1	4	3	1	1	2	2
	Phelps University	1	1	3	1	1	2	1
	Urban State University[b]	2	4	2	2	1	1	2
	Southwest State University	2	2	2	1	1	2	2
	Longmont College	3	1	1	2	2	2	2
Environmental studies	Phelps University	2	1	1	1	1	2	1
	Major State University	1	4	1	1	1	2	2
	Carver A&M University[b]	2	3	2	1	1	1	2
	Vernon College	3	1	1	2	2	2	2
	Walton State College	3	2	2	3	1	2	2
Microbiology	Major State University	1	4	3	1	1	2	1
	Southwest State University	2	2	3	1	1	2	2
	Mountain State University	2	2	3	1	1	2	2
	Middle State University	2	3	2	1	1	2	2
	Appleby State University	2	4	2	1	1	2	2
Sociology	Major State University	1	4	3	1	1	2	1
Computer Science	Major State University	1	4	3	1	1	2	1

[a] M = master's degree
B = bachelor's degree
D = doctoral degree
[b] Predominantly black institution
[c] Predominantly women's institution

Table 2.4. **Distribution of Interviewees**

By stakeholder group		By field of study	
Institutional administrators	85	Established professional	
Program administrators	95	Business	78
Faculty	167	Education	76
Students	184	Engineering	90
Alumni	147	Nursing	90
Employers	103	Theater	76
Total	781	Total	410
By minority status		Emerging professional	
African-American	60	Applied anthropology	100
Asian-American	12	Computer science	15
International	19	Environmental studies	71
Hispanic	11	Microbiology	89
Native American	3	Total	275
White nonminority	676		
Total	781	Traditional arts and sciences	
By sex		English	82
Men	430	Sociology	14
Women	351	Total	96
Total	781	Grand total	781
By institutional type			
National universities	303		
Regional colleges and	333		
universities			
Liberal arts colleges	84		
Specialized institutions	61		
Total	781		

concerned with how interviewees experienced their master's program, including its "character," its "quality" and value, and those attributes they felt contributed most to student and faculty learning. Rather than using these topics as a formal interview protocol, however, we chose to give each interviewee as much responsibility as possible for establishing the overall direction of the dialogue. To prepare interviewees for our open-ended interviews, we provided each, in advance, with a three-page description of the research project and our interview process.

In our interviews, we explained that we wanted to learn what they thought was important for us to know about their master's program. Some interviewees, to be sure, needed to be verbally prompted: Could you tell us what you expected from this program? What do you think are the most important characteristics of the program? What have you and others gotten out of the program? Generally speaking, however, people needed relatively little prompting. They not only described, interpreted, and evaluated their experiences but also often provided information and perspective on program history as well as external and internal factors influencing the program. Once they felt that we genuinely wanted to understand their views on the program and grew accustomed to the open-endedness of our interview approach, most interviewees seemed to enjoy establishing the general direction of the dialogue.

We tried to limit the amount of prompting with specific questions—because this would have tended to turn the dialogue into a testing ground for our emerging "themes," which may or may not have been interviewees' themes—but we inevitably provided interviewees with various interactive cues. Our notetaking, in particular, sometimes provided a stimulus to interaction. By pausing to take notes, we often communicated to interviewees that we believed what they had said was particularly important. They frequently responded to such cues by commenting on our notes, either explaining that what we had written was not that important or, as was more often the case, elaborating on the point. We also noticed during the course of the study that we became better at interacting with interviewees, such as noticing when they needed to pause and reflect and allowing these moments of silence. We found, too, that, as we became more skilled at listening, the people we interviewed often told us that they had learned a great deal about themselves and their program during the interview.

Upon reflecting on what the 781 interviewees told us, we want to emphasize that most people seemed to be remarkably candid with us. We attribute their candidness to several factors. For one thing, interviewees appreciated our promise to keep their responses confidential. For another, most interviewees seemed to accept our explanation that our aim was to listen carefully to their perspectives as the basis for understanding stakeholders' experiences—not to evaluate their particular programs per se. For still another, we often noticed how most interviewees, as positioned subjects, seemed to enjoy the opportunity to express their views about their master's program.

From our perspective, the validity of our interview approach was enhanced through what researchers in the social sciences refer to as "triangulation." To begin with, triangulation—collecting and analyzing data across multiple data sources—was built into our sample inasmuch as each of the stakeholder groups "stood" in different positions with respect to their programs. In broad terms, faculty and program administrators held the most permanent and interior positions, since they were formally responsible for the program and often had long-term "insider" perspectives. Current students and alumni held partly interior and partly exterior standpoints: they were intimately involved in their program yet were also "visitors" who passed through it. Employers and institutional administrators, meanwhile, tended to speak from exterior standpoints and, while gener-ally less informed than other stakeholders, provided a valuable check on insiders' perspectives as well as an alternative source of understanding.

Analysis as Positioned Subjects

Program-level Analysis

Just as triangulation was built into our case study design in the way we selected interviewees, it was also built into the analysis process in which we engaged as researchers. Since at least two of us conducted interviews in the same program at the same time, we continually engaged and "worked off" one another while we were in the field, frequently meeting over meals and during the evening hours to discuss our interviews.[22] These meetings helped us identify the occasional interviewee whose perspective seemed "out of kilter" with those of other interviewees.[23] They also helped each of us listen and react more independently of personal biases.[24] Moreover, our frequent interactions in the field helped us develop a better sense of our interview data, thereby enabling us to be more perceptive in our subse-quent interviews. In addition, whenever possible we also read beforehand all the written materials that we asked each program liaison to send us and thus were able to include these materials in our ongoing efforts to "triangu-late."[25]

Upon completing interviews in each case study, we summarized each and, using our tapes, transcribed long sections of many. One member of the research team then developed a case study summary (from 80 to 170 pages in length) based on all interview summaries as well as written docu-ments provided by the program. While completing this work, we con-tinued to triangulate and learn from each other's perspectives. In this fashion, we were able to use all the interviewees' perspectives to formulate a program portrait that incorporated what each had said and yet was more complete than what any one of them had presented.

The format we used for program summaries changed over time, as we discerned emerging themes in our interview data. By the midpoint of the study, we had established a format that helped us more quickly tune into various themes that we identified across interviews, while allowing us to retain the individuality of different stakeholders' voices. Our underlying purpose in producing these summaries was to understand, identify, and describe those themes that were shared by interviewees both within and across stakeholder groups in a given program. In effect, we attempted to renarrate, in their terms, the "stories" they told us about their particular program.

Cross-Program–Level Analysis

Our cross-program analysis, which mirrored the process we used in analyzing individual programs, began early in the study as we became attuned to themes, or patterns, in our fieldwork. Periodically, after several new program summaries had been completed, we paused to read and discuss them as a group. These discussions helped us discern patterns across programs, but we avoided drawing conclusions so that we would remain open to emerging themes throughout the duration of the study. As a result, we had a vast amount of relatively unanalyzed information by the time all the program summaries were completed and we were ready to begin our cross-program analyses.

We began the process of developing themes across the forty-seven programs in our sample by reading and discussing the individual summaries on a case-by-case basis. At first we were overwhelmed by the diversity of stakeholder perspectives. Despite this diversity, both across individuals and programs, we began to develop various themes that helped us to understand both similarities and differences across programs. Stakeholders in some programs, for example, spoke repeatedly about the sense of community in their programs, while interviewees in other programs described their experiences as more competitive and individualistic. Over the course of almost six months of intensive analysis, we developed patterns and themes that we tested and retested against our interview material. In so doing, we observed that many of the themes that stakeholders raised were ones we had not foreseen. It is noteworthy that many of the themes showed little association with attributes built into our sample, such as field of study, type of control, and a full- or part-time student population. Moreover, we realized that, depending on the characteristics and themes to which we were attuned, we learned different kinds of things about master's programs. We could clearly see that the meaning of our "data" changed depending on which themes we were using to make sense of them.

Throughout this period of analysis, our central problem was to decide which sets of characteristics across programs would allow us to develop an analysis that helped us most to understand stakeholders' master's experiences and one that accurately reflected the voices of the nearly eight hundred people we interviewed. To that end, we chose to view our interview material primarily in terms of five key types of decisions that stakeholders told us, directly and indirectly, they made about their master's programs. These five decision-situations were instrumental in the process we used to articulate four different types of master's programs which, from our perspective, embody the major differences among the master's programs in our sample. This analytical process is further explicated in parts 2 and 3 of the book.

Writing and Reading as Positioned Subjects

Conventional academic writing uses the present tense and the third-person passive voice, a textual style that presents the author as anonymous. From our perspective, this writing style makes invisible the very strength of our approach to inquiry, which assumes that we, like the people we interviewed as well as our readers, are positioned subjects who actively interpret and make meaning out of our interview material as we select certain themes, and not others, from individuals located in specific times and places. As Dorinne Kondo put it, "style and theory are inseparable in the process of writing" (1990, 48), and "the real challenge is *to enact our theoretical messages*" (43). Throughout this book, we try to use a writing style that "enacts" our positioned subject approach to the study.

During transitional passages in the book, when we want to involve the reader directly in the research and analysis process, we use the present tense and write in the first-person voice, self-consciously, or "reflexively" (as at this moment). Throughout most of the rest of the book—except when we quote directly from interviewees, when we present whatever tense they used—we use the past tense. When in past tense, we use the first-person voice when we want to remind the readers of our presence as interviewers and analysts and the third-person voice when we seek to engage the reader more imaginatively, as if "from the native's point of view" (Geertz 1983). We understand that some readers may, at first, find this unconventional use of tense and voice somewhat awkward, but readers of earlier drafts of this book have told us that they easily adjusted to it.

As part of our textual strategy, we also seek to pay attention to our readers as positioned subjects and, in turn, invite them to view us as positioned subjects. We strongly believe that readers will be better able to respond to our work if, as in a face-to-face conversation, they have enough information to position us in terms of our backgrounds and experiences. As Renato Rosaldo has noted: "Because researchers are necessarily both somewhat impartial and somewhat partisan, somewhat innocent and somewhat complicit, their readers should be as informed as possible about what the observer was in a position to know and not know" (1989, 69). We invite our readers to view us as positioned subjects (along with themselves and our interviewees); in so doing, we conclude the chapter by presenting personal sketches of those of us involved in the study.[26]

Clifton Conrad was born in North Dakota and grew up in an upper middle-class family. He was educated at major public universities in mainstream social science (history, political science, and sociology) and earned

PART TWO

DECISION-SITUATIONS

In part 1 we described the setting for the study. We reviewed the history of master's education in the first chapter, drawing attention to the perspectives of those who contributed to the published conversation about master's education. In the second chapter we described our research approach, which involved listening to almost eight hundred people selected from forty-seven master's programs from across the United States.

In part 2 we turn to our interview material and begin to present what we learned about how interviewees, as positioned subjects, experience master's programs. We organize our interview material around "decision-situations," which we define as types of circumstances in which stakeholders make decisions that influence how they and others experience their master's programs. While we emphasize that stakeholders had freedom of choice in these decision-situations, we note that choices in some circumstances were contextually constrained in varying degrees.

We chose this decision-situation approach as the initial pathway through our interview material for four reasons. First, in describing their master's experiences to us, many interviewees portrayed them (explicitly and implicitly) in relation to certain types of decisions that stakeholders made. Second, we came to appreciate that the choices stakeholders made in certain decision-situations were very instructive in helping us to explain variation in stakeholder experiences across the forty-seven programs in our sample. Third, we presumed that many of our readers would be interested in what we have learned about relationships between the choices stakeholders made in key decision-situations and the master's experiences of current students, program graduates, faculty, program administrators, and (for the most part, indirectly) institutional administrators and employers. Fourth, we believed that this approach to understanding how master's programs are experienced would be useful to readers as a "thinking device" as they review their own programs.

In completing our cross-program analysis, we identified five decision-situations that stakeholders typically encountered in their master's programs. We refer to three of these as "primary" decision-situations because they were especially useful in helping us understand variation, or differences, in stakeholder experiences. In order of their relative importance, the primary decision-situations are: approach to teaching and learning, program orientation, and departmental support. Two additional decision-situations, institutional support and student culture (in order of relative importance), further helped us to understand differences in stakeholder experiences. Since they were, on balance, slightly less helpful than the first three, however, we refer to them as "auxiliary" decision-situations. (This rank ordering of the five decision-situations is explained in chapter 5.)

In chapter 3 we present the three primary decision-situations and, in chapter 4, the two auxiliary decision-situations. In these two chapters, we provide a brief description of each decision-situation and the alternative choices within each. (The alternative choices in each of the five decision-situations are summarized in table P2.) We then illustrate each of the choices made within these five decision-situations by presenting a vignette that features a master's program from our study. We do this to provide readers with a contextualized understanding of the specific choices stakeholders made and to illustrate the consequences these choices had on their experiences with master's programs. Consonant with our "positioned subject" approach, we write these vignettes appreciatively or, in Geertz's words, "from the native's point of view." Across these two chapters, we present a total of thirteen vignettes.

In chapter 5 we seek to generalize about the overall master's experiences interviewees had across the forty-seven programs in our sample by developing a typology of master's programs. In discussing the analytical process we used to generate this typology, we explain how—on the basis of broadly similar choices stakeholders in the forty-seven programs made in the five decision-situations—we partitioned the cases into four "idealized program types." We note that stakeholders in each of the cases within these program types described their overall master's experiences in similar terms, though not all of them made identical choices in each of the five decision-situations. In short, while these decision-situations provided us with a useful tool for formulating four groups of programs, they did not provide the "whole picture."

In the last part of chapter 5 we name and describe each of the four idealized program types that we formed: ancillary, career advancement, apprenticeship, and community-centered. After summarizing the program

Decision-Situation 1: Approach to Teaching and Learning

Choices	1. Didactic	2. Facilitative	3. Dialogical
Overview	Faculty didactically transmit knowledge to students, emphasizing student mastery of knowledge.	Faculty facilitate knowledge transfer and generation, emphasizing student involvement in the rediscovery and generation of knowledge.	Faculty and students dialogically engage in critical questioning throughout knowledge transfer and generation processes, emphasizing mutual (faculty and student) rediscovery and generation of knowledge and meaning.
View of knowledge	Authoritative	Authoritative/contingent	Authoritative/contingent
Model of communication	Transmission	Interactive	Interactive
View of teacher and teaching	Hierarchical: Teacher is viewed as "authoritative expert" whose role is to transmit expert knowledge and skills didactically to students.	Participative: Teacher is viewed as "expert guide" whose role is to assist students in acquiring knowledge and skills through an apprenticeship approach.	Collaborative: Teacher is viewed mostly as "colleague" whose role is to interact dialogically with students in the teaching and learning of knowledge and skills.
View of learner and learning	Students are seen as "receivers" of didactically transmitted knowledge whose role is to acquire and "store" knowledge for future use.	Students are viewed as "apprentices" whose role is to understand, test, and apply knowledge to learn their craft.	Students are viewed as colleagues with ideas to contribute, whose role is to interact dialogically with faculty and other students.
Focus of teaching and learning experiences	Primary learning experiences occur in the classroom, where faculty rely heavily on lectures and lecture discussions to transfer knowledge to students. Laboratory, clinical, and fieldwork settings are viewed as supplementary learning experiences.	Primary learning experiences occur in the laboratory or field, where faculty use a variety of hands-on activities to apprentice students in the knowledge and skills of their craft. Classroom activities (lectures, seminars, discussions) are viewed as supplementary learning experiences.	Primary learning experiences occur within the context of a tacit "learning community," where mutual dialogue between faculty and students as colearners is encouraged through activities such as classroom seminars; laboratory, clinical, and field experiences; and out-of-class learning experiences.

(*continued*)

Table P2. *(Continued)*

Decision-Situation 2: Program Orientation

Choices	1. Academic orientation	2. Professional orientation	3. Connected orientation
Knowledge emphasized	Specialized theoretical knowledge	Specialized theoretical and applied knowledge	Generalized and specialized theoretical and applied knowledge (knowledge is viewed in "connected," dynamic terms)
Skills emphasized	• Research skills • Analytical and problem-solving skills • Communication skills (primarily written)	• Technical, field-specific, professional practice skills • Analytical and problem-solving skills • Communication skills (oral and written)	• "Big picture" skills • General and technical field-specific, professional practice skills • Analytical and problem-solving skills • Communication skills (oral and written)
Primary faculty	Full-time, Ph.D. faculty with minimal nonuniversity professional work experience	Combination of full-time Ph.D. faculty with some nonuniversity professional work experience and part-time adjunct faculty with significant nonuniversity professional work experience	Full-time, Ph.D. faculty, many with significant nonuniversity professional work experience

Decision-Situation 3: Departmental Support

Choices	1. Weak	2. Strong
Conditions of support	Master's program is not viewed as significantly enhancing financial or human resources, reputation, and mission of the department.	Master's program is viewed as enhancing financial and human resources, reputation, and mission of the department.
Kinds of support	Weak financial and symbolic support; weak faculty commitment to master's students	Strong financial and symbolic support; strong faculty commitment to master's students

Decision-Situation 4: Institutional Support

Choices	1. Weak	2. Strong
Conditions of support	Master's program is not viewed as greatly enhancing financial or human resources, reputation, and mission of the institution.	Master's program is viewed as enhancing financial and human resources, reputation, and mission of the institution.
Kinds of support	Weak financial and symbolic support to master's program, including nonsupportive faculty reward policies	Strong financial and symbolic support to master's program, including supportive faculty reward policies

Decision-Situation 5: Student Culture

Choices	1. Individualistic	2. Participative	3. Synergistic
View of peers and peer learning	Relatively isolated learners who have little to contribute to one another's learning	Participative learners who can contribute to one another's learning	Community of interdependent and collegial learners who synergistically contribute to one another's learning
Interaction patterns with peers	Individualistic peer relationships characterized by either highly competitive or isolated interactions	Cooperative peer relationships characterized by frequent and cordial interactions	Collaborative peer relationships characterized by frequent, synergistic interactions in which the "whole" is valued more than "individualistic parts"
Involvement in outside-of-class activities	Little to no student involvement in program; students occasionally form study groups with the intention of improving their own performances.	Moderate student involvement in program activities, including study groups, student-run social clubs, and student government associations	Heavy student involvement in program activities based on strong commitment among students to a vital student learning community

47

choices that stakeholders made in each of the five decision-situations, we briefly describe the overall character of stakeholder experiences in these programs. This typology, like the decision-situation approach, can be used by readers as a "thinking device" for reflecting on the character of their master's experiences and reviewing master's programs.

3

Primary Decision-Situations
Approach to Teaching and Learning, Program
Orientation, and Departmental Support

In this chapter we explore three decision-situations in which stakeholders made choices that influenced their experiences with master's programs. These include situations in which faculty and program administrators decided on their overall approaches to teaching and learning, the knowledge and skills around which to orient their programs, and the support they would provide to master's education. For each decision-situation, we outline the basic choices made by stakeholders then present a vignette drawn from our forty-seven case studies to illustrate each of these choices within specific settings.

Approach to Teaching and Learning: Didactic, Facilitative, or Dialogical

In analyzing and interpreting the forty-seven cases in our study, we came to understand that, in terms of the daily experiences of faculty and students, no decision-situation was more important than that concerning the overall approach to teaching and learning. With respect to this decision-situation, faculty and program administrators (individually as well as collectively) chose one of three approaches: didactic, facilitative, or dialogical.

In those programs in which faculty and program administrators chose a didactic approach, we learned that they embraced a generally authoritative view of knowledge coupled with a transmission model of communication. This authoritative view assumes that knowledge consists of theories and principles that exist "out there"—"universal truths" that exist independent of the knower—which have withstood exacting scrutiny and hence are not vigorously questioned in the classroom. From this viewpoint, to "know" knowledge is to acquire, master, and apply it. Faculty and

49

administrators who hold this authoritative view of knowledge tend to organize their teaching around a transmission model of communication: a sender (professor) encodes authoritative knowledge into signals (lecture and written text) and didactically transmits it to a receiver (student), who, in turn, decodes and stores the knowledge.

Faculty and students who adopted a didactic approach to teaching and learning enacted traditional, largely hierarchical, teacher and student roles. In defining themselves as "authoritative experts," faculty assumed responsibility (individually and collectively) for determining program and course content and transmitting knowledge to students. While faculty members often invited students to present their perspectives, seldom did they expect students to contribute original insights. Instead, faculty primarily cast students into a receiver role in which they expected students to concentrate on acquiring and "storing" knowledge for later use. In turn, communication was largely hierarchical and one-way and was viewed mainly as a vehicle for ensuring the accurate transmission of knowledge.

Faculty and administrators using a didactic approach grounded most of their program's primary learning experiences in lectures and lecture discussions. Many faculty members communicated to us that this approach—interspersed with periodic evaluations to ensure that students achieved mastery of the material presented to them—was their preferred method for transferring knowledge to students. In most of these programs, faculty treated laboratory, clinical, and fieldwork experiences as supplementary learning activities that reinforced students' mastery of the knowledge transmitted to them.

In a second set of cases, faculty and program administrators chose a facilitative approach to teaching and learning. In these programs, master's education was seen as an opportunity in which students not only acquired knowledge but also developed their individual capacities as generators of knowledge. For the most part, faculty and program administrators embraced a "contingent," as contrasted with an "authoritative," view of knowledge, and they adopted a two-way, interactive model of communication.

As we came to understand, those who hold a contingent view assume that all knowledge is continually being rediscovered, constructed, and scrutinized by people through interaction with others in specific settings. Knowledge is not seen as autonomous from but, rather, as intimately connected to the people who "know." While established theories and principles passed on in texts as de facto authoritative knowledge are considered important sources of understanding, people who embrace a contingent perspective understand these theories and principles as "true" when they rediscover their adequacy in each new situation they encounter. Rather than viewing authoritative knowledge as the only source of understanding, they also view the individuals involved in constructing meaning as important sources of knowledge and understanding.

Faculty and program administrators who held a contingent view of knowledge organized their teaching and learning around an interactive model of communication. As we use the term, *inter* refers to a reciprocal process, and *active* refers to who participates in this process, including faculty, the authors of texts, and students.

Faculty and program administrators who embraced a facilitative—in contrast to a didactic—approach were more participative and less hierarchical teachers, who viewed students as apprentices in their field. As we came to understand, faculty in these programs saw themselves as "expert guides" who facilitated their students' understanding of the knowledge and skills needed to practice their discipline by modeling techniques and engaging in joint problem-solving activities. For their part, students viewed themselves as "apprentices." They saw faculty both as accomplished experts who brought knowledge and experience to their teaching and as individuals who actively listened to, and sometimes learned from, their perspectives and ideas. There was a hierarchical dimension to faculty-student interactions in these programs, but we came to understand that communication was more two-way than one-way and that faculty viewed students less as receivers of knowledge and more as active contributors invested in the process of generating knowledge.

Faculty and program administrators who chose a facilitative approach to teaching and learning generally conceived of classroom-related lectures and discussions as activities that supplemented their program's primary learning experiences: intensive hands-on learning in experiential settings (scientific laboratories, theatrical productions, fieldwork experiences). In the context of these "learning laboratories," faculty members assisted students in learning the knowledge and skills of their discipline.

Finally, in a third set of cases, faculty and program administrators chose a dialogical approach to teaching and learning. Like those cases in which a facilitative approach was chosen, faculty and administrators focused their teaching and learning around two-way interactions that encouraged the discovery and generation of contingent knowledge. Yet, in these programs, we learned, interaction was more animated, collegial, and collaborative. Faculty as well as students so valued one another's ideas and experiences that they actively sought to learn from each other. Metaphorically, we came to understand this dialogical approach as a mutually evocative conversation in which faculty and students critically examined, interpreted, challenged, and rediscovered knowledge while, at the same time, they generated new knowledge and meaning.

Faculty and administrators who adopted a dialogical approach to teaching and learning assumed roles very different from those in which a didactic approach was used. Since faculty and administrators in these programs perceived students as experienced individuals who were important sources of ideas, they defined their role only minimally as transmitters of authoritative knowledge. By choosing to interact with students as colleagues, faculty frequently became colearners alongside students as they mutually examined and critically questioned knowledge and practices in their field. For their part, students saw themselves as individuals who had ideas and perspectives to contribute and hence defined themselves and their professors as teachers as well as learners.

Faculty and program administrators who took a dialogical approach to teaching and learning centered their program's primary learning experiences within the context of a tacit "learning community." In this setting, faculty and students participated in a variety of activities, including interactive classroom seminars, hands-on experiential learning, and informal outside-of-class conversations.

In many ways, the decision to take a dialogical approach to teaching and learning was similar to the choice to adopt a facilitative approach. In both instances, faculty became involved participants in the learning process, and, in turn, students valued faculty as active contributors to their learning. And, in both instances, communication was two-way, and faculty used cooperative and experiential instructional approaches. Yet there were significant differences. Faculty who embraced a dialogical approach were less hierarchical and acted more clearly as colleagues with students. Moreover, faculty and administrators in this set of programs were committed to nurturing collaborative learning communities in which distinctions between faculty and students were not considered a precondition for effective learning. Indeed, many faculty in these programs told us that hierarchical faculty-student interactions inhibited effective learning.

We turn now to three vignettes that illustrate the basic choices stakeholders made in this decision-situation. To represent a didactic approach, we present a vignette drawn from a nontraditional master's program in electrical engineering at United Technological University. We then feature a vignette from another electrical engineering master's program, at Moore A&T University, to illustrate a facilitative approach. Finally, we highlight Southern State University's nursing program as an example of a dialogical approach.

Engineering at United Technological University: A Didactic Approach

United Technological University (United Tech) is a nonprofit consortium established during the 1980s as a national university committed to serving the postbaccalaureate educational needs of engineers, technical professionals, and managers. To provide engineers with the opportunity to earn a master's degree while maintaining their employment, United Tech uses advanced telecommunications technology to deliver courses directly to the worksite. United Tech has no regular faculty, and, except for an office building where a small staff handles administrative matters and coordinates an extensive broadcast schedule, it has no campus. By providing an infrastructure that links faculty from participating universities with individuals in the workplace, United Tech offers students flexibility, choice, and convenience in pursuing their master's degree.

In 1990 United Tech offered master's degrees in seven engineering-related fields. The curriculum in each field was drawn up by a committee of faculty representing more than thirty participating institutions, and the courses were taught by faculty selected from these member institutions. Each of the more than three hundred corporate and industrial subscribers around the country operated a site at which students received live and videotaped graduate engineering courses—taught by participating faculty on their own campuses—via satellite.

Like all other master's programs offered at United Tech, the master's program in electrical engineering (EE) was anchored in the goals of the institution: to discover, disseminate, apply, and preserve knowledge. As the university bulletin put it, students were expected to "synthesize the delivered knowledge, to think critically, communicate effectively, and use knowledge intelligently and responsibly." To achieve these ends, EE faculty required master's students to complete a combination of thirty-three credits, including both general and highly specialized courses in an engineering subfield. Since United Tech did not require a thesis or project, the program consisted entirely of televised or videotaped courses.

Before our visit to United Tech, we had learned from university documents that the EE master's program was organized around the transmission of the most up-to-date knowledge in the field. An employer, who aptly summarized the views of many individuals we interviewed, put it straightforwardly: "This program feeds our engineers with a firehose." Like many other programs we visited, United Tech's main approach to teaching and learning was to educate students by didactically transmitting the latest knowledge to them. Instructional delivery was nontraditional, but instruction was not.

Stakeholders told us that great care went into the overall planning and evaluation of the EE master's program. To begin with, they emphasized that the program "utilized the expertise," as a United Tech brochure put it, of faculty "consultants" selected from the faculty of participating institutions. From the membership of this "graduate faculty," a chair for the program was appointed by United Tech's president. The chair was responsible for overseeing the program and assigning each new student an advisor. As United Tech administrators explained, the graduate faculty held at least one annual meeting and maintained communication through electronic mail, computer conferences, and teleconferences. Furthermore, they were responsible for regularly revising the curriculum to ensure that program content remained current.

While the graduate faculty ensured the program's overall quality, especially curriculum content, the chair and two university administrators (an academic coordinator and the academic vice president) were responsible for implementing the curriculum. Each term these individuals selected courses and instructors from the participating institutions, with the academic vice president making the final decision. We were told by those involved in these decisions that they used several criteria to select courses and faculty. One administrator explained, for example, that student demand was an important consideration and that United Tech occasionally polled potential students to find out what courses interested them. We learned, however, that, for the most part, decisions about what courses to offer and which professors to hire were based on identifying the "best courses" and the "best faculty." To this end, the electrical engineering program relied heavily on the nominations of participating institutions.

In our interviews with faculty, many conveyed their belief that a didactic teaching approach was, in the words of one professor, "the way for students to get in-depth knowledge." Without exception, faculty communicated this knowledge to students through classroom-based, satellite-transmitted lectures. When asked to compare differences in pedagogy between their undergraduate classes and United Tech classes, students and alumni of the program indicated that there was not much difference: listen to the lecture, absorb the content, go off by yourself and do the problems, and master the material. The primary focus was on "getting the content." As an administrator at United Tech elaborated:

> I think there is something about engineers and computer scientists. . . . They are much more turned on by the content and much more focused on the content. That's what it is that is important to them: the quality of the content. Other people, for some reason that is not abundantly clear to me, focus on presentation style, production quality, and it doesn't seem to matter whether it is good or bad content if it is broadcast quality. And engineers don't think that way. They don't care if it is "candid classroom" or not: the question is "what are they getting out of it?"

Although the videotaped lecture was the main vehicle for transmitting content, there was some interaction between faculty and students in courses. For one thing, several interviewees stressed that United Tech videotapes were not, as one faculty member put it, "dead." Rather, he explained, "we insist on teaching only when we have an on-campus section so that we have live students in the audience. When you're teaching it is usually only a small subset of students who ask 90 percent of the questions, and yet the questions they ask are frequently questions that an awful lot of other students have been pondering. So a videotape made in that format—with all of the questions live—actually has a lot of what I would call a 'living' nature to it." As one student remarked, however, students taking the course at the participating institution usually asked only "real technical" questions. A United Tech administrator told us that most courses also provided a brief call-in question period in which students could raise questions from their home sites. Students and faculty reported that relatively few students utilized this option.

In describing their experiences, several interviewees expressed concern about the relatively small amount of faculty-student interaction. Administrators as well as employers suggested that students sometimes miss "live interaction" owing to the delivery format of the program, although they emphasized that students had the opportunity to develop relations with faculty through long-distance communication (telephone and electronic and regular mail). And many faculty told us that the absence of direct faculty-student interaction was a limiting factor in satellite instruction. For several reasons, however, most students and alumni did not perceive this as a significant loss. First, as one student put it, engineering students were used to enacting a receiver role in the classroom, and thus their master's experience, in this sense, differed little from their undergraduate experience or, for that matter, from the experiences of master's students in "live" lecture halls on campus. Second, most said that they had the opportunity to interact with other employees in their workplace setting about what they were learning. An alumnus we spoke with indicated that for him interaction in the workplace more than compensated for any on-campus interaction he might miss:

> Well, I think the [on-campus] interaction—talking about the course and being enthusiastic and chatting with the professors, and so on—I view that as a substitute for what we have. Which is that we use that stuff [knowledge]—our careers depend on it. You get in there, you turn the tape off, you go back to your desk—and you do some of it, in real life. And you actually see the chip in six months. So maybe those guys [on campus] are kind of chatting and daydreaming about what they're going to do in a couple of years when they get their degree.

Throughout our interviews, we found a high degree of enthusiasm for the EE program, particularly for its emphasis on "cutting-edge" knowledge and for the effectiveness of its faculty in delivering that knowledge. Administrators at United Tech, though quick to point out that the program could always be improved, emphasized that long-distance technology and didactic teaching were well suited to master's-level work in engineering and that the program was meeting a vital societal need in providing working engineers with expert knowledge. The employers we interviewed expressed similar sentiments. One stated that the corporation he worked for believed the United Tech program was well worth the expenditure because graduates acquired knowledge that greatly increased their "efficiency" in the workplace. Another said that he was "pretty impressed" with the program and that he "likes the idea that the students are able to choose from what they consider to be the best classes from a variety of universities." Still another employer emphasized that United Tech courses had "direct value for research and development" in her corporation.

Faculty associated with the program expressed several reservations: the relative lack of interaction with students, the absence of a thesis requirement, an occasional problem in finding laboratories in which students could complete assignments, the technical challenges of long-distance instruction, and the nearly exclusive reliance on coursework. Yet, without exception, faculty expressed strong support for the program because it brought together some of the most highly regarded "authorities" in the field who, in turn, provided cutting-edge knowledge to students in what many interviewees referred to as United Tech's "state-of-the-art" courses. As one faculty member put it:

> Traditional education is ancient history. Most students today are part-timers. The mode of operation is shifting. The university will continue to be the backbone for engineering education, but it will need to accommodate more. This is the best of a no-win situation. With [United Tech's] program, you try and "milk the cream" from the best institutions in the country and provide this kind of educational experience to students. We must compete in the international marketplace. We must be competitive. This is an all-or-nothing game. [United Tech's] program provides students with some of the best national minds in engineering.

Echoing these views, another faculty member called United Tech students "incredibly lucky" because they can take courses from some of the "best and brightest in the field." This individual also noted in passing that the challenges of organizing material for broadcast were considerable. Perhaps because a tape "immortalizes a presentation in some way," he noted, faculty tended to prepare more carefully for these courses than for regular on-campus classes.

Students, too, were pleased with the content and overall approach to teaching and learning in United Tech's program. They appreciated the flexibility, choice, and convenience, and they valued the opportunity to learn from faculty considered to be experts in their field. Again and again, students and alumni talked about how United Tech provided the best courses from the "best universities in the country" and also offered greater depth and breadth of coursework than any single engineering program in the nation. For the most part, they indicated that their United Tech courses were better than on-campus courses (graduate and undergraduate) they had taken.

One alumnus reflected the generally positive response of students and alumni when he described his participation in graduation exercises at United Tech: "I felt a real sense of accomplishment . . . as I completed each and every course and applied it. I know that I'm much more theoretically based in a particular area, so there was this progression of competency, feeling of accomplishment, and then at graduation there was this step-function of 'wow.' Yeah, when they give you that hood, it's kind of like a recognition that, yeah, you're a master. Yeah, you definitely feel like a master."

In summary, we learned that, while United Tech's long-distance instructional delivery system distinguished it from many other master's programs, its overall approach to teaching and learning did not. In seeking to transmit the latest authoritative engineering knowledge to students, program administrators and faculty at United Tech capitalized on a one-way, didactic approach to teaching and learning. In so doing, interviewees believed United Tech's program was very successful at producing engineering experts who had "mastered" the latest cutting-edge knowledge in their field.

Moore A&T University: A Facilitative Approach

Moore A&T is a predominantly black public university located in a metropolitan area in the southern United States. Established as a "land-grant" college for blacks in the 1890s, the school introduced master's programs in the 1930s. In the late 1960s Moore A&T became a "regional university" and several years later a constituent institution in a statewide public system of higher education. Despite initiatives by university administrators to establish doctoral programs, A&T did not have doctoral programs when we visited the campus in 1990. It offered master's degrees in more than twenty fields to almost one thousand graduate students and enrolled over five thousand undergraduates.

Many interviewees told us that the School of Engineering was considered the "crown jewel" on the A&T campus and that the master's in electrical engineering was the largest and most visible of the five master's programs in engineering. Administrators and faculty said that the School of Engineering and the Department of Electrical Engineering enjoyed strong financial and symbolic support from university administrators.

At the time of our visit, more than 80 of the approximately 150 master's students enrolled in the School of Engineering had matriculated in the EE master's program. Most had enrolled directly after completing their undergraduate studies and attended on a full-time basis owing to the ample financial support available. More than a dozen students held fellowships, and most others received teaching and research assistantships during their first and second years, respectively. The sixteen EE faculty members had secured over two million dollars in externally funded research support during the previous year.

We learned from faculty and administrators that the primary mission of the EE master's program was to prepare and encourage students, especially African Americans, to pursue a doctorate elsewhere after completing their master's degree. As a former chair of the department put it: "We are bringing in talented black undergraduate students and then refocusing them toward graduate school. We have set the pursuing of doctoral degrees as a major priority." Faculty and students told us in recent years that the program had sent a substantial proportion of its master's graduates on to Ph.D. programs. At the same time, faculty and administrators also emphasized that they were committed to preparing engineers for the nonuniversity workplace. As a program administrator stated, "We have a special mission of taking students and turning them into highly competent engineers—whether they go on for the Ph.D. or go directly into the workplace."

To these ends, program administrators and faculty—under the leadership of the current and the previous department chairs—had focused on developing what one professor referred to as a "family image." As we came to understand, faculty and administrators had developed a shared commitment to teaching and learning in which each faculty member was expected to assume significant responsibility for "guiding," "apprenticing," and "mentoring" students throughout their master's experience. As one professor put it: "We all try to get our students prepared for Ph.D. work and the mainstream workplace, where they will not have one another for support. To do this we try to establish a balance between being too supportive and not being supportive enough, by being more caring than anywhere else."

On several occasions, faculty and administrators articulated the assumptions supporting their view of teaching and learning, including the assumption that students "learned best" by "doing" research with faculty guidance. A program administrator said that he and his colleagues felt strongly that "just one or two faculty can have a profound impact on a student." A professor elaborated on this perspective: "The mindset we create for our students is that we will give them every support service—such as access to tutorials—and that our faculty are very sensitive to being competent in the classroom, caring, providing lots of office hours and time for them. We will do everything we can to help make them successful." Faculty and administrators also emphasized that they held high expectations for students and that, as one administrator put it, "faculty could be very stern with students" if they were not fully committed to their studies. As one student told us, "Faculty here are incredibly supportive as long as you are industrious in your work."

Faculty and administrators implemented this facilitative approach to teaching and learning through a variety of faculty-guided, hands-on learning experiences. These included course-related projects, non-course-related projects, a thesis, and informal faculty mentoring. In addition, faculty strongly encouraged support staff to mentor students and students to support one another in their learning.

All EE master's students were required to complete twenty-four credits of course work. Faculty and students said that, while faculty sometimes lectured in the courses, it was their individual or group research projects—often guided by faculty—that were the center of their course experiences. Representing the view of many other interviewees, a graduate of the program told us:

> These projects are so important because the "real work" that you do is research. In almost all of the graduate [master's] classes you're supposed to have a project by the end of the semester. So these projects, with faculty help, give you the chance to learn how to do research and find out what your thesis is going to be about. For example, for one of my classes I had to design a traffic light controller—one that was not like the classic one. After doing that I realized that I wanted to go into this area. Then I went and talked to the chair and said, "What do you think?" And so I started to work with him. So I started with this little project [in a class] and found out what I wanted to do, and then I worked more than six months on my project.

In addition to course projects, interviewees emphasized that non-course-related research projects, conducted with faculty supervision, were a major feature of the program. Indeed, we were told that, since there was no departmental money for research (or teaching) assistantships, faculty used their external grant money to provide research assistantships to their master's students. First-year master's students were encouraged to identify a faculty member with whom they wished to work as a research assistant during their second year. At the same time, a program administrator mentioned, "faculty were free to attract students" with whom they wanted to work. Thus, faculty and students were, as he explained, "matched with one another, insofar as possible, with each student choosing their mentor." To ensure that matches were "good" ones, the department chair monitored the process and suggested "new matches," if necessary.

Students explained that they devoted much of their time to "doing research" with professors, both individually and in research groups. As an alumnus of the program put it: "Everything is in the lab. We had two students working on a project, and we went to national and international conferences, conferences where we presented our work. Most students worked in these 'mixed work stations,' and students really benefited from it." Many students said that they found "faculty-sponsored" laboratory research experiences both challenging and fulfilling. One told us, for example, that his mentor "depends on us to help with his research, but he gives us a lot of responsibility and guidance. He will get on your case every now and then if it's not going well, but, once we get things working and get good results, it's great and you learn a lot from him."

In addition to the projects students completed, interviewees explained that the thesis research and writing experience also was a central feature of the program. Although the program offered a nonthesis option, several stakeholders noted that faculty strongly encouraged students to take the thesis option—whether or not they planned to go on for a Ph.D.—and that almost all students did. Many faculty said that the opportunity to pursue independent thesis research under the guidance of a faculty member was important enough to justify their investment in this time-consuming activity. Students told us that the thesis was one of the most valuable aspects of their master's experience, especially the faculty guidance they received.

Interviewees also highlighted the value of informal faculty "mentoring" outside of class. One professor, for example, told us that faculty took their mentoring role so seriously that they only hired faculty who, in his words, "were multidimensional—faculty who are not only good 'research-and-grants' types but who have great teaching ability and care about students." Voicing a similar perspective, a program administrator said: "Here one must be really interested in advising students. Faculty are on campus from nine to five, and they are here for informal as well as formal contact. When we hire faculty, we stress this informal contact—that getting grants and publishing papers isn't enough. Like members of a small company, faculty have to be willing to be involved in many aspects of the master's program—not just their own specialty."

Students repeatedly told us that faculty provided outside-of-class mentoring in a variety of ways, from giving individualized help in the lab to developing students' knowledge and understanding of professional settings. An alumnus said, for example, that the department chair was constantly looking for professional opportunities for students:

> The chair and I were presenting papers at a conference in New Orleans. I was really impressed with the chair. He could have just sent me with a plane ticket. Instead, he said, "You're going to drive. Let's rent three vans and take fifteen more students." He just wanted to acquaint them with what was going on in the field. He paid for the whole thing just to have

them exposed to that. He told the students, "Go to any of the talks, whatever is going on. Go to those that you feel are interesting, but go and see how people are doing things."

Similarly, a program administrator stressed that he and his faculty colleagues informally interacted on almost a daily basis with students—in their offices, in the hallways, at various department-sponsored events, and through electronic mail.

Interviewees also noted that administrators and faculty encouraged technical staff to mentor students and that staff researchers responded accordingly. As one staff member explained: "What I do is work with students. . . . So we work together, and I show them how to use these tools because I'm there all the time." A program administrator, emphasizing that these support personnel were valuable resources for graduate students, said: "People in higher education don't think enough about how the support people can really help students. If I do my job right, I'm developing people [faculty and staff] who can do the work of helping students."

We also learned that faculty and program administrators encouraged students to learn from one another. One professor, for example, said that faculty "expected" their second-year master's students to mentor and "nurture" new students. As he explained, "Ordinarily, a program would have Ph.D. students doing that, but we have to use more senior master's students to help nurture the new ones." Similarly, a program administrator remarked: "Much of the learning for students occurs after class and in the labs, and it is group oriented—with students helping one another. When students get together and eat at McDonalds, then the groups start to form in the evenings, and they get together in the labs in different buildings and wrestle with things they have been working on. They come back and work with each other until midnight and then come in early in the morning. They come in on weekends."

Most A&T master's students and alumni told us that they learned a great deal from one another—in courses, working together on projects, and outside of class. Several said that, just as "faculty taught students," they actively "taught" one another. As one student put it: "In a small program like this, you really get to know one another. Our lives are tied together, socially and academically. We pull and push each other, to get everybody through . . . and so we stabilize each other and help each other. It's a source of motivation and stimulation."

Overall, interviewees were often effusive in describing the facilitative approach to teaching and learning in Moore A&T's engineering program. Faculty and administrators felt this approach was highly successful in helping students become more "self-assured professionals" who were skilled at doing research and "applying" and "producing" knowledge. Stakeholders also said that students began to embrace a contingent view of knowledge alongside an authoritarian view. Students became, as many faculty suggested, resourceful "problem solvers," who critically examined extant knowledge. Finally, faculty and administrators told us that they sent many "promising" students—African Americans and others—on to doctoral programs.

Students and alumni emphasized that they had grown significantly because of the faculty support they had received. One alumnus, for example, said that he had decided to enroll in the program because "faculty really worked with students to help them learn." He found that faculty did, in fact, "take more time" with him: "They help to develop your whole self versus just getting your degree. And I loved the one-on-one attention I got." An advanced student put this point in somewhat different terms: "This program has been a rite of passage for me and other students. Now we have a different way of approaching things because of all the research and independence and help from everyone. You get the 'big picture.' It definitely changes your outlook on things." Several students also made it clear to us that faculty were very helpful in encouraging them to pursue their Ph.D. degrees, and students who did not plan to go on for the Ph.D. told us that they felt very well prepared for the workplace.

Nursing at Southern State University: A Dialogical Approach

Like many regional institutions located in major metropolitan settings, Southern State University has grown rapidly in the last several decades. Since the 1960s, when Southern State first introduced master's and doctoral programs and became a full-fledged "university," many new graduate programs have been added. At the time of our visit, the university enjoyed considerable regional visibility as one of the largest nonresidential public universities in the South.

The evolution of nursing at Southern State mirrors the overall expansion of the institution. The baccalaureate program was initiated in the late 1960s, followed by the establishment of a master's program in the mid-1970s and a Ph.D. program in the mid-1980s. In 1990 the School of Nursing employed approximately thirty full-time faculty members. It enrolled more than one hundred students in its baccalaureate program, almost that many in its master's program, and a small number of doctoral students. Most of the students in the master's program were part-time, about one-fifth were minorities, and nearly all were female.

In reviewing information about the program prior to our visit, we noted that it appeared to be a traditional master's program in nursing. The program prepared individuals for advanced nursing practice as either clinical nurse specialists (CNS) or family nurse practitioners (FNP). Students who chose CNS preparation were expected to complete at least sixty credit hours, while students in the FNP specialization completed seventy-four units. In addition to taking core, research, and specialty courses, all master's students were required to complete a thesis or clinical research project.

Upon arriving at Southern State, we learned that the master's program in nursing had been undergoing major change. One of our first interviewees, a professor who had taught at Southern State for many years, told us that the School of Nursing had historically embraced a conventional approach to teaching and learning because, "to play with the 'big guys,' you had to use their rules. This is a male-dominated higher education institution, so you play it like that or else you're not viewed as being acceptable." Despite some resistance among a few nursing faculty, she noted, the faculty had begun to develop a new approach to teaching and learning which "didn't just belong to the faculty" but also "gave students a voice in their own learning." In much the same vein, another faculty member commented: "There are many of us on this faculty that are to a point now where we can't continue to teach the way we have. It's just too oppressive. We have to do it differently."

We learned that the faculty in nursing at Southern State had been engaged in what many referred to as a "curriculum revolution." Time and again, stakeholders told us that, over the previous several years, faculty and program-level administrators had scrutinized the foundations of their master's program, including its underlying purposes and its assumptions about teaching and learning. Although no new set of requirements had been developed, many interviewees indicated the program had already changed significantly within a short period of time.

When we asked faculty and program administrators what had sparked this curriculum revolution, they told us that, during the mid-1980s, many of them began to participate in a national debate centered around nursing education. Many attended national conferences of the National League of Nursing, which, they said, was at the forefront of a national movement to enhance the profession and redefine nursing education. They noted that most of the faculty were reading books and papers that encouraged them to rethink a variety of issues related to curriculum, particularly their perspectives on "knowledge" and "knowing" as well as their approaches to teaching and learning.

As a result of these activities and numerous discussions, faculty and administrators said that they began to reconceive their program. Several faculty indicated that they decided to develop a more two-way, interactive approach to teaching which would encourage students to take an inquisitive stance toward authoritative knowledge in their field and professional practice. As one faculty member explained:

> One of the things that we're trying to do is to raise the consciousness of students to things that people buy into without questioning. . . . If you accept things without questioning them, then you're buying in. That's what we try to do at the master's level—to get people to question the systems that they are in and the way things are done. For example, why do women and children have poorer health care, why aren't they valued more, why doesn't everyone have access? We want to give a bigger picture of the way the world is.

In a similar light, another faculty member told us that, above all, she wanted students to "question orthodoxy," to become more independent and, in our terms, more contingent thinkers. Similarly, a student stressed that faculty constantly urged students "to reexamine their values" and to "reexamine their own professional role in the health care industry." And other students and alumni emphasized that faculty constantly urged them, as one suggested, "to be free thinkers—they encourage thinking as opposed to just following strict guidelines."

Questioning orthodoxy, more than one faculty member stated, was central to the program. We came to appreciate that this questioning was inextricably linked to the teaching and learning approach faculty and program administrators chose for this program, namely, to encourage students to become active generators—as well as critical users—of knowledge. One faculty member captured what we have referred to as a dialogical approach to teaching and learning when she remarked:

> I don't know if you are familiar with the work, it was a qualitative study: *Women's Ways of Knowing*. That wasn't the only thing, but it was one of the things that helped some of us see that women, and others, but women have primarily been "received knowers"—that whatever an expert tells them, it must be true and I'll just accept that. And we have our students read that, and that helps to give them an idea of where we are coming from. It's that kind of thing that we're trying to do here. To make past "received knowers" into "creative knowers" and have them feel comfortable about what we do and know and telling students like, "Look, you have a lot of knowledge. You may not have been rewarded for it or it hasn't been valued or whatever, but you do have a lot of knowledge."

A program administrator used similar language to describe this dialogical approach: "One of the central elements that we've discussed over and over again is the notion of empowerment—empowerment in the sense of recognizing yourself as both a knowledge user and a knowledge maker." Another administrator told us that the program sought to cultivate "the excited student, who continues to be excited and is ready to embrace new knowledge and to look at old knowledge in different ways, piecing it all together in a pattern that will help them to be the scholars and leaders in the health care field."

In adopting this dialogical approach, most faculty associated with the master's program revisited their traditional approaches to teaching. Many said that they had greatly reduced the amount of lecturing they did and, instead, encouraged students to share their experiences, question assumptions, and develop their own interpretations. One professor provided an example of how faculty had set this new approach in motion:

> What we're doing now is sharing with each other and how it's working. Like, for example, in the pathophysiology course, the instructor who teaches the course has stopped lecturing. There are certain articles that are assigned for the evening, and she has told the students that this is your class, here are some things we might discuss, but we can do it in whatever way you choose to do it. Even some of the content has already changed— bringing in the critical thinking, the feminist perspectives, and questioning things that nurses often think are carved in stone. . . . And we're questioning that with the students. We're asking them if they think that's the way our knowledge really is.

Not surprisingly, the move away from a didactic approach toward a dialogical one had not been easy. One faculty member noted that coming to grips with this "new pedagogy" was "real powerful" and that "you can't do this stuff without being different yourself. You can't continue to teach old ways that you are teaching and have the 'curriculum revolution' happen, and it requires a fundamentally different relationship between faculty and students. We have to mourn for what we've done and are not going to do anymore." We were told that a few faculty in the program had not fully embraced the "new pedagogy."

Throughout our interviews at Southern State, faculty described how they had reexamined old assumptions and developed new perspectives on how they viewed their own and their students' roles in the teaching and learning process. As one faculty member explained, it was in preparing for one of her courses that she began to reconceptualize these "teacher" and "student" roles: "I had just finished this book about how 'received knowers' are set up in this way by educators, and it talked about all the things I had ever done in teaching and lectures. And again, I found myself in the place where I just couldn't do this." With the support of her peers, she completely reconceptualized her teaching approach, moving away from viewing students as receivers of knowledge to more active learners who had valuable insights and perspectives to contribute. "I began to recognize that students' experiences were valuable sources of knowledge," she said. "And I began to create opportunities for helping students to see that and to get them to share their knowledge in my classes."

Faculty and program administrators told us that this "new pedagogical approach" was based on a new understanding of teachers and students as collaborative, collegial learners engaged in a simultaneously enriching teaching and learning dialogue. As one professor put it:

> Teaching and learning is a mutual investment in a "continuing other"—it's an embeddedness in the process over a period of time with one or two individuals that you begin to trust and you begin to dialogue with in seminars. It's a dialogic, you begin to play out the process around their experiences. . . . These people need to be developed, and I need to be developed, and this happens from dialogue and reflection and making some mistakes and being confused and having to work it through. It requires a tremendous commitment to dialogue with students and really trying to see how their thinking is developing. . . . There are no teachers and students. We are all here learning. Some of us are more learned than others and vice versa.

Another faculty member expressed this idea in these terms: "One of the things that we try to do is independent thinking—critical thinking— taking responsibility for your own learning and knowing what you want from the program. . . . We try to let people [faculty] pick out how they'll implement those kinds of things, to make it a much more collegial relationship with the student—not as controlling. Having students take responsibility for where they want the course to go."

Most faculty and administrators noted that, although many students were initially hesitant to abandon their traditional role as receivers of knowledge, they developed confidence in their abilities to be active "knowledge constructors." One professor, for example, elaborated on this approach:

> Some students—by virtue of their past educational experiences—are very resistant to that. But eventually they learn to like it, and they accept that responsibility for leading the discussions, asking the questions, deciding on learning experiences, writing the kinds of papers that they think are useful for them. . . . Initially, some students think that they just need more knowledge of machines and scientific facts and those kinds of things. Then I try to tell them that it's not in the technology, it's in you. And the technology can work through you, but you have to have these other things within you to make nursing the best it can be.

In much the same vein, another faculty member provided this perspective:

> Many of the students still believe firmly that I am the expert. The question that they asked me last time at the beginning of class was, "When are you going to tell us the facts that we need to know?" And I said, "First of all, that puts me into a position of incredible power to assume that I know the facts that you need to know." The problem I have with somebody asking me "When are you going to tell me the facts that I need to know?" is the elitism; it's an inherently disempowering perspective for that person to think that somebody outside them can tell them what they need to know. There has to be some movement where people recognize not only that they have knowledge within themselves but that they have the ability to get additional information that they might need and make decisions about whether or not that material is valid instead of allowing somebody else to tell you that "this is what you need to know."

From our interviews with employers, we learned that faculty had, in the words of one professor, begun "to walk their talk." One employer noted that "a lot of the teaching is done between colleagues instead of the traditional way of the instructor coming to class to do the teaching; it's teaching by the class itself." She said that this "collaborative spirit" affected graduates, "who can't help but be changed by that experience." Another employer remarked that her master's-educated employees were very independent and autonomous: "These nurses aren't afraid to get out there and challenge major assumptions. They're more independent, more autonomous, and more creative."

Similarly, students and alumni emphasized that the dialogical approach to teaching and learning in particular, and the master's experience in general, had significant consequences for how they viewed knowledge and approached their professional practice. As one student told us: "Before I was just a robot. . . . I was a good staff nurse. But it wasn't like anything I can do now." Another student described the effects on her this way: "I discovered that I could be a free thinker, and I got this in the master's program. The master's gave me a path for a journey for a lifetime."

For their part, faculty and administrators in the master's program were pleased with the way their dialogical approach to teaching and learning had changed students from passive receivers of knowledge to more active generators of knowledge and understanding. One professor, with a full measure of pride, remarked that "students are cockier—they're more willing to say what they think." Another faculty said that a student recently told her that the program had changed her life. She continued: "They say things like that to us—that they can never go back and practice the way they did before."

Program Orientation: Academic, Professional, or Connected

Across the forty-seven cases in our study, we came to understand that faculty and program administrators made important choices concerning program orientation, a decision that often had subtle but nonetheless significant consequences for the master's experiences of students and faculty. We learned that faculty and program administrators chose one of three general orientations for their master's programs: academic, professional, or connected.

In broad strokes, the orientation decision-situation concerned the kinds of knowledge and skills faculty chose to emphasize in their master's programs. Faculty in one set of programs oriented their programs around the highly specialized (nonapplied) theoretical knowledge and basic research skills highly valued in academe and used primarily in college and university settings. In contrast, faculty in another set of cases focused on the specialized theoretical and applied knowledge—and field-specific technical skills—valued in professional, nonuniversity workplace cultures and settings. (By referring to "professional" nonuniversity workplace cultures, we do not mean to imply that academics are not professionals.) And faculty in a third set of cases oriented their programs around the generalized and specialized theoretical and applied knowledge and skills valued in both academic and professional workplaces. In effect, these latter faculty did not divide knowledge into the "generalized versus specialized" and "theoretical versus applied" dyads that distinguish "academic" and "professional workplace" cultures. Rather, they sought to understand and use knowledge independently of these traditional distinctions and to "connect" these various kinds of knowledge in their programs.

Decisions about program orientation were, to some degree, shaped by field-specific job market circumstances that generally were beyond the control of faculty and administrators. In some fields (such as sociology and English), for example, the master's degree was often viewed as a first step in securing academic employment, even though an uncertain professional, nonuniversity job market exists for master's-educated individuals in these fields. In others (such as theater and business), the master's degree was perceived mostly as a credential for professional advancement in nonuniversity workplace settings. In still others (such as education and microbiology), the master's was used as a vehicle for advancement either in higher education or in nonuniversity workplace settings. The institutional mission in many colleges and universities was oriented either toward the nonuniversity workplace or the academic workplace. In short, we came to appreciate that circumstances such as these may have influenced, though by no means wholly prescribed, the kinds of knowledge and skills faculty and program administrators chose to emphasize in their master's programs.

In those programs in which faculty and administrators chose an academic orientation, faculty made it clear to us that the knowledge and skills they most wanted students to learn were those highly valued in academe. They expected students to acquire a basic understanding of highly specialized and theoretical knowledge, which they contrasted sharply—and occasionally disparagingly—with applied knowledge. Further, they accentuated those skills highly valued in academic culture: research skills, analytical and problem-solving skills, and written communication skills.

In choosing this orientation, faculty usually viewed master's education, like doctoral education, as removed from the more technical and practical concerns associated with professional, nonuniversity workplace settings. They also emphasized the hiring and retention of faculty who demonstrated a commitment to academic values, usually placing great value on full-time faculty who had strong academic, as opposed to nonuniversity workplace, credentials. Although on occasion programs in professional fields temporarily engaged practitioners to help develop students' technical skills, faculty and program administrators expected the full-time faculty to do most of the teaching to ensure that the knowledge and skills they valued were acquired by students.

In those programs in which faculty and program administrators chose a professional orientation, faculty aligned their programs with the knowledge and skills valued in nonuniversity workplaces. While not minimizing the importance of specialized theoretical knowledge, faculty in these programs placed as much, if not more, emphasis on applied, practical knowledge. In addition, they stressed the acquisition of skills valued in the workplace, including technical, field-specific professional practice skills (such as clinical nursing skills, acting methods, or stock valuation techniques); analytic and problem-solving skills; and written and oral communication skills.

In this set of programs, faculty conceived of master's education as a time when students learned not only theory but also the everyday knowledge and practices of their profession. Accordingly, they sought to hire faculty who held academic credentials and had some experience in the nonuniversity workplace, either through previous employment or through current applied research projects or consulting activities. Moreover—and in sharp contrast to most programs with an academic orientation—these programs often hired full-time professional practitioners as part-time adjunct faculty. And many of these programs sponsored a variety of informal events at which invited workplace representatives provided students with "real-world" perspectives on their professional practice.

In the final set of programs—those with a connected orientation—faculty and program administrators brought together people involved in both university and nonuniversity workplace settings and, in so doing, embraced the knowledge, skills, and attitudes valued in both academic and professional cultures. By hiring full-time faculty with professional, nonuniversity workplace experience, as well as by developing ties with people in nonuniversity positions, these programs brought the knowledge and skills germane to both settings into the service of their more connected orientation. They accomplished this, in part, by not distinguishing—in terms of economic rewards and status—between those faculty who valued highly specialized (nonapplied) theoretical knowledge and those who preferred more generalized theoretical and applied knowledge. In effect, we learned that most faculty in these programs believed that theory and practice should not be separated into discrete "categories" of knowledge, each one associated with specified activities. Rather, faculty suggested that they viewed all knowledge in connected, dynamic, and inseparable terms.

Many interviewees communicated to us that it was faculty, and often program administrators, who established programs with this connected orientation and that the affirmative responses of students nurtured and helped to institutionalize it. As we came to understand, faculty in these programs were more responsive and open in comparison to the more goal-driven faculty who chose an academic or professional orientation for their master's programs. To illustrate, many faculty in these programs did not assume that people in university and nonuniversity workplace settings thought in fundamentally different ways, nor did they look more favorably on one group of individuals over another because they chose academic or professional careers. Rather, they generally treated all students, regardless of their career aspirations, as individuals eager to learn and enrich themselves. Moreover, many faculty also held the view that in both settings there were interesting and important technical and nontechnical goals to achieve.

Faculty who chose a connected orientation for their master's programs frequently told us that, in both university and nonuniversity settings, people constantly needed to rely upon and develop generalizations while also managing nitty-gritty details. As such, they stressed generalized and specialized knowledge that was both theoretical and applied.[1] These faculty also emphasized that in both settings the ability to see the "broader view," the "big picture," was a critical skill they sought to develop in their students. We also learned that general and technical field-specific professional practice skills, analytic and problem-solving skills, and oral and written communication skills were emphasized by faculty who chose a connected orientation for their master's programs.

We now present vignettes from three different institutions to illustrate the choices faculty and program administrators made with respect to this decision-situation. We include nursing at Barrett State Medical Center to illustrate a program with an academic orientation, education at Laramie University to portray a case in which faculty and program administrators chose a professional orientation, and environmental studies at Major State University to represent a program with a connected orientation.

Nursing at Barrett State Medical Center: Academic Orientation

Barrett State Medical Center, a specialized institution devoted exclusively to the health sciences, is a major public university within a statewide higher education system. It consists of four professional schools (nursing, medicine, dentistry, and pharmacy), graduate programs in the basic and behavioral sciences, several health policy institutes, and a medical center that includes several hospitals. Barrett State's student body is composed of mostly graduate students enrolled in either advanced professional or graduate programs in health-related fields such as microbiology, neuroscience, and psychology.

When we visited Barrett State in 1990, it was widely recognized as one of the leading health science complexes in the United States, what one professor described as a "high-tech, biotech university." Without exception, interviewees emphasized the university's commitment to maintaining its academic reputation as a prestigious research institution. To that end, senior-level administrators told us that the university was heavily dependent on outside funding and that a large proportion of its annual budget came from federal government and other external funding sources. One student's views on this topic reflected those of many interviewees: "Well, money is the almighty arbiter here. The faculty on this campus are hired because of their grant-producing and grant-getting ability and are tenured a lot on that. . . . The professors are very outspoken about saying 'Look, I'm here because I publish, because I've gotten these grants.'" A senior administrator at Barrett State put it forcefully when he said that all faculty, including those in nursing, needed to "publish big time" in order to establish themselves on campus.

We learned that the School of Nursing was strongly oriented toward the kinds of knowledge, skills, and values strongly associated with the academic culture at Barrett State. Faculty repeatedly emphasized that they were expected to engage in significant research, contribute to the "science of nursing," and join the ranks of nationally and internationally known nursing scholars. Many noted that the School of Nursing had a stellar external funding record, securing several million dollars annually in training and sponsored research grants. Nursing faculty and administrators likewise mentioned that their doctoral program was highly regarded in academic circles and recently was ranked as one of the best in the nation.

Faculty and program administrators at Barrett State told us that they intended their master's program to prepare individuals for a wide range of nursing roles, including clinical nurse specialist, administrator, teacher, and consultant. According to a program brochure, graduates were expected to "have a base of knowledge in a specific area of nursing" which would allow them to "participate knowledgeably in research activity and application" and "contribute to the formation of theory in nursing practice." To ensure that these expectations were met, students were required to take at least thirty-six units of specialized course work. In addition, students completed core nursing and research courses, a supplementary internship (practicum), and a written comprehensive examination or a thesis. According to several interviewees, faculty strongly "urged" students not to write a thesis but to take the comprehensive examination instead.

In describing their master's program, faculty, students, and employers variously referred to the curriculum as "hyperspecialized" and "balkanized." A program administrator, for example, said that the master's program was a "confederation of specialty areas rather than a unified curriculum." Likewise, a faculty member emphasized that the influence of external funds from what she called the "medical-industrial complex" had made the curriculum highly responsive on externally driven research topics (emphasizing "pharmacological intervention," for example, instead of other treatments and more prevention-oriented nursing).

In 1990 almost three-fourths of the approximately six hundred students in the School of Nursing were enrolled in the master's program. All master's students had at least one year of professional experience, and most attended part-time. There were close to one hundred full-time faculty, including a substantial number of clinical faculty hired on "soft funds" as well as a large contingent of nonsalaried adjunct faculty. The School of Nursing had relatively abundant supporting resources, including a separate office that provided services such as statistical consultation to assist faculty and students in developing proposals and conducting research and a learning resources center to help students and faculty in their assignments, research, and publications.

We learned that the master's program was heavily infused with the same academic orientation that permeated Barrett State and its School of Nursing. One program document we reviewed, for example, emphasized that the major purpose of the master's program was "to provide students with advanced knowledge in a specific area of nursing and with the knowledge necessary to participate effectively in research activity." It went on to state that the master's program "set forth an integrated body of knowledge with primary emphasis on presenting principles and theories rather than on developing skills and techniques for immediate practical application."

Further, this document noted that students must "demonstrate theoretical knowledge in a selected area of specialization," "use advanced theoretical knowledge in the practice setting," and be able to "critique and evaluate developed theory and research as they relate to the science base of nursing." In short, the program placed major emphasis on highly specialized, generally nonapplied, theoretical knowledge—the kind of knowledge most valued in academe.

Stakeholders confirmed that the emphasis on specialization and the acquisition of theoretical knowledge was the cornerstone of their program. As one student put it, "The faculty encourage you to find a specialty area because I think [Barrett State] prides itself on producing people who are specialists." One employer suggested that about 70 percent of the curriculum was concerned with "theory." And a student, whose views represented those of many interviewees, told us:

> The faculty really pride themselves on producing traditional people who have a conceptual framework and background on how to synthesize and analyze information, whatever information that is. But they try to give you that as a basis. . . . On top of that you come here to get a specific body of knowledge. . . . Probably the skill that I'm going to get that's going to be most valuable is an ability to look at systems and bodies of information analytically, to be able to critique them and see what's worthwhile in this body of knowledge in terms of patient care and to kind of throw out the rest of it.

The importance placed on theoretical knowledge, research, and higher-order thinking skills was reflected in faculty teaching assignments in the program. As one alumna of the program explained, the "regular" tenure-track faculty saw their job as teaching the theory and research in the program. As she and others noted, these faculty seldom had significant clinical experience and often had little interest in "application" and the "clinical side of things." One program-level administrator commented that the regular faculty simply did not have time to be involved in practice-related activities, much less to supervise "independent research" or theses.

Many interviewees emphasized that it was mostly the adjunct faculty who focused on the development of practitioner skills in students. We were told that students developed these skills in the "advanced practice" component of the master's program during their second year when they completed their internships. Since full-time regular faculty generally viewed them as supplemental learning activities, unsalaried adjunct faculty usually supervised students' internships or practica.

In describing their experiences in the program, interviewees spoke highly of two aspects of the program. First, many were impressed with the quality of the regular faculty, both in terms of their scholarly reputations and their command of leading-edge theoretical knowledge. Faculty expressed pride in the number of individuals in their department who had national and international reputations. Similarly, students and alumni conveyed great respect for the regular faculty's scholarly qualifications, research productivity, ability to attract sponsored research funding, and visibility in the field. One student, after telling us what an "honor" it was to have so many faculty at the leading edge of the field, remarked: "The saying is that if you didn't see it here, you won't see it, and that is—very much in a nutshell—how you feel about [the master's program]. And I think everybody who has come out of this program has to admit that. If you didn't see it here, it probably doesn't exist." Most of the stakeholders we interviewed told us that they especially valued the fact that faculty gave students, in the words of one employer, a "strong theory base."

Students, alumni, and employers also were pleased with the quality of interaction students had with adjunct faculty. One alumna described her experiences with adjunct faculty in these terms:

> They [regular faculty] had guest lecturers who would come in, . . . such as [an individual] who works in ambulatory care who is knee-deep in this stuff and is an excellent teacher. So when they have those kinds of people come in and teach rather than the faculty here who teach, it's great. It's great. We loved it. We hung on their every word. . . . They were my preceptors [internship supervisors] out there in the field, but they also came here on occasion and taught a class, and they were so great. They were "real" because they were telling you what's really happening out there and practice it in the real world—not this "ivory tower" that we used to call it.

Many stakeholders, however, were disappointed with other aspects of Barrett State's academically oriented nursing program. Students, alumni, and employers, in particular, expressed concern over the relative lack of attention given to advanced professional practice in the program. One alumna emphasized, for example, that there was not enough doing and clinical practice—that the little experience she had gotten was in her internship. Many students noted that the faculty seemed to be more concerned with preparing researchers than advanced practitioners. Similarly, employers often were dissatisfied with the full-time faculty's weak clinical backgrounds and their lack of interest in the practical side of nursing. One, the chief nursing administrator in a major hospital, remarked that many of the regular faculty "found it difficult" to walk the one hundred paces from the School of Nursing to the hospital. Another noted that the regular faculty simply were not involved in nursing practice and "care giving."

Closely connected, many interviewees were displeased with the disjuncture between theory and practice in the program. Students and alumni, for example, told us that the theory they learned in class was not linked to the internship they completed near the end of their program and that it was the adjunct faculty who helped them bridge the gap between theory and practice. The regular faculty, we learned, assumed that students could "apply the theory" once they learned it. And employers suggested that better bridges needed to be built between the "operations," or practice, side and the academic side of the program.

Education at Laramie University: A Professional Orientation

Laramie University, a private university in the western United States, is located in a metropolitan setting. Its campus suits Laramie's reputation as a "small university," an appellation frequently invoked by faculty, administrators, and students. As a small university, Laramie enrolls about six thousand students, almost one-half in its graduate and professional programs. Notwithstanding its modest size and strong commitment to undergraduate education, Laramie is very much a university: it offers programs in over forty fields of study, houses several major research institutes, and maintains an extensive library system.

For many years, faculty and administrators at Laramie had been involved in efforts to develop interdisciplinary programs, institutes, and centers. One of these initiatives, launched in the late 1960s, led to the establishment of the International Relations Teaching Institute (IRTI). Jointly sponsored by the Graduate School of International Studies (GSIS) and the School of Education, IRTI is self-supporting and employs three professionals, including the director of its master's program. As stated in institutional documents, the institute's main purpose is to "help classroom teachers become more knowledgeable and proficient at teaching global, social science, and educational skills topics" in order "to improve the teaching of precollegiate international and intercultural studies." To that end, IRTI offers credit and noncredit courses and workshops for teachers; develops and disseminates teaching materials related to major issues and problems in areas such as global awareness, environmental education, cultural studies, and bilingual/bicultural education; and provides consulting services to schools.

Through the School of Education and with the joint cooperation of GSIS, IRTI offers an interdisciplinary M.A. degree in curriculum and instruction with a cognate in international studies. Intended for working educators, the program is designed to enhance students' "teaching skills" in three major areas: (1) addressing major substantive issues in the world today such as conflict, change, communication, and interdependence; (2) planning and evaluating curricula related to problems that confront humankind; and (3) developing practical classroom strategies for translating awareness of issues into meaningful learning experiences for students.

Students began IRTI's forty-five-credit (quarter system) master's program during the summer when they enrolled full-time in an intensive nine-credit course on world politics for precollegiate teachers and a one-credit IRTI course. The world politics course was offered by GSIS. In subsequent semesters, students completed nine credits in the School of Education, including two research courses and a course in cultural foundations; a ten-credit IRTI "curriculum development laboratory" sequence; and seventeen credits of electives. In addition, a curriculum project and a comprehensive examination were required. After the first summer, most students completed their courses on a part-time basis during evenings and on weekends.

In 1990 IRTI's master's program enrolled approximately twenty students, most of whom were junior high or high school teachers. Although faculty from education and international studies were involved, IRTI staff administered the program and taught many of the courses. None of the three faculty in IRTI held a doctorate, but all had considerable experience in education as well as extensive practical experience in international education, including consulting, preparing teaching materials related to global education, and conducting workshops for teachers.

In our interviews at Laramie, we learned that the GSIS and School of Education faculty associated with the master's program often taught the kinds of knowledge and skills commonly associated with an academic orientation. Faculty and students told us that the interdisciplinary nine-credit world politics course was "content rich" and "theoretical" and that most of the courses in the School of Education and GSIS were organized around theoretical knowledge. Yet interviewees emphasized that the program was principally organized around a professional orientation that provided students with the applied knowledge, skills, and practical experiences that were expected to be most valuable to them in teaching and developing international studies/global education curricula.

The director of the master's program explained the program in these terms: "I think that the [IRTI] master's degree should be for practitioners as opposed to theoreticians, . . . and [I think] that we offer them the opportunity to acquire the kinds of skills which will make them better practitioners." Voicing similar sentiments, other interviewees said that the program emphasized "applied" and "practical" knowledge and focused on cultivating students' workplace skills—including pedagogical, problem-solving, communication, and interpersonal skills—and improving students' abilities to develop curricula and work cooperatively with others.

Faculty and students told us that the IRTI courses were designed to bring together the content provided in the intensive world politics course with the pedagogy offered in the education courses. As an alumna of the program put it: "It's like the Graduate School of International Studies feeds us the international study content type of stuff that we took in the summer. Then the School of Education gives us 'back-up' education classes. And then [IRTI] blends them together and offers us creative educational ways of presenting international studies." Indeed, IRTI faculty said that they offered the four-course "curriculum development laboratory" to help students relate their interdisciplinary experiences to their professional work as teachers.

We came to appreciate that IRTI faculty and program administrators relied on three basic strategies to help students apply what they learned in class to their professional practice. First, faculty emphasized an applied curricular focus in the program, in which students, faculty, and outside speakers were encouraged to discuss their real-world experiences with one another. Second, they relied heavily on practical learning activities designed to improve the teaching skills of their students. Third, and closely related, they required students to complete a major curriculum project.

IRTI faculty told us that they initially incorporated this applied curricular focus during the first quarter of their program when, concurrent with the world politics course, students took their first IRTI course. An IRTI professor explained how he used this course to help students apply global education concepts to their teaching and curriculum planning and to invite students to become active participants in their own learning:

> I'm the one who talks with students initially about how we're going to take this concept of, for instance, the concept of nation-states—which can be fairly ivory tower and esoteric—and translate that into something that third-graders [or ninth-graders] can do. . . . [Students] have to keep a log or a journal of ideas on a daily basis while they're in [the world politics course], but we also take them out, and I do things with them. I do some new games with them to supplement the intellectual, cognitive kinds of things they are doing. I take them out, and I give them the opportunity to talk about "how do you take this concept of conflict resolution and bring it down to make it work with the elementary children when we talk about global education?" It's not just a concept of things that happen on the other side of the world, but children have to be able to learn to get along with who's sitting next to them and to be able to play together in the schoolyard. And that's also global education. They [teachers] don't have to be talking about India to be a global educator.

Interviewees also told us that IRTI faculty regularly invited practitioners from the larger community, as well as other graduate students and faculty at Laramie University, to speak in their courses. One IRTI faculty member, for example, said that, in his course on "Third World Development," he invited female students from GSIS to participate in a panel discussion on the role of women in developing nations. Another professor noted that he brought international graduate students into his course to discuss their perspectives on global education.

Besides emphasizing an applied focus in their program, IRTI faculty oriented their courses around hands-on learning activities designed to enhance students' teaching skills. Students told us, for example, that faculty used games and simulations to encourage them to consider different teaching and learning styles when developing international studies curricula. As one student explained: "There were always some principles at work, like 'dependencia'—the way Third World countries are economically dependent on industrial countries. One of these games would easily illustrate this concept and help engage the students in substantive discussions of what dependencia is—questions like: Are countries prompted by necessity to be cooperative? So these things illustrate different approaches to teaching and development of curriculum." Another student vividly described her recollections of a class session devoted to games: "We spent time in one class playing the kinds of games kids would play and which have international learning consequences. We got so much from it that we forgot we were supposed to be learning from it. But when we looked back on it, we thought, 'What sorts of tricks do I have in my bag of teaching tools that I can use to have fun with the kids?' We were enjoying ourselves so much, too."

IRTI faculty and students also told us that field visits and community service were an important part of IRTI courses. These experiential learning activities were designed to encourage students to think creatively about ways of teaching international studies and to enrich their respect for different cultures. One student, for instance, explained that she worked in a homeless shelter as part of one of her classes:

> Now you might ask yourself: "What are a bunch of graduate students doing down at the local homeless shelter serving meals?" Most of us don't normally go down there. But we're studying international issues that affect a variety of people—there are all sorts of refugee movements going on. Now, if we're going to understand refugees traipsing across the border between Cambodia and Thailand, we can start by understanding it locally. At this homeless shelter, we're seeing a great variety of people who are homeless—often times for the same economic and political reasons as folks in Cambodia and Thailand.

A required curriculum project was the other major way IRTI faculty and program administrators oriented their program around the kinds of applied knowledge and practical skills valued in the professional workplace. As we came to appreciate, this project not only encouraged students, "to do something that they can take back and use in their class-rooms," in the words of a program administrator, but it also was an integral part of the applied curricular focus incorporated into all IRTI courses. Many stakeholders told us that the curriculum project was a key feature of the master's program.

Students began their curriculum projects during their first summer in the program and worked on them throughout the four-course IRTI curriculum laboratory sequence. In brief, students were required to develop a complete curriculum (including lesson plans) that they, and others, could use in their classrooms. During their first terms, students identified their topics and, with extensive feedback from practitioners in their schools, produced project outlines. As the director of the master's program put it: "Before they ever sit down to write their curriculum, they have to go to other people [in their schools] and talk with them about this. They have to be willing to compromise. They have to get others to buy in who are going to be involved in teaching this so they don't step on toes. It's a whole feedback system, which involves them in a dynamic change situation."

Students then developed their individual projects during the first three courses of the curriculum development sequence. IRTI faculty and students alike explained that a substantial portion of class time was devoted to discussing and critiquing student projects. As one faculty member described this process:

> Students bring their proposed plans to the class, and they bring multiple copies. The class is involved in giving each other feedback because . . . one of the skills that I want them to acquire is that they need to be good curriculum evaluators—not only writers, but evaluators. . . . They're given constant new input, which they then incorporate into their writing process. So, for instance, we open up with a night on writing—how you teach students writing skills. We follow that with a night on cooperative learning. We follow that with a night on critical thinking, followed by a night on learning styles.

In describing their program experiences, interviewees told us that they greatly valued the curriculum project because it was directly tied to their professional practice. One alumnus, for example, stated simply: "The curriculum project was great because we walked out with the actual curriculum in our hand." Another student said that the high school global studies curriculum she developed was being implemented in her school. And the director of the master's program, who noted that IRTI sometimes published student projects and marketed them throughout the world, explained that he valued these projects because they were meaningful "products." In his words:

It's a product. It's something they're very proud of, that . . . is a very tangible result of the year or two or three that they've gone through here. As I always say in my orientation sessions, "Why do you want to go through a master's program where you do a thesis which ends up on a dusty shelf somewhere?" . . . Master's degrees are for practitioners. Do something that you can use in the classroom that you're going to be proud of. And that's this. And that's what they walk out with.

While interviewees were most enthusiastic when discussing the curriculum project, they also spoke appreciatively about the program's emphasis on practical knowledge and skills. Indeed, many students stressed that the program enabled them to gain new perspectives and insights that enriched their pedagogical and curriculum planning skills. As one student put it, "Since I've been in this program, I feel like I've been able to offer much more in rewriting curriculum for our department."

To be sure, two individuals we interviewed were critical of the IRTI master's program. One, a faculty member in the School of Education, criticized the program for being "too practical and applied" and said it needed more emphasis on theory. The other, an institutional administrator at Laramie, expressed strong reservations: "I'll be very frank with you. I think that a lot that goes on in [IRTI] is very, very problematic—in terms of course work, the quality of course work, the level of course work."

Yet those interviewees directly involved with the program—faculty, students, and alumni—felt very differently. They spoke with great enthusiasm for the IRTI program. Time and again, stakeholders told us that graduates of the program were "doers" who had developed a broad range of skills that enhanced their effectiveness as teachers. One student, whose views reflected those of many others, evaluated the program in these terms:

> Over twenty years I've taught across the spectrum, from the best and brightest to the most impoverished and educationally deprived. And I really like what I see here [IRTI]—with new ideas on working with students, curricular development, philosophies—it really is plowing new ground. And I can say that from having been in the educational setting for so long. It's very refreshing and, I think, legitimate, that is, it's not appealing only because it's new—it's new, and it makes sense. It's new, and it's very applicable.

Environmental Studies at Major State University: A Connected Orientation

Established as a land-grant institution in the mid-1800s, Major State University has been one of the nation's leading public research institutions for over a century. The university offers master's and doctoral programs in over one hundred departments and enrolls more than ten thousand graduate students. Major State faculty annually attract millions of dollars in extramural research support, placing the university within the top ten institutions nationwide in sponsored research activity. Many of Major State's faculty are considered to be among the leading scholars in their disciplines.

While several master's programs at Major State relate to environmental studies, we chose the program that focused on the management of water resources. When we interviewed there in 1990, the Management of Water Resources (MWR) master's program was part of the Environmental Studies Center (ESC), a campuswide institute that housed seven research centers and various graduate programs.

In 1990 over fifty faculty—from more than twenty different departments representing the arts and sciences, engineering, business, law, architecture, and medicine—were affiliated with the MWR master's program.[2] Faculty members told us they became involved in the MWR program largely out of their strong commitment to addressing environmental problems from an interdisciplinary perspective—an opportunity, they said, that was not available or recognized in their departments. As the ESC director put it, "What's exciting about the program is that we have so many people, faculty, coming together out of their own interest and commitment, usually volunteering their time to work with students outside their own department, for which they get little or no credit, out of their commitment to understanding this world of ours—how, as specialists in their own area, they can work cooperatively with other specialists to understand the problem." A faculty member described this sense of commitment in this way: "This sharing with faculty from different disciplines, in this program, is very rewarding. . . . We share the conviction that this is really the way that this has to be done. It is not just an engineering problem, not just a political problem—it is all of it together."

We learned that MWR faculty not only had a strong commitment to the environment and interdisciplinarity but also had experience working in professional, nonuniversity workplace settings. One alumna, for example, said: "There are a lot of [MWR] faculty who have spent some time working in other jobs and can bring some business or real-world working experience, not academic, back into the classroom and share that." Indeed, many faculty told us that they had worked in government policy positions, in industry, or had done extensive consulting in both the public and private sectors.

In 1990 the MWR program enrolled approximately thirty-five students. The majority pursued their studies on a full-time basis. Most were in their late twenties and early thirties and had substantial work experience in places such as the Environmental Protection Agency (EPA), the Peace

Corps, and state and local government agencies. Many interviewees told us that the diversity in students' work experiences, as well as the variety of undergraduate majors they represented, enhanced the interdisciplinary character of the program. One student said, for example: "There were a lot of different perspectives of different disciplines. Some had been professionals for many years." A professor commented that the "MWR students in my courses ask interesting questions and try to get me to put what I'm teaching into a broader context—more so than the engineering students I get. . . . The grad students at [Major State] are good in general, but MWR students have a uniquely broad perspective on what they're studying."

Stakeholders repeatedly described the knowledge and skills emphasized in the MWR program in terms of what we refer to as a connected orientation. Interviewees emphasized that the MWR curriculum was designed to help students understand the dynamic and inseparable relationships between generalized and specialized—as well as between theoretical and applied—knowledge and skills. To this end, faculty and program administrators required students to take "breadth" courses in a range of disciplines, enroll in "depth" courses in one specialty area, and complete an intensive summer workshop.

MWR students were required to take thirty breadth credits distributed in the following categories: nine in "natural science and technology," nine in "water resources institutions and public decision-making processes," six in "analytical and design tools in water resources," and six in "synthesis and integration" (consisting of a core planning seminar and an interdisciplinary summer workshop). In addition, students were expected to complete fifteen credits in an "area specialty." According to a program brochure, these specialty credits constituted "an intensive program of courses designed to provide the individual with competence in a particular water-related area."[3] As a program administrator explained, this "depth-breadth requirement helped students develop 'a leg on both sides of the aisle.'" In other words, the curriculum emphasized interdisciplinary breadth of knowledge (traditional theory and research courses in both human institutions and behavior as well as in science and technology); a set of applied skills (practical courses in computer programming, statistical methods, technical writing, modeling techniques, and remote sensing); and integrative abilities (a hands-on seminar and workshop intended to help students synthesize information and knowledge).

Faculty and program administrators told us that interdisciplinary breadth was the cornerstone of the MWR curriculum. As the program chair stated, this interdisciplinary breadth was different from the academic specialization characteristic of most graduate education at Major State: "Any discipline is so specialized today that even getting a perspective on a subfield is a major accomplishment. So [doctoral students'] broadening has these boundary conditions on it. In contrast, people [in this master's program] ask all of the ugly questions about things that fall between the disciplines that relate to disciplines when you bring it into the realm of management—which, from a 'letters and science' point of view has a kind of negative, professional kind of connotation. It seems 'dirty'—like being a lawyer or business person." A professor told us that he and his colleagues believed the program's thirty-credit interdisciplinary breadth requirement was important because it allowed students the freedom to relate courses from a wide range of fields to their specific interests. In his words:

> Technical courses, water rights law . . . this is the nice thing about an inter-disciplinary program, you can take courses from all over—the ag [agricultural] school, the law school, letters and science, business school. . . . If students go into a more traditional [graduate] program, like the hydro-geology program, they don't have the flexibility that they have in the MWR program to do things like take water rights law. The MWR program is still focused, but there's a lot more flexibility for them to choose what's appropriate to what they want to do. What some of them want to do is the same as the students in my hydrogeology program, but the advantage of the MWR program—being course intensive rather than thesis intensive— is that they have more time to take courses.

Faculty emphasized to us that, in addition to the more generalized knowledge students learned in these interdisciplinary courses, students left the program with an appreciation for specialized knowledge. One professor explained that they "make sure that [students] don't just become generalists and think that they know 'it' [the field]. . . . In almost every discipline, there is more than meets the eye. You [have to] have a mindset that is willing and able to comprehend that—you have to be open to this fact in order to be effective. And the only way to ensure that is to be sure that you yourself have experienced some real depth in one area—so that you can appreciate the complexities of the depth that the other people on your team have."

This connection between "broad" generalized knowledge and "deep" specialized knowledge in the MWR curriculum was articulated by a program administrator:

> The MWR master's contrasts with the "convergent" education doctoral students get. Convergent knowledge—that's what expertise and special-ization is about at a research university. And oftentimes, you know, it's organized into higher and higher sets of associations and levels of infor-mation, so that people can develop this expertise and analytical where-withal. But we [as academic specialists] give ground on the kind of breadth area. Sometimes researchers are not interested in this kind of breadth—

how the parts connect. In order to pursue their work, they require very focused kinds of thinking. And that leads to my next point, which is that one of the kinds of things we are trying to accomplish in this kind of a master's program—it happens to be the MWR program, but it's true for any kind of an interdisciplinary program—is the breadth-depth dichotomy. What you do is attempt to give people sufficient breadth about connecting together unlike things and at the same time give them sufficient depth in an area or a couple of areas that they appreciate all about what is in a discipline and about what their limitations are. The more you know about how a particular field works—whether it's sanitary engineering, water chemistry, or agricultural economics—the smarter you are, yet the more you realize your own limitations.

The MWR program was not only connected with respect to the breadth and depth of generalized and specialized knowledge in its curriculum. Interviewees told us that the program also brought together the kinds of skills valued in both the university and the professional, nonuniversity workplace by requiring students to become skilled in practical techniques commonly used in both settings. These techniques were emphasized in regular coursework (six credits in the "analytical and design tools" category) and in the summer workshop.

As stated in a program brochure, the summer workshop was a "student-faculty team project on a contemporary problem in water resources" designed to be "a culminating experience near the end of the student's program." A former program administrator said that students and faculty collaborated in these workshops "on a question in the real world that has to do with managing a water resource—that involves people, institutional structures, reports, government, citizen groups, politicians, lawyers, and so forth." Each workshop was sponsored by an organization or group that was willing to work intensively with the program, cover basic costs, and consider implementing the recommendations included in the workshop report. A former program administrator told us that, throughout the workshop, faculty led students through "the whole process of figuring out what to do, negotiating among all the groups about various issues, showing them all the bases you have to touch in order to get a workable resolution."

Many students and alumni emphasized that the program "came together" for them during the workshop. Working under a deadline on a real-world problem, they learned how to take advantage of one another's diverse disciplinary and professional backgrounds to develop workable solutions to complex environmental problems. "I think for people who want to go into government work," one professor told us, "independent research experience isn't all that relevant to what they'll be doing in the long run. In these situations, you don't formulate the question. It's formulated by a client, and what you need are the technical and management skills to go out and get the answer. I think the MWR workshop provides a good model for that kind of experience—gives them experience working with other people in refining a question." Another faculty member said that what he "learned from this [MWR workshop] was that working with other people is a skill, and it's an important skill in the applied, practical world. These students are forced to learn that and to produce."

Alumni also told us that they found these workshops "extremely dynamic and extremely important." One alumnus, an employer at a state natural resources agency, said: "We [at my agency] learn a lot [from an MWR workshop] because they bring some high-powered ideas to it. There tends to be some innovative ideas here, partly because you're dealing with people who don't have the investment in the historic approach, who are able to get a more unbounded solution, who are able to take more risks."

In short, both in their course work and the summer workshop, the MWR program was oriented toward teaching students how to connect the tools, concepts, and approaches associated with both academic and professional "cultures" in order to solve complex environmental problems. Indeed, when we asked one student whether the program had an applied or theoretical orientation, he explained in slight exasperation that "anything can be looked at as either applied or theoretical—it's entirely up to what you do with it. I'm taking a hydrology course now that is entirely theoretical, but the applications are really evident. It's making that transition—using the theory in the program—that makes it applied." "Making that transition," according to a program administrator, occurs when "suddenly everything starts to fit in, you see how things interrelate. . . . For the people for whom it works, not only do you connect and link together focused pieces of information, but it all moves up to a different level of conception of how you look at it."

For one alumnus, the key to "making that transition" was the "concept of river basin management" which pervaded the entire program: "It's the notion that economists could study water resources management and never understand it, waste-water and flood control engineers could study it and never understand it, fisheries experts could, and so forth. You have to integrate all of these fields in order to understand the system." He elaborated on this point as follows:

> In my bachelor's degree, I kept hearing "assume no friction, assume weightlessness," things like that, for purposes of solving problems and analyzing systems. "To understand these things you have to make some simplifying assumptions." But you get into the real world—none of those assumptions are any good at all. [You solve problems] by forgetting all

those assumptions you were told to make and analyzing people and reactions. . . . I went from a master's in engineering from a major professor who [as an academic] was assuming all sorts of things into the MWR program where we spent all our time examining assumptions—in water resources management. . . . We spent our time examining assumptions about politics, rather than making assumptions.

Echoing this student's perspective, a professor described the connected orientation of the program in these terms: "The MWR program is valuable because it's interdisciplinary. It's applied. It brings people together. It gets people jobs. I mean, it makes the world a better place in a very clear way. *And* [interviewee emphasis] it advances knowledge because of its capacity to put things together in a new way that you only get through interdisciplinary work. So it has that kind of potential to really advance knowledge as well—in a more basic sense."

Alumni and employers repeatedly emphasized that they valued both the applied and theoretical—as well as the generalized and specialized—knowledge taught in the MWR program. One administrator told us, for example, that students "can say to employers, 'I understand not only theoretically but practically what it means to work on a problem like this.'" An alumna expressed this point in these terms:

I went into consulting and found that my training was extremely valuable. I ended up having to do policy work. I ended up having to go out and be able to interpret engineering and operations and then go back and tell my client what risks were involved. . . . I found that I adapted very quickly, whereas the geologist never figured out what was going on with the engineering, and the engineers couldn't look past the flanges to understand what was going on from a practical point of view or from a hydrogeologic, or geologic, or land-use type perspective. Seeing past that narrow discipline—having a multidisciplinary background—makes it much easier to do that.

Similarly, an employer noted that, in his experience, MWR students with strong backgrounds in the sciences had familiarity with the social sciences and those with strong social science backgrounds had familiarity with science. He said: "They'd seen each other's worlds, and, from an employer's perspective, I knew I was dealing with someone who had seen both—although I still needed to know what their undergraduate background was. The program really helps their thinking." A program administrator told us that, according to a recent alumni survey, many employers hired MWR students because "they had the broader view."

From our perspective, this "broader view" was linked to the commitment MWR interviewees had to learning whatever would best help them to solve environmental problems, regardless of disciplinary boundaries or traditional barriers between generalized versus specialized and applied versus theoretical knowledge and skills. A program administrator summarized the connected orientation of the program in this way:

> If all these [specialists], by themselves and in their disciplines, don't represent the solution, then who will link these together and formulate the alternatives? MWR people. And they can also work along the way stations [between the disciplines and the policymakers. They can act both as] an engineer and a natural resources professional, and so forth. . . . The strength of these people is the recognition that the individual disciplines are critical, important—that excellence is called for there. That the professions are an inherent part of the solution. That we all work together, knitting together alternative actions for ourselves as a world society. These kinds of programs [like MWR] have the potential to afford critical thinking on those subjects.

Departmental Support: Weak or Strong

Across the forty-seven cases in our study, we learned that faculty and program administrators faced another important decision-situation: whether to provide strong departmental support to their master's programs.[4] In a nutshell, faculty and program administrators reached this decision by evaluating the contribution their master's program made to their department's resource base, reputation in the academic and nonuniversity workplaces, and mission. In turn, support was variously expressed through the relative apportionment of departmental financial resources to the master's program, departmental faculty reward policies, and faculty allocation of effort to master's education.

In one set of cases in our sample, administrators and faculty chose to provide weak support to their master's programs. This decision was rendered most frequently by administrators and faculty in circumstances where doctoral, master's, and baccalaureate degrees were conferred in the same department. Many administrators and faculty told us that, while master's programs strengthened departmental resources, it was the doctoral and baccalaureate programs that enhanced the department's reputation and advanced its mission.

In making resource allocation decisions among degree programs, administrators and faculty in this set of cases provided minimal budgetary and space allocations to their master's programs. In addition, not least because many faculty were heavily engaged in major research projects and were strongly committed to doctoral education, these departments awarded the majority of their research and teaching assistantships to doctoral students. For the most part, laboratory and teaching assistantships were not offered to master's students who intended to pursue graduate work for a relatively short period of time.

The weak support provided by faculty and administrators in these master's programs was also manifest in departmental reward structures and the allocation of faculty effort to master's education. In general, faculty in these departments based promotion and merit reviews heavily on research-related activities (or, in a few cases, undergraduate teaching), depending on the institution's mission. For the most part, faculty did not allocate substantial effort to master's education, choosing instead to invest themselves in their departments' doctoral or baccalaureate programs. At some research institutions, in particular, faculty viewed the master's program as a screening device for selecting future doctoral students. In these departments, faculty did not develop close working relationships with master's students, explaining that this activity was a wasted effort, since they considered these students "untested high risks" who had not yet "made the final cut" into the department's doctoral program. In other departments, faculty told us that they preferred to work with doctoral students rather than master's students because the latter frequently left the university just at the time that they were "becoming useful" to them.

In a second set of cases, administrators and faculty chose to provide strong support to their master's programs. For the most part, interviewees told us that these master's programs generated sufficient financial resources to support their annual operations, enhanced the department's reputation in academe or in the nonuniversity workplace, and advanced the department's mission. In addition, we came to appreciate that there was a widely shared belief among administrators and faculty that master's students were valuable human resources in their departments, both as important sources of teaching and lab assistants and as resources for collegial learning among themselves and the department's other students.

Administrators and faculty in this set of cases expressed their support in several ways. They frequently allocated financial support for teaching, research, and laboratory assistantships for master's students, independent of the presence of doctoral students. They also developed departmental reward structures that encouraged faculty involvement in master's education. We learned, however, that, even when such rewards were absent, faculty in these departments nonetheless chose to devote substantial effort to master's education, a decision based heavily on the belief that they benefited from their relationships with master's students.

We turn now to two vignettes to illustrate the choices faculty and program administrators made in this decision-situation. We include the master's program in sociology at Major State University as an example of weak departmental support and the master's program in microbiology at

Appleby State University as an illustration of strong departmental support.

Sociology at Major State University: Weak Departmental Support

The department of sociology at Major State University is considered by many to be one of the "top ten" sociology graduate programs in the nation. The department consistently has received recognition as a premier program for "educating research scholars and scientists" and also earns top honors among its peers for the "scholarly quality of [its] faculty." Throughout our interviews, faculty and program administrators referred to themselves as research scholars, dedicated to advancing knowledge in their discipline and to developing a new generation of "professional [Ph.D.] sociologists." The department's orientation toward research and doctoral education complements—and, in this case, is nurtured by—the broader institutional culture of Major State University.

When we visited Major State's sociology department in 1989, about thirty-five graduate students were admitted to the master's program, all of them prepared to further their studies in one of the more than forty subspecialty areas offered by the department's fifty-five faculty members. We were told by many interviewees that, since the admissions process was highly competitive, the department only admitted students who intended to pursue the doctorate. As a matter of course, these students began their graduate studies in what faculty termed the department's "graduate program," with the first two years serving as the master's program. During this time, students were required to complete twenty-four credits of course work and to write and defend a master's thesis. On the basis of the scholarly ability demonstrated by a student in his or her thesis and oral defense, faculty decided whether to formally "pass" a student into the Ph.D. program. Students who were not accepted into the doctoral program were awarded a "terminal master's degree"; all others received a master's as a "degree in course." In 1989, of the approximately two hundred graduate students enrolled in Major State's sociology department, roughly seventy were completing "master's degree" requirements.

We were told that approximately 75 percent of all students eventually left the department with the Ph.D. degree and, of these, approximately two-thirds entered the professoriat. One administrator informed us that the department did not maintain student records on the remaining 25 percent, most of whom left with a terminal master's degree. "It isn't that I don't want to tell you," she explained, "it's just that we have all of this data on our graduate program, but we don't have anything on the master's program. I really don't know where our master's students go after they graduate. We really only have data on our Ph.D. students."

Positioned within an institutional setting where producing high-profile research, securing external funding, and training doctoral students were strongly rewarded activities, we learned that administrators and faculty in Major State's sociology department chose to focus their energies on doctoral education rather than master's education. Stakeholders repeatedly told us that the master's program provided minimal benefits to the department, with the exception of a few additional FTE (full-time equivalent) dollars generated by master's students. Several interviewees emphasized that the master's did "absolutely nothing" to increase their reputation in academe, much less to advance the research and doctoral missions of the department.

Faculty and administrators told us that they offered a master's program for one primary reason: it functioned as a convenient and low-risk means for determining which students should be allowed to advance into their Ph.D. program. As a program administrator explained, "The master's degree performs a gatekeeping function for us in this department. It helps us to gauge if the student really has the ability and the commitment to do the Ph.D. And we tell our students that. From the day they walk in that door, they're told that. The common expectation around here is that students come to Major State for the Ph.D. We [the faculty] don't look at the master's as a viable degree . . . we only view it as serving a gatekeeping function." For their part, students often referred to the master's program as "not a big deal." One student, for example, told us that the master's was really "just a hurdle. I really don't think there is a master's program here— it's more of a steppingstone, and, in some cases, a sign of failure. I really think it's intended as a two-year training period to prepare you for the Ph.D."

This "gatekeeping" function provided faculty with a strategy not only for selecting "promising" doctoral students but also for allocating resources between their master's and doctoral programs. In terms of student funding, for example, one program administrator told us that generally only second-year and post-master's students were provided with teaching or research assistantships: "You see, we admit many people that we can't fund right away. We have lots of doctoral students we need to support first. So, we tend to save our teaching assistantships for those people who come here on their own and turn out to be good students, and they get funded in their second or third year." Students reiterated this point, noting that, as master's students, they were considered "bad risks" for departmental funding. As one student put it:

The big issue among first- and second-year students is if you can get funding. . . . The department makes this attribution that, because you're somehow not yet worth funding, we chose not to fund you. I think, if you're going to let someone in the graduate program, you should fund them. If you can't afford to fund them, don't bring them in. It's really asking an awful lot of someone to have them work off campus, do all the requirements of graduate work, and still try and make the cut [into the doctoral program].

In addition to providing minimal financial assistance to master's students, we learned that faculty and administrators seldom allocated significant time or effort to master's students. As one professor explained, it was very important that master's students reached the "gate" as quickly as possible (usually no later than the end of their second year) because "we can't let them use up too much faculty time. Collectively, the faculty are only going to spend so much time with our master's students. So the more we have these students hanging around that we have to go to exams for and read theses for, the less quality time we have for those students who have made it [through the gate]. Our time is a real resource that the university pays for, and there's just a fixed amount of it to go around."

Students and alumni told us that faculty seldom spent time with them outside of class discussing research ideas or "providing much direction" on their master's theses. Yet few students criticized faculty in this regard. Rather, most expressed a perspective similar to one offered by a recent program graduate: "This department is geared for doctoral work. The master's is a gatekeeper—and an important one because it actually helps faculty determine where they should devote their time. To get tenure around here is really nuts. Faculty are just crazed. If we didn't have it [the gatekeeping function of their master's program], the resources of the department and the faculty could really be drained off."

Indeed, faculty and administrators told us that the departmental reward structure encouraged faculty to invest themselves principally in research and doctoral education. Many commented that junior faculty, in particular, were warned against spending too much time on teaching and other activities (such as advising nonpublishable master's theses) that failed to advance their own, and the department's, scholarly reputation. One professor summarized the views of many of her colleagues on this point when she remarked:

> Our clients, and our product, are our doctoral students. Our reputation . . . has nothing to do with our master's program. It has to do with the fact that our Ph.D.'s go out there and become famous sociologists at some of the best universities in the country. . . . We're sort of the equivalent of the major league draft in football, with our Ph.D. students locked in there with the best that the most prestigious universities have to offer. The people who have gone out of here with master's degrees, well, no-

body knows who they are. They don't do anything for us. They're out there doing competent work, I'm sure, but they don't contribute to our reputation as high-quality scholars or as a high-quality program. They're not always a good use of our time.

Characterized by weak departmental support from faculty and administrators, the sociology master's program at Major State University was, we learned, a "nonprogram," for the most part. Time and again, faculty and administrators referred to the master's as a degree in course and told us that they viewed their master's program mostly as a two-year sorting device for assessing students' suitability for doctoral work which wasted neither financial nor faculty resources. Departmental resources, including teaching and research assistantships as well as opportunities to work closely with faculty, were reserved for those who successfully passed through the "gate" and became full-fledged "graduate" students in the department. One faculty member aptly summarized the department's attitude toward its master's program when she remarked: "The master's is an anachronism in the department . . . it doesn't have an independent logic in any way. The ABD ["all-but-dissertation"] is a more meaningful degree than the master's degree, in my opinion. . . . I just think we should get rid of the master's program, period."

Microbiology at Appleby State University: Strong Departmental Support

Located in the midwestern United States, Appleby State University is a public, regional institution enrolling roughly ten thousand undergraduate and one thousand five hundred master's students. For the first ninety years of its history, the institution offered only baccalaureate programs. In the mid-1960s, however, Appleby State began to add master's programs to its curriculum, including a program in microbiology. By 1990 the institution offered thirteen master's programs, and it appeared likely that the university's goal to "strengthen the role and mission of graduate education" would soon lead to the establishment of more master's programs on this small, college-town campus. As one institutional administrator pointed out to us, the "move was on" to transform the university from a "teachers college into a top-tier comprehensive institution" by the turn of the century.

The master's program in microbiology was one of the first introduced at Appleby State University. Over the years, it has developed a niche for itself as a well-regarded regional source of master's-educated industrial and medical microbiologists. When we visited the program in late 1990, the thirty-credit thesis program enrolled fifteen students drawn mainly from within a seventy-five-mile radius of the campus. Of the five faculty who taught in the master's program, one also served as the biology department chair, and three were required to teach a minimum of six credits per term in the department's undergraduate program.

With significant undergraduate and graduate teaching and program responsibilities, faculty at Appleby State told us that they very much wanted university administrators to begin fulfilling their promise to support master's education on their campus. From their perspective, current levels of support for their program were weak at best. As the department chair put it, "This program has never been funded because the Graduate School doesn't have a budget on this campus. We are told to have a master's program, and then we have to finance it through the undergraduate allocation we receive from the College of Arts and Sciences. There is absolutely no institutional support for this program." A high-ranking institutional administrator frankly admitted that the institution lacked funds to support any of its graduate programs. "Right now," he explained, "this program comes off the hides of concerned [microbiology] faculty in the department."

Despite limited institutional support, faculty and program administrators at Appleby State chose to provide strong departmental support to their microbiology master's program. We learned that this support was based on their beliefs that the master's program greatly enhanced the department's overall reputation in the regional nonuniversity workplace and advanced their departmental mission as a place where faculty were, in the words of one faculty member, "really committed to students." "We feel," this faculty member explained, "that we help them get a job—either as Ph.D.-bound people or as people who want to work for a local industry. That's our real goal." In expressing their support, faculty and program administrators not only creatively secured financial support for their master's program, but they also allocated significant portions of their time and effort to master's students.

The attitudes that faculty and program administrators held toward master's students stood out as a distinguishing feature of the strong support they provided to their master's program. Not to be misunderstood, many faculty told us that they were committed to undergraduate students. At the same time, they said that master's students were valuable human resources in the department. A program administrator, whose remarks mirrored those of his faculty colleagues, made this point when he described his master's students as "important sources of collegial learning," who "continually challenge and force me to keep current with my research. They keep me thinking. I'm able to think and grow with them." Faculty likewise mentioned that master's students were an important resource for their department's bachelor's students, often noting that they served as mentors who modeled the excitement of advanced science to undergraduates.

This shared commitment to master's students influenced how faculty and program administrators procured and allocated scarce financial resources between their bachelor's and master's programs. Since the department received institutional budgetary support only for its undergraduate program, faculty and program administrators were forced to develop what one professor termed "some ingenious strategies" for generating funds for student assistantships and general operating expenses associated with the master's program. Among other strategies, faculty and program administrators indicated that they reallocated a small fraction of the department's undergraduate student assistance fund to support four quarter-time graduate teaching assistants and attracted enough external grant support to fund another three master's students as half-time research assistants. Many faculty also noted that the department chair "creatively coupled" equipment and supply requests to "demonstrated undergraduate needs" as a means for acquiring resources for their master's program.

Aside from financial constraints, we learned that Appleby State faculty and program administrators also dealt with institutional tenure and merit review policies that discouraged their involvement in master's education. Many faculty explained that, while the institution rewarded them for research productivity and undergraduate teaching, they were seldom recognized for their involvement in master's education. The institution expected faculty to teach twelve credits per term, advise scores of undergraduate students, serve on undergraduate committees, and maintain an active research agenda. Faculty efforts associated with master's education—including teaching master's courses, supervising master's theses, and advising master's students—were considered "overload" activities at Appleby State.

Despite this unsupportive institutional reward structure, faculty and program administrators told us that they nonetheless chose to allocate significant time and effort to their master's program. In the words of one faculty member, they did so because: "We like it. No one is forcing us to do this. The rewards outweigh the punishments for us. We take great pride and joy in interacting with our master's students." Yet another said:

> You have to understand that what makes this program go is the faculty. We have a very strong commitment to students. . . . You see, the microbiologists always had this desire for a master's program. They wanted to do research, and they wanted their students to have that research experience. So, they took care of it on an overload basis, and they didn't complain about it, and they didn't ask for time off or extra pay for doing it. The

reward was in the doing of it. Now I know altruism is not a very popular thing anymore, and people laugh at it, but it comes back in satisfaction. We're very proud of what we do with our master's students here.

This commitment to master's students also was communicated by a program administrator, who explained that, although the institution treated faculty involvement in master's education as a "peripheral" activity, the microbiology faculty did not treat their master's students in like fashion:

> We have had to make a personal commitment to this program. And, sure, we do this at our own expense in terms of time and lacking rewards. . . . But we're not like faculty at some Ph.D. institutions whose attitude is to tell their master's students, "just write a thesis, and we'll give you a master's degree." We just don't do that here, even though, just like at the Ph.D. places, we don't get credit for working with master's students. Those students at those research institutions who feel like they have an empty experience feel like they're on the periphery. And they are. But our students don't feel like they're on the periphery—they feel like they're in the limelight, they're in the mainstream. And I think that's a big point. Because, if students feel like they're on the periphery, they act like that.

Many students and alumni confirmed this administrator's and others' remarks. On numerous occasions, they emphasized that faculty expressed a genuine interest in learning from students. As one alumnus put it, the microbiology faculty at Appleby State were:

> always really interested in what we were doing, and it almost seemed like—well, we were like everybody getting together and doing this learning. . . . The professors they have here, as I remember them, are not ones who were just there to show off. And I really mean "show off"—how much they know and impress you. They were interested in a genuine attempt to get you to learn the information. . . . Faculty here don't just tell you what to do. I always felt as though I could come up with an idea and it wouldn't be shot down. I never felt belittled at all.

Students and program alumni also pointed out that faculty made time for them, listened to their ideas, and worked with them as colleagues in the research process. A first-year student provided us with an anecdote to illustrate this point:

> These faculty give their all with students. I remember this one day when I walked into my advisor's office and said "Gee, I wonder if this problem is because of this?" And much later I realized that that was off the wall and that if I had understood it as well as she did I wouldn't have said that. But you know what she said to me? She said, "You know, that's a good idea, let's sit down and take a look at that." And there are other faculty in this

program that do the same thing. They're really student oriented. There is a real genuine concern for student learning here.

Although positioned within an institutional setting that did not provide strong support to master's education, faculty and program administrators at Appleby State nonetheless chose to provide strong departmental support to their master's program in microbiology. They demonstrated this commitment by resourcefully "digging up" dollars to support their institutionally underfinanced program and allocating substantial time and energy to a program they knew would go unrewarded in the institution's reward structure. Faculty told us that they supported their master's program for one main reason: the satisfaction they experienced in working with master's students and watching them develop into "active, independent scientists." As one faculty member put it, "As I understand our role here, I think, by and large, we do master's education right. . . . And I think that role is to help people see their own potential as scientists . . . and to channel those talents. Our greatest pride is in facilitating [efforts by] people to make better lives for themselves."

4

Auxiliary Decision-Situations
Institutional Support and Student Culture

We proposed in the previous chapter that the decisions faculty and program administrators made concerning their approaches to teaching and learning, program orientation, and departmental support had important consequences for how stakeholders experienced their master's programs. In addition to these primary decisions, institutional administrators and students made important choices with respect to two auxiliary decision-situations that also influenced the character of master's programs. Institutional administrators chose whether to provide strong or weak institutional support to their master's programs, and students made decisions about what "type" of student culture to develop in their master's programs. In this chapter we discuss the choices interviewees made in these two auxiliary decision-situations and present a vignette to illustrate each of these choices.

Institutional Support: Weak or Strong

We learned that the choice to provide strong or weak institutional support for master's education was often shaped in part by institutional circumstances. At most national and regional universities, for example, institutional administrators and faculty were confronted by difficult decisions regarding the distribution of resources across bachelor's, master's, and doctoral programs. Likewise, at some regional universities, as well as liberal arts colleges, administrators and faculty struggled with support issues when they introduced master's programs in their historically undergraduate-only institutions. In these latter institutions, we were often told that debates over whether to provide stronger support to undergraduate or graduate programs had become increasingly heated in recent years.

Institutional administrators (including college deans, graduate deans, and vice presidents) based their support decisions on whether they felt master's programs enhanced their institution's resource base, reputation, and mission. In turn, they expressed their support for master's programs through financial and space resource allocations, institutional promotion and tenure review policies, and various symbolic gestures.

In one set of cases in our sample, institutional administrators chose to provide weak support to master's programs. Many administrators told us that these programs did not add substantially to their institutions' resource bases, markedly enhance their institutions' reputations, or contribute much to realizing their specific missions. In turn, these institutional administrators provided programs with relatively minimal budgetary and space resources and little symbolic support. Moreover, administrators seldom tried to alter institutional tenure and merit review policies to support faculty involvement in master's education—policies that, in almost all of these cases, tended to reward faculty much more for their participation in doctoral or baccalaureate education.

In a second set of programs, institutional administrators chose to provide strong support to master's programs. We learned from administrators that these programs generally posted balanced revenue-expenditure sheets and, in some cases, generated additional fund revenues for the institution (usually through student FTE or external funding). Similarly, they suggested that many of these master's programs contributed to the advancement of their institution's mission and reputation (through faculty scholarship and service activities, well-prepared prospective doctoral students, or highly marketable terminal master's professionals). In return, institutional administrators provided these programs with relatively strong pecuniary and nonpecuniary support, including adequate budgetary and space allocations, promotion and tenure policies that encouraged faculty involvement in master's education, and highly visible symbolic support both within and outside of the institution.

We now present vignettes from two institutions to illustrate the choices institutional administrators made in this auxiliary decision-situation. We include microbiology at Major State University to represent a program that received weak institutional support and Lake College's education program to portray a program that received strong institutional support.

Weak Institutional Support: Microbiology at Major State University

Considered a pioneering department in the development and expansion of microbiological research and teaching in the United States, the microbiology department at Major State University has long been recognized as one of the nation's most renowned centers for the study of microbiology. In 1990 the department's fourteen faculty members attracted more than two million dollars in sponsored research funding. Especially in light of the scholarly accomplishments of the faculty, a recent external review team used the term *world class* to describe the department.

When we visited the program in 1989, our program liaison informed us that students from all corners of the globe were attracted to the department. The department offered bachelor's, master's and doctoral degrees, and enrolled more than 250 undergraduate and 80 graduate students. Of the 30 master's students in the department, roughly one-third were enrolled part-time. Many interviewees told us that the demand for the university's graduates was high. Most undergraduate and master's students found employment as scientists or technical sales managers in pharmaceutical, biotechnology, and food industries. The majority of doctoral students eventually secured professorial positions, some in the nation's most prestigious colleges and universities, while those who left higher education usually pursued careers in industrial research laboratories or in government agencies.

In contrast to the doctoral program, which was established in the early 1900s, the master's program in microbiology was in 1990 a relative newcomer to the department. According to a program administrator, departmental faculty had made a "conscious decision" approximately ten years before to establish a "bona fide terminal master's program" that would allow students to prepare for emerging nonuniversity careers in biotechnology and other microbiology-related areas. From many stakeholders, however, we learned that the master's program in microbiology had not been strongly supported by institutional administrators. As one program administrator, whose view mirrored those of many others, told us, "We've had to be self-perpetuating because the institution doesn't provide the department with any resources for the program."

Institutional administrators told us that the master's program in microbiology did provide a few benefits. For one thing, they said that the program contributed graduate student FTE dollars to the institution. Moreover, they mentioned that it assisted faculty in determining which master's students they should "keep for themselves" in the doctoral program, and it sometimes provided students with a "slight edge" over bachelor's-prepared microbiologists in the nonuniversity workplace.

Yet institutional administrators more frequently emphasized that the program did not do much to enhance the institution's reputation, either in academe or in the nonuniversity workplace. Administrators compared the microbiology master's program with the department's doctoral program and, in so doing, remarked that the former did little to improve the university's reputation and mission as a premier public research institution. Rather, it was the department's doctoral program that successfully advanced these highly valued priorities at Major State University. As a result, campus administrators chose to provide weak support to their microbiology master's program. One senior administrator, who summarized the views of several interviewees, told us that allocating any more support for the program would not be "a particularly wise use" of already "scarce resources."

Many microbiology program administrators and faculty emphasized the weak support campus administrators provided to their program. One professor, for example, commented matter-of-factly that, "for all intents and purposes," the master's program "almost did not exist in the eyes of the central administration. There's almost no [institutionally funded] administrative anything to support this program. It's almost a hobby for faculty in the department." A program administrator told us along these same lines: "The program supports itself to a very large extent. . . . The department doesn't receive any institutional resources to pay anyone to administer the program. . . . One faculty member serves as the master's program advisor and as the admissions officer for the students, but he does this out of his own time. And we have no financial assistance to offer students in this program."

Program administrators and faculty also told us that institutional tenure and merit review policies did not adequately recognize their involvement in teaching and advising master's students. Rather, they explained, faculty were primarily rewarded for their involvement in doctoral education and research and their ability to attract research dollars to the institution. One microbiology professor, who had a strong record of sponsored research, expressed the view of many of his peers when he said that the emphasis placed on "grant grubbing" in Major State's reward structure often undermined faculty involvement in master's education. In his words:

> The way this university is run, there is no financial or political incentive for a faculty member to be involved with this master's program. There's just no incentive to do it. . . . If someone or some department does it, no one [in the administration] is going to care. I mean, they'll care, but so peripherally that it's not worth it. The only reason you do it—the same reason anyone teaches here—is that it's a matter of pride, of citizenship. You're not going to be rewarded. They're not going to give you a thing for doing it. And, in some fairness, you cannot penalize someone who's bringing in money for being a wretched teacher, or a wretched citizen, because that's not the basis on which they'll be hired away [to another institution]. . . . The reality of the situation is that people aren't hiring wonderful researchers because they're nice folks or because they do wonderful research. They hire them because they bring in sponsored research dollars, which the university skims. So, that's the inherent dilemma in this competitive situation. And all you can hope for is that people will do it

[involve themselves with master's students] because it's a matter of pride, of good citizenship.

Despite inadequate funding and nonsupportive institutional tenure and merit review policies, several microbiology faculty told us that they devoted considerable time and energy to master's students. One professor expressed his commitment to master's students in these terms:

> On this campus, we're so research oriented that we don't see the souls of our students. I think that's a mistake. We put them all in a box. I care about my master's students, even though they [administrators and many faculty at Major State] think that master's students are a waste of time, a waste of effort. . . . I don't think of these students or this program as second-class. I don't agree with that one damn bit. I consider the master's degree very valuable. I value the students. I value the subject matter they have to master. I think the master's is a very valuable step in a student's professional career.

We learned that, in a nutshell, institutional administrators at Major State based resource decisions on which programs delivered the best "rate of return" on their investment. With respect to this criterion, they emphasized that they did not view the microbiology master's program as a "wise use of resources" when compared to the department's doctoral program and therefore chose to provide it with weak financial and symbolic support. For their part, microbiology program administrators, faculty, and students criticized the weak institutional support their master's program received. They told us that the program survived, and prospered, largely on the basis of the "good citizenship" efforts of departmental faculty.

Strong Institutional Support: Education at Lake College

Lake College is a private liberal arts institution located in the midwestern United States. Established as a parochial teacher's college during the Depression era, Lake College enjoys a good reputation within its regional service area for educating baccalaureate-level teachers. In the early 1980s, following numerous requests from undergraduate alumni and area employers, college administrators and faculty decided to extend its teacher education mission to include graduate study. In 1990 Lake College enrolled more than 250 students in its thirty-credit master's of arts in education program. From its inception, the master's program in education at Lake College has been centered around an innovative delivery system designed to allow teachers to complete their studies through intensive evening, weekend, and summer course formats offered at seven satellite campuses located within a 150-mile radius of the college's main campus. Institutional administrators told us that they selected these sites strategically, offering courses in areas where alumni and employer requests for the program were particularly strong or establishing site locations that generally were not served by the state's public university system.

We learned that the decision to develop a master's program that combined a nontraditional instructional format with an off-site delivery system had two significant advantages for the institution. First, it boosted student enrollment at a time when the college was struggling financially. Second, the program generated favorable statewide recognition for the college. As such, institutional administrators at Lake College provided the program with strong support because it contributed to the institution's resource base and reputation as well as its mission. As we came to understand, institutional administrators expressed their support for the program through relatively strong financial resource allocations, supportive promotion and tenure policies for graduate faculty, and various symbolic gestures.

In elaborating on their reasons for supporting the program, college administrators emphasized that it advanced the institution's historic mission as a "teacher's college" dedicated to the "development of the whole person." As one high-ranking administrator at the college explained: "It only made sense, given our history, to develop a graduate program in education. Our undergraduate alums really wanted to continue their education along the same lines they had experienced as undergrads at [Lake College] . . . and we wanted to provide them with a graduate experience that reflected the college's broader mission of developing the whole person by stressing a professional approach to education that would help teachers use theory and praxis in their continuing development as 'master teachers.'"

Stakeholders told us that this "master teacher" emphasis not only reaffirmed the college's teacher education mission but also contributed to the development of a statewide reputation for the school. As a senior college administrator emphasized, Lake College had "gained a great deal of statewide visibility because of this master's program. It has helped us to develop an image as a strong education school—an important outcome in today's competitive higher education market." Employers stressed that the master's program was deserving of its growing reputation and praised it as a "mission-driven" program that differed from many other teacher education "credentialing operations." As one employer said, Lake College's "program isn't just a credential or an empty steppingstone [to a Ph.D.] or a passive learning experience. It's a hands-on experience where teachers really do become engaged, enthusiastic master teachers."

Several interviewees also emphasized that the master's program at Lake College received strong institutional support because it added much needed revenues to the college's financial resource base, an important consideration for this tuition-driven private institution. By coupling the emphasis on developing master teachers with an instructional delivery strategy that extended master's-level (graduate) educational offerings into previously untapped state educational markets, institutional administrators explained that their teacher education master's program reaped handsome financial and public relations benefits for the college. As one campus administrator told us, "There's no doubt. We're very pleased with the unanticipated financial returns this program has generated."

Not to be misunderstood, stakeholders communicated to us that college administrators viewed this master's program as much more than a money-making operation. One institutional administrator, for example, described the program as a "mission-driven operation. It is not a cash cow operation. . . . We insist on maintaining the quality of this program so that it does not become a fly-by-night operation. We're very concerned about these fly-by-night operations dominating the market and undermining the quality of teacher education. We have gone to great lengths to insure that [Lake College's] program quality stays high." A faculty member expressed a similar view:

> The program receives strong support from the administration. They perceive the program as important for the financial well-being of the college and for the mission it is fulfilling for the college and the broader community. Sure, we're a struggling, private institution, but the master's program never has been viewed as a "cash cow operation" here. The program is self-supporting and brings in a little extra money, for sure, but the administration knows that they can only milk a cash cow for so long without feeding it. They do worry about quality, and they have supplied additional resources to support the program's quality.

Indeed, many faculty and program administrators told us that the program received strong institutional financial support, particularly given the college's recent financial difficulties. They indicated, for example, that, over the past three years, institutional administrators provided general operating fund increases to keep pace with the program's escalating student enrollments, modest faculty development funds for graduate research and other scholarly activities, and four additional full-time faculty lines. The director of the master's program told us that, while "even more resources" were needed, "the college administration has shown a real commitment to this graduate program. Maintaining the quality of the program has been an institutional priority here, even though it takes lots of energy and lots of money to do this successfully."

Institutional administrators at Lake College also demonstrated their support for master's education by altering their previous undergraduate-only institutional promotion and tenure guidelines to accommodate—and reward—teaching and research at the master's level. As one senior administrator explained:

> Teaching is the most important thing we do here. It is a very critical activity
> in our promotion and tenure review process [at both the undergraduate
> and graduate levels]. But we also have a very broad definition of scholarly
> activity here, and we encourage and reward graduate faculty for their
> efforts in this area. We don't quantify articles here. Rather, we say that
> scholarly activity is any kind of engaged activity or dialogue in the field.
> That could mean published articles, applied research with local school
> districts, presentations at conferences, or organizing state- or nationwide
> conferences.

Faculty indicated that these guidelines supported their involvement in the master's program. Although salaries were low, faculty told us that they nonetheless stayed at Lake College because they appreciated the emphasis college administrators placed on "good teaching," applications-oriented research, and professional service activities.

Last, we came to appreciate that institutional administrators provided strong symbolic support by promoting their master's program to various constituencies in their off-campus activities. One administrator, for example, was a strong advocate of the program when he was involved with a statewide commission on quality control in graduate education. Many administrators likewise expressed strong support for the program's non-traditional delivery system and indicated their commitment to the program at various campus events.

In short, with strong support from college administrators, faculty and program administrators at Lake College developed a thriving, nontraditional teacher education program that was greatly valued by its constituents. Because the program attracted needed revenues and recognition for the institution and also advanced the college's mission, institutional administrators provided it with strong financial and symbolic support. We learned that the master's program, although relatively new, was becoming recognized, in the words of one employer, as "a totally good program" that nurtured "enthusiasm and zest in its alumni" and developed "highly professional master teachers."

Student Culture: Individualistic, Participatory, or Synergistic

Many students told us that choices concerning student culture—those attitudes, values, beliefs, and activities that shape how students interact with one another within master's programs—greatly affected their overall learning experiences. Across the forty-seven cases in our sample, we learned that students chose to develop individualistic, participatory, or synergistic student cultures within master's programs.

To be sure, choices that students made were frequently influenced by the environment in which they found themselves. Faculty in some master's programs, for example, made greater use of interactive classroom pedagogies that encouraged student dialogue. In still others, the curriculum included "immersion" experiences—such as extended-length group, field, and laboratory activities—that required frequent student interaction. And, in still other programs, faculty provided master's students with departmental space and financial resources to support student organizations and extracurricular activities. We learned that these environmental characteristics were present in many cases in which students developed participatory or synergistic student cultures. Yet, even when these environmental features were absent, students in a handful of programs still managed to build participatory or synergistic cultures. Thus, we came to appreciate, while environmental circumstances influence the decision-making process, students ultimately exercised choice over how they interacted with one another.

In a fairly substantial number of programs, master's students chose an individualistic student culture. In these programs, students frequently saw faculty as the primary sources of knowledge and viewed their peers as isolated learners who had little authoritative knowledge to contribute to the learning process. On numerous occasions, students told us that they learned best "on their own" rather than in interaction with one another.

This individualistic perspective on peer learning was expressed in the ways students interacted with one another in and outside of class. In some cases, students competed with one other, vying over limited goods such as graduate assistantships, high grades, admission into the department's doctoral program, and job opportunities. In other cases, the culture was less competitive but more isolated as students acted independently of one another in pursuing their own individual agendas. Along these same lines, students in these master's programs seldom became involved in outside-of-class activities, rarely choosing to socialize with one another or to form student organizations. Although students occasionally met outside of class to study for major exams or to work on assigned group projects, many told us that they only did so to improve their individual in-class performances. Students also limited their involvement in curricular or administrative issues related to their master's program, dismissing this as the "faculty's responsibility."

In a second set of programs, master's students chose a participatory student culture. Rather than relating to their peers as individual learners, these students viewed each other as active participants in the learning process. They frequently explained that they enhanced one another's understanding of course material and contributed perspectives useful to one another's professional growth and development. At the same time, however, students in these programs told us that they saw faculty perspectives as much more authoritative than those of their fellow students, even when faculty discouraged this attitude.

This participatory view of peer learning was expressed in the cooperative interactions students had with each other in these master's programs. Many, for example, engaged in frequent dialogue with one another both in and outside of class. They often formed study groups, meeting on a weekly basis to facilitate each other's understanding of course material. Moreover, students in a number of these programs developed and participated in student-run organizations—such as community service programs or journal clubs—that provided additional outside-of-class social and academic activities within the program. Frequently included among these organizations was an elected student government association that provided faculty and administrators with student suggestions for improving or altering administrative or curricular aspects of the program.

Finally, in a third set of master's programs, including a few cases in which there was minimal faculty support for their decision, students chose a synergistic student culture. Going beyond viewing each other as active participants in the learning process, these students developed an active learning community among themselves in which the "whole"—a community of interdependent, collegial learners—was "greater than the sum of its parts." In these cases, students told us, they learned "more from their peers than from their teachers." And, in contrast to students in participatory cultures, they treated their peers' perspectives as legitimate sources of knowledge and understanding, as important as those expressed by the program's faculty.

This decision among students to view their peers as colleagues who actively taught and learned from each other was expressed in an interdependent ethic, sustained both in and outside of class, in which students drew on each other's diverse life and professional experiences to expand their understandings of different concepts and events. In some programs, for example, including a few that largely served a part-time population, students established clubs, invited speakers, and sponsored social and academic events to nurture continuous interaction among themselves. They also took an active role in the administrative and curricular affairs of their master's programs, forming student government organizations that faculty took seriously. In several instances, for example, faculty approved student-initiated requests for new courses and specialized curricular emphases in their master's programs. Many students also illustrated their strong commitment to these programs by recruiting new students and serving as "peer counselors" to them during their first years in the program. Alumni likewise noted that they remained active in recruiting, networking, and placement activities long after graduation.

The choice to develop a synergistic student culture was similar in many ways to the choice to develop a participatory student culture: both reflected an appreciation and respect for one's peers—their experiences, insights, and knowledge—and their potential to enhance student learning and development; both exhibited a commitment to the importance of interactions with other students in and outside of the formal curriculum; and both showed a willingness to expand the curriculum of the program to include a wide range of outside-of-class learning experiences. Yet there was a critical difference between the two choices. In choosing a synergistic student culture, students more fully integrated each of these activities into their master's experiences. In so doing, they not only expressed strong respect for each other's experiences and contributions but also conveyed a firm conviction that their interdependent learning community, as a whole, was more valuable than the sum of its individual parts.

We now turn to three vignettes to illustrate the different choices students made in this decision-situation. We have chosen theater at Trafalgar College to represent an individualistic student culture, business at St. Joan's College to portray a participatory student culture, and environmental studies at Phelps University to illustrate a synergistic student culture.

Individualistic Student Culture: Theater at Trafalgar College

Trafalgar College is a regional, urban institution in the northeastern United States. While founded as a conservatory in the late 1800s, this private college gradually added bachelor's and master's programs in such fields as journalism, advertising, and speech pathology to round out its traditional curriculum in the performing, literary, and communication arts. Since introducing a master's program in theater three decades ago to complement its undergraduate program, Trafalgar has developed into one of the largest, multipurpose dramatic arts departments in the nation. Many of its baccalaureate and master's graduates have pursued successful careers in performance, technical theater, theater management, and theater education.

When we visited Trafalgar in 1990, the master's program in theater enrolled approximately thirty students. Roughly two-thirds were full-time students. Stakeholders told us that the students were a highly diverse group, both in terms of their academic and professional backgrounds as well as their career interests. More than one-half were recent college graduates or midcareer professionals, who sought training for careers in the theater, while the remainder were local elementary and secondary school dramatic arts teachers, who concentrated their studies in the program's highly regarded theater education courses. Few students had experience in the professional theater. Several interviewees commented that the program's student mix was fairly typical of the larger student population at Trafalgar. As one institutional administrator told us, the college deliberately admitted a wide range of students into both its undergraduate and graduate programs because "that's one of the things that we think Trafalgar is all about. We call it the 'Trafalgar Mystique.' We attract an eclectic student population, and we encourage and are proud of that."

We were told that Trafalgar's forty-credit master's program was flexible enough to accommodate the diverse interests of its students. Aside from four prescribed core courses and a comprehensive examination, students were allowed to create highly individualized programs of study which met their own career goals. Referred to as the "Trafalgar Way," this emphasis on individually tailored curricula and study was highly valued by most program stakeholders. As one professor told us, "We expect our master's students to be self-directed, and, as part of the Trafalgar Way, we give them that opportunity by allowing them to develop their own individualized programs of study." Similarly, an alumnus commented that the "fostering of individuality was a really good thing. I've been able to do what I wanted to do. I like the laissez-faire character of the program." Another student said she was delighted that faculty allowed her to "carve out" her "own strategy for learning."

In interviews with students and alumni, we learned that the Trafalgar Way had some influence on their decision to foster, to use our terms, an individualistic student culture in their master's program. Most students referred to their peers as "other students" with whom they seldom interacted and from whom they learned relatively little. Many said that they did—and, in some cases, preferred to do—most of their learning by themselves. One second-year student told us, for example: "I think I learn most of the stuff that I do on my own. Other students really don't help me much. . . . I don't really think I learn much from them. . . . I don't feel like I have much to share with the others, and I don't feel like I pick up too much from them, either." An alumnus, who had many years of professional experience as a high school drama teacher, voiced a similar perspective: "I did a lot of learning on my own. I can't say I learned much from the faculty or students. I guess I sort of learned in spite of them. And I think that a lot of good solid education takes place that way. . . . It comes down to self-motivation. And I was motivated to get something out of the time I was putting into this program."

The belief that the "best learning" occurred "on your own" was most distinctively expressed in the limited interactions students had with one another in Trafalgar's master's program. Many students said that, since they were so busy "doing their own thing," they rarely had the time, or did not choose, to interact much with their peers. "You have to be independent here," explained one second-year student, "because faculty expect you to be pursuing your own goals. You're expected to do a lot of stuff on your own—mount your own shows, work outside jobs, do your own class work. On the whole, I'd say most of us did these things individually. Sure, there was some camaraderie in class, but it's not like we left class skipping and holding hands. That just didn't happen." Another student noted that, although she wanted to interact with her peers, many of them were uninterested: "You know, I would meet people in class and start talking with them, and then they'd say they had to run off to a job off campus or to work on their own show. . . . My sense is that students really didn't want to see much of each other in this program."

When students did interact with one another, they suggested to us, these exchanges were characterized by either slightly competitive or serendipitous relations. One alumnus, for example, remarked that he "really enjoyed" the seminars he took because "I felt very challenged to get all of my reading done. There was a sort of competitive edge among students— you know, my seminar has to be as good as so and so's. You put a lot of time and energy into those seminars because you really wanted to show you knew your stuff." Other students said that they felt more isolated than competitive with one another. One alumna we spoke with told us that she went through her entire first year of classes feeling "completely disconnected": "I didn't know of a graduate niche. I didn't have any interchanges with my peers." She then explained that it was not until she became a teacher at a college-sponsored summer youth theater day camp that she "finally got to know people in my program. . . . There was a core of eight of us [master's students] there as teachers. We began to share ideas with one another, and, well, we became part of a unit. But, before that, you weren't a unit. . . . Up until then I had done most of my learning by observation and absorption by myself. It was just plain serendipity that I got to know these students in the summer."

We heard from many interviewees that the lack of interaction among Trafalgar's theater students may have been related to the dearth of graduate-only courses, performance opportunities, and space provided in their master's program. Several students noted, for example, that they seldom knew who their peers were because so many of their courses enrolled undergraduate students. As one alumna put it: "The graduate students—we didn't move through the program in a block. There was only one class that I had that was entirely made up of graduate students. Most of the classes were a mix of undergrads and grads, and in a lot of my classes there wasn't any distinction between bachelor's and master's students." Students and alumni also said that they had very restricted performance opportunities at Trafalgar, explaining that faculty often gave their primary attention to—and filled major production and performance roles with—

undergraduate students. Even the master's program director admitted that the college had "so few roles and so many talented undergraduates that, I'm afraid, we often don't have roles for master's students." Finally, students complained about the lack of space allocated to them, noting that they did not even have a central meeting area where they could, in the words of one student, "just plunk down and call this place home."

While these circumstances often seemed to limit interaction among master's students at Trafalgar College, students seldom chose to change them. To be sure, several students and alumni expressed disappointment at the lack of an active graduate student culture in the program. One second-year student, for example, explained that there was "not a well-defined graduate student niche here at all." Another second-year student, who was considered by faculty to be a "student leader," said that he felt "a whole lot of negative energy" in the program. Despite their concerns, we learned that students had not raised these issues with faculty or tried to alter the situation themselves. Instead, they chose to sustain an individualistic student culture in which they could do "their own thing" on their own time. As one student remarked, "You see, at Trafalgar, students are allowed to be individuals. And I really think that's the strength of this place—it lets individuals be individuals."

Participatory Student Culture: Business at St. Joan's College

St. Joan's College is a private liberal arts institution located in the western United States. Originally established as a woman's college in the Roman Catholic tradition more than a century ago, St. Joan's became coeducational in the late 1960s. A relative newcomer to master's education, the college awarded its first master's degree less than twenty years ago. In 1990 St. Joan's offered seven master's programs, most of which utilized a nontraditional delivery system designed to allow midcareer adult students to complete master's degree requirements through evening and weekend instructional formats.

When we visited St. Joan's in early 1990, faculty and administrators informed us that their master's in business administration (M.B.A.) program was the largest, and most profitable, graduate program on campus, enrolling more than 150 of its approximately 450 master's students. The program's director said that many of these M.B.A. students were in their mid-thirties, and most had ten to fifteen years of professional work experience. The majority were employed in middle management positions in government agencies, nonprofit organizations, multinational corporations, and smaller local industries. The program also enrolled a substantial number of foreign students, most from the Pacific rim, who, though often lacking professional work experience, were valued by faculty and students alike for their perspectives on international business and global economic issues. Almost all of the program's students were enrolled on a part-time basis.

Faculty, administrators, and students told us that M.B.A. education at St. Joan's College was intentionally broad based to facilitate the "career-transitioning" status of their student population, most of whom were seeking the degree to either "move up the corporate ladder" or to make a lateral shift into a different sector or specialty area in the business world. The thirty-credit program required students to complete fifteen credits of core courses—including advanced study in accounting, marketing, management, and international business—as well as a three-credit capstone business policy course. Students selected three courses from one of four specialization areas to round out their programs of study. Although the program was not specifically designed as such, several students and alumni said that they completed many classes with a "core group" of their peers. As one student put it, "Since I saw the same students class after class, that helped us to develop, if you will, a kind of cohort identity in the program."

Faculty, students, and alumni suggested that this "cohort identity" among students contributed to a friendly, open, and noncompetitive student culture in St. Joan's M.B.A. program. When we listened closely to these stakeholders, however, we realized that the "friendliness" of this program's student culture went beyond the experience of sitting in the same classes. Specifically, the appreciation students and alumni had for one another's perspectives influenced their decision to develop, in our terms, a participatory student culture in their master's program.

St. Joan's students repeatedly told us that they viewed each other as people with whom they could study, learn, and network. To use one alumna's phrase, students saw each other as "experienced professionals in an additional learning laboratory" where they facilitated and discussed their "school-related and profession-related ideas." In large part, this participatory attitude toward peer learning was nurtured by a shared respect for the richness of one another's professional experiences and real-world knowledge. "The biggest plus of this program—and what I most appreciate about it," explained one student, "is that I really like being with students who are in the real world. I like hearing about their experiences. I like that real-world edge." Another student commented that she was so impressed by the practitioner-based knowledge of her peers that she had often thought to herself, "Wow, what a neat bunch of students": "These students are so in touch with reality—they're really ingrained in the workplace. They're extremely reality-based in terms of being able to share what was really happening in the real world. . . . I feel so lucky. I've learned so much from them."

This student's perspective was reinforced by many of her peers. Yet a number of students and alumni also told us that, while their peers helped facilitate their understandings of course material with concrete real-world examples and provided them with an expanded professional network, they did not believe these peer learning experiences were sufficient in and of themselves. Indeed, when asked where the "real learning" occurred for them, these students and alumni almost always said that it was the program's faculty, not their peers, who were the "key" to their learning. As one second-year student put it, "I like sharing my professional experiences with people who are in the real world, but I really think the quality of the faculty at St. Joan's is the key to this M.B.A. program." When asked to elaborate, he added: "My peers have lots of real-world business experience, and they can provide me and other students in the class with a lot of good, concrete examples to illustrate a point, . . . but the faculty here are exceptionally good at linking theory with practice. They introduce me to new ideas and stimulate my thinking."

This notwithstanding, many St. Joan's faculty members told us that they encouraged students to view one another as valuable learning resources on real-world professional issues. In turn, students usually developed cooperative interactions with one another both in and outside of class. Within classes, for example, students conjoined one another in class discussions. In some instances, these discussions evolved into student-managed "learning episodes" in which students helped each other to make connections between course content and real-world practice. A first-year student provided a vivid anecdote of one such episode:

> I had a person in one of my classes who was working at a major record company. And the company has some advertising problems, and they were looking to go into some new areas. And one of the top executives at the company suggested that they put their label on a totally different kind of music than the label had been associated with previously. So this classmate of mine brought up the issue in class one day and asked us what we thought. And all the students said "Why are you going to do that? You have a solid issue with your label already. You're going to destroy your company's issue if you diversify like that." And then a few more students added: "Gosh, haven't you been in the class where we discussed strategic positioning in marketing?" And then he said, "Oh yeah, you're right." And so we helped him, and now he's trying to convince the top management that, instead of ruining the image, they should create a new label.

In addition to in-class peer learning, students extended their interactions to outside of class, often forming small study groups to prepare for exams or to work on team projects. As we learned from many interviewees, these in- and outside-of-class relationships among students produced a strongly cooperative learning ethic in St. Joan's master's program.

One alumna aptly summarized this cooperative ethic when she commented, "We [the students] constantly sought each other out and worked with one another on case studies and presentations. We worked very closely with one another. . . . We weren't trying to compete with one another because we all really just wanted to see each other succeed."

Although employed in full-time professional careers, many M.B.A. students at St. Joan's also participated in a number of outside-of-class social activities and student-run organizations. Students told us, for example, that they regularly discussed their courses and their own careers informally after class, sometimes over beer or coffee at a local diner. "We're [the students] just very friendly with one another in this program," noted a second-year student, "We go out with each other after classes all the time." We learned that many students attended student-initiated ski trips and picnics throughout the year. Moreover, interviewees informed us that students had recently established an M.B.A. Student Association, which took responsibility for coordinating social activities for M.B.A. students, networking the program to local employers and prospective students, publishing an annual alumni directory, and serving as the voice of student government in the program. Several students and alumni said that the program's director "listened to the association" and took its suggestions "seriously."

In embracing the view that they could learn from each other's professional knowledge and experience, students at St. Joan's College chose to develop a participatory student culture in their M.B.A. program. Although students emphasized that St. Joan's faculty were really the key to their learning, they were also convinced that, without the benefit of one another's diverse real-world perspectives, their overall master's learning experiences would have been diminished. As such, these students actively took part in building a student culture that not only acknowledged and encouraged students to learn from one another in class but also provided them with opportunities for informal outside-of-class learning through a range of activities, including study groups, team projects, and casual social gatherings. Perhaps one student best described the overall feeling of the student culture in St. Joan's M.B.A. program when he remarked: "You know, education is supposed to be a conversation. And in this program, it is."

Synergistic Student Culture: Environmental Studies at Phelps University

Established as one of the first graduate programs of its kind in the United States, the environmental studies master's program at Phelps University enjoys a reputation as one of the most highly regarded centers for the study of global ecosystems and natural resources policy in the world. The program boasts several renowned environmentalists as alumni as well as a number of distinguished faculty who have earned worldwide acclaim for their pioneering research in the field of natural resources. Given the program's reputation, it is not surprising that many program graduates are aggressively recruited by both public and private sector organizations.

Affiliated with one of the nation's most distinguished private universities, the School of Natural Resources at Phelps University attracts students from all over the world to its campus in the eastern United States. In 1990 more than 50 doctoral and 150 master's students were enrolled in the school and took courses from its 25 faculty. The majority of the master's students were in their middle to late twenties, and almost all entered the program with a minimum of three to five years of professional work experience, often in organizations such as the Peace Corps, the National Forest Service, and the Nature Conservancy. Approximately 15 percent were foreign nationals; almost a quarter held bachelor's degrees from elite, private liberal arts colleges and research universities. Although a part-time option was available, our program liaison told us that all environmental studies master's students were currently enrolled full-time in the program.

Intended to be completed in two years, this master's program was characterized by strong emphases on interdisciplinary and individualized programs of study. Designed to "accommodate the varying background preparations and career aspirations" of its diverse student population, the program had no prescribed, required courses. Rather, students were encouraged to construct individualized curricula in consultation with a faculty advisor while fulfilling three general degree requirements: a minimum of sixteen courses of their own choosing, an interdisciplinary "special project," and a three-week field module immediately prior to the first term in the program. In these modules, students participated in a number of team projects that introduced them to basic field techniques associated with natural resources management. Faculty and students told us that these "mods" helped to build an "esprit de corps" among master's students from the outset of the program.

We learned from stakeholders in Phelps' environmental studies program that, while students were required to develop and pursue an individualized course of study, they did not develop an individualistic student culture. To the contrary, interviewees repeatedly said that the "truly unique" feature of Phelps' environmental studies master's program was the strong sense of community students actively generated among themselves. One faculty member made this point when he remarked: "The most important thing that you should know about this program is that there is a powerful sense of community here. You put this bunch of students together who are all so bright, and who all care so much about environmental issues, and they develop this powerful sense of community and caring."

When we asked faculty, students, and alumni to elaborate on what contributed to this "powerful sense of community," they provided us with a range of responses—perhaps none more telling than their expressed belief that students in the environmental studies master's program viewed each other as "colleagues" who actively taught and learned from one another. Students repeatedly mentioned that they greatly respected their peers' diverse professional backgrounds and their willingness to share these experiences. One second-year student provided us with a sense of this collegial attitude when she commented, "The capabilities of the student body are tremendous here. We [the students] take lots of opportunities to learn about what other people have done and to teach others about our own professional experiences. Most of us have been in very responsible positions for two or four years, and we really do have a lot to learn from each other." A first-year student added: "There's an attitude among students here that we all bring a really good depth and breadth of knowledge and professional experience to this program. We're fascinated by our classmates here."

In contrast to the more hierarchical perspective on faculty "expertise" which students expressed in programs characterized by participatory student cultures, students in this program said that they viewed their peers as no less important and authoritative sources of ideas and knowledge than faculty. One alumna voiced this attitude when she told us: "There's no doubt in mind that I learned as much—if not more—from my peers as I did from the faculty." A faculty member corroborated this perspective, explaining that students "become very close to one another here. They share with one another. They teach each other as much as we teach them. They really value each other's professional experiences and what they can learn from each other. . . . I would even say that these students learn as much, and maybe even more, from each other as they learn from us."

Indeed, the collegial attitude among students strongly influenced the overall ethos of the Phelps environmental studies master's program. Reflected in their collaborative interactions and deep involvement in program activities both in and outside of class, students chose to develop what we have termed a synergistic student culture—a culture, we learned, that was grounded in their shared respect for peer learning and teaching.

Many interviewees told us that this collegiality generated synergistic, rather than competitive and individualistic, interactions among students in this master's program. Although we were told that Phelps students generally were "overly competitive" with their peers, we came to appreciate that this was not the case among the university's environmental studies master's students. In the words of one student, "Here, we try and learn from each other, not compete with one another." A professor elaborated as follows: "Although I think our classes are tough and demanding, our students will tell you that this is not an overly competitive place. There is a powerful sense of community in this program. People really work and learn from one another here. . . . These people are here because they really care. And when you put these bright, committed, experienced people together your see them develop an amazing synergism. This place is just bursting with their energy."

Students frequently pointed out to us that they were constantly interacting with their peers, either formally through assigned group projects or informally through casual discussions in the field, over dinner, or in the student lounge. "There's always lots of informal learning going on around here," explained one second-year student: "People hang out in the lounge, or you just run into someone on campus and you start talking. There's a lot of collegial sharing that goes on in this program." One alumna described how much students learned through their informal interactions with one another when she shared this story:

> I remember sitting at one of our student-organized social events and listening to my peers. The first-year students were so black and white—they thought that all foresters did was rape and pillage the land—and they were heavy into the conservation movement. Then I would listen to how the second-year students talked to them. They provided a more broadened view on things—they were more informed and less orthodox in their approaches. They spoke with a more holistic perspective on things. And I think that's where a lot of the real learning happened for us—in those informal discussions we had with each other.

Students in the Phelps environmental studies master's program told us that they so strongly valued the outside-of-class collegial interactions they shared with one another that they formed a variety of student organizations and initiated numerous student-run activities to expand and enrich the program's overall learning environment. One student, for example, explained that she and her peers organized several "natural resources clubs" in which they drew upon their professional experience to present a series of weekly forums on selected environmental topics to the campus community. Students were also actively involved in recruiting outside speakers for their annual lecture series. In addition, students sponsored social and service activities, including canoeing and backpacking trips, environmental education outreach seminars to local schools, and weekly T.G.I.F. ("Thank God I'm a Forester") parties. Students and alumni emphasized that these activities strongly contributed to the vibrant community life they experienced in this master's program. In the words of one student: "These activities provide a really strong sense of community here. It's fun. We have a good time together. Everyone really gets to know each other—we've become a very close-knit group. And, you know, other people like the community, too. We're considered the only normal people on this campus. Students from across the university flock to our T.G.I.F. parties because they really enjoy the community we've built up here."

Faculty likewise commented that these outside-of-class activities helped to build a strong sense of community among the program's master's students. "It's neat to see these students at their T.G.I.F. parties every Friday," one faculty member told us: "You can see that they share a special kind of camaraderie . . . that they've shared and learned a lot from one another. You can see that they've become each other's best friends."

Besides developing these outside-of-class teaching and learning activities, students also became involved in administrative and curricular activities related to the master's program. Under the leadership of the Student Affairs Committee, many interviewees explained that students had a strong governance voice in the program concerning issues such as minority recruitment and the implementation of new curricular specialization courses and tracks. Faculty and administrators told us that they respected the commitment these students demonstrated to the program, often noting that many of their suggestions were "great sources for change" which they "took very seriously." One faculty member, in fact, said that it was the master's students, not the faculty, who were "largely responsible" for the establishment of the school's "Tropical Studies Center": "It was probably one of the first ones created, although lots of places are now developing one. You know, I'd like to say it was the vision of the faculty that created it. But it was much more a vision—a demand, actually—of the students who saw the global scale problem as critical, and they demanded that the school do something about it."

Moreover, faculty stressed that the commitment and concern these students developed for their master's program often endured for many years after graduation. "Our alums are a great source of student recruitment for us," said a faculty member, "and they're also a great source for jobs for our current students." Numerous interviewees informed us that program graduates were so committed and their network so extensive that students, faculty, and even some employers affectionately referred to them as the Phelps "mafia."

In interview after interview, we came to appreciate that students in environmental studies at Phelps University chose to develop a synergistic student culture in their master's program. Animated by an attitude that they could both learn from and teach one another, these students embraced one another as full colleagues, engaging in synergistic interactions through an extensive network of student-initiated outside-of-class activities and organizations. We learned that these interactions fostered in students both a genuine respect for the depth of one another's knowledge and a strong commitment to their vibrant student community. Perhaps one student provided the most telling testimony to this communal spirit when she remarked: "I just love this place. . . . There's such a nice group of people here. There's a real down-to-earth feeling in this program. It's that feeling and this sense of history and community that really makes the ethos of this place."

5

Decision-Situations and
Program Types

As we stated in the introduction to part 2, we began our cross-program analysis by identifying five decision-situations that helped us to understand stakeholder experiences across the forty-seven cases in our sample. We gradually came to appreciate that the process of focusing on the choices stakeholders made in these five decision-situations helped us to understand overall differences in interviewees' master's experiences across these cases. With this in mind, we used the decision-situations as an analytic device to help us differentiate cases on the basis of the character of stakeholder experiences. In so doing, we were able to develop a typology of master's programs in which we identified four "idealized program types".[1] In this chapter we elaborate on this cross-program analytical procedure and name and briefly describe the four types of master's programs which resulted from our analysis.

Analytical Strategy

We began to develop a typology of master's programs by first considering the choices stakeholders in each program made in the five decision-situations.[2] Organized by field of study, table 5.1 displays our interpretations of the choices stakeholders made.

Our analysis was then guided by the following question: What standard should we use to help us sort the forty-seven cases? In response to this question, we established a sort order that was based on a single standard: that decision-situations should be sequentially ordered in terms of their relative contribution to helping us explain variation in stakeholder experiences. Thus, we first sorted the forty-seven programs by the decision-situation that, from our perspective, accounted for the greatest

Table 5.1. **Choices in Decision-Situations**

Institution	Field	Approach to Teaching and Learning (Didactic Q, Facilitative W, Dialogical Z)	Program Orientation* (Academic Q, Professional W, Connected Z)	Departmental Support (Weak Q, Strong W)	Institutional Support (Weak Q, Strong W)	Student Culture (Individualistic Q, Participative W, Synergistic Z)
1 Major State	Business	Q	Q*	Q	Q	Q
2 Parks-Beecher		Q	W	W	W	Z
3 Peterson		Q	W	W	W	Q
4 Pierpont		Q	W	W	W	W
5 St. Joan's		Q	W	W	Q	W
6 Chester	Education	Q	W	W	W	Q
7 Lake		Z	W	W	W	Z
8 Laramie		Z	W	W	Q	Z
9 Major State		Q	Q*	Q	Q	W
10 Southwest State		Q	W	Q	W	Q
11 Major State	Engineering	W	Q*	W	Q	W
12 Middle State		Q	Q*	Q	Q	Q
13 Moore A&T		W	Q*	W	W	Z
14 Prestige State		W	Q*	W	Q	Z
15 United Tech		Q	W*	W	W	Q
16 Barrett State	Nursing	Q	Q*	Q	Q	Q
17 Major State		Q	Q*	Q	Q	Q
18 Peterson		Z	Z	W	W	W
19 Southern State		Z	Z	W	Q	W
20 Western State		Z	Z	W	Q	W

120

#	Institution	Discipline				
21	Helena State	Theater	Z	W	W	N
22	Major State		Q	Q*	Q	Q
23	National Conservatory		W	W	W	N
24	Phelps		W	W	W	N
25	Trafalgar		Q	W	Q	Q
26	Atlantic State	Applied anthropology	Q	W*	W	Q
27	City-State		Z	Z	W	W
28	Land-Grant		Q	W	W	W
29	Southeast State		N	N	Q	N
30	Southwest State		N	N	W	W
31	Longmont	English	Z	N	W	N
32	Major State		Q	Q	Q	Q
33	Phelps		Q	Q	Q	Q
34	Southwest State		N	N	W	W
35	Urban State		Q	W	W	Q
36	Carver A&M	Environmental studies	W	Q*	Q	W
37	Major State		Z	N	Q	W
38	Phelps		N	N	Q	N
39	Vernon		Z	N	Q	N
40	Walton State		Z	N	W	W
41	Appleby State	Microbiology	Z	Q*	Q	N
42	Major State		W	Q*	Q	W
43	Middle State		Z	Q*	W	N
44	Mountain State		Q	Q*	Q	W
45	Southwest State		W	Q*	W	N
46	Major State	Computer science	W	Q*	W	W
47	Major State	Sociology	Q	Q	Q	Q

In the Program Orientation column, the symbol Q stands for those programs oriented exclusively to academic culture, Q for those programs oriented largely, but not exclusively, to academe; W stands for those programs oriented exclusively to professional workplace cultures, and W* indicates programs largely, but not exclusively, oriented to professional workplace cultures; Z represents programs oriented largely toward both cultures.

Table 5.2. **Program Types and Decision-Situations**

Institution	Field	Approach to Teaching and Learning: Didactic Q / Facilitative W / Dialogical Z	Program Orientation: Academic Q / Professional W / Connected Z	Departmental Support: Weak Q / Strong W	Institutional Support: Weak Q / Strong W	Student Culture: Individualistic Q / Participative W / Synergistic Z
Ancillary programs						
1 Barrett State	Nursing	Q	Q*	Q	Q	Q
2 Major State	Business	Q	Q*	Q	Q	Q
3 Major State	English	Q	Q	Q	Q	Q
4 Major State	Sociology	Q	Q*	Q	Q	Q
5 Major State	Nursing	Q	Q*	Q	Q	Q
6 Major State	Theater	Q	Q*	Q	Q	Q
7 Middle State	Engineering	Q	Q*	Q	Q	Q
8 Phelps	English	Q	Q*	Q	Q	Q
9 Major State	Education	Q	Q*	Q	Q	W
10 Mountain State	Microbiology	Q	Q*	Q	Q	W
Career advancement programs						
1 Trafalgar	Theater	Q	W	Q	Q	Q
2 Southwest State	Education	Q	W	Q	W	Q
3 Urban State	English	Q	W	W	Q	Q
4 Atlantic State	Applied anthropology	Q	W*	W	Q	Q
5 St. Joan's	Business	Q	W	W	Q	W
6 Peterson	Business	Q	W	W	W	Q
7 Chester	Education	Q	W	W	W	Q
8 United Tech	Engineering	Q	W*	W	W	Q
9 Land-Grant	Applied anthropology	Q	W	W	W	W
10 Pierpont	Business	Q	W	W	W	W
11 Parks-Beecher	Business	Q	W	W	W	Z
Apprenticeship programs						
Environmental		W	Q*	W	Q	W

#	Institution	Major					
2	Major State	Computer science	W	Q*	W	Q	W
3	Major State	Engineering	W	Q*	W	Q	W
4	Major State	Microbiology	W	Q*	W	Q	W
5	Prestige State	Engineering	W	Q*	W	Q	N
6	Moore A&T	Engineering	W	Q*	W	W	N
7	Southwest State	Microbiology	W	W	W	W	N
8	National Conservatory	Theater	W	W	W	W	N
9	Phelps	Theater	W	W	W	W	N

Community-centered programs

#	Institution	Major					
1	Appleby State	Microbiology	Z	Q*	W	Q	N
2	Middle State	Microbiology	Z	Q*	W	W	N
3	Laramie	Education	Z	W	W	Q	N
4	Helena State	Theater	Z	W	W	W	N
5	Lake	Education	Z	W	W	W	N
6	Major State	Environmental studies	Z	N	W	Q	W
7	Southern State	Nursing	Z	N	W	Q	W
8	Western State	Nursing	Z	N	W	Q	W
9	Phelps	Environmental studies	Z	N	W	Q	N
10	Southeast State	Applied anthropology	Z	N	W	Q	N
11	Vernon	Environmental studies	Z	N	W	Q	N
12	Peterson	Nursing	Z	N	W	W	W
13	City-State	Applied anthropology	Z	N	W	W	W
14	Southwest State	English	Z	N	W	W	W
15	Southwest State	Applied anthropology	Z	N	W	W	W
16	Walton State	Environmental studies	Z	N	W	W	W
17	Longmont	English	Z	N	W	W	N

amount of variance in stakeholder experiences across cases (and so forth across all the decision-situations). On the basis of this stepwise sorting process, we eventually arrived at the sort order displayed in table 5.2, with "approach to teaching and learning" as the first decision-situation (that is, as the decision-situation that accounted for the most variance across cases) and "student culture" as the last decision-situation (that is, as the decision-situation that accounted for the least variance across cases). Through this analytical process, we developed four program types that differed significantly in terms of the overall character of stakeholder experiences. In the following discussion, we provide a step-by-step discussion of how we sorted the decision-situations in the process of developing our typology.

Before elaborating on our sorting process, we introduce two caveats. First, in using an analytical procedure that depends on the order in which decision-situations are sorted, we do not mean to imply that stakeholders made decisions in any particular order—or always consciously. In several of the newly established programs in our sample, stakeholders described a fairly orderly decision-making process that accompanied the establishment of their master's program. In most programs, however, choices regarding the five decision-situations were made incrementally—and often in light of various departmental or institutional contingencies. Second, while we found our decision-situation strategy to be a useful analytic device for helping us to identify program types, we emphasize that we were careful not to become prisoners of our analytical approach. In other words, we viewed our decision-situation sorting method largely as a tool for understanding variation in stakeholders' experiences. In some instances, as shown in table 5.2, cases were classified in the same program type even though stakeholders made different choices in particular decision-situations. In the end, therefore, we classified these cases as members of the same "program type" on the grounds that stakeholders described the overall character of their experiences in similar ways. (Readers who are not interested in the details of our sorting process may wish to bypass the following discussion.)

First Sort

We began our analytical process by selecting the decision-situation that, from our perspective, accounted for the most variance across cases: approach to teaching and learning. As displayed in table 5.3, we found that the groupings produced by sorting on this decision-situation helped us to identify three clusters of cases: twenty-one didactic, nine facilitative, and seventeen dialogical. While the programs in these three clusters differed significantly from one another in terms of stakeholders' experiences, we observed that there were important differences among some of the programs within the cluster of twenty-one didactic cases. Stakeholders in the nursing program at Barrett State Medical Center, for example, described their program to us in terms very different from those of interviewees in the education program at Southwest State University. Because these differences were not well explained by our first sort, we decided to conduct a second sort.

Second Sort

We next partitioned the case studies according to choices made in a second decision-situation: program orientation. As displayed in table 5.4, we found that incorporating this decision-situation divided the didactic cases into two clusters that helped us understand important differences among the twenty-one cases. As shown in table 5.4, ten of these twenty-one cases had an academic orientation, and the remaining eleven had a professional orientation. (Not all of the cases within the third and fourth clusters made identical choices regarding program orientation, but we retained them in these clusters on the grounds that they were similar to other programs in their respective groupings in terms of the character of stakeholders' experiences.)

Sorts on the Four Remaining Decision-Situations

Following our second sort, we asked ourselves if each of the four groups resulting from the first two sorts adequately differentiated the programs in our sample in terms of the overall character of stakeholder experiences. By comparing table 5.4 and table 5.2, it is clear that we decided that the members of each of the four groupings resulting from these first two sorts were sufficiently similar to be considered members of the same program type. Before making that decision, however, we continued delineating finer groupings among the programs by sorting on the remaining three decision-situations (the programs in table 5.2 are ordered by all five decision-situations, whereas those in table 5.4 are ordered only by the first two). In so doing, we realized that the choices made in these forty-seven programs with respect to departmental support (decision-situation 3) further supported—except for a subset of two programs within the second group—the groupings formed by the second sort. As we continued this sorting process, we also decided that the smaller groupings formed by the last two decision-situations did not substantially contribute to our understanding of program types. As we earlier suggested, however, the last two decision-situations were still important because they gave us a better understanding of important similarities and differences both across and within the four types of programs we had formed.

On the basis of our analysis, we identified four idealized program types: ancillary, career advancement, apprenticeship, and community-centered. We label these clusters "idealized" program types because we do

Table 5.3. **First Sort: Decision-Situation I**

Institution	Field	Decision-Situation	Approach to Teaching and Learning (Didactic Q, Facilitative W, Dialogical Z)	Program Orientation (Academic Q, Professional W, Connected Z)	Departmental Support (Weak Q, Strong W)	Institutional Support (Weak Q, Strong W)	Student Culture (Individualistic Q, Participative W, Synergistic Z)
1 Atlantic State	Applied anthropology		Q	W*	W	Q	Q
2 Barrett State	Nursing		Q	Q*	Q	Q	Q
3 Chester	Education		Q	W	W	W	Q
4 Land-Grant	Applied anthropology		Q	W	W	W	W
5 Major State	Business		Q	Q*	Q	Q	Q
6 Major State	Education		Q	Q*	Q	Q	W
7 Major State	English		Q	Q*	Q	Q	Q
8 Major State	Nursing		Q	O*	Q	Q	Q
9 Major State	Sociology		Q	Q*	Q	Q	Q
10 Major State	Theater		Q	Q*	Q	Q	Q
11 Middle State	Engineering		Q	Q*	Q	Q	Q
12 Mountain State	Microbiology		Q	W	W	Q	W
13 Parks-Beecher	Business		Q	W	W	W	Z
14 Peterson	Business		Q	Q	Q	W	Q
15 Phelps	English		Q	W	W	Q	Q
16 Pierpont	Business		Q	W	Q	W	W
17 Southwest State	Education		Q	W	W	W	Q
18 St. Joan's	Business		Q	W	Q	Q	W
19 Trafalgar	Theater		Q	W	W	Q	Q
20 United Tech	Engineering		Q	W*	W	W	Q
21 Urban State	English		Q	W	W	Q	Q
1 Carver A&M	Environmental studies		W	Q*	W	Q	W
2 Major State	Computer		W	Q*	W	Q	W

#	Institution	Field					
3	Major State	Engineering	W	Q*	W	Q	W
4	Major State	Microbiology	W	Q*	W	Q	W
5	Moore A&T	Engineering	W	Q*	W	W	N
6	National Conservatory	Theater	W	W	W	W	N
7	Phelps	Theater	W	W	W	W	N
8	Prestige State	Engineering	W	Q*	W	Q	N
9	Southwest State	Microbiology	W	Q*	W	W	N
1	Appleby State	Microbiology	N	Q*	W	Q	N
2	City-State	Applied anthropology	N	N	W	W	W
3	Helena State	Theater	N	W	W	W	N
4	Lake	Education	N	W	W	W	N
5	Laramie	Education	N	W	W	Q	N
6	Longmont	English	N	N	W	W	N
7	Major State	Environmental studies	N	N	W	Q	W
8	Middle State	Microbiology	N	Q*	W	W	N
9	Peterson	Nursing	N	N	W	W	W
10	Phelps	Environmental studies	N	N	W	Q	N
11	Southern State	Nursing	N	N	W	Q	W
12	Southeast State	Applied anthropology	N	N	W	Q	N
13	Southwest State	Applied anthropology	N	N	W	W	W
14	Southwest State	English	N	N	W	W	W
15	Vernon	Environmental studies	N	N	W	Q	N
16	Walton State	Environmental studies	N	N	W	W	W
17	Western State	Nursing	N	N	W	Q	W

Table 5.4. **Second Sort: Decision-Situations 1 and 2**

Institution	Field	Approach to Teaching and Learning (Didactic Q, Facilitative W, Dialogical Z)	Program Orientation (Academic Q, Professional W, Connected Z)	Departmental Support (Weak Q, Strong W)	Institutional Support (Weak Q, Strong W)	Student Culture (Individualistic Q, Participative W, Synergistic Z)
1 Major State	English	Q	Q	Q	Q	Q
2 Major State	Sociology	Q	Q	Q	Q	Q
3 Phelps	English	Q	Q	Q	Q	Q
4 Barrett State	Nursing	Q	Q*	Q	Q	Q
5 Major State	Business	Q	Q*	Q	Q	Q
6 Major State	Education	Q	Q*	Q	Q	W
7 Major State	Nursing	Q	Q*	Q	Q	Q
8 Major State	Theater	Q	Q*	Q	Q	Q
9 Middle State	Engineering	Q	Q*	Q	Q	Q
10 Mountain State	Microbiology	Q	Q*	Q	Q	W
1 Chester	Education	Q	W	W	W	Q
2 Land-Grant	Applied anthropology	Q	W	W	W	W
3 Parks-Beecher	Business	Q	W	W	W	Z
4 Peterson	Business	Q	W	W	W	Q
5 Pierpont	Business	Q	W	W	W	W
6 Southwest State	Education	Q	W	Q	W	Q
7 St. Joan's	Business	Q	W	W	Q	W
8 Trafalgar	Theater	Q	W	Q	Q	Q
9 Urban State	English	Q	W	W	Q	Q
10 Atlantic State	Applied anthropology	Q	W*	W	Q	Q
11 United Tech	Engineering	Q	W*	W	W	Q
1 Carver A&M	Environmental studies	W	Q*	W	Q	W
2 Major State	Computer	W	Q*	W	Q	W

#	Institution	Major					
3	Major State	Engineering	W	Q*	W	Q	W
4	Major State	Microbiology	W	Q*	W	Q	W
5	Moore A&T	Engineering	W	Q*	W	W	N
6	Prestige State	Engineering	W	Q*	W	Q	N
7	Southwest State	Microbiology	W	Q*	W	W	N
8	National Conservatory	Theater	W	W	W	W	N
9	Phelps	Theater	W	W	W	W	N
1	Appleby State	Microbiology	Z	Q*	W	Q	N
2	Middle State	Microbiology	Z	Q*	W	W	N
3	Lake	Education	Z	W	W	W	N
4	Helena State	Theater	Z	W	W	W	N
5	Laramie	Education	Z	W	W	Q	N
6	City-State	Applied anthropology	Z	N	W	W	W
7	Longmont	English	Z	N	W	W	N
8	Major State	Environmental studies	Z	N	W	Q	W
9	Peterson	Nursing	Z	N	W	W	W
10	Phelps	Environmental studies	Z	N	W	Q	N
11	Southeast State	Applied anthropology	Z	N	W	Q	N
12	Southern State	Nursing	Z	N	W	Q	W
13	Southwest State	Applied anthropology	Z	N	W	W	W
14	Southwest State	English	Z	N	W	W	W
15	Vernon	Environmental studies	Z	N	W	Q	N
16	Walton State	Environmental studies	Z	N	W	W	W
17	Western State	Nursing	Z	N	W	Q	W

not wish to imply that stakeholders in cases within any one of the four types had nearly identical experiences: they did not. Yet, as we attempt to show in the chapters in part 3, we learned that stakeholders in each of the respective program types often experienced important aspects of their programs in much the same way. Thus, on the assumption that our sample of forty-seven cases is broadly representative of master's programs in the United States, we suggest that most of the master's programs in this country (subject, as always, to further verification) are likely to fall into one of the four program types identified here. At the same time, we emphasize that this idealized typology is, like any social construct, an artifact of its historical time and place. With this caveat in mind, we briefly describe each of the four program types in the following section.

Naming the "Idealized" Program Types

Ancillary Programs

We identified ten ancillary programs in our sample of forty-seven programs. As shown in table 5.2, with only a few exceptions, the same choices were made by stakeholders in each of the five decision-situations in these programs. All ten chose a didactic approach to teaching and learning, an academic orientation, and provided weak departmental and institutional support. And, in all but two of the ten programs, students chose to develop an individualistic student culture. This overall consonance of stakeholder choices, especially in the first three pivotal decision-situations, yielded an "ancillary" character, which was unique to this group of master's programs and which helped us understand how stakeholders experienced these programs. Specifically, we learned that stakeholders experienced their master's programs largely in relation to, and subordinate to, the Ph.D. programs offered in their departments, that is, as ancillary. In both professional and arts and sciences fields alike, stakeholders across these programs told us that they viewed the master's as a pre-Ph.D. "scholarly training experience," regardless of whether students intended to pursue the Ph.D. degree. Moreover, most faculty and administrators said that they considered master's education as subordinate to doctoral education and their research, and many students and alumni communicated to us that they had felt like "second-class citizens" while in these programs.

Career Advancement Programs

Our sample has eleven career advancement programs. Stakeholders in these programs chose a didactic approach to teaching and learning and a professional orientation for their program. In addition, faculty and program administrators in all but two of the programs chose to provide strong departmental support. In terms of auxiliary decision-situations, institutional administrators provided strong institutional support in all but four of the programs, and students developed individualistic student cultures in all but four of the programs. Stakeholders across the career advancement programs—almost all of which were in professional fields—told us that they viewed their master's programs largely as a client-centered, career-oriented, "expert training" experience in which faculty provided students with the knowledge, skills, and credentials needed for advancing their professional careers in the nonuniversity workplace.

Apprenticeship Programs

We identified nine apprenticeship programs in our forty-seven case sample. Faculty and program administrators in all nine chose a facilitative approach to teaching and learning and chose to provide strong departmental support to their master's programs. In seven cases, faculty and program administrators selected an academic orientation for their master's programs, whereas a professional orientation was preferred by those stakeholders in the other two cases. In terms of the two auxiliary decision-situations, campus administrators chose to provide weak institutional support, and students developed synergistic student cultures in more than half of these programs. Across the nine apprenticeship programs stakeholders told us that they understood their master's programs as an apprenticeship experience in which faculty—as "master craftspersons"—actively and consciously invested in their profession by facilitating students' educational development as young apprentices intent on becoming contributing members of their guild.

Community-centered Programs

We identified seventeen community-centered programs in our sample. Faculty and program administrators in these programs made similar choices in the first three decision-situations. In all seventeen cases they chose a dialogical approach to teaching and learning and provided strong departmental support. In terms of program orientation, faculty and administrators in all but five of the seventeen programs chose a connected orientation. As regards the auxiliary decision-situations, institutional administrators provided strong support in slightly over one-half of the cases, and students chose to develop either synergistic or participative student cultures. Stakeholders viewed their master's programs as community-centered experiences in which faculty and students, as collegial participants within a learning community, actively sought to serve their professional and broader social communities by generating critically informed understandings and approaches to issues in their respective fields.

## PART THREE

A TYPOLOGY OF
MASTER'S PROGRAMS

In part 2 we described master's programs at both the individual case and cross-case level. In chapters 3 and 4 we presented vignettes from thirteen different master's programs, each of which illustrated the consequences of a specific choice made in one of five decision-situations. In chapter 5, using the choices stakeholders made in the decision-situations as a tool to guide our analysis, we developed a typology of master's programs which classified the forty-seven cases within our sample in terms of the overall character of stakeholder experiences. The four idealized types of master's programs we formed are: ancillary, career advancement, apprenticeship, and community-centered.

In part 3 we devote a chapter to each of the four program types. In each we present a single case study portrait followed by an "idealized portrait" (abstracted from all cases in the program type) of the featured program type. Although we begin each case study by describing the circumstances in which the interviewees were positioned—such as institutional and program history, mission, reputation, program requirements, faculty and student characteristics—our primary emphasis in these four chapters is on explicating the overall character of stakeholder experiences as communicated to us in interviews.

In portraying the views of the people who animate the case studies in the following four chapters, we attempt to communicate the generalized perspectives of our multipositioned stakeholders. Our intention in doing so is to leave readers with a contextualized understanding of the overall character of these four program types. Throughout these case studies, we use extended direct quotations, as we did in the vignettes presented in chapters 3 and 4. At the same time, however, we also (in the words of an English professor at Longmont College) "keep our voices in there," thereby reminding readers of our role as positioned subjects who listened to and interpreted stakeholders' perspectives.

In the idealized type part of each of these four chapters, we draw on all the cases included in the program type to delineate an "idealized" portrait that necessarily deemphasizes the uniqueness of individual cases in order to describe those common characteristics that, in our interpretation, broadly represent the particular ideal type. We define *idealized type* in much the same way that Max Weber (1947) used the concept of "ideal type," namely, as an abstract and general construct developed through observation and comparative analysis. We made three assumptions that guided our construction of idealized types. First, each idealized type should provide insights that describe stakeholders' overall experiences and, at the same time, differentiate them from those of stakeholders in other idealized types. Second, each idealized type should not only describe—but also accentuate—themes across cases. Third, while our analysis would be based on what stakeholders across cases communicated to us, we, as researchers, would assume responsibility for constructing idealized types. We emphasize that typologies, including our own, should not be viewed as "rigid classifications" (Mitroff and Kilmann 1978; Neumann and Bensimon 1990), and we invite our readers to do likewise.

When presenting each idealized portrait, we first locate the member programs with respect to considerations such as field of study and type of institution in which they are located. Next we describe the overall character of the program type and the purposes that stakeholders articulated for these programs. Following that, we identify and elaborate on features that we believe are characteristic of the program type; in so doing, we illustrate how stakeholders experienced these features in their master's programs. We conclude by describing how stakeholders evaluated their overall experiences.

Throughout each of the four chapters included in part 3, we occasionally note, sometimes only parenthetically, relationships between choices made in the five decision-situations and the purposes and features that are represented in the idealized type. In these chapters, however, our main emphasis is on overall stakeholder experiences—not choices in decision-situations. Hence, we try to refer to decision-situations unobtrusively, not least because choices in decision-situations and stakeholder experiences were so closely connected with each other that to separate them would have created misleading distinctions.

6

Ancillary Programs

English at Major State University

While its land-grant mission and history reflect a strong commitment to public service and undergraduate education, Major State University's national reputation is unmistakably anchored in its commitment to research and doctoral education. This allegiance is manifest in highly visible research and scholarship by faculty, significant external research funding (several hundred million dollars per year), and the training of large numbers of Ph.D. students, including many who assume professorial positions in prestigious colleges and universities throughout the nation. As one high-ranking administrator at Major State told us: "As we see it, reputation is made through leadership and research accomplishment plus the contributions made by doctoral graduates of the program over time. If you have a good track record in putting out Ph.D. students that do a good job, that's a major component of your reputation. . . . The master's really only contributes insofar as it provides a very fine way in which you can screen for the most capable [students] to move on to the Ph.D."

Within this institutional context, we were not surprised that faculty and administrators in the Department of English were strongly committed to the scholarly training of advanced graduate students. We were told repeatedly that research and doctoral education were their major concerns and that they judged their effectiveness as a department primarily by the success of their doctoral graduates. Given these priorities, we came to understand that faculty and administrators defined their master's program largely in relation to, and subordinate to, the Ph.D. program—hence our appellation *ancillary*.

When we visited the English department in late 1989, total graduate enrollment exceeded two hundred students, with more than one-half enrolled at the master's level.[1] Admission to the master's program was highly selective. Most students were from out of state, including a substantial number of foreign students but few minorities from the United States. The program enrolled a handful of students over the age of thirty, but the majority were in their mid- to late twenties. Almost all students were enrolled on a full-time basis. Interviewees told us that about one-fourth of all entering master's students intended to leave the program with a terminal master's degree. The remainder planned to pursue the Ph.D. degree in the department.

Approximately fifty full-time faculty were employed in the Department of English. Representing all traditional specializations and a wide range of theoretical perspectives, many were considered leading scholars in their fields. While most senior faculty were male and in their fifties and sixties, interviewees told us that the department had recently hired a number of younger faculty (most of whom were female) who brought, in the words of one faculty member, a "diversity of critical perspectives" to the department.

Throughout our interviews we learned that the master's served primarily as a steppingstone to the Ph.D. program and a faculty "screening device" for the Ph.D. One professor illustrated this steppingstone purpose when he remarked: "At a place like this the M.A. program is just conceived of as the first part of the Ph.D. program. We invite you, and you come here to get an M.A. You don't have to go on for the Ph.D., but, on the other hand, the program is designed for the Ph.D." Echoing similar sentiments, an alumnus suggested that the "master's was basically a Ph.D. master's program. Everyone approached the courses the same way. You just happened to be fulfilling a master's requirement, that's all."

Interviewees also emphasized that the master's program served as a screening, or selection, device for the Ph.D. program. One professor, for example, described the master's as a "weeding-out" program in which faculty evaluated master's students in terms of their suitability for doctoral study. An alumnus told us: "It's a revolving door master's. And you just came in and did it—however you can do it, however you can hang on with your bloody fingers and do it."

In addition, several faculty mentioned that the program accommodated students who wished to pursue the M.A. as a terminal degree. One faculty member said, for example, that the master's provided an "opportunity" for public school teachers to broaden their knowledge and increase their salaries, that foreign students often found the degree prestigious and useful when they returned to their native countries, and that some students used the degree to enter careers in journalism and public relations. An institutional administrator noted that, while the master's in literature qualified students to teach English at the community college level, this was "not a very big part of what we do at this institution."

As a steppingstone to the Ph.D., the master's curriculum was designed to provide students with "a background in English and American literature, along with an introduction to methods of critical analysis and to the study of the English language or composition theory," as stated in a program brochure. As one professor put it, "The M.A. program in literature is a very cut-and-dried program designed for someone going on for the Ph.D." To this end, students took an introductory research course in critical methods, four courses in American and English literature, a breadth course in language or linguistics, and an elective course. In addition, the twenty-one-credit master's required students to demonstrate (by course work or examination) reading competence in one foreign language and to pass a comprehensive examination. A thesis was not required. Students were expected to complete their master's degrees within one year.

In conceiving the master's largely as a scholarly training experience that prepared students for doctoral study, faculty emphasized that they designed the program around the kinds of knowledge and skills traditionally valued in academe. Besides a broad base in English and American literature, students were expected to be knowledgeable about specialized theories and methods of literary criticism. A program administrator articulated the academic orientation of the program when he remarked that he and his colleagues "still have the old-fashioned view that education is about increasing one's knowledge and one's awareness": "I mean, if one is looking for any kind of a skill for a student coming out of the master's program, it's analytical skills. For me, it's the analytical skills combined with the rhetorical skills of being able to present what you have to say in a way that is both orderly and, one would hope, exciting. I really don't think you could ask for much more than that."

We learned from interviewees that, at the master's level, faculty used three basic instructional strategies to prepare—and screen—students for doctoral study. First, to ensure that students acquired a base of specialized theoretical knowledge, faculty emphasized academically demanding course work experiences in which the instructor assumed responsibility for didactically transmitting knowledge to students. Second, faculty expected students to acquire a body of knowledge on their own through developing a critical understanding of the sixty texts included on the basic reading list for the comprehensive examination. Third, and closely linked to the role of the master's program as a Ph.D. screening mechanism, faculty placed heavy emphasis on evaluating each student's scholarly potential through his or her performance in class and on the comprehensive examination.

Throughout our interviews, we were told that the master's program was, in the words of a faculty member, a "very faculty-controlled program" that was organized around "demanding" courses. Although master's students occasionally took advanced seminars in the department, most master's courses (including some offered to undergraduate students as well) followed a straightforward format that, in our terms, focused on the transmission of authoritative knowledge through a didactic approach to instruction: the instructor lectured, students read the assigned material, there was some class discussion, and students demonstrated mastery through course papers and examinations. While there was variation in this basic pattern, most interviewees stressed that the program was instructor centered. Many students and alumni highlighted the "strong personalities" on the faculty—personalities, they suggested, that were on display in the classroom as well as in the hallways and departmental offices. As one program graduate, currently a Ph.D. student in the department, put it: "Certain identities are held within the department, and they are not of subtext. They are on the surface, and they are carried around openly and self-consciously portrayed, and the identities are shifted around what are called 'ways of knowing,' and that, I think, describes a lot of the professors. Basically, in a spiritual sense, faculty live and die by those identities. I mean, they spend their whole lives forming them."

In describing themselves as teachers, faculty explained that they, above all, sought to challenge students by establishing rigorous expectations for them. One professor, for example, contrasted the master's with the bachelor's program in English in these terms: "It's more harried, it's more hurried, it's more pressure. Students want to sit around and encounter books on an intense personal level, but it isn't very much like that here." Another faculty member said that entering master's students had "a real hard time picking up the signals that the game has changed," but they "came to appreciate" that graduate study in the department was a formidable challenge.

Echoing these sentiments, students and graduates emphasized the demanding nature of faculty instruction. As one alumnus of the program put it: "I would say that the first semester of the M.A. year is the most emotionally and academically demanding, taxing, and sometimes frightening experience I've ever had. [It's captured by] two thoughts—of feeling exhilarated with what I was learning (though sometimes confused) and of being very happy that I had done this, but at the same time feeling somewhat as an outsider." A current student described her feelings this way: "The thing that works for me is just being pushed. I like having more expected of me than I feel that I can do just when it comes down to it. I definitely do feel challenged. Certainly my writing has been challenged.

I've gotten much better. I think I've learned a lot. It's just been so psychologically draining."

While acknowledging the considerable benefits of studying under faculty who held high expectations, most students and program graduates suggested that faculty often were so demanding that, as students, they had experienced levels of stress which inhibited their development. One student said: "The master's program is much more all-consuming than undergraduate work. I pretty much don't do anything but work, and I think about work all the time. And it's a lot of worry. I don't know how the people who have families, how they deal with it. I don't have anything like that, and I still can't, . . . I mean, I'm dealing with it—but not always feeling very sane." Another alumna described her experience in the program in these terms:

> The master's program is sort of like a "boot camp." It's the "boot camp mentality" [among faculty]. You can sense they're saying "I did it. Damn it. It was hard. And I'm going to make everybody else suffer." I resent the boot camp mentality. I thought they were making it hard on us because they saw some value in making it hard. I think faculty believe that if they make it hard enough and unpleasant enough a lot of people will quit, and they only want the people who can stick it out [and go on for the Ph.D.]. That's ridiculous. I think that's just stupid. You're not going to get the best people because you made it really hard. You're going to lose some people who would be very good but didn't like that life-style.

Interviewees pointed out that faculty, alongside what they required in courses, expected students to acquire a substantial body of knowledge on their own by becoming thoroughly familiar with the works included on the reading list for the comprehensive examination. Taken at the end of the program, this six-hour written exam tested students on their knowledge of approximately sixty texts. Interestingly, several students and alumni stated that, although admission into the Ph.D. program was determined largely by one's performance on this exam, relatively few of the works on the reading list were presented in master's courses.

As a third and closely related instructional strategy, faculty placed substantial emphasis on evaluating students, through informal interactions as well as their performance in class and on the comprehensive examination, in order to screen students for the Ph.D. program. Interviewees repeatedly told us that faculty relied on first-semester grades to decide on teaching assistant awards for second-year students and used the comprehensive examination as the official gateway to the Ph.D. program.

This emphasis on evaluation greatly influenced the way students experienced their master's program. Many students and alumni said that it often meant that they, as one student put it, "were supposed to toe the line" and conform to faculty expectations without "ruffling feathers." An alumnus expressed this perspective when he commented:

> As a student, there's a kind of decorum or posture that you should be careful to assume, I think, in class because you're afraid of alienating someone who you need desperately professionally at the time. . . . You don't want to piss anybody off. I felt like I was walking on eggshells with people. There were very significant messages which were being imparted by faculty as to whether the department was going to employ you or not [as a teaching assistant] and whether the professors were taking you seriously.

Students and alumni also told us that the faculty emphasis on evaluation fostered an individualistic culture in the program in which "excessive student competition," "grade grubbing," "isolation," and "anxiety" were widespread. One graduate, for example, remarked that it "bred a fair amount of paranoia among students about their professors: whether their professors approved of them, whether they would pass them on exams, and whether they were going to get through this place." Another graduate of the program defined her master's as a "grueling" and anxious experience in which students were "consumed" with receiving high grades and successfully passing their comprehensive examinations. As she explained, "A strong effect of this structural situation [faculty evaluation and screening] is that the students, far from supporting one another as fellow sufferers, actually avoided interacting with each other. We were placed into strongly competitive relationships. I was terrified the whole time I was in the program."

In much of the same spirit, another graduate bemoaned the lack of community in the program by contrasting it to the department's Ph.D. program:

> That sense of community that the Ph.D. students have, part of that is that they are teaching together, and part of that is that the burdens on them are not so great—they have time to develop a sense of community. There was no sense of community in the master's program because of the rigors of the program. It's grueling, and you don't have time to develop the kind of camaraderie that people expect. . . . You don't have time to talk about any ideas. All you have time to do is keep grinding out stuff. Keep reading it, keep grinding out work. That's the program. There's no time for reflection.

That faculty and administrators were aware of the stress master's students experienced was reflected in this program administrator's remarks: "They talk about preparing for the master's exam, they talk about how they can complete the master's program in a year, and they start talking about the M.A. reading list the first week they are on this campus, and, eleven months later, they walk away exhausted with their master's degree."

Throughout our interviews, many stakeholders pointed out that faculty were more committed to Ph.D. students and their own research than they were to master's students. Faculty frequently said that they placed a much higher value on doctoral education because it was "not worth their effort" to "invest" heavily in master's students since they might not continue on to the doctorate. More than one faculty member suggested that they did not award teaching assistantships to first-year students because they first wanted to make sure that students were "Ph.D. material."

Master's students and alumni often expressed disappointment with the lack of faculty commitment to students and to the master's program in general. Several complained about the lack of faculty mentoring and said faculty often were "inhospitable" to their needs. One alumnus put it this way: "I'd really do something about this collegiality thing. It's easy enough to say that professors are really busy. But, ideally, they should do something—like an open house or having their class over to their house. I'd do something like that." Another graduate offered this explanation for the absence of strong faculty commitment to master's students:

> I guess my problem is that, having survived this long, I tend to get more cynical about changing things. It's not cynical, it's seeing more of the picture, so it's very easy to say that professors should spend more of their time with the students, and I think that's true, but then the whole system needs to be changed so that's rewarded. Professors are trying to get tenure and so on. If they spend their time "palling around" with M.A. students, then they couldn't get their books published. So, in order to make the M.A. better, the whole institution would have to be changed.

In describing their overall experiences in the program, students and program graduates repeatedly characterized the master's as, in our language, an ancillary experience in which faculty defined the master's principally in relation to, and subordinate to, the Ph.D. program. Most students and alumni said that the subordination of the master's—through faculty-controlled instruction, excessive demands on students, heavy emphasis on evaluation, and generally weak faculty commitment—fostered a strongly individualistic and competitive master's experience in which students often felt isolated from one another and "invisible" to faculty. A program graduate, who had earned a departmental fellowship and admission into the Ph.D. program but chose to attend law school instead, illustrated this point when she compared her experiences in the master's program to those in law school: "It was very hard to distinguish yourself in the master's program. In law school, you can get recognition, say, a great final exam or law review. In the master's program I wasn't distinguished from anybody. It's sort of embarrassing to admit that I wanted them to recognize me. But the fact is that they didn't. I was nothing. I felt there was no personal interest in the master's students. The master's students were invisible."

This notwithstanding, faculty and administrators emphasized that the master's provided students with a rigorous Ph.D. steppingstone experience and was an effective device for screening applicants to the doctoral program. Those students who were allowed and chose to pursue the Ph.D. likewise mentioned that, in many ways, the master's experience was a valuable academic—albeit boot camp—experience that prepared them well for doctoral study. As one student put it: "The master's program is a really good program for what it sets out to do: To give us a broad background in English literature, a base to build on so that we can go on and study something in depth, give us a real good critical background. I also think it's intimidating. But, overall, it's a really solid program."

Almost everyone we interviewed indicated that the master's was best understood as a "predoctoral experience" rather than as a "program." Indeed, for the majority of master's students—those who were not admitted into the Ph.D. program and those who chose to finish their formal study at the master's level—the master's was viewed more as a "consolation prize" than as a "legitimate" degree. One alumna, for example, said that, of the forty or so M.A. students who entered the program when she did, only four or five went on to receive their Ph.D. degrees. In her words: "It was an ugly program. And people were disillusioned. They came in thinking either I'm sure I want to do the Ph.D., or I think I want to do the Ph.D., and that's why I'm here. People didn't come in thinking I'm just going to get a master's and quit." In much the same way, another program graduate said that most people expected to go on for the Ph.D., "but then, on the other hand, the vast majority of people don't go beyond the master's. So they have a program that's set up as preparation for the Ph.D., when, in fact, the people who take it end up not getting a Ph.D."

Most students and alumni also emphasized that a master's degree from the program had little cachet in the job market. As one graduate noted: "a flat M.A. in English is almost a worthless piece of paper. You have a very remote chance of getting a job if you have an M.A. in English." This individual suggested that there was a disjunction between the master's and the job market, namely, that the program taught students to be literary critics but the job market for English M.A.'s was primarily for composition teachers: "And that's the absurdity of it all," he remarked. "You learn all of this literature so you can go out and teach what is a comma, what is a sentence, but you've never had any background in it." Another alumnus candidly told us that the program failed those students who did not go on for a doctorate. In his words, for these graduates the master's program in English at Major State "was just a charade."

Understanding the Ancillary Idealized Program Type

Our case study of the master's program in English at Major State University portrays one ancillary program and alludes to the choices its stakeholders made in the five decision-situations discussed in part 2. With few exceptions, these same choices were made by stakeholders in nine other master's programs included in our sample. All ten chose a didactic approach to teaching and learning, an academic orientation, and provided weak departmental and institutional support. And, in all but two of the ten programs, students chose an individualistic student culture.

All ten of the master's programs we classified as ancillary were housed in departments or schools that offered baccalaureate as well as doctoral degree programs. Eight of the programs were situated in national universities, and two were located in regional institutions. By field of study, these ten cases represented two arts and sciences disciplines (English and sociology) and six professional fields (nursing, theater, business, engineering, education, and microbiology). Six of the eight programs at national universities were located at Major State University (English, sociology, business, nursing, theater, and education) and one each at Phelps University (English) and Barrett State Medical Center (nursing). The two programs housed at regional institutions included the master's program in engineering at Middle State University and the master's program in microbiology at Mountain State University. All but one of the ancillary programs (English at Phelps University) were located in a public institution. (Table 6.1 identi-

Table 6.1. **Distribution of Case Studies in the Ancillary Idealized Program Type**

Pseudonym Institution	Field of Study	Degree Levels
Case Studies at National Institutions		
Barrett State	Nursing	B.S., M.S., Ph.D.
Major State	Business	B.S., M.B.A., Ph.D.
Major State	Education	B.A., M.A., Ph.D.
Major State	English	B.A., M.A., Ph.D.
Major State	Nursing	B.S., M.S., Ph.D.
Major State	Sociology	B.A., M.A., Ph.D.
Major State	Theater	B.F.A., M.F.A., Ph.D.
Phelps	English	B.A., M.A., Ph.D.
Case Studies at Regional Institutions		
Middle State	Electrical engineering	B.S., M.S., Ph.D.
Mountain State	Microbiology	B.S., M.S., Ph.D.

fies the ten cases by institutional type, field of study, and degree levels offered.)

We now sketch a portrait of the ancillary idealized program type by considering major similarities across the ten cases as a whole. In the first part of this section, we briefly summarize our interpretation of the overall character of these programs and discuss two key purposes stakeholders articulated for their programs. In the second part, we discuss three features that, based on interviews with stakeholders across these programs, are characteristic of the ancillary program type: the emphasis placed on student mastery of basic theoretical knowledge and skills through faculty-directed scholarly training; the "marginalization" of professional (non-university) workplace-related knowledge and experiences; and the weak administrative and faculty commitment provided to master's education and master's students. In the third and final part, we examine stakeholder perspectives concerning the overall quality and value of their master's experiences.

Character and Articulated Purposes

Stakeholders across these ten cases communicated to us that they experienced their master's program largely in relation to, and as subordinate to, the Ph.D. program, that is, as an ancillary activity in their departments. Interviewees, including those in professional as well as arts and sciences fields, repeatedly characterized the master's primarily as a pre-Ph.D. "scholarly training experience," regardless of whether or not students intended to pursue the Ph.D. A student in sociology at Major State, for example, described his master's experience as a "two-year training period to prepare you for the Ph.D."; a professor at Mountain State said that the master's program in microbiology gave students the "opportunity to get their basic scholarly training" for the Ph.D.; and a Barrett State administrator mentioned that their master's program in nursing was becoming "secondary to the doctorate" as they increasingly organized it around the training and selection of students for their Ph.D. program. Moreover, most faculty and administrators across all ten cases emphasized that they considered master's education subordinate to their involvement in doctoral education and research, and many students and alumni in these programs told us that they felt like second-class citizens.

We came to understand that the ancillary character of stakeholder experiences was related to two purposes that faculty and program administrators articulated and that other stakeholders corroborated. First, in varying degrees, faculty and administrators in all ten cases told us that master's education should support doctoral education as a steppingstone degree that provided students with the scholarly background and training to pursue the doctorate and which gave faculty the opportunity to screen students before admitting them into their Ph.D. program. Second, stakeholders noted that an accompanying, albeit secondary, purpose of the master's was to fulfill their university's public service mission by serving as a terminal degree for students who were not invited or did not wish to pursue a doctorate.

Program faculty and administrators communicated their first purpose—that the master's should provide students with a steppingstone experience and faculty with a screening device for selecting students for the doctoral program—when they spoke at great length about their commitment to the "traditional model of graduate education" widely used in the arts and sciences. This model, for all intents and purposes, is tailored almost exclusively for doctoral education. Located in institutional settings in which doctoral education, faculty research, and grants were highly valued, most faculty and administrators associated with the ten ancillary programs indicated, explicitly or implicitly, that they embraced these institutional values as their own and viewed participation in their master's programs as an ancillary activity.

Stakeholders in the five universities (three national and two regional) housing the ten ancillary programs informed us that their institutions were strongly committed to this traditional model of graduate education. A nursing professor, for example, who represented the views of many interviewees at Major State, described the university as "big, impersonal, and tough": "It's recognized every year as one of the top ten research institutions in the country. Anybody that's gone here as an undergraduate knows that the faculty . . . are buried in research and doctoral education—and not master's education." A nursing professor at Barrett State characterized her institution as a major "high-tech, biotech" university that was mostly interested in research and training new Ph.D.'s. And, at Phelps University, stakeholders indicated that Phelps' prestigious national standing was based largely on its reputation in doctoral education and faculty research.

Interviewees in both regional universities likewise conveyed that their institutions had embraced a traditional model of graduate education, largely as a means of developing a national reputation for their campus. We learned that, at Middle State University, institutional administrators and many faculty had focused on building a "national reputation" for their institution for over a decade. In the context of explaining the rapid expansion of graduate education at their institution, several interviewees emphasized that Middle State was positioning itself, as one institutional administrator suggested, "to join the ranks of the top fifty institutions in the country" as a major producer of doctoral graduates and research. Many faculty pointed out that the new president was deeply committed to doctoral education and research, as reflected in the number of faculty he had rejected for tenure owing to "weak" publication records.

Institutional administrators and faculty at Mountain State repeatedly told us that they were committed, as one institutional administrator put it, to converting Mountain State from a "cow college" to a "real university." As one microbiology faculty member explained: "The big picture is to make [Mountain State] a first-class research institution. If we're going to be recognized nationally as a serious research institution, we have to have strong Ph.D. programs." One senior institutional administrator—who opined that a "master's degree is silly" if a student has any serious interest in a Ph.D.—unambiguously stated that she and other top-level administrators were committed to enhancing Mountain State's reputation through placing increased emphasis on research and the training of researchers at the doctoral level. Another institutional administrator said that "new faculty are expected to do 25 to 50 percent teaching and 50 to 75 percent research" in order to earn tenure at the university.

Most faculty and administrators in the ten ancillary programs mirrored the orientations of their respective institutions by adopting this traditional model of graduate education in their departments. At Major State, for example, stakeholders in all six of the ancillary cases—nursing, education, business, theater, English, and sociology—emphasized the centrality of doctoral education and research in their departments. One education professor, for example, told us that his department had a "world-class reputation that was based on the quality of faculty publication records," while a sociology professor mentioned that faculty saw doctoral students as their department's "product": "The people who have gone out of here with master's degrees, well, nobody knows who they are. They don't do anything for us." Most faculty and administrators in nursing at Barrett State Medical Center and English at Phelps University echoed the same overall preference for doctoral education and research. At Barrett, for example, one professor said that, "while the mission of the school is to prepare advanced clinical types and then researchers, in reality it is to prepare people for involvement in research and for contributing to nursing science."

These themes were reiterated by faculty and administrators, as well as students, in the engineering program at Middle State and the microbiology program at Mountain State. Many faculty at Middle State stressed that they wanted to be recognized as one of the "top ten or at least top twenty-five" engineering departments in the nation. A longtime faculty member in microbiology at Mountain State remarked that, a decade earlier, the faculty decided to build a national reputation for the department by taking "someone else's model and adapting it": "We hired new faculty based on their research records and their potential and capabilities. It was a purposeful decision. We are trying to compete with the real universities."

In describing their allegiance to this traditional model of graduate education, faculty and administrators in the ten ancillary programs communicated to us that their master's program was designed mostly to support doctoral education. They made it clear that their master's should accomplish this purpose by serving both as a steppingstone experience in which students received the scholarly training and background needed to pursue the doctorate and as a screening device for faculty to select individuals for their doctoral program.

Faculty and administrators in sociology and English at Major State articulated the steppingstone intent of their master's programs when they described the master's largely as a "degree in course." To illustrate, one sociology professor explained: "The master's may be the terminal degree for a large proportion [of entering students], but it will always be considered in between the bachelor's and the Ph.D. [in this department]. And I don't see a track where people who get a master's go and do something different than what people who get Ph.D.'s do. It's just that they're going to a different, a lower level." A student in the same department put it this way: "What I didn't understand before I went back to graduate school was that in the Department of Sociology you simply didn't just get a master's. It was a master's in preparation. It's only a preparation point for Ph.D. work." Another sociology student said: "There isn't really a master's program here. They give you a degree that's geared toward the Ph.D. level, and you enter [Major State's] sociology graduate program only with the idea of getting a Ph.D. It's more of a steppingstone." Along these same lines, a graduate student in English described their master's as a "Ph.D. master's program."

Although stakeholders in the other eight cases did not view their master's program exclusively as a degree in course, they often suggested that its primary intent was to provide students with the scholarly training needed to "step" into Ph.D. programs. The microbiology program at Mountain State is a case in point. One faculty member, for example, told us that faculty "did not differentiate between the M.S. and the Ph.D." in their department. A former program administrator expressed a similar outlook: "My master's students—my good, solid master's students—just go smoothly into the Ph.D. program, here or elsewhere." And another professor remarked: "Right now, the degree is halfway to the Ph.D. . . . It's a mini-Ph.D."

To be sure, in all of the ancillary programs, save the two exclusively degree-in-course programs, faculty and administrators noted that there was some tension between faculty who saw the master's principally as a steppingstone and those who placed equal emphasis on the master's as a steppingstone and as a terminal degree. In the end, however, we learned that the steppingstone objective was the primary focus in each of these programs. As an administrator in Major State's education program put it:

I think there is a fundamental tension between preparing a person who intends to go on for a Ph.D. versus the person who sees herself as a practitioner—as a classroom teacher who wants to get from a master's degree ideas, skills, and knowledge that will help her to become a better teacher. Faculty members divide themselves along these lines. My feeling is that the faculty members who are responsible for developing the master's degree in the field of secondary education range across those who only see it as the preparation of a research scholar and those who see the master's degree as the first step in the doctoral process. And then there are other faculty members who are very field oriented—very committed and concerned about improving the effectiveness of classroom teachers. . . . But clearly the program leans toward the research-oriented bias. . . . The master's really is preparation for the Ph.D.

Another Major State education faculty member, who referred to the same tension between preparing "practitioners" and preparing "scholars," said that the unmistakable tendency in the department's master's program was to "emulate a Ph.D. program."

We came to appreciate that this tension was greatest in three cases advertised as "terminal programs"—English at Phelps University and theater and business at Major State. Notwithstanding these tensions, however, many interviewees stated that, in each of these programs, faculty and administrators continued to view the master's primarily as a predoctoral scholarly training experience for students. In the theater program at Major State, for example, faculty and administrators said that they primarily designed their M.F.A. around the kinds of scholarly training needed to prepare graduates for university teaching positions. Similarly, faculty and administrators in Major State's master's in business administration program told us that their program was oriented, in large measure, around scholarly training.[2] While most graduates in this program did not intend to pursue a doctorate, some did use the degree as a steppingstone to the Ph.D., especially those "handpicked" by faculty as promising doctoral students.

Across all ten ancillary cases, faculty and administrators also emphasized that the master's supported their doctoral program by serving the faculty as a screening device for their Ph.D. program. As noted earlier, an administrator in Major State's sociology program told us that the master's served an important gatekeeping function by helping faculty "gauge if the student really has the ability and the commitment to do the Ph.D." A microbiology professor at Mountain State expressed a similar outlook, stating that he and his colleagues viewed "the master's as a screening device and a default degree for students who can't cut it." A nursing alumna from Barrett State also remarked, "In the last few years faculty seem to be using the master's program primarily as an opportunity to judge potential Ph.D. students."

In addition to serving their doctoral programs as both a steppingstone and a screening device, faculty and administrators in the ancillary cases presented another, albeit secondary, purpose for their master's programs: they should serve their public service mission by offering the master's as a terminal degree. Interestingly, it was this second purpose that addressed the needs and, in many cases, expectations of the largest proportion of students in these programs: in all but one of the ancillary programs, the majority of master's students were either not invited or did not choose to pursue a doctorate. A representative case was the master's program in education at Major State University. This program enrolled many teachers who wanted a master's degree in order "to move up the salary scale" in their school districts. As one program administrator explained, in recent years their master's enrollment had been fueled by licensure requirements, which led to the development of a "backdoor" student population: "Because teachers have to upgrade their credential and they do that as a special student, they suddenly realize that they have all of these credits that they really might as well apply toward a program. As a result, a number of our students enter our master's program through the back door." A professor told us that, although their program had "very pragmatic value" for students, most faculty nonetheless viewed this aspect of the program as a low-priority "service activity." As he explained:

> The master's in secondary education is almost a service degree. It's a service by making it available to students. The faculty orientation here . . . it's a very strong research-oriented faculty. Fairly frequently what we do at the master's level is a part of our public service obligation, and so we spend a lot of time talking about the research, what's going on in an area, trying to think with the master's students about the application of that. But most of the faculty see themselves as researchers and view the teaching at the master's level as part of their service obligation to the university.

There was some variation across these ten cases in terms of how faculty and administrators viewed the master's as a terminal degree. At one extreme, faculty and administrators in the two degree-in-course programs (sociology and English at Major State) and the English master's program at Phelps saw the terminal master's degree largely as a symbolic "reward" to students for their efforts. A Major State English professor, for example, explained that the program sought "to accommodate terminal students like teachers and foreign students," but, he added, "it ain't a big part of what we do here." And at Phelps a professor told us: "English is not a full-blown program. Not forgotten or neglected, it just seemed to develop. Rather than being a program, it's that we have some people who come for a year to do an M.A." At the other extreme, faculty in Major State's master's program in business said that they provided a solid terminal master's program that was relatively important to them since so many students enrolled with the clear intention of finding positions in the nonuniversity workplace. Despite this variation, we learned from most administrators and faculty in the ancillary programs that providing terminal master's education for students was secondary in importance to preparing students for doctoral education.

From our perspective, the two purposes interviewees articulated for their master's programs—to support doctoral education by serving as a steppingstone and screening device and to provide a terminal degree for students who do not continue on for the Ph.D.—were closely related to the decision-situation choices they made in the ten ancillary programs. In order to provide prospective doctoral students with the scholarly preparation to pursue the Ph.D., faculty chose a didactic approach to teaching and learning (decision-situation 1) and an academic orientation in their programs (decision-situation 2). In seeking to fulfill their university's public service mission, faculty and administrators in most of these programs also chose to offer the master's as a terminal degree—without substantially altering their primary focus on teaching students the kinds of highly specialized, theoretical knowledge and skills needed for doctoral study. Accordingly, they viewed master's education as subordinate to doctoral education and hence chose to provide weak departmental support (decision-situation 3) and weak institutional support (decision-situation 4) to these master's programs. Finally, and particularly in light of the emphasis faculty placed on using the master's as a competitive screening device for the Ph.D. program, students chose to develop individualistic student cultures (decision-situation 5) in most of the ancillary programs.

Characteristic Features

In analyzing our interviews across these ten cases, we came to appreciate that the purposes faculty and administrators articulated for their master's program, as well as the decision-situation choices stakeholders made, helped inform our understanding of the ancillary idealized program type. By focusing on the overall character and features of this program type, we present a more encompassing interpretation of stakeholder experiences in these ten programs. In reviewing our interviews, we came to understand three distinctive features as broadly characteristic of the ancillary program type: the primary emphasis on student mastery of basic theoretical knowledge and skills through faculty-directed scholarly training; the marginalization of (nonuniversity) workplace knowledge and workplace-related experiences; and weak administrative and faculty commitment to master's education and master's students.[3]

Basic Theoretical Knowledge through Faculty-directed Scholarly Training Student acquisition and mastery of nonapplied, specialized theoretical knowledge was a pronounced feature in the ten ancillary programs (decision-situation 2). As we discussed in chapter 3, the master's program in nursing at Barrett State emphasized theoretical and academic knowledge and was focused on student acquisition of "an integrated body of knowledge with primary emphasis on . . . principles and theory rather than on . . . developing skills and techniques for immediate practical application." Barrett State faculty and administrators were not alone in emphasizing specialized, theoretical knowledge in their master's program. A Major State nursing professor, for example, said that she and her colleagues were proud that they offered the M.S. degree rather than a Master's of Science in Nursing (M.S.N.) because, "if our degree is given by the graduate school, then it means it emphasizes a fair immersion in the scientific basis of knowledge." In a similar fashion, an administrator in Major State's education program told us that their master's courses focused on empirically based "content knowledge" rather than on anecdotal "tricks-of-the-trade" techniques: "Our faculty says you ought to get as much knowledge in your head as a teacher as you possibly can . . . not just a bag of tricks."

Students and alumni across these ten cases also emphasized that acquiring specialized theoretical knowledge was a fundamental aspect of their master's experiences. A nursing student at Major State, for example, described the master's program in these terms: "What we get is theory, the current research, the current thinking [in this program]. The feeling I get from the faculty is that they realize that we know day-to-day, nitty-gritty clinical stuff. They have the expertise in the big, broader theory." An education student at the same institution explained that his classes "weren't just general education stuff or philosophy of education or all of that crap you had to take to get certified. Instead, you learned a lot of current theory and research." And a Major State sociology student said that, during his master's experience, "a central idea was pounded into my head, and I feel very strongly about that: theory has to come first."

To facilitate student mastery of basic theoretical knowledge, we learned that faculty in ancillary programs primarily employed a faculty-directed, didactic approach to instruction (decision-situation 1). In this approach faculty transmitted the basic theories and concepts (authoritative knowledge) of their respective discipline and, in turn, expected students to master this knowledge. While they presumed students would raise questions about the knowledge and information being presented, faculty expected students to do so in their role as receivers, or "consumers," of knowledge. A brochure published by the Barrett State nursing program aptly conveyed this "recipient" role: "Functionally, within academic nursing, master's programs occupy a mid-point between the 'received view' approach that must be taken in pre-licensure undergraduate programs and the fundamentally questioning view of doctoral programs. . . . Master's graduates act as consumers and questioners of doctoral research findings."

Interviewees across the ancillary programs told us that this faculty-directed approach to instruction was expressed primarily through classroom-centered lectures and lecture discussions. As such, students took most of their graduate credits in courses rather than in thesis credits or in internships, practica, and the like. To illustrate, an English professor at Phelps described the master's program there as "a year of course work": "Students come in and take courses for a year. I think they can write a thesis but I don't think it's required." In all but one of the ancillary programs, master's students occasionally (frequently in several programs) took courses along with doctoral students; in three of the programs, students were allowed to complete a portion of their course work in undergraduate courses that offered graduate credit. Despite their overall emphasis on providing students with scholarly training, faculty in only one-half of these ancillary programs—microbiology at Mountain State and education, sociology, nursing, and theater at Major State—required students to complete a thesis or major project.

Within courses faculty relied principally on lectures—didactic instruction—to transmit theoretical knowledge to students. Although professors in some programs occasionally "turned classes into seminars," it was only in Phelps' English program, in which master's students took the same classes as first-year doctoral students, that faculty made seminars widely available to master's students. Yet, even in these seminars, a Phelps English professor said that most faculty used a "lecture style with encouraged interruptions," and very few tried a "Socratic" teaching approach. As an alumna of the program told us, "Because there were about twenty-five people in a class, almost all of my classes invariably turned into a lecture."

Faculty across the ten ancillary programs suggested that they defined themselves as scholars whose teaching responsibilities were twofold: to introduce students to a variety of theoretical perspectives and to "model their expertise" for students. The Major State education program serves as an interesting case in point. One professor proudly told us that master's students "walked away with their heads spinning at the frequency with which they encountered questions that [had] never occurred to them. They are exposed to orthodox and rival perspectives: neo-Marxist, feminist, and international perspectives." A music education professor said that he modeled "good teaching" for his students: "The one thing I do every day in front of the kids is to act as a model—sometimes I do it vocally, sometimes if my trumpet is around I pick it up, sometimes I dance—but I provide the musical spark as a model."

In describing their coursework experiences, many students and alumni talked about the respect they had for faculty as knowledgeable scholars and intellectuals. In Major State's sociology program, for example, an alumnus referred to faculty as "scary-smart professors": "What makes the faculty good is that they know everything. They know everything in the world. I have a lot of respect for the faculty, and it's not really related to their teaching. . . . I have been exposed to the way they are when someone is presenting research and the way they respond to that. And it's just amazing how quick they are." Similarly, students in the theater program at Major State emphasized that faculty challenged them intellectually. As one student put it, "We are pushed to our limits."

While many students and alumni said that they appreciated studying under "outstanding scholars" and acquiring a substantial base of theoretical knowledge, a large number also remarked that they did not always appreciate being "lectured to," much less being expected to assume a fairly passive role in their courses. A student in the microbiology program at Mountain State, for example, told us that one of his professors was a "leading researcher" in the field but was "an awful teacher." As he put it, the professor "just lectures straight from the book." An alumna of the same program suggested that many faculty did not expect students to assume an active role in their classes, and, as a result, "students tended to be sheep or parrots" in their interactions with faculty.

Marginalization of Workplace-related Knowledge and Experiences

While faculty in the ancillary programs placed primary emphasis on scholarly training and student acquisition of theoretical knowledge, we learned that most faculty also incorporated supplemental workplace-related knowledge and experiences in their programs.[4] This was usually inserted into these programs through "professional practice" activities (such as internships, practica, and laboratory experiences) in which students applied knowledge learned in their classes to "real-world problems." These activities were taught by full-time faculty and, in some instances—as in the two nursing programs—by clinical and adjunct faculty. In addition, some faculty in the ancillary programs occasionally invited practitioners from the field to share their perspectives in courses.

Many students and alumni told us that the hands-on learning they completed, and the interactions they had with practitioners, while engaged in these professional practice activities greatly enriched their master's experiences. A Barrett State nursing alumna, for example, described the program's adjunct faculty as "dynamic":

> I was so happy to have met them. They were my mentors when I was in school, and they were people that I had heard about from other students,

and I think as a group they're an extremely intelligent lot, and they really know their nursing. . . . When these people come in and teach rather than the [full-time, tenure-track] faculty here who teach, it's great. We loved it. We hung on their every word. We had our tape recorders on those days, and it was just great. They were real because they were telling you what's really happening out there in practice in the real-world—not this "ivory tower" stuff. The people who worked and stayed in the ivory tower, most of them we could do without.

Notwithstanding these accounts, we learned that most full-time faculty and program administrators marginalized workplace-related knowledge and experiences in their master's programs. This marginalization occurred in two major ways. First, most faculty did not consistently introduce workplace-related knowledge and perspectives into their courses. Second, faculty seldom emphasized hands-on learning experiences (such as group projects, case studies, and clinical, laboratory, and performance activities) to help students link theory with practice. In general, interviewees attributed these omissions to the "narrowness" and "hyper-specialization" of faculty, their lack of involvement in professional practice, and their attitude that applied, or practical, knowledge and workplace-related experiences were less valuable than "pure" theory. This latter point reflected these faculty members' shared perspective that the master's degree was primarily "useful" as a steppingstone degree to the theory-based and specialized research activities associated with doctoral study.

The nursing, theater, and business programs at Major State illustrate this tendency among faculty in ancillary programs to marginalize workplace-related knowledge and experiences. Many nursing program administrators and faculty candidly told us that they were not involved in professional practice, nor did they stay in close touch with clinical faculty in the program. As a program administrator put it: "So few of our faculty are actively involved in practice. It's just the nature of the tenure-track faculty member: You can't do everything. . . . [But] we need at least to have a tie between the research faculty and the practice faculty—other than students." Students, alumni, and employers were more critical. One student said that "most faculty have not practiced in decades" and that "some research-oriented faculty have told me that they rely on those of us coming into the program to tell them what problems need to be studied." An alumna remarked that the regular faculty "didn't model clinical skills," while many students suggested that they wished faculty would incorporate more hands-on learning experiences into their courses. Echoing these sentiments, an employer criticized the program for placing too little "emphasis on clinical expertise and more on the theoretical": "In [Major State's] nursing program, there is a belief among faculty that, if you have the theoretical framework, you can apply it to clinical practice. My view is that it is a fairly weak program clinically." And another employer simply said: "There aren't enough faculty in the program who are really tuned into reality. They have a lot of people who are into research. It is a protective environment for faculty where practice gets the short end of the stick."

Interviewees in the theater program at Major State voiced similar concerns. One alumnus, for instance, told us that the program "minimized hands-on experience," while another said that students were not encouraged to work in local repertory theaters while completing their studies. And an employer, a director of a regional theater company, criticized the program for being too academic. In his words:

> There's a lack of ongoing exchanges between this program and professionals in the field like myself—who are not invited to teach, to work with students. Students are not being invited to the theaters to do internships. Faculty are not querying us on a regular basis as to what our needs are, what the failures of the graduates are, what their strong points are. . . . Faculty in the program don't have the time to spend with professionals or hire professionals. From our point of view, we don't know why there's that lack of inquiry [on the part of faculty], but it's clearly there. . . . In short, very little happens between the faculty giving out the M.F.A. degree and those of us doing the hiring. Many students don't understand how the theater works or what it is all about.

Finally, in Major State's business program, students said that they often were frustrated by the lack of practical and "concrete" knowledge in their program. As one student put it: "Academe is a world by itself—part of which is publishing papers and part of which is developing models with little boxes with arrows and dashes. Those of us who have worked are more interested in how business works on a day-to-day basis than in academic models about organizational theory and behavior. It's really nice to be exposed to that, but we really want more concrete knowledge." Another student added: "Pedagogy should develop students' ability to analyze complex, real-life situations by means of writing more papers, working on projects, doing more class presentations. That's the kind of experience you should get out of an M.B.A. program, but we really aren't getting that experience here."

Weak Administrative and Faculty Commitment to Master's Education

One theme above all others cut across our interviews in the ancillary programs: institutional and program administrators, as well as faculty, treated master's education and master's students as subordinate to doctoral education and doctoral students and subordinate to faculty research. Students and alumni, in particular, told us that this weak administrative and faculty commitment was so pronounced that they often felt like second-class citizens.

To begin with, we learned that few master's students in the ancillary programs received monetary support from institution-wide funding sources (decision-situation 4). In some cases institutional policies severely limited aid to master's students, while in others institutional administrators chose to limit funding support. At Barrett State, for example, an institutional administrator informed us that university policies and guidelines largely precluded support for master's students in nursing, with most fellowship money going directly to doctoral students. Similarly, we were told that, at Major State, master's students were seldom funded from institutional sources except for fellowships awarded to individuals who were perceived as especially promising potential doctoral students. As an administrator in Major State's education program put it, "Master's students are at somewhat of a disadvantage for institutional funding because of the large number of Ph.D.'s and the emphasis on doctoral students."

Many students and alumni explained that they felt "inferior" to doctoral students because they did not receive institutional, or program, financial assistance. A sociology student at Major State, after telling us that only a few master's students received funding, said rhetorically, "If you can't afford to fund students, don't bring them in." A Phelps English student put it more sharply: "I think we're treated very differently. Doctoral students get funding. Master's students get nothing."

Faculty and administrators in the ten ancillary programs also pointed out that institutional administrators rarely provided support for master's education, even in the form of symbolic gestures, such as public statements of support. Moreover, many explained that, since university-wide promotion and tenure policies emphasized faculty research achievement, there was little incentive for them to invest in master's education and master's students. As an employer familiar with the nursing program at Major State told us: "There's a real problem with the way the university tenures faculty. Research and doctoral education—not master's students— are what count." A business professor in the same university elaborated on this point:

> Any faculty member who spends his time on teaching is going to get "had" at this institution. There are no incentives in the system for developing new courses or for teaching. None. You don't get paid for that. All people care about is that you're not bad. You get rewarded for one thing: what research you publish in which journals. The faculty that are responsible to students—you know what happens to them? Five years down the road, they're denied tenure. An M.B.A. program needs high-quality pedagogy

and the institution isn't set up for that. We have to give a life raft to people who are taking risks to be involved in pedagogy and not just research.

An alumna of Mountain State's microbiology program commented that the institution's tenure and promotion policies were "breeding a new kind of scientist":

a kind of self-centered publish-or-perish type who doesn't care so much about students. . . . The [prototypic] new faculty member is a high-tech, Wall Street businessman sort of scientist. They are getting to be self-centered little capitalists. There is a new emphasis on getting those grants. What would you think of somebody [referring to several professors in the program] who, every chance they got, would tell you how many people were in their lab, how much grant money they had attained, how many publications they had? That's the type of person they are. The new faculty [in the program] are pushed to get grant money, and they are always complaining about teaching undergraduates or master's students.

In light of the weak institutional support provided to master's education—coupled with the widespread view among faculty that the master's was primarily a steppingstone degree to the Ph.D.—we were not surprised that administrators and faculty at the department level also provided relatively weak support to their master's program (decision-situation 3). We learned that only two of the ten ancillary programs had been comprehensively reviewed within the previous decade and that stakeholders in most of the other ancillary programs believed a program review was long overdue. An employer of graduates from Major State's nursing program echoed the sentiments of many interviewees when she said: "I don't know when the master's curriculum has been revised. It's been on autopilot for so many years." She added that, with ten times as many master's students as doctoral students, "a major overhaul was called for."

Interviewees across the ten ancillary programs likewise criticized faculty and administrators for their lack of concern about establishing an effective placement mechanism for master's graduates. In most programs, stakeholders told us, administrative and faculty involvement in placing master's graduates was limited mostly to posting job announcements on the departmental bulletin board. An administrator in the English program at Major State, for example, candidly "confessed" that he had not "thought about job placement for master's students much": "We're inclined to place our Ph.D. students because they are being placed in universities. People with M.A.'s don't try to get university jobs, and they disperse in various ways. So in a sense we don't know about how our master's graduates are placed. I don't have any records of what these people do." Only Major

State's M.B.A. program had a placement office, albeit a meagerly staffed and underfinanced one. In the words of one business professor, the "placement office was a disaster." An administrator in this program remarked that students were "herded through the office like cattle" and that most of the faculty in the program saw "no need for a placement office or don't care one way or the other if they have it."

Given their interest in doctoral education and research, most faculty in the ancillary programs told us that they chose not to devote much time or energy to master's education or master's students. One Major State education professor explained that it was reasonable for faculty to direct their attention away from master's education because "Ph.D. students are contributing to the world of research, and faculty see research as contributing to salvation, with much broader implications than teaching a few master's students." A Barrett State nursing faculty member made the point in this way: "Master's students are seen less as individuals than doctoral students because, while the goal of the master's program is education, research is what faculty do."

Faculty expressed weak commitment to master's education and students in myriad ways. Interviewees often told us that faculty devoted relatively little time and effort to their teaching. As a business student at Major State explained: "Quite a few of my professors were not as ambitious as they should be—not devoting enough energy to their teaching. They give multiple choice exams to graduate students." An employer of Barrett State nursing graduates criticized faculty for spending too much time "traveling the international circuit" and not enough on their teaching. And an alumnus of Middle State's engineering program said that, although faculty expected "master's students to learn on their own, it was awful": "Faculty are interested in students insofar as they can be useful to them in their research, and the students also did the lab teaching. Faculty almost never showed up for teaching labs."

In several programs faculty emphasized that they were unwilling to spend much time supervising theses. As an engineering faculty member at Middle State told us: "Supervising master's students is a one-way street. Master's students are around only about two years, which is not time enough to do good research. To do good research, you almost have to be a Ph.D. student." In other programs faculty incorporated a nonthesis option. At Barrett State a nursing professor remarked that she and her colleagues "personally encouraged" students to take the nonthesis option: "We don't have time for mentoring unless a student's thesis is related to a faculty member's line of research and that student looks like they're going on for a Ph.D." For their part, many students and alumni criticized faculty for their indifference to a thesis requirement. As an engineering student at Middle State put it: "The nonthesis option degrades the prestige of the master's degree. It's just an easy way out for faculty and students."

Finally, students and alumni repeatedly told us that they felt slighted by faculty in various "little ways." A graduate of the Phelps English program, for example, pointed out that master's graduates were not invited to departmental diploma ceremonies. And several nursing students at Major State mentioned that they had difficulty finding three professors to serve on their comprehensive examination committees.

To be sure, some faculty in ancillary programs expressed concern about master's students. And, in a number of instances, students and alumni told us that there were individual professors who were interested in their work. This notwithstanding, students and alumni across the ten ancillary programs generally felt neglected—by their institutions, by their departments and by individual faculty members. As an alumna of the English program at Major State put it: "To be honest with you, I didn't receive a lot of support and encouragement, period. The terminal master's students were really rather second-class citizens. . . . I certainly had the feeling that because we were not going on for the Ph.D. that we were, in a way, second-class. The reason I chose to do this master's was to try it out, and I didn't understand until I got into it that this was the way it was." Similarly, a Major State sociology student remarked: "You really aren't treated well until you get to the Ph.D. level. . . . Before that, you're a grunt." And an English faculty member at Phelps said that "to be a master's student here is to be pretty marginal, very marginal, actually . . . a second-class citizen."

Overall Stakeholder Evaluations of Ancillary Program Experiences

To recapitulate, stakeholders across these ten cases communicated to us that they experienced their master's program largely in relation to, and as subordinate to, the Ph.D. program, that is, as an ancillary program. We learned that the master's was given definition by faculty and administrators and viewed by students, alumni, and employers primarily as a "scholarly training" and steppingstone experience, a graduate degree in course which also accommodated students who sought the master's as a terminal degree. In addition, we learned that the master's often served as a Ph.D. screening device for faculty. And, because faculty and administrators treated the master's program as secondary to the Ph.D. program and viewed master's students as ancillary to both doctoral students and their research interests, many master's students and alumni told us that they felt like second-class citizens.

Throughout our interviews in the ancillary programs, stakeholders expressed their perspectives on the quality and value of their master's experiences. On the one hand, many remarked that master's education provided students with a fundamentally sound pre-Ph.D. experience, one that equipped them with a foundation of specialized theoretical knowledge and skills. In those fields in which there was a strong demand, many students and alumni also told us that their master's degrees were valuable as credentials in the nonuniversity workplace. Faculty and administrators also said that their master's programs played a valuable role in supporting their Ph.D. programs. On the other hand, many students, alumni, and employers raised serious concerns about their master's programs. Many students, especially those who did not pursue the Ph.D. and who found the degree relatively meaningless in the workplace, saw the master's as a "consolation prize." Moreover, many employers, students, and alumni emphasized that these programs were inadequate as terminal master's programs because they seldom provided graduates with adequate workplace-related knowledge and experience to enhance their professional development.

Sound Academic Experience   Many stakeholders in the ten ancillary programs, especially faculty and administrators, suggested that students had a "sound academic experience" while enrolled in their master's program. This experience was especially valuable for students who continued on to doctoral study.

Faculty and administrators frequently told us that the primary ingredients of a first-rate master's program were "an outstanding faculty as reflected in their research productivity and their national reputations" and "excellent resources." On the basis of these criteria, many faculty evaluated their program favorably. In Major State's nursing program, for example, one professor remarked: "We have an excellent, well-prepared faculty. They are experts in their content areas, and they do interesting research." An administrator in the same program stated, "The quality of our master's program is based on the quality of the faculty—where they got their degrees, the kind of research they are doing, and so on—and we stack up very well."

Albeit with many more reservations, not least because they often felt like second-class citizens, students and alumni in the ancillary programs also assessed the academic quality of their master's programs favorably. Many noted that they benefited from "being around faculty with outstanding reputations and research accomplishments" and from attending "first-rate institutions with excellent resources." In the words of a Major State education student, "Faculty here are people that are well known in their fields, people on the leading edge of what's happening nationally, and that is a plus."

In commenting on the sound academic experience students had in these programs, faculty and administrators stressed that students acquired a solid foundation of "theoretical knowledge and perspectives" and enhanced their analytical and written communication skills. As an education professor at Major State put it: "I know that when I talk to former master's degree students of mine, and they compare notes with people who've done master's work elsewhere, they feel like they've been challenged—they've had their treasured preconceptions crushed by a wider variety of mental architecture bearing on education. . . . They feel like knowledgeable teachers pretty much in command of the field, and they celebrate the knowledge that they've acquired through graduate study." A faculty member in Major State's business program said that "students in our program, unlike in 'training camp' M.B.A. programs, do well because they have developed the ability to think, to be analytical, critical thinkers. We teach students how to learn."

Students, alumni, and employers reiterated these faculty remarks. An employer associated with Major State's nursing program, for example, said that their graduates "have more knowledge": "I really believe they just plain have more knowledge, so they can analyze and synthesize better. But it's because they have a better knowledge base." Students also appreciated the theoretical knowledge and skills they learned while in these programs. As one education student at Major State told us: "I've learned how to read research. I've learned what to look for. I've learned to look at the results, to look at the statistics and to say, 'Does the kind of data they've gathered here, and the statistical methods they've used—are they legitimate?' This skill will be valuable to me as a learner and in walking back out into a classroom." In much the same way, a student in Barrett State's nursing program said he had developed a "good conceptual framework and learned how to synthesize and analyze information": "Probably the skill that I'm going to get that's going to be most valuable is an ability to look analytically at systems and bodies of information. [The master's program has] been extremely intellectually stimulating to me."

The Master's Degree as a Credential in the Job Market Although administrators and faculty in the ancillary programs rarely commented on the "career advancement" value of the master's degree, students and alumni in fields in which a master's degree provided cachet in the job market told us that their degrees often helped to advance their professional careers. For the most part, these fields included nursing, business, engineering, microbiology, and education.

Students and alumni in these fields frequently valued the master's because it broadened their contacts with leaders in the field and helped them find better jobs. One Barrett State nursing student, for example, said that simply being in the master's program "will open doors for you": "Faculty and students are connected nationally and internationally, and the people you have as professors and make friends with are going to be the nursing leaders of tomorrow." Nursing students and alumni at Major State expressed similar sentiments, emphasizing that the master's credential was needed to "move up the ladder in the field." As one student put it: "I think the reason we go for a master's is because the credential is demanded, so I guess there's not a lot of choice. If I want to do more things, then I have to get the credentials to be acceptable to employers. And the master's from this program is an excellent credential."

Students and alumni also valued the master's because it increased their salaries. A student in Major State's nursing program, for instance, noted that a master's was worth a salary increase "in the neighborhood of eight thousand dollars." Likewise, students and graduates of Major State's education program pointed out that the master's credential, and the accompanying credit hours, were instrumental in increasing their salaries. As one alumna put it, "The master's helped me meet my original major objective—to make a lot more money."

In the same vein, students and graduates in the business, engineering, and microbiology programs emphasized the benefits associated with the master's as a credential in the workplace. An alumnus of Major State's business program, for instance, told us that he had "greater credibility" because he had that degree: "So I am a fuller person for having done it, and, from an image perspective, when you look at the marketplace, it's something that people can see and say, 'Oh, you have an M.B.A.' It helps on the image side." And an alumnus of Middle State's engineering program aptly summarized the views of many students and alumni enrolled in those ancillary programs producing graduates in fields with strong employment demand when he said: "What I got from this program was money, prestige, and more marketability."

Valuable Support for Ph.D. Programs and Faculty   Faculty and administrators in the ancillary cases told us that they valued their master's programs because it supported their Ph.D. programs in two important ways. First, many noted that master's students brought in revenues that helped to maintain or increase the total number of full-time faculty in the department and, in some instances, helped to generate funds that could be used for the Ph.D. program. In Barrett State's nursing program, for example, an administrator commented that "having several hundred master's nursing students provided a safety net for the program since the number of nursing students determined the number of faculty." In Phelps' English program a faculty member told us that, for every master's student admitted, the university placed a thousand dollars into the departmental "slush fund." He added that this fund exclusively supported the Ph.D. program. (In about one-half of the ancillary programs, some students and alumni speculated that their department offered a master's degree "primarily to make money.")

Second, faculty and administrators in the ancillary cases repeatedly emphasized that the master's provided an excellent screening device for the Ph.D. program. In the two arts and sciences programs at Major State—English and sociology—many faculty said that the most valuable aspect of the master's program was the role it played in, as one sociology professor put it, "separating the wheat from the chaff." Although faculty in the eight other ancillary programs indicated that they placed less emphasis on this screening function, they nonetheless valued the master's as a vehicle for evaluating students' suitability for doctoral study.

In addition, a few faculty in the ancillary programs forthrightly told us that they personally benefited from master's students. A microbiology professor at Mountain State, for example, said: "You need graduate [master's] students because they do all the dirty work. They come in, run the computer. I don't have the time to do it, so they spend all night running the program and come in with all the results in the morning. I learn from them, but they've done all the dirty work. So they [master's students] are a tremendous plus." And an education faculty member at Major State explained that he and his colleagues valued master's students because, in his words, "a lot of us prefer to teach graduate-level courses [as opposed to undergraduate courses], and the only way we are permitted to do that is if there are enrollments. . . . It's clearly self-interest."

Consolation Prize for Students Not Earning the Doctorate   When we interviewed in the English program at Phelps University, a student who had not been accepted into the Ph.D. program told us that she accepted her fate with equanimity. "There is always a certain magic about saying you're going to [Phelps]," she explained. "It impresses people, and I will always have that diploma to hang on the wall." While taking pride in the prestige of her master's degree, she also viewed it as a consolation prize. Many students and alumni in most of the other nine ancillary programs felt similarly, especially those individuals who had planned but were not invited to pursue their Ph.D. degrees and those in fields in which the master's degree had little cachet in the workplace. As an alumna of Major State's English program told us: "The master's degree was a consolation prize for students who didn't go on for the doctorate. And most students didn't."

Indeed, many faculty and administrators in the ancillary master's programs candidly told us that the master's degree was little more than a consolation prize. As a professor in Phelps' English program put it: "The cynical thing, and the nice thing, about the [Phelps] M.A. degree is that it in no way represents any unique or special qualification beyond a year in the Ph.D. program." A faculty member in Major State's sociology program made the point this way: "If somebody came to me and said they wanted to get a master's degree, I would strongly discourage them from doing that in sociology. That would be crazy. . . . Because this degree isn't worth anything, in my mind, unless you have a Ph.D."

Limited Value in Preparing Practitioners for the Workplace   Students, alumni, and employers occasionally told us that the scholarly training students received in ancillary programs contributed to their professional development as practitioners in the nonuniversity workplace. Moreover, some employers—especially in business, engineering, nursing, education, and microbiology—suggested that, in varying degrees, they used the master's degree as a key criterion for selecting and promoting employees. Yet there was another far more pronounced theme that ran through our interviews with students, alumni, and employers in the ten ancillary programs: by marginalizing workplace-related knowledge and experiences and treating the master's as subordinate to the Ph.D., they suggested, these master's programs did not adequately prepare students as practitioners for the nonuniversity workplace.

Students and alumni repeatedly emphasized that faculty seldom related theoretical knowledge in their field to applications in the real world; often were uninformed about developments in the workplace; only occasionally brought practitioners into their classes to discuss professional issues; and generally "neglected" students who planned to return to the workplace after completing their master's degree (the majority of students in the ten ancillary programs). Students often said that their master's program was "too academic," "impractical," and "unrelated to the real world." In turn, many concluded that their master's experiences did not, as one alumnus of Middle State's engineering program put it, "fully prepare people for the workplace." And in some programs, particularly in the arts and sciences, students and alumni suggested that there was a "disjunction" between the program and the workplace. In the English programs at Phelps and Major State, for example, alumni told us that their master's did not adequately prepare them for teaching composition or for other field-related careers such as journalism.

While few employers dismissed altogether the nonuniversity workplace "value" of master's education, many criticized faculty and administrators for inadequately incorporating practical knowledge and workplace-related perspectives into their programs. An employer of Major State's M.B.A. graduates, for example, believed the program's "curriculum could be greatly improved by more practical education": "Students are missing the nuts-and-bolts and are too much involved in theory." Similarly, with respect to Major State's theater program, an employer told us that the program was "too broadly based in academics and the curriculum too far removed from what's happening in real-world theater"; another said that it "tries to be all things to all people, and, as a result, the terminal master's gets shortchanged." This criticism—that, by "accommodating" master's students while placing major emphasis on doctoral education, faculty and administrators diminished the potential workplace value of these master's programs—was expressed by employers, students, and alumni in all the ancillary programs.

We came to understand that stakeholders across these ten cases had mixed views about the overall value of their programs. On the one hand, many interviewees were pleased with the scholarly training students received and the credential value of the degree in those fields in which the master's had cachet in the job market. Moreover, many administrators and faculty appreciated the role that their master's programs played in supporting their departments' Ph.D. programs and individual faculty. On the other hand, faculty and administrators viewed the master's largely in relation to, and as subordinate to, doctoral education and their research. As such, most students and alumni felt neglected by faculty and considered the master's a second-class, or, in our terms, an ancillary experience. Moreover, because relatively little emphasis was placed on workplace-related knowledge and experience, many stakeholders believed these programs inadequately prepared practitioners for the workplace.

7

Career Advancement Programs

Business at Peterson University

Peterson University is a private, regional institution of more than twenty-eight thousand undergraduate and graduate students located in a major metropolitan center in the northeastern United States. Established as a one-room business institute in the early 1900s, Peterson is now a full-fledged university that offers degree programs in more than sixty fields of study across eight schools and colleges. Guided by its motto, "opportunitas," the university is dedicated to providing practical professional educational "opportunities" to largely first- and second-generation college students. As one senior institutional administrator told us: "Opportunity is at the core of Peterson University. This institution began as a very practical place that trained working-class people for the business profession. That culture has carried through to today. The theme is still here. . . . We really try to provide opportunities for our students. We're a very career-oriented kind of place."

Individual career opportunity and practical education were oft-repeated themes in our interviews with individuals associated with Peterson's master's of business administration program. Since it first began to offer master's courses in the late 1950s, Peterson, as described in a program brochure, has been committed to its original mission to "prepare individuals for successful management careers" through an instructional program that balances "real-world practical applications" with a rigorous grounding in the "theoretical principles of business."

We learned from many interviewees that, in the past few years, Peterson's "no-nonsense, career-oriented" approach to business education had earned the program national recognition as a place that produced highly skilled graduates for corporations. Several referred us to a recent reputational study of over three thousand colleges and universities that had ranked Peterson in the top 10 percent of institutions with alumni holding executive positions in the nation's leading corporations. We also learned that, in a recent newsmagazine poll, business school deans on the eastern seaboard—citing alumni achievements, practical orientation of the curriculum, and faculty willingness to develop close working partnerships with business—had ranked Peterson as one of the "top" regional graduate schools of business in the eastern United States.

This recent wave of national recognition was greatly valued by institutional and business school administrators at this strongly tuition-dependent university. Because it competed for students with more than a dozen other local graduate schools of business, Peterson faculty and administrators emphasized to us that institutional reputation and visibility were critical "selling points" that enhanced the credibility of their product in a rapidly shrinking—and fiercely competitive—market for M.B.A. students. "In 1984," explained one high-ranking institutional administrator, "our M.B.A. graduate student enrollment peaked at four thousand students. Then, in 1987, the Wall Street crash hit. The M.B.A. market went through the floor. Here, at [Peterson], we dipped to about twenty-seven hundred students in 1988. Then the [business school dean's] survey came out in [a national magazine], and more and more people learned that a part-time program could compete with the Ivies [Ivy League schools]. Our enrollment increased to about thirty-three hundred in 1990." While they told us that their national visibility would eventually pass—though their reliance on tuition revenues would not—Peterson faculty and administrators said that they had launched an aggressive public relations campaign to keep their M.B.A. program in the spotlight. "It's a matter of survival for us," one professor explained: "Student enrollment is our bottom line. Our existence is based on someone else's demand. Since this institution is so dependent on tuition revenues, we have to do what we can to hold our own in this competitive market. It is simply a matter of good business for us."

When we visited Peterson's School of Business in 1990, total graduate school enrollment numbered over thirty-five hundred students, with roughly thirty-three hundred in the school's M.B.A. program. Program administrators and faculty expressed pride in the academic ability of their students; several told us that students had good undergraduate academic records and performed relatively well on the Graduate Management Admissions Test (GMAT). Roughly 90 percent of Peterson M.B.A. students sought their degree on a part-time basis during the evening and held jobs such as investment banker, financial analyst, and computer specialist during the day. The great majority were in their mid- to late twenties with four to seven years of professional work experience. Approximately 40 percent were female, another 15 percent were foreign nationals, mainly from the Pacific rim.

Peterson listed about ninety full-time and one hundred adjunct faculty in its 1990–91 graduate catalog, yielding a student-faculty ratio of nineteen to one. One-tenth of Peterson's faculty were female; roughly one-half were at the rank of associate professor or above. All of the full-time faculty and about three-fifths of the adjunct faculty held doctorates or law degrees, and some had professional business experience. Peterson also offered a doctoral and an executive M.B.A. program, but in 1990 only about fifty students were enrolled in this program.

As stated in the program's official brochure, Peterson's seventy-two-credit, predominantly part-time M.B.A. program was designed to "provide students with both a broad managerial perspective and a specialized expertise." To this end, students took courses in three core areas: (1) business foundation courses aimed at teaching students how to "integrate theoretical concepts from business disciplines and apply them to complex, companywide management problems"; (2) advanced skills courses designed to "furnish students with the analytical tools" needed to solve business problems; and (3) a seven-course specialization sequence intended to provide students with "functional expertise within a subfield of business." Additionally, students were required to pass proficiency examinations in basic business computing applications, quantitative methods, and business writing.

From program administrators and faculty, we learned that the purpose of their M.B.A. program was to prepare, in the words of one business professor, "practitioner-experts" for the nonuniversity workplace. Time and again, they told us that the program sought to provide students with the specialized theoretical and applied knowledge and skills necessary to certify them as "experts" in financial accounting, marketing, management, investment banking, or corporate planning. The director of Peterson's graduate business programs described this expert orientation as follows:

> We have a terminal professional degree that is intended to serve individuals who plan to pursue careers in the business world. As a terminal degree, we want our M.B.A. to indicate to employers that our students have achieved a number of things. First, the degree shows that they're educated in general business, so that, no matter where they go, they'll be respected as educated business professionals. Second—and more importantly—because our M.B.A. requires a specialization in a functional area of business, this says to employers that our graduates are not only educated but that they're also somewhat of an expert in a particular area.

Another professor offered an additional perspective on the purpose of Peterson's M.B.A. program: "We're here to really service industry by preparing students with a kind of practitioner expertise for job opportunities available in our region. We realize that most of our students come to us for an M.B.A. because they believe that, without the degree—no matter how smart or how diligent they are—the road to the corporate office is blocked. . . . I'd say we're a boot camp, if you will, that prepares students with the expertise and the credential to move forward in their companies." Students and alumni also articulated this perspective, with several noting that one of the primary reasons they selected Peterson's M.B.A. program was because it focused on practical expertise. As a second-year student put it, "I chose [Peterson] because they had a reputation for being a school that was practical. I heard the professors weren't all theory but that they taught you what you really needed to know out in the real world. That was important to me. I wanted my M.B.A. so that I could get a better job—I sure wasn't doing this just for fun. This degree was for real."

In preparing students as experts for the business world, we learned that Peterson's faculty and administrators utilized three instructional methods in their M.B.A. program. First, in traditional lecture-centered courses, faculty used a didactic approach to transmit business theories and principles (authoritative knowledge) to students. Second, faculty occasionally supplemented the theory in their lectures with a variety of practical, hands-on learning activities, including case studies. Third, sensitive to students' needs for real-world information, faculty often invited experienced business professionals to teach in the program as either guest speakers or adjunct faculty.

Throughout our interviews, faculty communicated to us that they viewed business theories and principles as a basically "well-founded" and "set" collection of knowledge that was, for the most part, not open to debate. Many suggested that their primary responsibility as professors was to "pass on" this knowledge in an objective manner, primarily through traditional classroom-centered lectures. As one professor put it:

What we teach in business is pretty well founded in terms of the functional areas and methods. . . . In terms of methods, there are two: you listen and regurgitate back, and the other is the case study. And most schools don't do much else besides teach in these two ways. Sure, there are variances within these two methods, but there isn't as much, for instance; it's very different than sociology, where there's a lot of ego involvement and a great deal of room for a personal point of view. There is room for that in business, but you can teach business by staying aloof—by staying away from the subject and not pouring yourself into it. And what we teach in

business—if you just looked at the curriculum of this school and compared it to others, you would see that we all teach the same thing. There
isn't much variance in that, either. . . . There isn't much freedom or flexibility in business education. That's the way it is. There is a body of knowledge that needs to be passed on.

Interviewees emphasized to us that Peterson's business faculty viewed
themselves as experts whose role was to deliver specialized knowledge
and skills to students. One professor, for example, said that he considered
himself the expert in the classroom because, in his words, "after all, I know
what my customers [the business community] need, and students are
ignorant, and they don't know what they need." Students supported this
view of the faculty role. As one alumna explained, "I wanted professors in
my M.B.A. program who would be definite in their goals and experts in
their fields. I didn't want a course where students did reports and spoke all
the time and that was the course. After all, I was paying money to hear the
professor—I don't mind if students get up and speak during class—but I
wanted to learn from the professor. They're the experts. So I chose classes
where I could have that." Along these same lines, a faculty member said:
"With these students, I pretty much am the expert. Nobody is going to
challenge me on what I have to say. It rarely ever happens. These students
really expect me to dispense information—they sort of look up to you as
the major focus of information. So I do the best job with that as I can."
Students often mentioned to us that they were impressed with the
expertise of Peterson's full-time business faculty. "I'd describe them as
accessible, knowledgeable, well-credentialed, well-reputed professors,"
remarked one second-year student. "I've learned a lot from them." An
alumna noted that she felt like faculty had fed her "intravenously": "It was
almost like a 'fix.' I really looked forward to going to class and hearing what
the professor had to say." For their part, faculty told us they took pride in
their ability to impart information to students in a highly competent, even
entertaining, fashion. As one professor put it, "We have very dedicated,
committed teachers walking down these corridors. They may not be the
most published, but they are very dedicated to teaching the discipline."
Another professor remarked, "We have some excellent teachers here. I
think a really good teacher is someone who—well, our classes are two and
one-half hours long. You really gotta know your stuff, and you gotta get
these people to listen to you. Sometimes I wonder if a good teacher is more
of a showperson than anything else."
While the program was primarily lecture driven, interviewees indicated that faculty used hands-on learning experiences to supplement the
theoretical orientation of their lectures. The practice component of this
"theory-to-practice" pedagogical approach—in which students first

learned the theory then applied it to a practical problem—took many forms, including case study simulations, group projects, and cooperative education internships (which were primarily filled by the program's small number of full-time students). When faculty told us why they introduced this practice dimension into their courses, we frequently heard variations on this senior professor's reasoning: "The practical element is so important. We need to see if students can relate the theory to real-world situations." He went on to explain that, by observing how "students analyzed cases and formulated their answers to case study problems," he was able to evaluate the level of practical expertise students were developing. "My bottom line is this: with a case study, I can test and see if students know how and where to apply the knowledge and the tools. And that's what I want this M.B.A. program to do—to develop people who know when, where, and how to use the tools to solve business problems."

Students and alumni enthusiastically described their hands-on learning experiences, often providing us with vivid stories reflecting the importance they placed on learning practical, real-world business skills. One student, for example, described a case study she completed in which she analyzed two Fortune 500 companies that were considering a merger and developed a report that discussed the "pros and cons" of such a consolidation: "I worked so hard at it. I really had to learn how to read and analyze business spreadsheets and how to use that information to support my recommendations. . . . It was really rigorous, but I think it was one of the most valuable things I've done at [Peterson]." Other students and alumni told us that they greatly valued the real-world case studies and group projects they had completed in the program. As one student put it: "When I have to go out and actually collect financial indicators from my own work setting for a case study, I really feel like I'm being bumped up to another level of education. It's no longer hypothetical, it's real-world stuff. In this program, somewhere along the line, after faculty make you learn the theory, they then make you deal with the realistic, and that moves you up to a different level of thinking. That's what I enjoy."

While pleased with these hands-on learning activities, some students and alumni expressed frustration at the individualistic and competitive relations they often experienced with their peers as they worked on assigned group projects. "There are so many commuter students here," said one second-year student, "that you're sort of forced by default to do things independently because . . . nobody wants to give their time. I mean, we end up talking before class and then after class and then, after that, everyone goes their own way." Another student added, "Yeah, and sometimes tempers flare because some students are really grade conscious, and others just sort of want to come in, take their classes, and skip out without pulling their own weight."

Faculty were aware of, and no less frustrated by, these concerns. As one professor told us: "I want my students to work in groups because I want them to learn how to cooperate and how to build off of each other's specialized expertise . . . but the whole concept of a 'subway university' . . . often causes logistical problems with getting students together to do the group work. It's troubling for me and for some of the students, I think." For their part, students suggested that these "logistical" difficulties, particularly when combined with competitive peer interactions, not only short-circuited many group projects but also contributed to, in our terms, an individualistic student culture in the program. "And that's too bad," said one student, "because a big part of your M.B.A. program should be interacting with your fellow students and the groups you work with as well as the time you devote to your studies. At [Peterson] you never learn how to work as a team. Instead, you really are forced to do things independently here."

In addition to the specialized and applied theoretical knowledge and skills faculty provided to students through classroom lectures and hands-on learning experiences, we learned that Peterson faculty also utilized business professionals in their M.B.A. program. Through such formal arrangements as hiring adjunct practitioner faculty and inviting local business leaders to be "executives-in-residence," administrators and faculty capitalized on the experiences of individuals who, in the words of one professor, "passed on their practical business knowledge and expertise to our students." This practical edge, said one program administrator, was important because "this school wants to be responsive to what our students really think is important. And there are so many academics in business schools that are writing for each other in very elite journals that they become so far removed from what the profession is really interested in. And that is not the case here. . . . The type of faculty we have here is responsive to what managers really think is important."

Many stakeholders emphasized that they strongly valued the real-world expertise of Peterson's adjunct faculty. One employer, who was also a graduate of the program, said that the courses students completed with adjuncts "were very valuable for them": "These students get to work with people who have some real world experience which is a real plus. I remember when I was at [Peterson] I had courses with adjuncts who were just outstanding. . . . I think that when students get to work with these top-notch people it's a real plus. . . . These students have the practical know-how that's really valuable to me as an employer." A student voiced a similar perspective: "I think the administration hires a lot of adjuncts because they want students to get that practical experience. . . . The adjuncts I had forced me to do the hard, practical work of becoming fluent in business indicators and knowing how to read them at a moment's glance. I walked away from those courses feeling really satisfied. I knew I had the tools to make it in the business world."

Notwithstanding these favorable comments about the real-world orientation of its curriculum and adjunct faculty, many interviewees cautioned us that Peterson's M.B.A. program was in the midst of change. Administrators and faculty recently had decided to pursue accreditation for their M.B.A. program from the American Association of Schools and Colleges of Business (AACSB), a decision that was not reviewed favorably by all stakeholders. For the most part, faculty and administrators believed that AACSB accreditation would provide their program with enhanced credibility that could significantly improve their reputation, and their "survival," within a fiercely competitive and saturated M.B.A. academic market. As one program administrator stated:

> The absence of accreditation has hurt us in this M.B.A. market. Up until the early 1980s, [Peterson] had many nonaccredited competitor schools— at least six that I can think of. Those schools were granted accreditation in the early to mid-1980s. Since that time, they've used their accreditation as a competitive tool to attract students. . . . I believe that we need to get accreditation because we need to continue to build confidence in our students that this is a good school. That's the only way that we can improve our enrollments. And, I can tell you, in this market most business schools are having big problems with enrollment.

When we asked a faculty member if they were seeking accreditation more as a means for "keeping up with the competition" than for evaluating program effectiveness, he responded: "Something that I've always said is that when we get AACSB accreditation, it's really only going to eliminate a negative. It doesn't really provide us with a positive. It simply says, 'Now you're accredited. Your unaccredited status is no longer there.' But I still think we need it as a strategy to convince potential students and potential donors and others that we've got a 'quality' product."

Convinced that the accreditation "stamp of approval" would enhance the school's image and its enrollment, program administrators and faculty had begun to alter their M.B.A. program to meet AACSB standards. One program administrator told us that these standards had already affected the program's curriculum, mission, and faculty recruitment and promotion policies. Another administrator elaborated on the point:

> This university used to be known as being a highly applied place in the business sense because we had a lot of people who were out there working and were teaching here with terminal master's degrees. And this particular flavor is being changed by AACSB accreditation because now we're hiring young Ph.D.'s—we're trying to get people with business experience—

but the researchers are not going to be out there in the profession as much as they are in the academy. . . . It's a trade-off, I know. But my feeling is that it's worth it.

On the other hand, students, alumni, and employers repeatedly told us that they did not believe that accreditation was worth the "trade-offs" involved. Many explained that they feared AACSB's accrediting "standards" would jeopardize the vitality of Peterson's practice-centered program. "I came to [Peterson] because I knew the professors here were out in the business world and not straight out of academia," remarked one alumna. "I'm really afraid accreditation could change that." An employer voiced the same concern: "I know that AACSB has put pressure on the program to get more Ph.D. faculty. I'm sure that [Peterson] is going to lose some of their best adjuncts because of this. This Ph.D. requirement is silly—I mean, some of [Peterson's] adjuncts are worth their weight in gold, Ph.D. or no Ph.D."

In what we came to understand as an ironic twist, these stakeholders, in contrast to some faculty and administrators, were not convinced that AACSB accreditation would improve the quality or credibility of Peterson's program among students or employers. An alumnus, who had recently completed a term as president of the business alumni association, told us: "The thing that absolutely amazed me when we brought up the issue of accreditation to alums was that they were really dead set against it. I thought they would be interested in anything that increased the prestige of their degree. But they were violently opposed to accreditation because they knew that the school would have to cut back on adjunct faculty." A student analyzed the faculty and administrative rationale for accreditation as follows: "I think [Peterson] is just too concerned with their own prestige and competing with the Ivy League. . . . I came to [Peterson] because it was known as a practical school. They should just focus more on that—the practical side of business—rather than trying to be something they're not. If they would ask for more feedback from students, they'd hear we're more interested in practicality than prestige."

Whether or not AACSB accreditation would improve Peterson's "reputation," many interviewees believed the program was already very successful in producing knowledgeable, skilled practitioner-experts. Indeed, many students and alumni said that they left Peterson's M.B.A. program as confident, skilled business professionals who had the specialized theoretical and applied knowledge as well as the practical skills needed to improve their performance in the workplace. As one alumnus, a vice president and partner at a prestigious "Big Six" accounting firm, explained: "The courses I took at [Peterson] were excellent for giving me the technical skills and expertise that I needed to perform. It gave me the basics and the specialized knowledge. I couldn't be where I am today without this knowledge." A second-year student remarked: "I feel as though I'm better equipped now than I was two years ago. I know my quantitative, data analysis, and business writing skills are much stronger. I'm much better off—I'm not the same businessperson I was two years ago." Another student said: "Yeah, I feel like I have the knowledge now. I feel like I can really run spreadsheets, do cost-benefit analyses, and write effective marketing strategies. This has really given me the confidence to go out there and be a little more demanding about what I want. . . . I really feel like I can be very effective in the business world now."

Employers strongly supported these student and alumni accounts, giving high marks to Peterson's M.B.A. program and its graduates. "It has been our experience that [Peterson] graduates perform," stated one employer at a major international bank. "They have always come to us ready and prepared to work." Another employer noted that he was pleased with the "pragmatic edge" of his Peterson employees:

> I like the fact that these students seek the [M.B.A.] degree as a sidelight interest. . . . I know that they're committed. And I like that they have practical business experience under their belts. My [Peterson] grads have a more pragmatic edge to them than some of the other M.B.A.'s in this company. They are stronger on the practical applications of business. They can roll up their sleeves, and they're not afraid to get involved in messy work. My [Peterson] graduates can perform right away. And, as an employer, that's very useful to me.

Another employer provided this bottom-line assessment: "Whenever I need a person in my tax division, I look for a [Peterson] M.B.A. Their graduates are competent, highly skilled professionals. They have the practical expertise that my company needs."

Besides evaluating them as highly skilled practitioner-experts, many faculty and employers remarked that they were impressed with the ambition of Peterson's M.B.A. graduates. As a faculty member told us: "Our students are people who work hard on the job, and who have had to work hard to get through school. They are not people who have been born into privilege. They are high performers and therefore high achievers. These people do the M.B.A. on an overload basis, taking courses at night while working hard all day on the job. That tells you something about a person— that they've got the wherewithal and the drive to succeed. . . . It's this work ethic, I think, that makes our M.B.A.'s outperform others." Indeed, most of the students and alumni we spoke with suggested that they pursued their M.B.A. degrees because they wanted to advance their professional careers. As one alumna put it: "I am ambitious, and I am extremely competitive. . . . I decided to get my M.B.A. because I wanted a career change and I wanted something better for me. . . . During those five years that I worked to earn that degree, I felt like I almost neglected family and friends. I was so goal oriented. I was interested in what the degree could do for me—I wanted a job where I could work up to my abilities and be challenged and be rewarded for my achievements. . . . My [Peterson] M.B.A. helped me to get that job—they helped me get in the door."

Peterson's motto, opportunitas, seems to be at the heart of their School of Business. During the late 1980s program administrators and faculty seized the opportunity to utilize their emerging visibility as one of the top business schools in the eastern United States to advance their reputation both within academe and in the nonuniversity workplace. Meanwhile, students and alumni used their M.B.A. degrees to give them, in the words of one student, "a leg up on the competition" within the highly competitive world of business. In short, as we came to understand, Peterson stakeholders were bound together by a common commitment to advancing their careers, whether they were climbing the reputational ladder against competing business schools or the corporate ladder in the nonuniversity workplace. Perhaps the point was made best by an alumnus who offered his "most important impression" of Peterson's M.B.A. program: "I'd say [Peterson] is known as a very practical school where people go to get an education that will improve their abilities to perform in the workplace. Yeah, the people who go to [Peterson] go there because they want to get ahead in the business world."

Understanding the Career Advancement Idealized Type

In our case study of Peterson's business program, we alluded to the choices stakeholders made in the five decision-situations discussed in part 2. To a large extent, the same choices were made by stakeholders in ten other master's programs in our forty-seven-case sample. All chose a didactic approach to teaching and learning (decision-situation 1) and a professional orientation for their programs (decision-situation 2). Additionally, faculty and program administrators in nine of the eleven cases provided strong support to their master's program (decision-situation 3). In terms of the auxiliary decision-situations, campus administrators in seven of the eleven cases provided strong institutional support (decision-situation 4), and students in the majority of these cases developed individualistic student cultures (decision-situation 5).

The eleven career advancement programs represented four types of institutions and six different fields of study. Of the four program types we identified, the career advancement programs had the largest number (seven) in private institutions. Three were located at national universities, including the M.B.A. program at Pierpont University and the applied anthropology programs at Land-Grant University and Atlantic State University. Another six programs were in regional institutions: the M.B.A. programs at Parks-Beecher University (a predominantly black institution) and Peterson University; the English program at Urban State University (a predominantly black institution); the theater program at Trafalgar College; and the teacher education programs at Chester College and Southwest State University (the only two programs in regional institutions in which the department also conferred the doctorate). Finally, one specialty and one liberal arts college were represented in the career advancement grouping: the electrical engineering program at United Technological University (United Tech) and the business program at St. Joan's College. (Table 7.1 identifies the eleven case studies by institutional type, field of study, and degree levels offered.)

We now look across these eleven cases and develop a portrait of the career advancement idealized program type. We begin by describing the overall character of these programs and present two key purposes that stakeholders articulated for them. We then elaborate on five features that, based on interviews with stakeholders across these programs, are characteristic of the career advancement program type: a heavy reliance on highly prescribed curricula; a theory-to-practice pedagogical model; a widespread use of practitioner guest lecturers and adjunct faculty; a "customer-friendly" service model; and strategic support faculty and administrators

Table 7.1. **Distribution of Case Studies in the Career Advancement Idealized Program Type**

Pseudonym Institution	Field of Study	Degree Levels
Case Studies at Regional Institutions		
Chester	Education	B.A., M.Ed., Ed.D.
Parks-Beecher	Business	B.B.A., M.B.A.
Peterson	Business	B.B.A., M.B.A.
Southwest State	Education	B.A., M.A., Ed.D.
Trafalgar	Theater	B.A., M.A.
Urban State	English	B.A., M.A.
Case Studies at National Institutions		
Atlantic State	Applied anthropology	B.A., M.A.A.
Land-Grant	Applied anthropology	B.A., M.A.I.S.
Pierpont	Business	M.B.A.
Case Studies at Liberal Arts Institutions		
St. Joan's	Business	B.B.A., M.B.A.
Case Studies at Specialty Institutions		
United Tech	Electrical engineering	M.S.

provided to their master's programs. We conclude the chapter by considering how stakeholders interpreted and defined the overall quality and value of their experiences.

Character and Articulated Purposes

Interviewees across the eleven career advancement cases communicated to us that they viewed their master's programs as a client-centered, career-oriented, expert training experience in which faculty provided students with the essential knowledge, skills, and terminal credentials necessary to advance their professional careers in the nonuniversity workplace. A program administrator at Parks-Beecher University expressed this overall character when he told us that their M.B.A. program "provided the most contemporary theories and practices to students so that they can compete effectively in the job market": "Our expectation is that our graduates will become leaders in Corporate America." Likewise, a faculty member at Chester College remarked that their education program "created effective practitioners" who were "firmly grounded in the established and newly emergent approaches to teaching." And a professor in Southwest State's education program described their master's in education as a "quick and convenient certification and ticketing agency that helps teachers climb the salary scale."

Students and employers in these eleven cases understood their master's programs in similar terms. A student in Urban State's English program, for example, told us that he viewed his master's as an inexpensive and convenient way to "get the content and the skills" he needed "to become a more creative writer" and, on the way, to "pick up the credentials" that would allow him to teach in a high school or community college. And an employer associated with United Tech's engineering program noted that this master's program provided students with a "flexible and convenient education" that equipped them with the know-how to become productive professional engineers.

We came to understand that the client-centered, career-oriented, expert-training character of the eleven career advancement programs was shaped, in part, by two program purposes that faculty and program administrators articulated and virtually all other stakeholders embraced. First, faculty and program administrators told us that a major purpose of their terminal master's programs was to "pass on" to students the established knowledge, skills, and attitudes of their disciplines. This knowledge, in their view, was the essential ingredient that students needed as master's-educated providers of expert services. Second, stakeholders said that an equally important purpose was to deliver the kinds of instructional services and educational products that would meet their clients' demands for "certifiable expertise" appropriate to their professional career advancement in the workplace.

This first purpose—the idea that a terminal master's program should pass on to students an established body of knowledge and skills—was aptly communicated by a professor in Pierpont's M.B.A. program when she said: "Faculty in M.B.A. programs know exactly what we're doing. . . . We know the fundamental base of knowledge we need to provide to our students, and that's what we teach them. We know that they must be taught principles x, y, and z because we know exactly where they're heading and what kinds of jobs they're going to get. So the knowledge to be taught is fairly well set—we know what they need to know, and we provide them with the training." Along these same lines, a United Tech program administrator told us: "At the master's level our purpose is to get students to specialize—to give them in-depth knowledge in one area. . . . So our faculty transfer a specialized body of knowledge to our master's students, and we expect them to be able to synthesize this delivered knowledge and then to use this knowledge intelligently and responsibly later in their work as professional engineers." Most faculty and program administrators in the career advancement programs similarly emphasized that the transmission of an established, well-defined core of disciplinary knowledge to students was a key purpose in their programs.

Throughout our interviews, faculty and program administrators also suggested that an equally important purpose of their master's was to deliver educational services that would satisfy their clients', both students and employers, need for certified expert training. A faculty member at Peterson's School of Business matter-of-factly described this purpose as follows:

> The M.B.A. has become a necessity in this society. Employers have legislated that, if you don't have the M.B.A. training and the piece of paper to prove it, you can't get into this corporation and advance. . . . I think the M.B.A. is analogous to legislation requiring seat belts. Remember the days when seat belt wearing was not legislated? How many of us wore them? And then they were legislated. Cars now come with automatic seat belts—you don't have a choice but to wear them. I mean, these seat belts capture you. Well, today, the M.B.A. has become legislated, too. And we, as faculty in business schools—well, that's what we do, that's what our job is. We have a responsibility to meet the business community's demand for M.B.A.'s. We are the seat belt manufacturers for the business world.

Faculty and program administrators in the two applied anthropology programs similarly designed their programs to service their clients' needs for expert training. As a faculty member at Atlantic State put it: "We have a very clear model of what we are trying to do here: we are not training academic researchers; we are training people who are going to be very sophisticated spokespeople for the discipline in professional careers outside academia. . . . This program is designed to provide students with the knowledge, skills, and credentials necessary to practice anthropology outside of academic settings." The same pattern of responding both to client requests and to external market demands was also reflected in the other business, education, and engineering programs included in the career advancement grouping.

This belief that master's programs should deliver expert services to satisfy their clients' needs was also expressed by students and alumni. Many indicated that they enrolled in their respective master's programs because they offered the promise of delivering both the knowledge and the credentials necessary to advance their professional careers in the non-university workplace. An alumnus of Land-Grant's applied anthropology program made this point when he remarked: "I wanted the degree to learn how to run and design my own projects and to conduct my own evaluations. Without the degree, I didn't have enough legitimacy and expertise in this professional field to do that. I was at a dead end. [Land-Grant's] program helped me to get the degree and the knowledge I needed for more professional autonomy in archaeology." Similarly, an engineering student said that he chose United Tech's program because, in his words: "I wanted to gain knowledge that would be useful to me on the job. I wanted to stay up-to-date in the field. [United's] program promised me the content. And I knew the M.S. would look good on my resume."

To be sure, not all of the students we interviewed expressed interest in "gaining knowledge" as a means to increase their individual performance in the workplace. Some told us that they pursued the master's solely for its credential value. An education student at Chester College, for example, remarked: "I didn't choose Chester because I was interested in learning anything. I just needed that teaching certificate and, at [Chester], you could get a master's and certification in nine months. And that seemed like a great idea to me." A business student at Pierpont likewise told us: "I chose this program because it was a strategic move for me. The [Pierpont] M.B.A. will mean that I am a member of the business elite, and that will help me a lot with my own career ambitions." Whether they pursued master's study primarily for the expert credential or for both the credential and expert knowledge, students and alumni in the career advancement programs almost always viewed master's education instrumentally. Most suggested that they sought, and valued, their master's degrees because it helped them obtain a pragmatic end: increased status as credentialed professionals equipped with the knowledge and skills needed to advance their careers.

Employers also emphasized that they expected master's programs to respond to their needs for well-trained and credentialed practioner-experts. An employer of United Tech engineering alumni, for example, said: "Technical obsolescence is a major problem in this field. A master's program needs to provide our employees with the technical knowledge if we're to remain up-to-date with our R & D [research and development] activities." In much the same way, an employer of Pierpont M.B.A. graduates noted that his company recruited only from those business schools where they felt "confident" that students had been "trained" as experts.

The widely shared belief in the career advancement programs that master's programs should actively respond to, and meet, external market demands for appropriately trained and "certified" professional experts was reinforced by two internal conditions common to most of these programs: a heavy reliance on tuition-driven revenues and, in a few cases, a strong commitment to public service. To illustrate, seven of the eleven career advancement programs were situated in private institutions. Except for Pierpont's heavily endowed business program, the other six programs in private institutions relied on enrollment-generated tuition dollars to meet the bulk of their expenses. As we learned from many stakeholders, these tuition-driven programs often embraced a client-centered focus to sustain their financial viability. At Chester College, for example, where tuition revenues comprised over 90 percent of the institution's budget, according to one professor, the institution could not tolerate programs that did not make a profit: "We're so tuition-driven here you just never know when they [the administration] are going to wipe things out. I know the college is out to make money. I saw the whole faculty in special education wiped out in one year because their program was no longer considered a money-making thing. Programs need to be profitable here to survive." Similarly, we learned that the strong public service orientation in the three career advancement programs in public institutions reinforced the commitment of program administrators and faculty to respond fully to their clients' needs. A professor in Urban State's English program, for example, told us that, since their program was in a predominantly black institution, they had a responsibility to meet their community's demand for "better teachers for the urban schools. . . . We are an urban university, and there are things that we can do that are relevant—urgent things—we must keep ahead of the public schools."

From our perspective, these two program purposes were closely related to the decision-situation choices stakeholders made in the eleven career advancement programs. Committed to transmitting to students the authoritative knowledge of their respective disciplines and to meeting their clients' needs for certifiable expert training, faculty and program administrators chose to rely mostly on a didactic approach to teaching and learning (decision-situation 1) and to orient their programs around the specialized theoretical and applied knowledge valued in the professional, nonuniversity workplace (decision-situation 2). In addition, since these programs often supported their department's tuition-driven funding formulas and service missions—and, in some cases, enhanced their department's reputation among employers in the nonuniversity workplace—faculty and program administrators in most of the career advancement programs provided strong departmental support (decision-situation 3).

Characteristic Features

Upon reviewing our interviews from these eleven cases, we learned that five features were broadly representative of the career advancement program type. From our perspective, these features—viewed in relation to the program purposes faculty and program administrators articulated and the choices stakeholders made in the five decision-situations—shaped the overall character of interviewees' experiences in the career advancement programs. These five features are: a heavy reliance on prescribed "core" and "specialization" course work; a theory-to-practice pedagogical model; a widespread use of real-world practitioners as guest lecturers and adjunct faculty; the incorporation of customer-friendly instructional services designed to facilitate student and employer requests for responsive, convenient, and flexible master's education; and (in most programs) strategic support by faculty and administrators to their master's programs.

Heavily Prescribed Curricula   Faculty and program administrators in the career advancement programs frequently centered their master's curricula around required core and prescribed specialization courses.[1] Students were expected to complete their core requirements prior to enrolling in prescribed specialization courses.

Core requirements accounted for at least 40 percent of the course work in all but two of the eleven career advancement programs. In general, these included theory and methods courses that were centered around teaching students "essential" disciplinary understandings that faculty believed students needed before they focused their studies in one specialized area. As a faculty member in Pierpont's M.B.A. program explained:

> The faculty know what constitutes the core material in business, . . . and we all have agreed on what knowledge should be addressed in our core courses. Our core curriculum courses tend to be stable, and the knowledge in them seldom changes. In the core we teach the essential body of conceptual knowledge and decision tools from economics, behavioral science, and quantitative analysis on which business is based. We believe

that students need an understanding of this core knowledge before they can move into more specialized courses.

All but one of the career advancement programs also required students to complete a prescribed number of courses in one disciplinary "subspecialty," or "concentration" area—usually amounting to between four and six courses of the total curriculum.[2] A faculty member at United Tech, where students completed a six-course specialization sequence, told us that this requirement was particularly important; in his words: "In electrical engineering today, you have to have a master's degree because that's where students finally take the specialized courses. You need that specialized knowledge for cutting-edge activities. That specialized content is really important." An administrator in Atlantic State's applied anthropology program spoke to this same point when he mentioned that they were adding four new specialization tracks to their program. "We need them," he said, "because our students need the in-depth knowledge, skills, and anthropological perspective to market themselves as specialists in this growing field."

Many interviewees suggested that the combination of core and specialized courses improved student performance by providing them with both the "big picture" and specialized expertise. As an engineering alumnus at United Tech put it:

> If an engineer's education was just very focused and not into providing a broad-based education, it wouldn't be providing everything that you need [to be a productive engineer]. A fixed curriculum forces you into a required broad range of courses. . . . Without these courses, there are a lot of parts of the discipline that you wouldn't take the time to learn—you'd just work in those areas that you were particularly interested in or involved with. And, to become really well rounded, you need to take a full course of study. Graduate education requires you to take courses you wouldn't otherwise take but end up being glad that you took.

Along these same lines, an administrator in Parks-Beecher's business program articulated this breadth-depth curricular strategy when he remarked: "We want to prepare our students with a broader, general management perspective [while, at the same time, furnishing them with] systematic study in a particular area of concentration. . . . We believe this approach provides students with the necessary knowledge and skills to perform successfully in the competitive business environment."

Theory-to-Practice Model of Pedagogy Many interviewees across the eleven career advancement cases communicated to us that faculty frequently used, in our words, a theory-to-practice pedagogical approach in their programs. This pedagogical approach paralleled the overall curricular strategy faculty utilized in these programs: just as faculty required students to complete core courses prior to enrolling in specialized content areas, they didactically transmitted theories and concepts to students through classroom-based lectures before having them "apply" this knowledge to real-world problems through hands-on learning activities, including case studies, group projects, and internships. In so doing, faculty divided theory and practice into two discrete categories, each characterized by distinct instructional activities.

This "meat-and-potatoes" approach, as a professor in Parks-Beecher's business program called it, was incorporated into nearly all of the career advancement programs. Faculty in Atlantic State's applied anthropology program, for example, first supplied students with what one professor termed the "epistemological bedrock of the field" through a six-course core curricular sequence before requiring them to apply this theoretical knowledge in a real-world, semester-long internship experience. Students in Chester College's education program were initially exposed to what one professor described as a "good dose of theory that laid a foundation for their careers" before they could take their practicums in surrounding schools. In Trafalgar's theater program, students completed basic theory courses before developing independently designed, hands-on, applications-oriented "special projects" courses to round out their programs of study.

While most faculty attempted to pay equal attention to both theory and practice, several interviewees pointed out that some faculty made teaching "the theory" their first priority. These faculty, in particular, held firmly to the view that students needed to be equipped with requisite theoretical knowledge before they could effectively engage in practical problem-solving activities. As a faculty member in Pierpont's M.B.A. program put it, if students were not provided with a solid foundation of conceptual knowledge and business tools during their first year in the program, the practice activities they later engaged in would be little more than "practice-without-reference-to-knowledge" exercises.

Faculty and program administrators in the career advancement programs relied heavily on a combination of lectures and lecture discussions as their principal method for transmitting theoretical knowledge to students (decision-situation 1). This approach was consonant with the belief shared among many faculty that, as experts in their fields, their principal responsibility was to communicate disciplinary knowledge effectively to students. A professor in Pierpont's M.B.A. program expressed this view when she told us that faculty should cast themselves in the role of a "translator" who "communicates theoretical concepts to students in an interesting, challenging, and relevant way." A United Tech program administrator expressed a similar outlook, stating that their engineering faculty were "master's of material," who took seriously their responsibility to transmit "cutting-edge knowledge" to students. He added that the program went to "great lengths" to ensure that faculty "effectively communicated" this knowledge to students, often using independent evaluators to carefully "monitor and assess" the quality of faculty lectures.

This didactic teaching approach often was favorably reviewed by students and alumni, who told us that they appreciated being taught by "well-regarded" faculty who supplied them with what many suggested was a valuable "stock of knowledge." As an alumnus of Parks-Beecher's M.B.A. program put it: "In a field like business, information is power. I had some faculty who ran their classes like military boot camps. You were expected to listen to them and to learn the knowledge. Some of those classes were really valuable. I learned the basics of becoming a financial engineer in those classes." A student at United Tech said that he enjoyed being taught by some of the country's "best and brightest engineering faculty," who "pumped theory" at him. In his judgment the emphasis faculty placed on "the content" was especially valuable because he was taking these courses because he knew he "had deficiencies in some areas"; in his words, "I wanted the content to be able to do my job better." Students and alumni in other programs provided comparable accounts, with most accentuating that faculty were the "established experts" from whom they expected to receive information.

We learned from many interviewees in the career advancement programs that faculty also stressed the practical applications of theory in their courses. In this practice component of their theory-to-practice pedagogical approach, faculty utilized various interactive and hands-on activities—such as case study simulations, group projects and presentations, required and optional internships, and fieldwork experiences—designed to assist students in applying theoretical knowledge to practical problems. In only two of the eleven programs did the practice component involve the completion of a thesis or a project.

We learned from faculty and program administrators that these practice activities helped them to accomplish three broad instructional objectives in their master's programs. First, it enabled students to test themselves in real-world situations. Second, it allowed faculty to assess students' "mastery" of theory. Third, it provided students with the opportunity to refine their professional skills.

In regard to the first objective, faculty told us that hands-on learning activities gave students, in the words of an Atlantic State applied anthropology professor: "that half of the experience that we academics can't give them. There they are, actually working on a day-to-day basis in an institutional setting and experiencing firsthand how different [from academe] the time rhythms are, the language, the discourse, the office politics. So there are lots of awareness shocks that come out of that experience. . . . Being a practitioner is about practical intelligence." Indeed, most faculty pointed out that case study simulations, individual or group projects, and internships related to real-world practical problems helped students "bridge the gap" between theoretical and practical knowledge in their programs.

Career advancement program faculty also noted that these practice activities were helpful in regard to a second instructional objective: assessing student mastery of theoretical knowledge. Many suggested that requiring students to apply theoretical knowledge to practical problems helped them determine if students had mastered the theoretical material presented to them in their courses. A professor in Land-Grant's applied anthropology program, for example, told us that, once faculty finished teaching students basic archaeological theory, they tried to get the students "out into a field school where they can learn survey training, reconnaissance training, and get some experience with major excavations": "After that, we encourage them to go get internships with federal agencies doing cultural resource management work. Then, when we get them back at the university, we can talk to them and assess and critique what they did in the field by putting their experiences back into a broader framework."

Many students we spoke with were aware that faculty used hands-on activities to assess their mastery of theoretical content. As one business student at Pierpont explained, "Faculty want us to apply theory in the case studies, and, even though they try and teach us that we should use theories only as guides, when it comes to test time the bottom line is that they expect us to give them the right answers based on the right theories." The belief that hands-on, practice-oriented activities served as useful mechanisms for evaluating how well students "mastered" theories presented to them through lectures illustrates the priority faculty assigned to ensuring that students left their programs armed with, in our terms, authoritative knowledge from which they could draw in solving real-world problems.

Students and alumni repeatedly emphasized that they strongly valued opportunities to apply theory to practice in their programs. As they explained, these hands-on practical activities taught them a variety of techniques and methods which greatly improved their performance in the workplace. Students in the four business programs, for example, stated that the case studies they completed helped them to "really learn" how to use electronic spreadsheets and statistical tools and how to "read financial indicators at a glance." Students in the two applied anthropology programs likewise indicated that their internship experiences provided them with the chance, in the words of a Land-Grant student, "to apply what I had learned in class in a real-world setting. Here I was studying to become a museum curator, and I was able to work in a museum and apply what I had learned about museumology to practical matters like cataloguing, conservation, and exhibition production."

Last, faculty and program administrators said that they expected the practice component of their master's program to meet a third instructional objective: refining students' analytic, quantitative, writing, oral presentation, and (in some cases) teamwork skills. A professor at Land-Grant University explained, for example, that he required archaeology students to submit written reports on their field excavations: "I tell them that if you don't analyze the material and get it in print—even in a contract report—then you're no different than a pot hanger. So, the writing becomes a practical and necessary skill that's emphasized in our field school." Many business professors likewise suggested that case studies were an effective method for strengthening students' analytic, writing, and quantitative skills. Students could not have agreed more. "The case studies really forced me to be analytical and to learn how to use quantitative data to back up my arguments," explained an alumnus of Parks-Beecher's M.B.A. program. "They taught me that there is no one best solution to a business problem but, rather, that it's whoever can support their argument best." Another business student, this time at St. Joan's, stated that the case studies he completed helped him to "hit on all the fundamentals." In his words, his "writing, analytic, and interpersonal skills have really improved."

In some programs—particularly those at Parks-Beecher, Pierpont, St. Joan's, and Land-Grant—faculty told us that they used hands-on instructional activities to develop teamwork skills in students. One Peterson business professor represented the perspective of many faculty in these programs when he remarked: "I require my students to do group case studies and to make group presentations for three reasons. First, I think they need to know how to cooperate. Second, I think students can learn from one another—build off of each other's specialties and expertise. Third, I think groups foster more creativity than individuals on their own." Like this faculty member, professors in St. Joan's and Pierpont's master's programs in business also required students to complete cooperative projects in out-of-class study groups. As one Pierpont professor told us: "I think the study groups are pivotal to students' experiences here. . . . We try and emphasize a culture of shared learning and cooperation, rather than competition, among our students. Working in study groups on case studies helps to nurture teamwork skills in our students."

In these four programs, faculty- and student-sponsored activities—such as required group presentations and projects as well as informal study groups, student clubs, and outside-of-class social activities—encouraged cooperative and participatory student relations (decision-situation 5). A Pierpont business student conveyed this cooperative ethic when he said: "Teamwork is really valued here. Being an individualist can get you blackballed here. . . . Here, we're pulled together. And that, I think, is good for the business world. You learn how to be a team player."

Students in these four programs were eager to learn from one another, often suggesting that "team" learning experiences were a highlight of their master's experiences. As a Land-Grant applied anthropology student put it, "You're bound to get close when you spend the summer with someone in a tent [in the program's field school]. We really batted ideas around. I learned a lot from those people that summer." Expressing this point differently, students at Parks-Beecher stated that, although they pursued the M.B.A. to advance their individual careers, they realized the importance of teamwork in the business world and eagerly sought to cultivate this skill by actively learning from one another throughout their master's experiences. "Sure, we're all here for a purpose," one second-year student remarked. "But we all know that there's room for all of us out there. We do learn from each other . . . it's just an expectation upon students by students here. You learn from the second-year students during your first year of the program, and then you hand that knowledge down during your second year. . . . We're a family here, and we try to help each other out."

Many students in the seven other career advancement programs, however, told us that they did not seek to develop or improve their teamwork skills during their master's experiences. In most of these programs, students suggested they were so focused on "acquiring knowledge" from expert faculty to improve their career performances that they seldom chose, or desired, to learn from their peers within or outside of class (decision-situation 5). An engineering student at United Tech, for example, told us: "I came here for the content. . . . I like being able to do the majority of the course work by myself." And an alumnus of Southwest State's education program said: "I expected my professors to profess. That's why I came to grad school. I wanted to get more of the substance. I didn't want to sit and listen to what other students thought about the issue. I wanted to hear the professor's perspective."

Practitioner Adjunct Faculty and Guest Lecturers   The widespread use of experienced, real-world practitioners as adjunct faculty and guest lecturers was the third characteristic feature we discerned across the eleven career advancement programs.[3] We learned from faculty and program administrators that "practitioner-adjuncts," as a business professor at Peterson described them, were involved in these master's programs in a variety of ways. Three of the four business programs, for example, had endowed semester and yearlong executive-in-residence faculty positions for which corporate leaders were brought on campus to serve as "consultants" on practical business issues. Especially in the business and applied anthropology programs, faculty invited local industry and government leaders to guest lecture in their courses. Indeed, in many career advancement programs, experienced practitioners were hired as adjunct faculty to teach specialty courses.

Full-time faculty and program administrators stressed one reason in particular for involving practitioners in their master's programs: since they often had limited professional experience in the nonuniversity workplace, they relied upon the practical expertise of real-world adjuncts to teach students the "nitty-gritty" knowledge, skills, and attitudes of their professions (decision-situation 2). A business professor at St. Joan's illustrated this point when he remarked:

> There's a place for theory in these programs, for sure, but that's just one piece of the puzzle. The other piece includes the practicalities of the workplace. Here we try to hit on both by using a lot of seasoned professionals to teach the practical side of things. Sure, a lot of new Ph.D.'s know the theory, but, when it comes to applying it, they have to use case studies from a book because they don't have any practical experience. Our adjunct faculty know how to take the theory, apply it to a real-life practical experience, and then demonstrate how the theory can be translated into money for a corporation's pocket.

Along these same lines, an administrator from Pierpont's M.B.A. program said that their adjuncts and guest lecturers "broaden our students' experience": "We're actually finding that these people can be more effective in the classroom translating real-world information to students than the Ph.D. people because they know the ropes—they know how the real business world operates." For the most part, faculty in the career advancement cases voiced variations on this theme, emphasizing that practitioners greatly contributed to their students' abilities to apply theory to practice.

Students, alumni, and employers in these programs often spoke appreciatively about their interactions with practitioner-adjuncts. An employer of Chester's education alumni, for example, said that the program's adjunct faculty brought "realistic and practical" perspectives to the classroom. A business alumna remarked that the adjunct professors at St. Joan's taught "relevant, interesting information" that was "connected to the practical realities of the workplace. . . . They gave me insights into the real world of business. They emphasized the serendipitous nature of business—that it wasn't all logical and rational." Similarly, a Peterson alumna told us that she greatly valued the "proven theories" adjuncts taught her in class:

> In general, if they [the adjuncts] gave us theory, they would say here is theory A, B, C, and D. Then they would tell us that they knew for a fact that Theory B worked because they were using it in their own business

right at this moment. . . . In other words, they were telling me practical information rather than just plain theory and [they applied it to their own experiences and told me if it worked]. I learned that, just because Theory A sounds logical, it doesn't mean it works. Yes, it sounds very logical, but, when you get out there in the real world and you're dealing with clients, it's a whole different ball game.

In addition to viewing practitioners as important "translators" of theoretical knowledge and sources of practical knowledge, faculty and program administrators in the career advancement programs also suggested that practitioners effectively communicated to students the norms and mores that informed their particular profession's practice in the real world. Many faculty believed that this important socialization function was best accomplished by workplace practitioners, since they often only had first-hand experience of a scholarly professional life. As one Peterson business faculty member put it, "These practitioner-adjuncts are people who work in industry—like financial and marketing executives—they can effectively pass on their real-world experiences to students [because] . . . they know what 'flies' in the business world. Sharing that information with students is important if you're trying to prepare students adequately for the type of opportunities that are available in the workplace." A Parks-Beecher business professor made this point from a slightly different perspective: "We [the faculty] say that the purpose of this program is to prepare African-American students with the knowledge and skills to move into leadership positions in corporate America. . . . The corporate representatives who are involved in our program help our students understand the image of corporate America and how to fit into that image. If anything, it seems like we need to approximate the corporate norm more than a 'majority' program if our graduates are to get good jobs."

Practioner-adjuncts in the career advancement programs taught students real-world professional behaviors and attitudes in formal workshops and during informal interactions that occurred in and outside of class. In the four business programs, for example, corporate representatives sponsored workshops and seminars that focused on such topics as "dressing for success," "tips for climbing the corporate ladder," and "managing the interview process." A Parks-Beecher business alumnus spoke for many alumni and students when he said that these seminars "help us understand the culture of corporate America." Another Parks-Beecher student explained that, although a corporate representative at an interviewing workshop advised him to change his haircut, this advice did not annoy him because, in his words: "I understand that they're trying to mold me in the image of what they want to see. And I think that's fine as long as you know what you're buying into." Students and alumni from programs in other fields provided similar accounts. An archaeology alumnus from Land-Grant University, for example, told us that while working with practitioners "in the field," he learned that mutual respect and teamwork were a "big part of thinking and acting like an archaeologist." And an alumna of Chester College's education program stated that, during her outside-of-class practicum experience, she began to "learn the ropes of the profession": "I mean, I was watching these fantastic teachers interacting with their students, modeling their behaviors for me—you know, what they thought an effective teacher should say and do with students." For the most part, students, alumni, employers, and full-time faculty in the career advancement programs communicated to us that most practitioner-adjuncts were very effective at translating practical, context-specific know-how to students and socializing them into the practices of their respective professions.

Customer-Friendly Service Model   In reviewing our interviews from these eleven cases, we discerned a fourth feature characteristic of career advancement programs: a pronounced emphasis on customer-friendly instructional and administrative services. In most of these programs, faculty and program administrators responded to student and employer demands for "full-service expert training" by providing them with convenient "nontraditional" instructional delivery approaches; cordial and entertaining instruction; and responsive, client-centered career placement services.

Convenient Nontraditional Instructional Delivery.   Many faculty and program administrators told us that they incorporated nontraditional instructional delivery approaches into their master's programs to respond to employer and student demands for convenient, part-time master's instruction. A senior administrator at United Tech, for example, told us that the school developed a satellite-based, long-distance learning approach to engineering education to serve a targeted "niche market":

> Our niche is not our delivery system . . . that's just the means for serving our niche market. Our niche market is the audience we have chosen—we provide advanced education to professional engineers employed full-time in the workplace. . . . I think the convenience and flexibility of our [satellite-delivery] approach meets a real need out there in the marketplace. Sure, I think if you took most of the students at [United Tech] and asked them "Would you rather go off full-time to M.I.T. and get your master's, or would you rather get it from [United Tech] on a part-time basis while you work?" I think most of them would say, "If I had a choice, which I don't, I guess I would like to go off and immerse myself in a graduate program at a prestigious university and get it that way. But I have a family,

I'm six years into my career, and I'm not going to do that even if I could afford it. I will not sever myself from my job and go away to get a degree." So, I think most of them see it as a trade-off, and they think that our program is a pretty good alternative for getting their master's degree.

A program administrator in Peterson's M.B.A. program offered a similar perspective: "We realize that we're not a Harvard or a Wharton. . . . We know what our target market is: we're a commuter-type school, and we cater to a primarily evening population because there is a big demand for a part-time M.B.A. program in this market. Our students need the flexibility to come and go when they want and to buy into a system where they can take a semester off if they have to travel or they get an extra assignment at work. We try to be responsive to our student's needs."

The nontraditional delivery formats used by the career advancement programs included innovative off-campus delivery systems—such as long-distance satellite-based instruction and videotaped lectures—as well as on-campus "extended-day" programs in which students completed their studies through evening, weekend, and summer courses.[4] In the education and English programs at Chester College and Urban State, for example, faculty scheduled courses in the evenings and summers to accommodate part-time students. Besides offering most of their M.B.A. courses in the evenings, faculty and program administrators at St. Joan's also provided students with the option of completing a variety of intensive four-week and weekend-only courses. And, in Southwest State's education program, master's courses were offered both on campus during the evenings and summers and at nearly fifty off-campus locations throughout the state. According to one professor, these off-campus sites were so convenient for students that they literally could complete their entire master's degree "without ever setting foot on [Southwest State's] main campus."

Many students and alumni told us that the nontraditional instructional delivery approaches utilized in the career advancement programs were very customer friendly. At United Tech students said that they preferred their videocassette tape-delayed courses to traditional, on-campus day classes. As one alumnus put it: "I really like the tape-delay format because I can take the tape home, sit on the couch, get a bowl of popcorn, and watch it there. It's really nice because I don't take notes that fast, and sometimes I need to rewind the tape so I can get the idea down in my notes." Another alumnus described the benefits of the videotaped lecture format as follows: "It allowed me to watch the lectures when I was in the right frame of mind for learning. It also allowed me to rewind the tape and listen to parts of the lecture that were not clear during the first viewing. I think all universities should study some of the revolutionary methods that [United Tech] has pioneered." Students in other programs expressed appreciation for convenient evening, weekend, and intensive short-course instructional formats. As one student at Chester College said, "I really like the fact that [Chester] realizes that we are full-time working professionals and schedules most of their graduate courses at night." A student at St. Joan's remarked: "This program is really flexible and convenient for me. It accommodates itself to meet my needs."

Employers provided us with similar accounts, often noting that customer-friendly instructional approaches conveniently met their needs without "losing" their employees to full-time study. An employer of United Tech's engineering alumni put it this way:

> We really want our engineers to get enhanced skill sets, but we don't want to send them away to school. We're on highly goal-driven production schedules here. This approach works, and it's really convenient. If we have to transfer an employee to another location, the master's program sort of moves with them. If they need to go to another site for six weeks, they can pick up their videos and continue on with their education. And the approach is particularly good for American corporations, since a lot of them are moving to remote sections of the country where they don't have access to good postsecondary education.

Employers of Chester and Southwest State education students also appreciated the convenience of evening, weekend, and summer instructional formats. "I depend on master's courses to renew teachers," noted one employer associated with Southwest State's program, "and I'm very glad this program makes it easy for teachers to get those courses. The program is very convenient and flexible." These comments were echoed by many employers we interviewed who had hired graduates from the St. Joan's, Peterson, Urban State, and Land-Grant master's programs.

Cordial and Entertaining Instruction. We learned from many career advancement program faculty and administrators that their attentiveness to "instructional delivery" involved more than providing conveniently scheduled courses to their customers. Most informed us as well that they viewed themselves as talented pedagogues who placed a high priority on "delivering" instruction to students through exemplary teaching "performances" in class and cordial interactions outside of class. An education professor at Chester College expressed the views of many faculty in these programs when she remarked: "The essence of [Chester's] program is quality teaching. That's what we do here. That's paramount in our thinking."

Faculty took pride not only in their ability to translate effectively to students the knowledge of their discipline but to accomplish this in an entertaining, customer-friendly way. A faculty member in Urban State's

English program, for example, told us that he actively tried to teach his students literary criticism by "teaching on adrenalin": "My teaching is like a theatrical performance. I try to give my students as much content as I can, but I realize that you also need to deal with the human factor of mental exhaustion in a three-hour class meeting. I really have to know how to orchestrate the material—how to make it interesting." In Pierpont's business program, a faculty member similarly remarked that many of the faculty were "superb performers" who were at once "incredibly entertaining" and effective in the classroom. She described several of her colleagues as "matinee idols" who regularly made the "lights go on" for students.

These faculty and program administrator perspectives were frequently echoed by students and alumni across the eleven programs. We came to understand that many students thought of their professors as "sages on the stage" who presented entertaining lectures and course activities. A business student at St. Joan's, for instance, remarked: "The first course I took in this M.B.A. program was from a battle-scarred businessman . . . it was great. It was like watching a movie! I listened to his every word." In a similar vein, students in Pierpont's business program said that many of their faculty were "blue-chip" professors who not only "knew their stuff" but, in the words of a second-year student, also could impart it in a way that "lit up the room with humor." An alumnus of Land-Grant's archaeology program simply described his professors as "great communicators": "They knew how to illuminate points in class and to make them stick with you."

In our conversations with faculty and program administrators, we learned that positive teaching evaluations were considered very important because students were viewed as "paying customers" upon whom their programs' financial and reputational futures depended. As a United Tech program administrator put it: "We serve an unforgiving group of consumers. Our faculty have to be 'on' to keep our customers [in the program]." Likewise, a faculty member in Chester's education program said: "Our students are here on a business venture, and they are highly motivated. They want their money's worth, and they are extremely demanding of teachers. We take their demands very seriously around here. . . . I can tell you that, if student reviews are not good, you won't be rehired." (Chester College faculty are employed on single- and multiple-year, non-tenure track contracts.) Indeed, many interviewees told us that faculty and administrators took their "customers'" feedback so seriously that they developed elaborate teacher evaluation protocols for which students were major judges of teacher performance.

Numerous stakeholders also informed us that faculty extended their customer-friendly approach to their outside-of-class interactions with students. Many students, for example, said that most faculty were "available and accessible" outside of class to assist them with course-related or aca-demic advising questions. As one business student at Peterson put it: "I think the faculty are very sensitive to the needs of many of the students here—they are there when you need them. Lots of them give out their home telephone numbers and encourage us to call when we have ques-tions about the material in class." An English alumna from Urban State expressed a similar perspective: "The faculty were really helpful, . . . the advising was excellent, and the faculty always made time for you." Even students in United Tech's engineering program—in which faculty were usually hundreds of miles from students—said that professors promptly answered their questions. As one student commented: "If I have a ques-tion, I'll usually E-mail [electronic mail] or FAX [facsimile] it to my pro-fessor. The profs usually answer my question that same day."

Faculty were responsive to students' requests for out-of-class as-sistance for several reasons. To begin with, many said they enjoyed inter-acting with students and watching them develop into seasoned profes-sionals. Others suggested that it was their "responsibility" to be available for "individual consultations" with their so-called customers. In a nutshell, faculty articulated one overarching rationale for the cordial and friendly interactions they had with students outside of class: they wanted students to have a comfortable, enjoyable experience in their program. A professor in Peterson's business program summarized the viewpoint of many faculty in the career advancement programs when he remarked: "I can see an advertising campaign for the school saying that, 'if you came to [Peterson], you could be very happy and comfortable here.' We [the faculty] try to create a comfortable climate for students here."

Client-centered, Career Advancement Services. We learned that most career advancement programs offered a variety of customer-friendly services to respond to the "career advancement" requests of students and employ-ers.[5] The most visible of these included corporate and alumni networking opportunities and career planning and placement services.

Although mentioned by interviewees in the education and applied anthropology programs, it was especially in the four business programs in which "networking" between students and employers was seen as a vital component of the master's experience. In these programs, administrators, faculty, and support staff sponsored networking seminars, luncheons, and parties to facilitate the job search and recruitment process for students and employers. At Parks-Beecher, for example, administrators in their career planning and placement office began each school year with a "kickoff" reception where students were provided with information on several For-tune 500 companies that recruited at the school. Then, over the course of the next few months, the office invited representatives from many of these firms to give formal presentations to students describing their company. At Peterson, Pierpont, and St. Joan's, interviewees emphasized that such networking opportunities enriched the career placement services that students and employers expected. As a St. Joan's student said to us: "The dean says upfront that one of the purposes of this program is to network with students, professors, guest lecturers, and corporate representatives. And that happens. Networking is very important here."

Stakeholders across these four business cases told us that program alumni were actively involved in networking activities. Both business programs at Peterson and Parks-Beecher, for example, had formal student-alumni mentoring programs. Pierpont's alumni sponsored parties for newly admitted students and encouraged them to become "members of the Pierpont family." One Pierpont student, for instance, remarked that upon her admission to the program she received a "barrage of phone calls" inviting her to an alumni-sponsored cocktail party in New York City. "The alums really made you feel wanted," she explained, "they all seemed to know my name when I arrived!" And, across all four programs, students told us that program alumni also helped them find jobs. Students at Parks-Beecher, Peterson, and St. Joan's said that they often contacted program alumni to help them with initial job inquiries at various corporations. And at Pierpont one student summarized a perspective shared by many of his peers when he said to us: "We're told to use [Pierpont's] alumni to help us get jobs. I've been told the [Pierpont] 'old boy network' is so strong that it will open any door in New York City."

Interviewees in the six career advancement business and education programs also described the comprehensive career planning and placement services that their programs offered. In each of the four business programs, for example, staff associates assisted students with a variety of job preparation activities including interviewing and résumé-writing workshops, on-campus employer recruitment visits and job interviews, and individualized job search referrals to prospective employers. Three of the four business placement offices also provided employers with attractive books containing a complete listing of student résumés. Moreover, the placement offices associated with the business and education programs published annual reports that chronicled such relevant statistics as the percentage of recent graduates employed, places of employment, and salary distributions.

For the most part, students and employers described these placement services in flattering terms, remarking that they were friendly places where staff eagerly responded to their needs. An education student at Chester College commented that everyone she interacted with at the career services office "was really helpful": "They really helped me to get a good placement." And an alumna of Peterson's business program told us:

"The placement people are very helpful . . . they really do try to get you interviews. They try to network you with lots of alumni and employers. So far, I've interviewed with many employers and have received a job offer from AT&T. The placement office has really met my needs."

Many faculty and program administrators communicated to us that their placement offices were an important component of the customer-friendly service model used in their programs, precisely because they "met" their customers' "needs." As one Pierpont business professor put it: "Our placement office is supposed to keep our students and employers happy—they're supposed to please the customer." A program administrator at Parks-Beecher similarly remarked: "Our students come here expecting to get good jobs. We do everything we can to help them get good jobs." Indeed, employment statistics from some of these programs indicated that they effectively met their customers' employment needs. In all four business programs, more than 90 percent of all graduates found jobs within their selected interest fields, and 94 percent of Chester College's education graduates were employed within a year of graduation.

Strategic Administrative and Faculty Support   Program administrators and faculty in nine of the career advancement cases indicated to us that they had strategic reasons for investing considerable personal time and energy in master's education (decision-situation 3). We came to understand that these reasons were related to a more or less well-articulated "reputation-enrollment-resources" strategy: faculty anticipated that, if they invested effort in targeted master's-related activities, this would enhance the overall reputation, enrollment, and resource base of their department, including the master's program.

Interviewees in the career advancement program emphasized the strategic benefits associated with a "solid" program reputation. In a few cases faculty and program administrators told us that their program's well-regarded reputation in the workplace enhanced the overall visibility of their institution and, in turn, encouraged college and university administrators to provide more resources and symbolic support for their programs.[6] In almost all cases faculty and program administrators said that their particular program's reputation was a pivotal selling point in attracting students to their departments. As an education faculty member at Chester College put it: "Our reputation attracts students to the program. I know that we have a reputation for producing good practitioners."

This reputation-enrollment-resources strategy was embraced by faculty and administrators in programs located in both publicly and privately controlled institutions. Faculty and administrators in Atlantic State's applied anthropology program, for example, told us that they recently revised their curriculum in hopes of strengthening the program's reputation and attracting more students to their severely underenrolled program. Faculty and program administrators at private institutions were even more emphatic about the salience of this reputation-enrollment-resources strategy. Many stressed that a downturn in reputation could seriously jeopardize the financial viability of their master's programs since their budgets were based primarily on enrollment-generated tuition dollars. As an administrator in Parks-Beecher's business program put it, "If, for some reason or another, we couldn't place our grads in high-paying positions in corporate America, I know we could not compete with some of the best schools in the country in attracting students or corporate recruiters to our program." This, she added, could spell financial disaster for the program.

Faculty and program administrators in almost all of the career advancement cases told us that they strategically targeted—and invested in—their program's customer-friendly activities. In explaining their reasoning, we frequently heard responses similar to one provided by a business professor at Pierpont University: "We realize that our program is market driven and that we must respond to our market. . . . What we are really trying to do here is to keep our customers happy. Our job is to please the customer—to be responsive to their needs." Indeed, many faculty suggested that their customer-friendly services did "keep customers happy" by responding to their requests for expert training through a combination of convenient instructional delivery approaches, exemplary teaching performances, and cordial in- and out-of-class faculty-student interactions.

Time and again, faculty and program administrators across these nine career advancement cases communicated to us that their "investments" in customer-friendly instructional and placement activities yielded handsome rewards for their programs. Many faculty, for example, indicated that their graduates often "networked" the program to workplace colleagues and contributed time and money to their alma maters. One Pierpont faculty member linked this alumni loyalty to the positive interactions former students had with faculty: "Our alumni are so devoted because we're so devoted to them while they're here. . . . We realize that our alumni are our greatest strength."

Faculty also emphasized that the time they devoted to developing customer-friendly relations with employers often produced a cadre of employers who regularly hired their program's graduates. A professor at Parks-Beecher, for example, said that many faculty and administrators in their M.B.A. program understood that "corporate America is the consumer of M.B.A.'s": "If they don't like our product, they'll go to another supplier." Consequently, he noted, they often invited corporate representatives to participate in various class and extracurricular placement activities to provide them with a "firsthand look" at their students and program. These efforts, he claimed, produced a fine payoff for the program: "Right now over one hundred of the nation's Fortune 500 corporations regularly recruit here. I think that says something for our program. If employers didn't like what they saw, they wouldn't keep coming back."

These "strategic investments" did, in fact, often produce the "results" faculty and program administrators anticipated. In most of the nine cases in which faculty provided strong strategic support to master's education in their departments, these master's programs were characterized by healthy student enrollments, at least adequate financial resources, and a generally well-regarded reputation in the nonuniversity workplace.

There were, however, two programs in the career advancement grouping in which faculty and program administrators did not provide strategic support to master's education (decision-situation 3). With over one thousand students taking classes in nearly fifty field-based service locations, we were not surprised that Southwest State's full-time teacher education faculty rebelled against the customer-friendly expectations institutional- and program-level administrators expected them to fulfill. One professor explained their situation as follows:

> The faculty in this program really want to serve our students, but we also want to ensure that there is some degree of quality in what we're doing. Right now, I think we're so service oriented that we've become a kind of Statue of Liberty institution. You know, give us your weak, your feeble, give us everybody, and we'll take them all and be a torchbearer for education. I think that's a mistake. Our faculty are incapable of meeting all the demands—they're stretched too thin. . . . There's just too much pressure to provide these classes and meet student demands and, at the same time, try and maintain a quality program.

At Trafalgar College we learned that many faculty and program administrators strategically invested their efforts in the college's baccalaureate, not the master's, theater program. As a result, their undergraduate program was characterized by strong student enrollments, considerable resources, and, we were told, a reputation as one of the "finest" undergraduate theater programs in the nation. The converse held true for the master's program: not only was it underenrolled and underfinanced, but also many stakeholders suggested that its reputation was, in the words of one alumna, "at best, mediocre."

Overall Stakeholder Evaluations of Career Advancement Program Experiences

Stakeholders across the eleven cases in the career advancement program type often communicated to us that they experienced these programs as places where faculty and program administrators attempted to provide students with the knowledge, skills, and terminal credentials that would help them to advance their professional careers in the nonuniversity workplace. Throughout our interviews, stakeholders constantly evaluated the overall quality and value of their master's experiences. Many interviewees told us that students not only had a comprehensive expert training experience that improved their professional performance in the workplace but also walked away from these programs with a career advancement credential that was valuable in fields (notably business, engineering, and education) with strong nonuniversity job market demand. In addition, employers suggested that these master's programs benefited them by serving as an inexpensive screening device for evaluating prospective employees for new jobs and current employees for promotions and salary increases. Notwithstanding these positive evaluations, stakeholders in several programs were less sanguine, emphasizing that their master's programs seldom provided students with the expert training and credentials needed to improve their performances and ensure their professional success in the nonuniversity workplace. Below we elaborate on these broad evaluative themes.

Comprehensive Expert Training for Students   Many stakeholders positively evaluated the comprehensive expert training experience that faculty provided to students in the career advancement master's programs. Students, alumni, and employers stressed that their expert training was particularly valuable because it equipped students with a "solid foundation" of knowledge and skills, enhanced their professional confidence, and markedly improved their on-the-job performance.

Many students and alumni told us that, while they originally enrolled in their master's programs expecting to earn a "quick and easy" expert credential, this motivation was often, in the words of a Pierpont business student, "stood on its head" as they experienced firsthand the emphasis faculty placed on student mastery of theoretical knowledge and professional skills in these programs. As an education student at Chester College put it:

> I really didn't enter this program thinking I'd get this huge amount of knowledge placed on my shoulders. I looked at it like a trade school where I could get the certification and some basic "how to do this and that." I thought of it as a necessary part of the education field. But, when I look back on the experience I've had at [Chester], I can say that I learned not just the how-to. I got some theoretical background to it. I guess I was defining trade school wrong. I think, whenever you learn how to do something, you should also learn the why. At [Chester] I got both—the how and the why. It was more than the trade school I thought it would be.

Along these same lines, a Pierpont business student said she was "totally surprised" that a "vocational training school" could be as "intellectually challenging as [Pierpont] was." As she explained: "I was completely cynical before I came here. I felt the M.B.A. was to be purchased—you know, pay sixty thousand dollars for a ticket. I didn't think the education would be at all stimulating. . . . But, it's funny, I've had a much more powerful experience here than I ever thought I'd have. I got lots of stimulation. I've been challenged."

In addition to providing students with theoretical knowledge and enhancing their professional skills, many interviewees emphasized that these programs also strengthened students' analytical, quantitative, and, in some cases, oral and written communication skills. A student in Land-Grant's applied anthropology program, for example, told us that he had learned how to "write succinct papers" and how to "repackage papers and analyses for different audiences." An education student said that Chester's program helped her learn how to "effectively present" a lesson to "school kids at their own level": "you know, at a level that's challenging for them but isn't over their heads." And an alumna of St. Joan's remarked that, although her interpersonal skills were "to the right of Atilla the Hun's" prior to enrolling in their M.B.A. program, by the time she graduated she "had learned how to deal effectively with people." Many faculty and employers agreed with these student accounts, often noting that, in many cases, program graduates had developed strong analytical and problem-solving skills.

Not surprisingly, students and alumni also told us that their confidence to pursue a demanding professional career had grown as they successfully completed difficult assignments and challenging courses. A second-year business student at Peterson University, for example, told us: "After taking the courses and learning the knowledge that I have at [Peterson], I feel much more confident now—I really feel like I can be very effective in the business world now." An alumna of Land-Grant's applied anthropology program voiced a similar change in outlook: "I've learned a whole new range of skills through this program, and I feel a lot more self-confident in my ability to go out and get a curatorship in a small museum now. I feel like I could really do that now." And a Parks-Beecher student, whom we interviewed two weeks before he graduated from business school, candidly remarked: "Prior to my coming here, if I had been offered the same job, I don't think I would have done very well at it. But now I have the knowledge, the skills, and the confidence to succeed."

For the most part, alumni in most of the career advancement programs greatly valued the knowledge and skills they acquired for one major reason: their expert training experiences significantly improved their professional performance in the workplace. An alumnus of Parks-Beecher's business program, for example, said that, although he found his program "painful initially," it was "well worth it for me in the long run. Once I got my job here at the bank, I realized that the course work had really prepared me as a financial engineer. I'm a much more creative, disciplined problem solver now than before my master's program. That master's program gave me the credibility, the skills, and the knowledge to become successful in the business world." An alumnus of Land-Grant's applied anthropology program likewise mentioned that the "technical and theoretical knowledge and skills" he learned during his master's gave him "the technical expertise" to "outperform my counterparts in the workplace": "The program gave me the skills to be in a totally different arena than the rest [of my counterparts] because I learned the theory and I learned how to write papers and draft budgets. And the program taught me that I had to talk to people and deal with a problem rather than rushing in and telling them what to do."

For their part, faculty and employers often commented that their programs produced alumni who not only had, in the words of a Parks-Beecher business professor, a "solid, basic foundation of knowledge and skills in their disciplines" but also were skilled at applying their knowledge to the workplace. Many employers emphasized that it was precisely for this reason—that master's graduates could "perform" as experts in their work settings—that they often gave high marks to these master's programs. One middle-level manager, for example, told us that he was so impressed with the improved on-the-job performances of his United Tech master's-educated engineers that he conducted a survey to convince top-level management that this master's program benefited their company. His conclusions:

> I couldn't believe the results. Most of these master's-trained engineers told me that they were more effective, usually by an average of 33 percent more than before the courses. I was hoping they would say maybe 5 percent more effective—but 33 percent more effective! I then interviewed their project supervisors, and they all corroborated that [these master's-educated engineers] were more effective. . . . What really matters in the workplace is whether or not you can perform. Our [United Tech] grads perform. I'm really overjoyed with [United Tech's] program.

An employer of archaeology graduates from Land-Grant's applied anthropology program provided a comparable assessment: "These graduates really can perform. The grads I hire from [Land-Grant] demonstrate a level of technical expertise that is really acceptable quality to me. They know how to do the job right." And an employer of Peterson business graduates simply stated: "I think Peterson's master's program is very strong. It gives you the basics and the specialized knowledge. . . . Their graduates know how and when to use the tools. That's valuable to me as an employer."

Stakeholders associated with several of the eleven career advancement programs, however, were noticeably less sanguine about the education students received. According to their accounts, these programs often were not valuable for students and employers because they seldom provided students with the knowledge, skills, and credentials needed to perform successfully in the nonuniversity workplace.

Many interviewees emphasized that these programs were so diffuse that faculty seldom could agree on their overall purposes and curricula. A faculty member at Trafalgar College, for example, told us: "This program is trying to be all things to all people. We are trying to prepare theater generalists, theater educators, and advanced practitioners for the professional theater. We, as a faculty, can't resolve what we should be offering or what we should be focusing on. As a result, our students often don't get the specialized training they need." A Southwest State education professor described the department's master's program in these terms: "No single coherent strand holds it [the program] all together. Our core set of courses are really only a core in title, not in content. . . . We need to get a much clearer idea of what the purpose of our master's program is and what we want to teach in it."

Indeed, many students and alumni in these several programs reiterated these faculty remarks. A student in Trafalgar's theater program, for example, mentioned that, since faculty seldom "zoned in on what was important," he did not receive the "appropriate training" necessary to become a director in the professional theater. "They didn't provide the courses or the individual attention I needed," he explained, " and I know that, if I had to do it all over again, I wouldn't come here. This program did not meet my needs." An applied anthropology student in Atlantic State's program voiced a similar perspective: "There is little agreement among the faculty in this program about the skills they believe every practicing, applied anthropologist should have. I'm not even sure the faculty can articulate what those skills are—in fact, I think the faculty emphasize different skills. I think if this program continues to market itself as a professional program, it should agree on the skills it's teaching to students." She added that students were "disappointed" with the absence of focus in the program and seriously questioned whether matriculation was a worthwhile investment: "I know that half of the first-year students are thinking about dropping out of the program. They're disappointed with the courses, and they're hearing that a lot of graduates from last year didn't find jobs."

In large part because these students and alumni believed they did not receive the focused expert training they expected, many suggested that they left these programs with little more than a credential. When we asked an alumnus of Southwest State's education program to tell us about the value of his master's experience, he gave this response: "You want to know what I think about the overall worth of this master's program? Well, I wouldn't say it's worthless or a complete waste of time, because it's neither. After all, it gave me the credential I needed to move up the salary scale in my district. But, professionally, it did not radically improve my teaching, and it sure didn't improve the quality of my life." A graduate of Trafalgar's theater program made the point this way: "All I got out of this program was a credential. The program didn't live up to my expectations at all. It was like a bachelor's of fine arts program, if you ask me. And I had a much stronger learning experience in my bachelor's program than in this master's program. I don't feel like I got as much out of this program as I put into it, that's for sure."

Career Advancement Credential   Stakeholders in many of the career advancement cases told us that they valued these programs for another reason: they provided the student with a credential that advanced his or her professional career (through expanded job opportunities, an improved salary, or both). These positive reviews were mostly expressed by interviewees in those fields with strong employment demand, such as business, engineering, education, and archaeology (a specialization within Land-Grant's and Atlantic State's applied anthropology programs).

Time and again, students and alumni evaluated their master's experience in terms of the career advancement value their master's credential had in the nonuniversity workplace. In the words of an alumnus from St. Joan's business program: "The real value of the program for me has been the improved job opportunities. Once I received the degree, doors magically opened for me. A whole new world of career opportunities was at my disposal." A Parks-Beecher business alumnus provided a similar assessment: "The M.B.A. has been a very valuable degree for me because it credentialized me within the business community and helped me to get a good job. More important, the money I've made has been very significant. Last year, after being on the job for only two years, I got a superior rating and an end-of-the-year bonus that was 45 percent of my base salary."

Faculty and program administrators also emphasized the career advancement value of their master's programs, often using the placement rate of their graduates as a yardstick for evaluating program quality. As an administrator at Parks-Beecher explained: "A good measure of success in any master's program is what your students do with their degree—where they go with it and if they get jobs in the field. Our students get great jobs in Fortune 500 companies when they leave here. Our placement rate is over 90 percent. And our students also get good salaries—we're in the top twenty M.B.A. programs in the country as far as starting M.B.A. salaries are concerned. Those statistics, I feel, say something about the quality of this business program." Along these same lines, an education faculty member at Chester told us that nearly all of their master's graduates found teaching jobs within one year of graduation from their program. From her perspective, Chester's placement rate was indicative of the quality of its program and the "regard employers have for our graduates."

Not all stakeholders across the eleven cases, however, were pleased with the career advancement value of their master's degrees. For the most part, these included students who were pursuing careers in fields with weak nonuniversity employment demand. Students and alumni in Atlantic State's applied anthropology program told us, for example, that, while several of their archaeology graduates found "good jobs," they questioned if there was a legitimate nonuniversity job market for master's-educated cultural anthropologists. As one alumna put it: "I think a little truth in advertising is needed in this program. I think the jobs that faculty envision students will get are just not out there. No one in my graduating class has found a job after an entire year."

Finally, although most interviewees gave high marks to the career advancement value of the master's credential in the nonuniversity workplace, some faculty were disgruntled with the "credential-driven" motivations of their students. A Pierpont business professor expressed this view when he said:

> I just think that too many people in M.B.A. programs come for the credential. Sure, a lot of doctoral students see the Ph.D. as a credential too, but it's not as severe as the number of M.B.A. students who do. The M.B.A. students come for the purpose of going through the recruitment process—that's why they're here. They want to be part of that meat market, because they're here for the credential more than they're here for the education. They want the M.B.A. to get ahead, not because they want to learn . . . it's a mentality. That's the mentality that drives them to come here. They're credential oriented when they come here.

Inexpensive Screening Device for Employers   Many employers in the career advancement cases said that they valued these master's programs because they provided an inexpensive screening device for selecting prospective employees for new jobs and current employees for promotions and salary increases. This screening function was most strongly emphasized by employers associated with the business and education programs, although a few applied anthropology and engineering employers spoke to this point as well.

An employer associated with Pierpont's business program expressed the screening value of M.B.A. programs when he remarked, "M.B.A. programs save corporate training dollars by educating these students for us, and, at the same time, they give us the opportunity to cherry pick their best students as our prospective employees." This employer, a corporate executive with one of the nation's leading financial investment firms, then added that he sent his corporate recruiters to the "nation's most elite business schools" to "skim off the cream" of the graduating class. Similarly, an employer of Land-Grant's archaeology students told us: "The master's is valuable for us because it lets us know that they have the technical expertise to write the reports and to do the job. By federal law, we have to have at least a master's-education person to sign off on our reports. So we hire master's people because we know we are getting a higher-quality product at a relatively lower cost to fulfill a mandated responsibility for us." Faculty and students in the business programs were "well aware" that employers viewed their M.B.A. programs in this fashion. One Pierpont administrator, for example, explained to us: "Over the past few decades, with the growth in access to undergraduate education, the screening-for-quality function played by the bachelor's degree has become less effective for employers: there are just too many bachelor's-trained people out there now, and many of them are not well trained. So employers now rely on M.B.A. schools to screen out a more elite group of business professionals to help make the hiring process easier." A faculty member in Parks-Beecher's business program likewise remarked: "[Parks-Beecher] is serving as a screening device for corporate America, and I think that's why companies keep coming back to this campus. This school credentials black Americans for the corporate community."

Many interviewees explained that this screening function was not restricted to hiring new employees. Employers, faculty, and students in both education programs, for instance, told us that employers frequently used the master's degree as a basis for raising teacher salaries. In United Tech's engineering program, several interviewees noted that employers often required bachelor's-trained engineers to earn a master's before they could be promoted into managerial or research and development positions. In the words of one United Tech employer, "The master's lets us know that they're technically current—that they can perform at a higher level."

Although some students and alumni evaluated their master's experiences more positively than others, most stakeholders in the career advancement programs were generally pleased with the overall quality of their master's programs. We came to understand that interviewees valued the expert training and workplace credentials students received in these programs.

They did so, in large part, because they fulfilled an instrumental objective both students and employers held for these master's programs: the production of practitioner-experts who had the essential knowledge, skills, and terminal credentials necessary to advance their professional careers in the nonuniversity workplace.

8

Apprenticeship Programs

Electrical Engineering at Prestige State University

Prestige State University was founded as a public land-grant institution in the mid-1800s. By the early twentieth century, it achieved international recognition as one of the leading universities in the world and has been widely recognized for its excellence in doctoral education and research ever since. Over the past seven decades, many of its programs have consistently ranked in the "top ten" in national reputational rankings of graduate programs. Prestige State's School of Engineering consistently has been rated as one of the best in the United States, and its Department of Electrical Engineering, which was among the founding departments of the school, has likewise been considered as one of the finest in the nation.

When we visited the electrical engineering program at Prestige State in 1990, interviewees emphasized that doctoral education and research were highly valued on the campus. A high-level institutional administrator, for example, told us that, although some institutional effort was "given to master's programs in professional areas like social welfare, engineering, public policy, business, and journalism," master's education was generally not as highly regarded, nor as strongly supported, as doctoral education.

We learned from many electrical engineering faculty and program administrators at Prestige State that, while they embraced the larger institutional emphases on doctoral education and research, they also chose to devote significant effort to their master's program. Faculty and program administrators emphasized that master's education was important to them because it developed students into skilled "young professionals" for the engineering field. One faculty member, whose comments reflected those of many of his departmental colleagues, articulated this perspective as follows:

> I think there's a tendency nowadays in our field to say that, if students really want to do engineering work, to be engineers in our profession, then most of us would like to see them go on and do master's degrees. It's partly for that reason that [we help them] get this first bit of experience on what it's like to be involved in a large project—to design something, build it, and so on. Another thing is that the field has gotten to be so broad that it's very hard to give them the principles of the profession in four years. And there's a tendency to feel that bachelor's students, if they try to go out and practice their profession, will not really wind up being engineers. They'll wind up doing work related to engineering—like working in sales or management—but not working in real engineering. The master's is more or less where the professional level is in engineering.

To develop students as young professionals, EE faculty and program administrators communicated to us that they viewed the master's as an opportunity for students—with guidance from faculty as well as doctoral students—to enhance their understandings of the knowledge and skills associated with the professional practice of engineering. As one program administrator explained, the "goal" of their master's program was to "develop students into young professionals to a point where they can continue their own education without the necessity of formal enrollments." He said that he and his EE colleagues did this by teaching students how to read research literature, deal with ambiguous problems, plan and execute a project, and work with people.

Along these same lines, a professor told us that "the general intent of this master's program is to try and give the students some experience that is similar to what they might get involved in when they get out in industry and do a project. That generally means that a student is going to be working with a large group doing a piece of a project rather than a more individual arrangement." To accomplish this, he explained, students were required to join a laboratory research team in which faculty—and, more often, advanced doctoral students—taught students how to interact with others as team members and how to go about designing, executing, and interpreting results from a research project. From our perspective, this process of having faculty and doctoral students facilitate students' professional understandings of the knowledge and practices of their field closely resembled a medieval guild apprenticeship system in which master artisans prepared apprentices for membership in their guild by involving them directly in the work of their profession.

This apprenticeship emphasis was reflected in the requirements for the EE master's program. In addition to completing twelve units of graduate-level course work, students were required to spend the remainder of their program (twelve units) conducting research with faculty and doctoral students in a "project laboratory." Students also were expected to complete a thesis or project report, study full-time, and finish the program in no more than three academic semesters.

Consonant with the department's high-profile reputation, admission into Prestige State's electrical engineering department was highly competitive. In 1989 the department admitted about 15 percent of all individuals who applied. The average Graduate Record Examination (GRE) score of admitted students was at the ninety-fifth percentile, and about one-fifth of the newly enrolled students had won "highly competitive external fellowships." Of the approximately 350 master's and 150 doctoral students in the department, about 15 percent were women, 7 percent were underrepresented minorities, and 30 percent were foreign nationals. Graduate research and teaching assistantships were offered to all admitted students.

At the time of our visit to Prestige State, the electrical engineering department employed more than eighty full-time faculty. Faculty research support had increased two and one-half times during the 1980s and averaged several hundred thousand dollars per faculty FTE (full-time equivalent). We were informed that faculty managed eight large research projects (involving from three to fifteen faculty, twelve to fifty master's and doctoral students, and one to twenty industrial sponsors) and roughly forty medium-sized research projects (involving from one to three faculty and three to twenty master's and doctoral students), while also maintaining individual workloads of about twelve bachelor's, four master's, and two doctoral students. Many faculty had received local, national, and international honors, including a substantial share of Prestige State's institution-wide teaching awards.

We learned from interviewees that faculty and program administrators used two instructional strategies to develop students as highly skilled young professionals. First, professors used a faculty-guided, experiential learning approach to teach students the knowledge and skills associated with professional practice in engineering. Second, faculty taught students how to interact with one another as professionals both by modeling collegial behavior for students and by requiring them to complete a variety of cooperative team research projects.

Faculty and program administrators repeatedly told us that the "best way" to teach students "how to think and act like professional engineers" was to get them involved, under the guidance of faculty, in a variety of experiential learning activities. Most of these learning experiences took place in research laboratory settings in which students, with assistance from faculty and doctoral students, were expected to use their understandings of engineering theory to solve challenging real-world problems. As the EE departmental brochure stated, these hands-on, laboratory-centered experiences were particularly important because they provided students with "more than the solid grasp of theoretical principles that course work can provide": "Students must also learn how to marshal resources, work on a research team, plan a long-term project, and make independent judgments. These skills, indispensable to scientists and engineers who will do significant work in the field, are developed in students through their involvement in individual and group [laboratory-centered] research projects." Many interviewees emphasized that "taking courses wasn't enough" to develop students into skilled professional engineers. As a program administrator put it, the way to make students "pros" was not to have them "sit in more classes" but, rather, to get them actively involved in "doing the real work of engineering."

In short, we came to understand that it was largely because faculty wanted students to develop a professional perspective on their field that they emphasized hands-on, laboratory-centered learning experiences more than traditional classroom-based activities. From their standpoint, developing this perspective was particularly important since beginning master's students often had a "textbook" (or, in our terms, an authoritative) understanding of knowledge: students assumed that, if they followed the correct procedures and produced a solution to a problem that matched the answer provided in the text, they had "found" the "single right answer." Several faculty emphasized to us that, as students addressed undefined problems in the lab and grappled with ambiguous procedures for solving them, many gradually cast off textbook understandings and began to develop, in our terms, a more contingent perspective. Students began to appreciate that, depending on the way they defined a problem and worked through it, there were often several "right" solutions. A program administrator explained how the laboratory experience helped students make this transition:

> In this master's program, all the students have to do some kind of research project for their master's degree, and, for most students that get their bachelor's degrees at public universities, that's their first experience at this kind of thing. They're making the transition from being very passive, sitting in the classroom and listening to what the professor has to say, and regurgitating information from a textbook where everything is sort of all laid out [to actually having to solve a problem where the answer is unknown.] This is the first time, I would say, where they are confronted with uncertainty. They have to go and read some original literature in the field. They have a task to do, and they are not told how to do it.

While hands-on, experiential learning activities were the focal point of Prestige State's EE master's program, students also completed four in-depth specialty courses to complement their work in the lab. In addition, students were encouraged to attend one or more of the approximately twenty-five weekly seminars given by departmental faculty and representatives from local industries. A program administrator, for example, told us that he strongly encouraged students "to listen to faculty, doctoral students, and industry experts talk about their work [in these seminars] and to get acquainted with these people": "I think this is really important because students begin to see what they're interested in. Once they find something, I tell them to go around to the faculty during their office hours and say, 'I'm interested in project work in your area. This is my background, and these are my interests. What do you suggest?' At that point the student is assigned to a 'shared laboratory area,' and they become a member of a research team."

Interviewees emphasized that it was in these teams that students, as apprentices, acquired knowledge and refined their research skills while working with faculty and advanced doctoral students. As leaders of research teams, faculty and doctoral students generally used what we have referred to as a facilitative approach to teaching and learning: as expert guides, they taught students their craft both by modeling their professional artistry and by encouraging students to test and apply their understandings of engineering theory and principles to real-world problems in the laboratory.

Many interviewees told us that Prestige State's engineering faculty and doctoral students modeled for master's students how professionals thought about and practiced their discipline. One faculty member, for example, said that he encouraged students to forgo a "textbook answer" approach to engineering problems by modeling his own contingent understandings of knowledge in the field. In his words:

> I tell students that I don't know exactly what the right answer to the problem is, that there may be more than one acceptable answer. I could be saying to a student, "I'm not even sure whether you're going to be able to prove that your solution is better than some other solution. It has to be a good solution that meets the requirements. There may be no right answer." And, in fact, sometimes I'll have two or three students working in parallel on the same problem—different approaches to the same problem [so they can understand that there can often be different solutions to the same problem].

Faculty also facilitated their students' development by requiring students to complete hands-on laboratory projects that allowed them to practice their skills. Interviewees told us that faculty, and often doctoral students, initially assisted students in defining the research problem, pointing out relevant literature, and exploring alternative testing procedures and analytical approaches. As students began to refine their re-search and problem-solving skills, faculty expected them to work more independently as professionals in the lab, consulting them only as needed. As one faculty member explained: "During a student's first year here, [he or she] is getting acquainted, so I give some direction. . . . By the second year, though, the student should start running. He [or she] should be coming to me every week or twice a week and saying, 'Here's the problem I'm working on, and here are the different possibilities I see as I move toward a solution.' And it's at that time that I would try to be helpful." This individual also noted how doctoral students helped master's students to learn their craft:

> I'll often say to one of my doctoral students, "Look, we've got a great crop of master's students here—somebody for you to teach and to help work with you." They were beneficiaries of that at the beginning [of their mas-ter's program] themselves. And they almost always say, "Great, I love it." . . . In the larger research projects, students have group meetings with faculty members at "x" intervals. And they also meet individually with their research advisor, but there's a lot of collaboration and a lot of orientation by senior graduate students of younger graduate students [here].

Many students and alumni told us that they greatly valued the hands-on research projects they completed under the guidance of Prestige State's faculty and doctoral students. One alumnus, for example, mentioned that these experiences were "more like 'real life' than something cooked up in a textbook." Another alumnus said that she was at first "shocked" by the amount of independent learning faculty expected her to do, but, in her words, "with graduate-level work, we only have our professors, and you just go read [by] yourself and look for answers": "That was a big change. . . . The professors didn't tell you everything—they would tell you where to look, but then you had to figure it out yourself." Another alumnus remarked, "I learned the most in those research projects—learning from my advisor and from the Ph.D. students in the group."

Many interviewees told us that these laboratory-based research proj-ects provided students with more than the opportunity to practice and hone their research and problem-solving skills. Faculty, in particular, stressed that these projects also helped students develop their communi-cation and teamwork skills. As a program administrator explained, teach-ing students how to interact effectively with others was viewed as an important aspect of their development as professional engineers:

> The worst thing, in my opinion, is a person who works in isolation and doesn't know how to work with other people in the field. . . . Some

students, when they come to the university, expect that they're going to learn everything from their professor. And I tell them when they come in, "You're going to learn more than half of what you learn while you're here from your fellow students. It won't be from your classes or your professors." . . . And some of them are a little shy and would rather go off alone and study in the library, and I say, "Forget it." You know. "That's not what this is all about. You have to work together in teams, and you're going to have to learn from each other. And there are a lot of very smart people around here, and you can learn a lot from them."

A professor pushed this perspective further when he remarked that learning how to work cooperatively in a group of professional colleagues was the most valuable lesson their master's students learned. As he explained:

Some people might think the research experience is valuable because students specialize. That's a benefit. But I don't view that as primary. I would say that the master's degree is still relatively unspecialized. The idea is that the particular area you choose to do your advanced course work in or that you do your project in is not as important as the experience of these other things, you know—doing the research and dealing with a research problem, dealing with a group of people who are trying to get different pieces of it done and having to coordinate with them. It's that experience that I think is much more interesting.

Prestige State faculty and program administrators made it very clear to us that, in their department, faculty were expected to interact with one another in a collegial—and collaborative—manner. This kind of interaction, they explained, provided students with a model for how they expected engineering professionals to associate with one another. One professor spoke to this shared understanding when he said:

There is an established culture in this department which is "be the best and use limited resources most efficiently and collaborate." Collaboration is a fact in our department. There are so many people collaborating in our department, and this is very unusual in top-ranked departments. . . . We run things differently around here. We have shared facilities, shared laboratories, joint projects, shared offices for students from different research groups. It's sometimes funny how it works. Sometimes, actually, the collaborations don't start with professors. They start with the students. So the students work together first and then tell the professors.

We learned that the collegial relations faculty generally had with one another set the tone for student interactions in Prestige State's electrical engineering department as well. Students in the program developed, in our language, a synergistic student culture in which they actively learned from, and taught, one another as colleagues. A program administrator told us that faculty consciously nurtured this student culture, noting that they "worked hard to promote collaboration [among students]—self-consciously, deliberately, and purposefully": "We try to tell them they're doing a good job at every possible opportunity. We try to put a very positive value on collaborative activity." An alumnus, who is now a professor in the department, provided a vivid description of the synergistic nature of student interactions he experienced as a student in the program:

> I learned a lot from the courses, I learned a lot from the professors, but I learned most of it [engineering] from the other students because we worked very closely together. We were very updated on what other people were doing. We had such an integrated program . . . students were doing state-of-the-art projects across the spectrum—so, if you knew the students well, and knew what they were doing, when you graduated you were pretty much state-of-the-art. . . . While I was a student here, I really enjoyed the learning process.

He added that master's and doctoral students frequently worked together and learned from one another, with doctoral students often establishing the standard of excellence by which master's students evaluated their progress.

Another alumnus provided a similar account when he remarked: "There were a lot of brilliant—really, I think, smart—students around. And we would work together, and we would get different feedback. . . . I think I got more, in a sense, from the other students, although maybe at the time I didn't feel that way—I thought I learned more from faculty. But looking back now I think I learned more from the interactions I had with other students." And an alumna described the student culture—and the professional interactions students had with one another—in these terms: "The graduate students are pretty much together. . . . People would be working on different areas of research, and it was kind of nice to know other areas of research too. It was kind of like 'work together and learn together'—that kind of environment."

In describing their overall experiences in the program, students and alumni repeatedly characterized their master's as, in our words, an apprenticeship experience in which they developed a more professional perspective on knowledge and skills in their discipline as well as a better understanding of how professionals interacted with one another in the field. One alumnus, for example, told us that the hands-on research projects he completed in the lab helped him to "really understand" his craft from a professional perspective. In his words: "Of course I heard about important underlying principles in my graduate courses, and in my undergrad program too. But I didn't really understand the full impact of them. But, with my master's program, I really understood what they meant because I got to work at a workstation and just try things out, experiment with things. I really got the full impact of [those underlying principles] in my master's program. It kind of opened up my eyes." Other students and alumni emphasized that the program enhanced their ability to analyze and solve problems in ways they never did as undergraduates. Several students and alumni also told us that they had become more independent and creative problem solvers. And almost all alumni said that they developed a fuller sense of professional identity as a result of their master's experiences. As one alumnus put it: "I left that program feeling really invested in the profession. I felt like a professional engineer."

Most employers also were pleased with Prestige State's electrical engineering program. One employer, for example, told us that he was so impressed with the "professionalism" of Prestige State's electrical engineering master's students that his company "didn't even bother to call the references listed on these students' résumés." Another employer said that he considered the program's alumni so "top-notch" that his firm offered them salaries that were 10 to 30 percent higher than those of graduates from other electrical engineering departments. Still another employer mentioned that his company, a multinational computer firm, strongly valued the "sophistication" of Prestige State's EE master's students. He candidly remarked that the company's recruiters greatly enjoyed visiting the program, telling us that "asking a recruiter to go to Prestige State is like asking kids if they want ice cream."

Understanding the Apprenticeship Idealized Type

Our case study of Prestige State's electrical engineering program illustrates the third type of master's program in our typology, the apprenticeship type. In broad strokes we learned that the nine cases in this program type had a character akin to a medieval guild apprenticeship system in which faculty, as "master artisans," prepared young apprentices to become contributing members in their professional guilds.

As with the ancillary and career advancement programs, we identified and became attuned to the overall character of this program type after completing the decision-situation analysis presented in part 2. In brief, stakeholders in the nine apprenticeship cases made broadly similar choices. All chose to utilize a facilitative approach to teaching and learning (decision-situation 1) and to provide strong departmental support to their master's program (decision-situation 3). In seven cases faculty and program administrators selected an academic orientation for their master's programs, whereas a professional orientation was preferred by stakeholders in the other two cases (decision-situation 2). In terms of the auxiliary decision-situations, campus administrators provided weak institutional support (decision-situation 4), and students developed synergistic student cultures in just over one-half of the cases (decision-situation 5).

As displayed in table 8.1, the nine apprenticeship programs in our sample varied considerably with respect to institutional type, number of degree levels offered, and discipline. Four were located at national institutions in departments that also granted bachelor's and doctoral degrees. Three of these cases—an electrical engineering program, a computer science program, and a microbiology program—were located at Major State University, while the fourth was Prestige State's electrical engineering program. A fifth program, theater at Phelps University, was also housed in a national university, but this department conferred the master's degree only. Three other apprenticeship programs were located at regional institutions and were offered by departments that granted both the baccalaureate and master's degree: environmental studies at Carver A&M University, electrical engineering at Moore A&T University (both predominantly black institutions), and microbiology at Southwest State University. The theater program at National Conservatory College (NCC), a specialty institution that conferred exclusively the master's in fine arts degree, was the other program in the apprenticeship group.

Our presentation of the apprenticeship ideal type, based on interviews with stakeholders across the nine programs, is separated into three parts. First, we describe the overall character of these programs and discuss two key purposes that stakeholders articulated for their programs. Second, we elaborate on three features that are characteristic of the apprenticeship program type: the strong emphasis faculty placed on "doing-

Table 8.1. **Distribution of Case Studies in the Apprenticeship Idealized Program Type**

Pseudonym Institution	Field of Study	Degree Levels
Case Studies at National Institutions		
Major State	Computer science	B.S., M.S., Ph.D.
Major State	Electrical engineering	B.S., M.S., Ph.D.
Major State	Microbiology	B.S., M.S., Ph.D.
Phelps	Theater	M.F.A.
Prestige State	Electrical engineering	B.S., M.S., Ph.D.
Case Studies at Regional Institutions		
Carver A&M	Environmental studies	B.A., M.A.
Moore A&T	Electrical engineering	B.S.E.E., M.S.E.E.
Southwest State	Microbiology	B.S., M.S., Ph.D.
Case Studies at Speciality Institutions		
National Conservatory	Theater	M.F.A.

centered" teaching and learning; the collegial relations among program participants; and the commitment faculty displayed toward master's education and master's students—a commitment grounded in their allegiance to developing "future professionals" in their field. Third, we discuss interviewees' interpretations of the overall quality and value of their master's experiences.

Character and Articulated Purposes

We came to appreciate that stakeholders across the nine apprenticeship cases understood their master's programs as, in our terms, guild apprenticeship experiences in which faculty, as master artisans, consciously invested in their profession by facilitating students' educational development as apprentices intent on becoming contributing members to their guild. To wit, an administrator in the theater program at National Conservatory College picked up their college catalog and read to us: "At [NCC], it is the responsibility of the experienced artist [which all faculty at NCC are] to continue his growth both through ongoing training and through the experience of passing on this knowledge to younger members of the profession. Similarly, the young actor . . . can strengthen his skills and approach theater artistry only under the guidance of active working professionals in an environment where standards are high and the emphasis is on creative growth and quality." He then emphasized that faculty expected students to have this same desire for sustaining and contributing to the profession: "I think acting is a calling. It's like the priesthood. There are people who are just called to do this kind of work, whatever it is—acting, artistry, science. . . . Our faculty want students who act on that intuition . . . people who want to continue the art and the performance of it."

Likewise, a program administrator in Southwest State's microbiology program told us that he and his faculty colleagues viewed themselves as professionals dedicated to helping students become invested professionals:

> We tell [our new students] that they have four semesters to become a competitive pro. We try to impress on them that we know what the market is and that we can help them shape themselves so that they can be competitive. . . . We keep our vitas on file so our students can see who we are. We want them to understand that they are working with pros. . . . We tell them that we will help them become pros but that they have to have fire in their belly, they have to be self-starters, because all faculty can do is point them in the right direction.

This same individual stressed that faculty wanted students who were committed to developing themselves as future "contributors to the profession . . . who are buying into the discipline, into the basic science, as a contributor—rather than as a voyeur who is just taking courses": "We don't want anyone here who is here to 'get their master's'—I hate that phrase."

Indeed, many students and alumni in the apprenticeship programs told us that they pursued master's study because they wanted to become contributing professionals in the field. One theater student, for example, said that he chose to invest three years of his life in Phelps' M.F.A. program because, in his words: "I wanted to become totally immersed in the field. . . . I wanted to work with professionals who would teach me the craft of playwriting so that, upon leaving the program, I would have the knowledge, the ability, and the confidence to exercise the craft." An alumnus of Prestige State's engineering program provided a similar perspective: "I decided to get the master's because . . . I wanted to enhance my ability to learn more so that I could pursue new professional directions— particularly to move into research and development work. I wanted to meet faculty who had interests similar to mine so that I could learn from them. I really didn't go for the master's because I would make more money in my job but because I really just wanted to learn more."

This emphasis on investing in the profession—either as professors who worked in the guild and "gave back" to it by mentoring young apprentices or as students who learned the "craft" and became contributing members in the field—captures the overall character of the nine cases represented in the apprenticeship program type. Consonant with this character, faculty and program administrators articulated two guiding purposes for their master's programs. First, they emphasized that the major purpose of master's education should be to prepare students for membership in their professions through an apprenticeship educational model. Second, they said that their master's programs should serve as "testing grounds" where students could explore their interests and decide how they wanted to contribute to a particular profession, as employees in the nonuniversity workplace or as college or university faculty trained at the doctoral level.

Interviewees told us that the major purpose of their master's programs was to apprentice students to the advanced knowledge and skills associated with their respective crafts. An NCC theater professor, for example, made this point unambiguously: "The apprenticeship model is the primary method we use to teach our students in this program. In my opinion, it forms the ideal way to train students in their craft." A Southwest State microbiology professor expressed this purpose in less direct terms, noting that his department's master's program sought to develop students who had the "knowledge and skills [associated with] being a scientist." "To me," he said, "the master's is not so much a proving ground as simply the learning ground for how to 'do' science, not just 'learn' science. And I think the way to do that is to get them working in the lab with me and with other students and to get them started doing the real work of science."

Throughout our interviews, faculty and program administrators also articulated another purpose for their master's programs: that they provide students with the opportunity to determine for themselves where they could make their strongest contributions to the field. A Major State microbiology professor expressed this purpose as follows: "I think a very important aspect [of the master's program] is to look at a person's heart. And I mean this sincerely—[to help students] find what they want to do. . . . I try to tell students that you're getting a master's but really your avenues are expanding. And they expand in many ways: you can go into industry, you can go into a clinical laboratory, you can even go on and get your Ph.D.—but that this is a time for you to evaluate your life also—and make some decisions."

Many faculty in the apprenticeship programs told us that they urged master's students to develop their interests in those areas where, in the words of a Major State engineering professor, they felt a strong "stake in the profession." Students developed this sense of commitment, he explained, by "talking to people, by reading, . . . by feeling [they] have a stake in engineering and are likely to take an interest in it and begin to read newspapers and technical magazines": "[You can tell when students] feel like they have a stake in the community [because] they try and understand the issues at a profound level."

Especially in the seven science and engineering programs, faculty advised students to engage in basic and applied laboratory-related research work to help them decide whether they wanted to work as master's-educated practitioners in the nonuniversity workplace or as doctorally prepared university faculty or industrial research scientists. Faculty in these science and engineering programs conceded that they often encouraged students to follow in their footsteps as academic faculty and researchers. Many students, alumni, and employers agreed, suggesting that, while faculty communicated their appreciation for the work done by nonuniversity practitioners in their fields, they often expressed the opinion that "real science" was done in universities, where there was more freedom of inquiry.

In a similar manner, faculty in the two theater programs stressed the importance of providing students with multiple opportunities to explore their interests and to develop their own stakes in the profession. Phelps and NCC faculty told us that they promoted this "professional self-discovery" process by encouraging students to experiment with a variety of "risky" theatrical roles, methods, styles, and techniques. As one NCC faculty member put it: "Our program's philosophy is to treat everyone as an individual and to push them to find their strengths as an actor. Other programs mold students to fit their vision of 'this is what an actor should be.' We try to have students create their own mold instead of having them fit into our mold."

In contrast to their colleagues in the seven science and engineering programs, theater faculty and administrators, as active theater artists themselves, urged students to enter professional, rather than academic, careers. Several individuals told us that they hoped students would some-day share their knowledge with aspiring, younger members of the profession (either as college teachers or as professional mentors assisting their understudies), but they had designed their programs primarily to allow students to test their interests in, and to determine how they wanted to contribute to, what they described as the real (that is, nonuniversity) professional theater.

From our perspective, these two articulated purposes were related to the decision-situation choices that faculty and program administrators made in the nine apprenticeship programs. To develop students as young apprentices for entry into the profession, faculty and program administrators chose a facilitative approach to teaching and learning (decision-situation 1) in which students worked closely with faculty in learning the principles and practices of their craft. Similarly, to develop their students for either research-based nonuniversity careers or doctoral study, faculty and program administrators in the seven engineering and science cases chose an academic orientation (decision-situation 2), one that accentuated specialized theoretical knowledge and research skills. In contrast, faculty in the two theater programs, in line with their purpose to develop artists for the theater, chose a professional orientation that highlighted specialized applied and theoretical knowledge as well as various field-specific, professional practice skills. Finally, because faculty and program administrators across all nine cases believed that the master's was critical to developing students into contributing members for their professions, all provided strong support to their master's programs (decision-situation 3).

Characteristic Features

In analyzing our interview material from the nine cases, we identified three characteristic features of the apprenticeship program type. Viewed in relation to the purposes articulated, and the decision-situation choices made, by stakeholders in these programs, these features shaped the overall character of interviewees' experiences in the apprenticeship programs. These features include the strong emphasis faculty placed on "doing-centered" teaching and learning activities—such as laboratory work and theatrical performances; the emphasis on collegial relations among program participants; and the commitment faculty made to preparing "future professionals" in their field by investing in master's education and master's students.

Doing-centered Teaching and Learning   We learned that most faculty and program administrators in the nine apprenticeship programs utilized a doing-centered approach to teaching and learning in which students practiced their crafts on a regular basis under the guidance of experienced faculty (decision-situation 1). This doing took place mostly in the laboratory or onstage, rather than in traditional classroom settings.

The major reason faculty and program administrators gave us for using a doing-centered approach was their conviction that professional practice, whether in the laboratory or onstage, was the "only" way for students to learn their respective crafts. A microbiology program administrator at Major State illustrated this perspective when he said:

> The only one thing [you should know about the master's curriculum] is that you come in to do science. The game is that biological science is a laboratory exercise. It's not a course work business. . . . The best thing we can do for folks is to have them take a couple of appropriate advanced courses and then get them onto a bench. And hopefully they realize that they know enough to learn anything they need to know. . . . It's a question of coming in and interacting with folks in the lab and realizing how to approach problems scientifically. . . . There's not a heck of a lot of reason for more formal course work.

Similarly, a Phelps faculty member suggested that a doing-centered learning approach was central to teaching theater: "With all respect for academe, sometimes the philosophical mind is far removed from the rest of your body. And theater is a dirty, concrete, tangible entity—you have to dig your hands into it to understand it well. . . . You can't teach theater separate from its life onstage. Theater is not about notes—it's about a real language and people interacting."

To be sure, the emphasis on doing in the lab and onstage did not preclude the need for traditional, lecture-based courses in these programs. Many faculty and administrators told us that they required students to enroll in core courses centered around established theories, concepts, and traditions in their fields. In all of the apprenticeship programs, however, faculty repeatedly stressed that these core courses were valuable only insofar as they provided students with requisite background knowledge— what one Prestige State electrical engineering faculty member referred to as "the necessary tools" in a student's "toolbox"—which would facilitate their hands-on learning experiences in the laboratory or on the stage.

Faculty and program administrators suggested that they used a doing-centered approach for one other reason: students were able to shed narrowly defined textbook understandings and develop a broadened and more contingent perspective on principles and practices in their fields only when engaged in the hands-on work of generating, testing, and applying knowledge. Put another way, faculty in the apprenticeship programs told us that, although most students were generally skilled at comprehending timeless principles and textbook examples, it was only when they entered the lab or went onstage and grappled with complex experiments or performances that they began to grasp that things did not always work out "according to the textbook." An employer of graduates from Major State's microbiology program, who had been a professor in the program prior to assuming his current position in a biotechnology firm, made this point when he explained that his profession did not need "science historians":

> It's easy for a student who does not come out of a research-based laboratory program to look at science almost as an accounting of what went on in the past, almost as history. In other words, he can understand what advances were made, but he may not know how they were made because he has not been in the lab to discover these principles for himself. . . . We need people who go into the laboratories and develop things and do things in new ways. A student who is taught by a professor who understands that and who teaches in that mode makes that transition into their work much more effectively than someone who knows the principles but doesn't know how they were discovered or what it's really like to face raw data and have the experience of trying to pull together a synthesis of what's going on and where to go. . . . Working with experienced professors and getting involved in hands-on lab work are essential in developing this perspective in students.

Stakeholders across the apprenticeship cases said that faculty implemented a doing-centered approach to teaching and learning in two major ways. First, faculty modeled for students their ways of understanding and practicing a particular craft. Second, faculty encouraged—and, in many cases, required—students to participate in hands-on learning activities.

In our interviews we learned that faculty were often deeply engaged in doing what they referred to as the "real work" of their profession. Faculty did not just talk about practicing their craft, they actually "did it." Many faculty told us that this doing orientation strongly influenced their teaching approach: most sought to model for students their understandings of knowledge and practices in the field while working with them in hands-on, doing-centered activities onstage or in the laboratory. A microbiology faculty member at Southwest State, for example, said that "having done [experimental work], you have a feeling for how to teach it. To talk about your own work makes the students know that it can be done, makes them feel comfortable that they can make advances, and that induces them to go into science—to have someone doing it who is their teacher." A professor in Major State's computer science program likewise remarked that the hands-on work he did in building computer hardware influenced the way he understood, then taught, the discipline to students:

> [I think that] you learn the theory in a hands-on way in computer science. . . . What I mean by theory is there are ideas that get employed in building computers . . . specific software, specific techniques and data structures that are used. The theory for me is: "Here are the different ways you could do it. Here are the alternatives. You might choose this technique for these reasons, the advantages of this one versus that one." That's what I mean by the theory. I don't teach "Here's how they did it on this machine." I use examples to say "You can do it this way" and "Look how they did it on this machine," but we don't teach one machine and say "Here's how they do it."

Students and alumni told us about, and often expressed appreciation for, the emphasis faculty placed on modeling and sharing their crafts with them. A second-year microbiology student at Southwest State, for example, mentioned that her advisor "required that [she] spend twenty hours a week in the lab, even if [she] didn't have things to do": "I know he wants me to see what's going on. . . He wants me to watch what he's doing and to learn from him." An alumnus of Moore A&T's engineering program indicated that his advisor constantly modeled his professional practice with students: "He always told us to come to the lab, and he would work with us. . . . I saw some of our group working until midnight with him. . . . He really wanted to get students involved. He wanted to teach us how to do science. And he was always there, doing it right in front of you." And a first-year drama student at NCC said: "What's wonderful [about this program] is that our instructors are going through the same process as we are. That's the big difference between [NCC] and other programs where the teachers don't act. These faculty constantly show us what they are striving for. It's very special."

Many students and alumni also communicated to us that, in working with faculty, they developed a more contingent perspective on knowledge and practice in their field. A second-year student in Major State's computer science program, for example, said that professors taught students how "to think analytically, not just memorize": "They help you get the whole picture and to know how to analyze it from many different points of view. They make you think about other factors to take into consideration, instead of just a narrow, 'textbooky' point of view." A Major State electrical engineering alumnus recalled how his advisor was constantly "modeling for us how you go about doing research in electrical engineering. He was candid about it. He would talk about confusions he had about particular problems and whether this was going to be a fruitful avenue to pursue. . . . That was, I think, when I first began to think like an engineer."

We learned that even as faculty facilitated their students' development as apprentices by demonstrating their artistry, they also stepped aside and encouraged students to discover for themselves the intricacies of their respective crafts. In keeping with their doing-centered approach to teaching and learning, faculty in the apprenticeship programs did this by requiring students to participate in a range of experiential learning activities, which included, among others, scientific and theatrical laboratory work, presentations at professional conferences and performances in professional theatrical productions, and the completion of a "culminating project."

Faculty and program administrators across the nine apprenticeship cases told us that they involved students in various hands-on projects in their respective "laboratories" almost immediately upon entering the program. These projects took many different forms, such as solving scientific problems at the bench, performing "ensemble" work onstage, and spending time developing software on personal computers. In their role as expert guides assisting their apprentices, faculty provided students with challenging problems and projects to get them started in these doing-centered activities. As a faculty member in Major State's microbiology program explained:

> I think master's students should get into the laboratory and start working on solving interesting, "do-able" scientific problems. Since they're new to the laboratory experience, I don't expect my students to be able to walk in here and choose a particular problem. It's my job to do that—to give them a few choices. I usually give them a problem that's more limited in scope so that they'll experience success [in solving it]. Then I generally explain the approach they should use, but I expect that they will design everything that is specific to the experiment. . . . I expect them to run the experiment— from setting it up from scratch, conducting it, taking the data and analyzing it, writing it up, and verbally presenting it. . . . I want them to learn how to do the work of a scientist . . . how to start thinking on their own and functioning independently in their work.

The faculty in the two theater programs viewed the laboratory assignments they gave students in similar terms. In NCC's program, for example, faculty assigned master's students challenging, open-ended problems, such as: "prepare the first act of this play without props" or "write and stage a one-act play" as an ensemble with other students. The aim of these open-ended assignments, as one member of NCC's theater faculty put it, was "to have [students] grapple with what theater is—their responsibility to the audience, the process of collaboration, what themes are important to them, how they personalize information. It's really the foundation of their training." NCC students performed their work in front of faculty and other students in "master classes," where they received feedback on their developing skills as artists in the craft.

Many students and alumni in the apprenticeship programs described their experiences in these laboratory settings with great enthusiasm. Interviewees, for example, told us that they so enjoyed these hands-on learning activities that they intentionally spent many hours participating in them. A Prestige State engineering alumnus said he was "in the lab all the time" because "that's where the action was in the program." An alumnus of Phelps' theater program likewise remarked that he and his peers were involved in theatrical activities "all the hours we were awake": "The learning process at [Phelps] is not just that you learn certain skills. It's not like a regular master's program. It's more like life. . . . You try and suck up as much of this [the opportunities for theatrical performance] as you can while you're there because it is three years of gold."

Still other students and alumni emphasized that they appreciated these hands-on laboratory experiences because they provided them with a taste for what "real professionals" in their fields actually did. As a second-year microbiology student at Major State put it: "The hands-on experience—learning how to do things in the lab—that's been really important to me. I learned how to do things in the lab as an undergraduate, but it had no comparison to what I've found real research laboratory work to be like. I've gotten a really good taste of that in the master's program." A Phelps play writing student voiced a similar account, noting the importance of being involved in stage productions:

> It's important to have the opportunity to practice interacting with other people in theater—understanding what it means to have a budget, what it means when a director wants a script now because the designers need to know things about the play. So it turns into knowing how to deal with that word *deadline*. Nothing happens until the playwright does it. And, if you don't do it, people get irate. You understand that part of the process because you have to do it in this program. And it's a *real* part of the process in this field.

Many students and alumni said that they also valued hands-on laboratory experiences for helping them both to develop broader perspectives on their crafts and to hone their own practices in the field. A Major State engineering student explained to us, for example, that, by applying his understandings of engineering theory to "real" problems in the lab, he had begun to "get a good handle on what the first principles mean" and the basic skills he needed to "really hone":

> For me, I think it goes back to this basic principle thing: In engineering you can't just learn how to read resistor codes and then you're a good engineer. You have to have the understanding and the insight behind it. I'm developing that in this program by going into the lab. Actually, it's become

a part of me—these equations, everything I've learned. Going into the lab and applying it, . . . I feel like I've gotten a much better handle on what it really means to be an engineer.

In addition to working in their respective laboratories, stakeholders across the nine apprenticeship programs told us that faculty encouraged students to participate in still another type of experiential learning: presenting their work to colleagues at professional conferences or in public theatrical productions. We came to appreciate that this doing-centered activity was closely linked to the emphasis faculty placed on developing students as contributing members of their professions. Indeed, many faculty told students that part of the "ethic" of being a professional was sharing their work with other members of the field. As a program administrator in Southwest State's microbiology program put it:

I tell my students to make their research of publishable quality because, if they don't, they're nothing more than a dilettante. [I tell them that], if you don't publish or present your work, you've wasted funding, our [faculty] time—that you're just a hobbyist. I want students to share their work with other people in the discipline. . . . So we get them off to a regional meeting as fast as we can, as soon as they have any real data. We get them in the lab as fast as we can. . . . When a student who has been lit up by an area has presented their research, they get a big sense of pride.

Many students and alumni indicated that they did, in fact, share their work publicly with others in the field, often noting that these experiences were extremely worthwhile. A second-year student in Southwest State's microbiology program explained, for instance: "[My] advisor really encourages us to interact with the scientific community at meetings, outside of the school—to get out and show our work. This gets you more in touch with the real world. Professionally, this is wonderful: as a master's student you can show that you've presented your work and that you've had some abstracts reviewed. And then it doesn't seem that frightening anymore—to make that transition from the academic world to the job site." A faculty member in Major State's microbiology program likewise described how one of his master's students, after presenting her research at a professional conference, came to realize that she could contribute to her field:

I recently had a student present a poster at the Annual Meeting of the American Society for Microbiology. After she had made her presentation, some of the very best people in the field came up to her and started to talk to her about her work. Later that day she said to me, "Oh my gosh, I've done something that's really important here. . . . When I was working on this research, I really didn't grasp how important, maybe even nationally, my work might be." And that event triggered it for her. She came back to campus a whole different person.

Faculty across the apprenticeship programs told us that they required students to engage in one concluding experiential learning activity: the production of a culminating product.[1] Not surprisingly, these "culminating projects" took different forms. Faculty in the seven science and engineering programs required students to write up their laboratory research in a thesis or project paper. In the theater programs, faculty expected students to produce a show, assume a major acting role, or design production then had them submit a written report that analyzed and described the entire process.

Many apprenticeship program faculty suggested that these culminating projects provided students, as apprentices, with a challenging hands-on opportunity to prove to their professors and themselves that they had achieved an advanced level of competence in their disciplines. As a professor in Major State's engineering program put it: "I think the master's degree implies a greater level of proficiency in your craft, and, without actually getting into some research problems, I don't think that [developing greater proficiency] is possible. . . . The big difference is the thesis project. The student has to become somewhat more independent and learn how to complete a piece of work and summarize it on paper. At the end of that experience, they walk away with a lot more under their belt."

Many students and alumni emphasized that, in completing these culminating projects, they refined their skills and enhanced their self-confidence. An engineering student at Major State, for example, said: "I think the thesis really has helped me to develop my skills . . . because I had to produce a finished product at the end, a product that worked and was useful and was original. And that was something I never did as an undergrad. As an undergrad, I basically studied from a book. . . . You didn't work on something that was tangible, that you could point at and say 'This thing works; this is something that is useful to somebody. That product—that's something I now take a lot of pride in.'" A Carver A&M environmental studies student articulated a similar outlook: "The thesis is helping to make me more professional. I have to be more independent, I have to write well, I have to think. . . . I've become much more observant, and I'm much more serious about what I'm doing. I feel a lot more confident because I think I have the skills to really do this stuff now." And a theater student at Phelps told us that her culminating project helped her to "know [she] could do this [theater administration] successfully": "I wasn't afraid of it any longer. I felt confident—that I knew I had the skills and the understanding of the work to be able to do it well."

Collegial Relations among Program Participants   In addition to requiring students to learn by actively performing, or doing, scientific research or theatrical work, faculty and program administrators in the apprenticeship programs also emphasized that professionals should learn how to interact with their other guild members in a respectful, collegial manner. Faculty and program administrators said that they taught this ethic by modeling it in the collegial relationships they shared with fellow faculty members and with students.

Faculty and program administrators told us that they wanted students to be able to interact collegially because they believed this was essential to enhancing their own, as well as others', contributions to the field. As a microbiology professor at Major State put it:

> I think the goal in science now is we put a man on the moon not because we had a bunch of Nobel laureates [working separately on it] but because we had a bunch of people working together with a whole bunch of different expertise, as a team. We're not the Louis Pasteurs anymore, who do an experiment by themselves and no one else is trying to crack the same problem. We've got team approaches to science now, and I think I'm in that philosophy. I want to have students, when they walk into a team, know that they're a team player in their expertise. [I want them to know that] they're damn good at what they do but that they can contribute [as a team player]—that there's a person right along side of them that's very good in physiology and a person who is very good in something else but that they can get together with these other people and that they can put another man on the moon if they want to.

In a similar way, a Phelps faculty member said that students in the school's theater program were required to assume roles outside of their specialty areas because they needed to "respect what their colleagues do in the theater": "Theater is not a one-person activity. It's a group effort. People have to learn how to get along with one another to put on a successful production."

One way faculty and program administrators taught students this teamwork ethic was through example—by interacting with one another as colleagues and treating each other with mutual respect. A Southwest State microbiology faculty member, for example, said that her relationships with departmental colleagues were like a "little piece of heaven": "The faculty here like each other and are respectful of one another." A program administrator in Moore A&T's engineering program described their faculty as "one big family": "We show lots of respect and collegiality toward one another. And we tell faculty that they need to do that with students too."

We came to appreciate that these collegial and respectful faculty interactions also entailed a dimension of personal humility. As one Major State microbiology faculty member put it, "arrogance isn't worth very much" in his department. An engineering professor at Prestige State also expressed this point: "Usually in top departments you have one god here and another god there, and the gods don't talk to each other. Everybody has this rose garden of their own, and nobody intrudes. . . . [But,] in this department, we're willing to share the research glory here. I think the era of 'single hero—change the world' has gone, at least as far as engineering is concerned. The products are very complex today and take a lot of people with different expertise working together." A program administrator in NCC's theater program, who annually renewed or failed to renew faculty contracts, told us: "Back stabbing is not allowed here. Those people are let go. We do not tolerate prima donnas."

As noted, collegiality also characterized faculty-student interactions in the apprenticeship programs. Interviewees repeatedly told us that faculty nurtured this collegiality by encouraging students to share their ideas with them and by responding thoughtfully. A Major State microbiology student illustrated this point when she remarked: "The rapport that is built up [between professors and students] is done in the journal clubs, the courses, and in the lab. There's a lot of give and take [because] the professor is not in an adversarial or tutorial position; he's kind of part of the gang if he's any good at all." A student in Carver A&M's environmental studies program likewise said that professors treated students respectfully, rarely "shooting down their ideas": "They really want you to learn. . . . They're successful professionals, but they're also down-to-earth human beings who talk to you at your own level. They never talk down to you." And a professor in Phelps' theater program communicated the respect he had for his students and their ideas when he said: "Faculty are the listeners here. . . . We put the students' learning first. We want students to have the opportunity to take risks and to test out their ideas. . . . When these fail— or succeed—we sit down with them and talk about why they worked or didn't work."

Not surprisingly, we learned that the generally collegial interactions faculty shared with one another and with students helped to establish the ambience, in part, for the way students related to one another. Students across all nine apprenticeship programs communicated to us that they respected one another and sought to enhance one another's learning through collegial, rather than competitive, interactions (decision-situation 5).[2] The following exchange between two microbiology students at Southwest State illustrates the collegiality among students in this master's program:

[Student 1:] I learn a great deal from the other students. No one is afraid to talk about their research, and nobody's going to stab me in the back if they find out what I'm doing.

[Student 2:] Yeah, it's really different than when I was at [another university]. There students didn't enter each other's labs. Everyone wanted to keep their work top secret, and there was a lot of sabotage—ugly things like unplugging people's refrigerators, even in the cancer center. I didn't like that at all. At [Southwest State] the doors to the labs are always wide open. I like that.

Engineering students and alumni at Major State described a similar student culture in their master's program. A second-year student said, for example, that he "never felt pressed by a sense of competition" with his peers: "We were always working together. I mean, I really think I learned just as much from other students in the lab as I did from the professors." An alumnus provided a similar account:

Certainly a rewarding and significant aspect of the program for me was working with other students in the lab. . . . A lot of times we would be working together on a project in the lab, and we'd find ourselves saying, "Geez, this is neat stuff" and "There are neat ideas here." We were just getting absorbed in the ideas. And . . . there was the case of finding, in our research, interesting connections to other fields and we formed a solution. . . . It was also the case that, when I had a particular problem with my research, I could catch somebody else and say "Hey, this is what's going on right now" and just have a sounding board, and I played that role for somebody else a few times. That was valuable.

In our view, a Phelps theater student aptly expressed the centrality of a collegial ethic in the apprenticeship programs. In describing her master's experience, this individual said that she learned, both from faculty and through her own interactions with other students onstage, that collegiality and collaboration were essential if professionals were to contribute to their fields: "I think it's up to us, to make sure that the people who leave here, the next generation, will think in terms of a collaborative art. . . . We, as artists, have to educate each other and create that sense of collaboration here and carry it with us so that, when we run into people later on who don't work that way, we can encourage them to be more collaborative—because it just fosters everybody's well-being."

Strong Faculty Commitment to Master's Education and Master's Students Across the nine apprenticeship cases, faculty and program administrators told us that they considered master's education a vitally important opportunity to develop highly skilled, contributing professionals in their fields. We learned that this conviction strongly influenced their decision to provide strong support to their master's programs, even when institutional administrators did not. (Of the nine apprenticeship cases in our sample, for example, more than one-half received weak institutional support.)[3] Their support, in turn, was reflected in their comments about the significant amount of time and energy they devoted to master's students (decision-situation 3).

As we came to appreciate, apprenticeship program faculty and administrators often supported their master's programs largely out of a sense of "allegiance" to their discipline; as faculty, many wanted to contribute to their fields by helping develop a new generation of skilled professionals. A faculty member in Prestige State's engineering program, for example, said that faculty in his department felt strongly that master's education was a necessary, and critical, step in the development of "real engineers" for the field. He "encouraged" all of his bachelor's students "to get their master's" if they wanted to do "real engineering." Likewise, a Major State microbiology professor stressed the value of the master's degree: "I think it's a very important part of training professionals for the field; it expands students' options and their careers." And a theater faculty member at Phelps told us that, in his program, he and his colleagues were committed to developing the "next generation of theater artists."

We would be oversimplifying if we suggested that this shared belief— that master's education could significantly enhance the caliber of members in a given profession—was, in and of itself, sufficient to justify the commitment of apprenticeship faculty and administrators to their master's programs. Indeed, many of these stakeholders told us that master's programs also contributed to a department's resource base, reputation, and mission. For the most part, these programs not only pulled their weight in terms of budget allocations per enrolled student, but they also produced alumni who enhanced their departments' reputations with nonuniversity employers and, particularly in the academe-oriented programs, with doctoral program faculty. And almost all of these master's programs also fulfilled a clear labor force demand, thus advancing their departments' community service missions.

Faculty and program administrators in the apprenticeship programs demonstrated their commitment to master's education in a variety of ways. To begin with, many stakeholders emphasized that faculty provided financial assistance to master's students. In Prestige State's engineering program as well as in the microbiology programs at Southwest State and Moore A&T, we were told that faculty aggressively sought and secured funding to support, either through teaching or research assistantships, all master's students who requested financial assistance. In the two theater programs, faculty allocated a substantial percentage of departmental tuition dollars to finance student scholarships and grants, supporting approximately 80 percent of their M.F.A. students. Even in those programs in which departmental student assistance dollars were limited, such as in Major State's microbiology program, many faculty hired master's students to work as laboratory or research assistants with research funds from outside the university.

Many interviewees also indicated that faculty were committed to helping students find employment in their respective professions upon graduation, either as Ph.D. students or as practitioners in the nonuniversity workplace. A faculty member in Major State's microbiology program said, for example, that he not only helped students "get in contact" with industry professionals but that the department also invited recruiters to interview master's students for various professional positions in the nonuniversity workplace. He added that faculty were also "very helpful" in placing their students in doctoral programs. Similarly, faculty in both theater programs told us that they spent considerable time preparing students for what one NCC program administrator described as the "grueling work of professional auditions." A Phelps program administrator remarked that faculty made "elaborate arrangements to get [master's students] out into the job market": "We cooperate with two other major schools to present our new actors to 250 professional casting directors through a one-hour ensemble production, and we ensure that each actor is a member of the Equity Union before they leave. We help our designers develop portfolios." Further, many interviewees mentioned that faculty used their own informal networks, via colleagues and alumni in the field, to help their master's students gain admission into doctoral programs or to secure professional employment outside the university.

Many students and alumni corroborated these accounts. One Moore A&T engineering student, for example, remarked that the chair "made a book of 120 pages of résumés" of students in the department and distributed it to every company represented at a recent on-campus employers' fair. An alumnus of Major State's microbiology program said: "Faculty always gave us lots of advice. And the newsletter that the department put out listing all the recruiters and the programs they set up to help you learn how to interview—all of those things were very helpful. So I thought the faculty really were helpful in getting me a job." And theater students at Phelps told us that, once they were admitted to the program, "faculty made a real commitment" to them. This commitment, they suggested, often included the unspoken promise that faculty would not only help students prepare for professional jobs but that they would also connect them with someone, either an alumnus or a professional colleague, who might audition them as well.

Perhaps the strongest indication of how committed faculty and administrators were to their master's programs was reflected in the time and effort they devoted to students. Faculty told us repeatedly that they took that "little bit of extra time" to provide students with individualized help and feedback. As one program administrator in Major State's microbiology program put it, "Even though we're real short of human resources, we do try to provide a lot of personal help for our students." A program administrator in Phelps' theater program said that faculty often worked with students in individualized tutorials, providing the instruction and feedback that students needed. And a Carver A&M environmental studies professor emphasized that he and his colleagues were "highly accessible": "There is almost unlimited counseling and mentoring in this program for students."

Students and alumni across all nine apprenticeship programs expressed similar views, telling us that, in the words of one Major State microbiology alumnus, faculty sometimes went "above and beyond the call of duty." A student in Phelps' theater program, for example, said that his advisor read "every word of every play" he wrote and provided individualized feedback to him on their strengths and weaknesses. A Southwest State microbiology student told us that faculty in that program "would stay in their offices until midnight to explain something to you": "Almost all of the professors are like that. They're concerned that we learn the material. They really care about us." And a Moore A&T engineering student summed up the personalized attention faculty in many of these apprenticeship programs gave to their master's students: "Faculty really take time with you here. They help you develop your whole self versus just getting your degree."

Finally, many students and alumni emphasized that their professors were committed to their being "contributing members" of their respective guilds. An engineering student at Major State, for example, said that he felt like he was "part of something important": "I wasn't just another grain of sand on a whole beach. I was really doing things other than just doing my homework. I was made to feel like I was part of something that mattered." An NCC theater student also expressed this point: "The faculty here made me feel like I was part of the profession. It was really special. I mean, they publicly introduced us to the audience as 'The Future of the American Theater.'"

Overall Stakeholder Evaluations of Apprenticeship Program Experiences

Across these nine cases, we discerned that stakeholders often understood their master's programs as guild apprenticeship experiences in which faculty, as expert guides, prepared students to become contributing members of their respective professions. Time and again, interviewees positively evaluated the overall quality and value of the experiences they had in these master's programs. Students and alumni emphasized that they had a beneficial professional development experience in which they not only learned the knowledge, skills, and practices of their craft, but they also developed self-assurance as contributing members to their fields. Moreover, interviewees told us that students frequently left these master's programs with a changed perspective on their professions, one, they suggested, that was rooted in a broadened appreciation for their field. In addition, many faculty and program administrators said that they greatly valued their involvement in master's education in large part because they took pride in developing new generations of well-prepared, highly skilled professionals. At the same time, however, stakeholders in the majority of the apprenticeship cases articulated one major concern: institutional support was not sufficient to allow faculty and program administrators to enact fully an apprenticeship educational experience in their master's programs.

Beneficial Professional and Personal Development Experience for Students   Many interviewees communicated to us that, in three related ways, students had a beneficial professional and personal development experience in the apprenticeship programs. First, students and alumni emphasized that they greatly benefited from learning under the guidance of experienced faculty. Second, students and alumni told us that they valued the high level of technical proficiency they had developed in their field. And, third, students and alumni expressed appreciation for the opportunities they were given to develop a strengthened sense of self-confidence and professional identity.

Students and alumni told us repeatedly that they valued learning the knowledge, skills, and practices of their respective crafts from outstanding faculty, who were, in the words of one Southwest State microbiology student, "really interested" in individual students. An alumnus of this microbiology program said that, although he "learned a lot" from many professors, it was his advisor who "really had a major influence" on him: "He taught me a few impressive concepts and had a very impressive vision of microbiology. He was a really interesting person—you know, a real inspiring kind of guy. He helped me get so interested in the field that I decided to go on for my Ph.D." This interviewee further noted that he was thankful to have had the opportunity to develop his scientific skills under his advisor's "care," particularly since his Ph.D. advisor [at a different institution] had been, as he put it, "no mentor, that's for sure." Many other students and alumni also emphasized that they appreciated learning their particular craft from professors who, in the words of one NCC alumnus, were "really experienced in the field themselves": "They were our coaches . . . people who cared enough about us to give us constant feedback so that we could become more independent, creative artists."

Students, alumni, and employers in the nine apprenticeship cases also valued the way these programs significantly improved students' technical proficiency as practicing professionals. Students in the academe-oriented science programs, for example, said that they often developed a solid understanding of specialized theoretical knowledge in their fields and improved their research and analytical skills. As a Major State microbiology alumnus put it: "[My master's] provided me with a good theoretical basis for what I was doing. That's the bottom line. . . . It was a whole new way for me to develop my cognitive skills—like knowing how to analyze data, interpret data, the skills of critical review." A Carver A&M environmental studies alumnus provided a similar appraisal: "I became much more observant over those two years. I had to learn how to think things through. And I had to learn how to really do research to understand the scope and the range of the problems I was dealing with in the lab."

Corroborating student and alumni accounts, employers noted that graduates from the science-based apprenticeship programs often came to them with a wealth of specialized theoretical knowledge and highly developed research and problem-solving skills. An employer associated with Major State's microbiology program, for instance, told us that its graduates really understand what it is like to work in a laboratory: "[They know] how to face the frustrations of research work, how to work through problems, how to get things done. . . . These grads know how to do it; they know what to do at the bench because they've done it in their master's program." Similarly, a professor who had recruited several of Southwest State's master's graduates into his department's doctoral program said, "[Southwest State] grads are very well prepared for doctoral study; they have both the theoretical background and a good grounding in the mechanics of doing research."

Interviewees from both theater programs likewise emphasized that students' technical skills were greatly improved because of their master's experiences. One NCC student said that her acting had become less stiff and more "natural": "I move more freely now." An NCC employer elaborated on this point: "[NCC] graduates know how to talk; their speech is better. They have a kind of energy—a kind of approach to the material—where you say to yourself, 'OK, this actor has been trained well.'" And an employer associated with both the NCC and Phelps programs remarked that he was delighted with the quality of their alumni: "In those programs there is a level of technical training that is sufficiently rigorous that students leave these programs having acquired certain skills. They are able to speak in any foreign dialect. They know how to project their voices so that they can be heard in any theater in the United States. They know how to scan a line of Shakespeare. They are able to discuss Sophoclean versus Euripidean theater without any difficulty."

Many stakeholders across the nine apprenticeship programs also told us that students gained self-confidence and strengthened their professional identities during the course of their master's experiences. Not surprisingly, interviewees suggested that, as students became more "accomplished" in their craft—through successfully completing challenging assignments and their culminating projects—they matured into more self-assured professionals. A graduate of Major State's engineering program described this change as follows:

> It was during my master's program that I developed a sense of professional confidence. . . . It took me three years to acquire some basic electrical engineering knowledge and to finish my thesis, and, at that point, I finally had confidence in myself—in my intelligence and my ability to work hard and grapple with solving problems. The contact I had with my advisor and my fellow students added to the sense that I can go into the lab and tackle and solve problems. It was a maturing process as an engineer, and certainly the maturing has continued. A significant part of my becoming comfortable as an electrical engineer happened in my master's program.

A Major State microbiology student described in different terms the shift to greater self-confidence which she experienced:

> It's when you can help someone solve a problem that you think "I'm not so dumb after all. I can think of that. I helped somebody." Doing that really makes you feel like you're a microbiologist: it's like you've learned all of this stuff, but deep down you don't know how much you know until somebody quizzes you or tests you or just asks you a question in the lab. And when somebody does that and you can actually answer them and talk like a microbiologist, you think school really helped. I mean, you begin to believe that you really are a microbiologist!

Students and alumni from both theater programs likewise told us how they had become, to borrow a phrase from one Phelps alumna, "self-confident theater professionals" by completing challenging projects. A second-year student at NCC said:

> One of the school's philosophies we hear around here all the time is: "only by attempting the absurd can we achieve the impossible." And students are encouraged to do a lot of that around here—to take risks and try out new things. That's been really valuable for me. I've tried risky things, and I've failed, but it was in failing that I discovered my own voice and the

impact I can have on an audience. I actually found my edge by going beyond it. I believe that an actress must dare herself to fail; otherwise, she will just fit into someone else's mold instead of creating her own mold.

Employers reiterated these student and alumni perspectives, often describing their master's-educated employees as "confident professionals." A theater director who hired many NCC graduates, for example, told us that she saw "a kind of professionalism" about the way NCC alumni approached their craft: "You can see that they know their way around a script or a reading. There is a kind of sophistication about their approach." An employer associated with Major State's engineering program likewise remarked: "My master's-trained employees are real go-getters; they tend to act a lot more independently than many of my other employees. They're just a lot more confident that they can start and finish the task."

Many faculty also emphasized that students developed into more self-confident professionals during their master's experiences. A professor in Major State's microbiology program said that many of his master's students cultivated "a scientific maturity" and added: "I don't think they necessarily would have gotten [it] if they had worked as a technician in industry. The master's degree really gives students the opportunity to learn how to think scientifically. . . . They have to be able to design experiments, to have broader views of what the implications of results might be, to have a broader knowledge base. As a result, they begin to have a more professional image of themselves, and I think that's important." In much the same way, a Phelps faculty member explained that, although many of her dramaturgy students, upon entering the program, felt "confused" about their place in the theater, by the end of "three years of collaborative work with others in the numerous productions, these students feel confident with who they are and where they come from and where they are going to. They know what dramaturgy is and what their role is [in the professional theater]."

"Appreciative Practice" Degree for Students and Alumni   Many students and alumni across the apprenticeship programs told us that they also valued their master's experiences for helping them to develop a new perspective on knowledge and practice in their respective fields. As we came to understand, this new perspective entailed the concept of "appreciation" in two senses of the word: "to grasp the nature, worth, quality or significance of" and to "value or admire highly" (as defined by *Webster's Ninth New Collegiate Dictionary*).

Students and alumni explained that one of the most valuable aspects of their master's experiences was developing the capacity to expand and enrich their understanding of their particular craft by learning, in the words of a Southwest State microbiology student, "how to see how things fit together—to get a bigger picture on the field." As a Phelps M.F.A. alumnus metaphorically put it, her master's helped her become "a broader thinker": "I really think I expanded my horizons. I think I broadened myself. . . . It's sort of like [Phelps] took me to the top of the hill; now I can see everything. The program helped me to climb a really steep hill and to look out and see what's really out there [in the field]." A student from Major State's microbiology program provided a similar perspective: "I've come out of this program with a different perspective on the field. Theoretically, I have a better understanding of what everything means. I have the big picture. And this has helped me to go out and attack research from a different angle; it's just a whole different way of looking at it. I don't just do it the way I'm told to do it anymore. I mean, I'm no longer just a pair of hands; I'm also thinking about the research and what it means. So I think there is a big difference in me."

Many students and alumni suggested that this "big picture" perspective gave them a new appreciation for their particular discipline and for the value of their master's degree. Several students explained that, while they originally pursued the master's degree to hone their skills and to earn a valuable workplace credential, these objectives became less pronounced as they developed a dual appreciation for the inherent worth of knowledge in their fields and their role, as professionals, in contributing to it. An alumnus from Major State's engineering program articulated this change in outlook as follows:

> I initially expected to get my master's degree so that I could go out and get a job in industry and that the degree would then lead me into good management possibilities. Things changed for me as I pursued the degree, however. I became just academically quite enamored with electrical engineering during my master's program because, well, I began to regard it as a kind of interdisciplinary hunting license, if you will. Electrical engineering, as a field, is so broad that you can converge into so many areas—physics, computing, mathematics. . . . It was a less confining area for me than physics was. I find this very exciting and rewarding.

Along these same lines, an alumnus of Major State's microbiology program told us that, while she originally pursued the master's to become "credentialed" for her position in an academic laboratory, during the course of her experience, she began to notice "a big difference in [her] contributions at work": "Things began to fall together for me. I began to integrate things, to see the big picture. I began to hold my head up in the scientific community. . . . I began to see myself as a scientist who could contribute to the field. . . . And, really, that's the bottom line." And a Major State engineering student commented that his master's degree was valuable "not just because it says M.S." on his résumé: "I learned a lot more about the field of electrical engineering, and I began to know exactly what kinds of jobs I would be good at—what kinds of jobs were out there and what kinds of jobs were important. . . . The degree, for me, isn't so much money and prestige as doing what you want to do. I don't see it as just a credential. . . . I see it as a way of channeling myself."

Indeed, we spoke with many students and alumni across the apprenticeship programs who told us that, by the time they neared completion of their master's studies, their interest in the master's degree as a credential had been largely replaced by their new appreciation for knowledge in their field and their role as contributors to it. Perhaps one Phelps alumnus best described this "appreciative practice" view of his master's degree when he remarked: "This program has increased my thirst for study and knowledge and understanding of my craft. I guess that says it all."

Satisfaction in Contributing to the Guild: Faculty and Program Administrator Perspectives   Apprenticeship program faculty and administrators constantly told us about their involvement with master's students— interacting with them in the lab, listening to their ideas, and helping them mature into contributing members in their profession. We learned that the "mentorlike" relationships faculty had with students, coupled with the professional success rate of many of their graduates, was very satisfying for faculty and program administrators. Many told us that they particularly valued their master's programs because they enjoyed helping students develop into well-prepared, highly skilled contributing members of their professions, or guilds.

Many faculty across these programs remarked, for example, that they found it "personally satisfying" to get students "excited" about their field. As a faculty member in Major State's microbiology program put it: "I enjoy teaching students about cutting-edge research. . . . When students have professors like that, I think that their excitement becomes evident in their students. There's a kind of ripple effect. It's satisfying to be involved in teaching students that excitement, getting them involved in the field." A microbiology professor from Southwest State's program provided a similar perspective: "I like to get students excited about doing research. I like to see . . . when they begin to take pride in their work. That's enormously gratifying for me."

Many faculty and program administrators also took considerable satisfaction in the high placement rate of their graduates. Faculty members in most of the science and engineering apprenticeship programs said that their master's graduates were eagerly recruited by corporate representatives and often had little difficulty gaining admission into doctoral programs. And, in both of the theater programs—a field that has a relatively low placement rate overall—faculty and employers proudly told us that many of their alumni were employed in a variety of professional theater settings.

Employers often pointed out to us that faculty had every right to feel "proud" of their program's alumni. An employer associated with Prestige State's electrical engineering program, for example, said that his company aggressively recruited from this master's program, whose graduates have had tremendous success within the company: "Their graduates can be productive for us right away." An employer from Moore A&T's engineering program likewise remarked: "I have no hesitations about hiring an A&T graduate. They are very well prepared in the fundamentals." Similarly, an employer of Southwest State's microbiology alumni commented that he was impressed with the "highly skilled and competent" individuals he had hired from the program. Employers associated with the two theater programs provided similar perspectives, frequently noting that NCC and Phelps M.F.A. students were considered to be among the most talented and well-trained emerging theater artists in the United States.

When faculty and program administrators reflected on the overall quality of the graduates they prepared for their respective disciplines, many enthusiastically expressed satisfaction in completing "a job well done." As a faculty member in Carver A&M's environmental studies program put it: "I'm really pleased with our students; we have a few that have gone on for Ph.D.'s and M.D.'s [doctors of medicine] and a few others who are working in industry. . . . And, professionally, I'm really proud of that. There's some ego there too—I'm proud of what I do. It's always gratifying to see a student that you taught go on to get their doctorate." Similarly, a program administrator from Southwest State's microbiology program explained that the faculty "take what we do here very seriously": "It's my personal belief that, when you graduate a student, they should be competitive with graduates from other schools. Ours are. They get good jobs in industry, and we have some students who go on for Ph.D.'s, and they do very well in their studies. We're proud of the product we put out here." Finally, a program administrator in Major State's engineering program told us of the satisfaction he took in preparing master's-educated professionals for the field:

> In my opinion, every one of these master's graduates is a very precious resource, and I want to make sure that they get their money's worth and they leave this place feeling that it was good for them. So, in that sense, there are many benefits that come back to you from this point of view, and it's not just financial. . . . I think people genuinely care. I was very impressed when I had these alumni dinners at how intensely they felt about their education and how they really cared about the future of the depart-

ment. It was very revealing to me. And I came away from a number of these meetings feeling that we had really done something well for those students and for our field.

Insufficient Institutional Support   Stakeholders in a majority of these apprenticeship cases expressed concern about one "trouble spot" in their master's programs: many believed that inadequate institutional support undermined their efforts to realize the full benefits of what we have labeled an apprenticeship educational model. Faculty and program administrators frequently told us that, if they were to enhance the overall quality of the apprenticeship experience, they needed additional funding to improve their laboratory facilities as well as revised institutional reward structures that recognized their instructional efforts.

Stakeholders in a number of apprenticeship cases emphasized that crowded and deteriorating laboratory facilities, coupled with the never-ending problem of outdated equipment, limited the amount and quality of hands-on experiences they could provide to master's students.[4] A Major state microbiology program administrator told us, for example, that the scientific laboratories in his department were literally "decaying at the seams": "I have to use duct tape to keep pipes together in my lab." Without adequate equipment and laboratory space, this program administrator indicated that he could not train students in the state-of-the-art techniques they needed as skilled professionals in their field. The problem was more severe at Carver A&M, where the administrator of the environmental studies master's program described the following situation:

> We simply don't have the laboratory space and the equipment to provide our students with enough exposure to laboratory techniques that they'll need when they leave [Carver A&M] and go into industry or onto Ph.D. studies. You need labs and equipment to run an environmental toxicology master's program. We're severely lacking in both. In the past, some of our faculty have tried to get around this by bringing their master's students up to [a nearby public national university] to work in their labs. These students need to learn more about scientific techniques, how you go about solving problems in the lab, how you use state-of-the-art equipment. . . . We need more space for labs and better equipment in this master's program. And, since this program receives absolutely no institutional funding at all—we have no graduate assets to speak of—I doubt that this will change.

Carver A&M students made it clear to us that the absence of laboratories and equipment had a major impact on their experiences in this master's program. As a second-year student put it: "We really need better facilities and equipment. It's a big deal to us if an undergraduate business student comes over for a biology course and breaks a dish or messes up a centrifuge. I just really wish we had our own equipment and our own facilities." An alumna of the program, who is currently a doctoral student at another institution, likewise said: "The equipment is so old at [Carver A&M] that it is hard to learn good techniques on it. I really feel it put me at a disadvantage when I got into my doctoral program."

Even where faculty and program administrators suggested that institutional administrators did support their master's programs—symbolically, if not financially—some indicated that they also struggled with space and equipment resources. At Southwest State, for example, where institutional administrators identified the microbiology department as the "model for their campus," faculty told us that they had insufficient laboratory space and equipment to provide adequate instruction to students. One program administrator made this point bluntly: "This institution hasn't developed the kind of infrastructure and general consciousness about the resources and time that is necessary to run a program like this." A faculty member elaborated: "Some of our labs are a mile away from our offices." That's less than ideal. And the labs we have here [in this building] are small and overcrowded. I have equipment flowing into the hallways." And a second-year student said: "The labs are really overcrowded. . . . And sometimes we don't even have the basic materials to complete our experiments. Sometimes the microscopes don't even work. I've been to a couple of the community colleges around here to use the stuff in their labs. It's much better than what we have here."

Coupled with these resource constraints, many faculty and program administrators told us that institutional reward structures, including promotion and tenure policies, were largely unsupportive of their involvement in master's programs.[5] Centering their comments largely under the umbrella of "teaching versus research," these interviewees emphasized that the personalized attention and individualized guidance they provided to students—what they classified as "teaching activities"—were not as highly valued in their institutional reward structure as obtaining external grant dollars and publishing widely in peer-reviewed journals. A faculty member in Major State's engineering program, for example, said that his institution, by rewarding research-related activities disproportionately over teaching, seriously undermined the time that many faculty could realistically devote to master's students. In his words:

> What you need to understand is that everything in this university is run on a shoestring. We're told [by institutional administrators] that they don't have enough money to pay our salaries, so we are told to bring in money from the outside. . . . It's like each faculty member is a small business bringing in grant money for the university. So we're doing that. And our

pay raises depend on that—far more than publications or teaching. . . . I mean, faculty are on a conveyer belt here. Let me give you an example. Our Ph.D. qualifying exams reflect this conveyer belt quality: it's difficult to get a faculty member to stay for more than one hour at them. Just imagine what our master's program is like if the Ph.D. [program] is like that. A master's student is hard-pressed to get a lot of attention from faculty. There definitely are some of us who do it, but we are not rewarded for it. . . . You have to remember that, given the pressure to get grant money and publish here, teaching becomes a marginal activity among many faculty. . . . There are not rewards for being a good teacher at this institution. It's not rewarded at all.

Another interviewee associated with Major State, an employer who recently left a professorship in the university's microbiology program, expressed a similar viewpoint:

I think that it's very important that research universities have both this training mode and the research mode. I think the university struggles with how to do that. I did a lot of teaching when I was at [Major State], and I took great pride in it. I really enjoyed it. I never felt that the university knew how to evaluate that though. In other words, the university realizes that it should, the department realizes that it should, but, in the final analysis, how your research is going is 90 percent of what you get evaluated on—not how good you are as a teacher. There needs to be more of a balance in there somehow. You need both. And I don't think the university knows how to do that.

A second-year microbiology student added her own perspective on this issue when she said: "Teaching is just as important as research, in my opinion. I mean, I've had some teachers who only care about the research, and they don't do a very good job teaching. . . . I would rather have a little bit weaker of a researcher and a stronger teacher than the other way around. You're going to get experience in the lab eventually, but, to get that background and the other things that you need, you really need some people who are really kind of showing you the way and are interested in you."

Faculty and program administrators in many of the other apprenticeship programs told us that, while they believed it was important to provide their students with individualized instruction and personalized attention, this was seldom rewarded in their universities. As a result, they were often frustrated in their attempts to realize fully an apprenticeship model in their master's programs. At Carver A&M, for example, a program administrator said that, although university administrators boasted about their tremendous success in mentoring African-American students onto medical

school or doctoral study, they were changing tenure and promotion policies to reflect a greater emphasis on grants- and research-related activities.
Indeed, a high-ranking institutional administrator at Carver A&M told us
that faculty would soon be evaluated "90 percent on their research and 10
percent on their teaching." And even in those programs in which there
was no tenure by design (such as the theater program at Phelps), faculty
stressed that institutional policies nonetheless failed to reward teaching-
related activities.

While some faculty and program administrators expressed concern with
the weak institutional support their master's programs received, we
learned that stakeholders were generally very pleased with the overall
quality of these apprenticeship master's programs. Students and alumni,
in particular, greatly valued learning from those they thought of as master
artisans, who facilitated their professional development as contributing
members in their fields. Perhaps an NCC faculty member best expressed
how valuable this apprenticeship experience was for students when he
read the following account an alumna had written about her master's experience:

> Since I left [NCC], I have acted professionally in more than forty plays and
> two PBS [Public Broadcasting Service] films, taught workshops at the high
> school, university, and graduate level, and appeared solo before more
> than three hundred audiences as an 'affiliated artist.' During that time,
> and I say this with pride, I've felt like a member of a medieval craft guild.
> After serving my apprenticeship at [NCC], I traveled for many years and,
> ever since, have contributed to a wide range of projects under various
> masters.

9

Community-centered Programs

English at Longmont College

Longmont College, located in a picturesque New England town, is a well-endowed liberal arts college enrolling about two thousand students. While it has long been known for its undergraduate programs, the college also offers several master's programs that extend and complement its undergraduate liberal arts focus. One of these is the master of arts in English, a seventy-year-old summer program that has operated as a relatively autonomous unit of Longmont College. During the program's six-week summer sessions, students and faculty reside at the college's conference center, which is located a few miles outside of town. This center consists of large, well-kept, old wood-frame buildings set among spacious lawns and surrounded by low mountains.

According to the program's catalog, faculty and administrators associated with Longmont master's program in English attempted to provide students with a "congenial natural environment" conducive to sustaining the "intellect and the spirit in a refreshing balance of society and solitude," while concurrently providing them with time to discover not only literature but also "place and community." The catalog stated further that the program's historic emphasis "has always been the personal bond between teacher and student, upon the creative and critical, rather than the mechanical and pedantic, and upon the liveliness of writing, literature and theater." Every one of the stakeholders we interviewed supported these statements: they told us repeatedly that they experienced this program as a time for community and as a place for liveliness and creativity. Interviewees also emphasized a quality that was not described in the catalog. They spoke at length about how, tucked away in this idyllic setting, they became much more aware of the larger society in which they worked during the rest of the year. In so doing, they indicated that the program often strengthened their professional commitment, and enhanced their capacity, to "make a difference" when they returned to their regular jobs.

Longmont administrators—who chose not to hire full-time, tenure-track faculty for this summer's-only master's program—recruited the majority of their roughly thirty faculty members (approximately one-third of whom were women) from institutions such as Yale and Princeton as well as from British institutions such as Exeter and Oxford. Most of the faculty were literature scholars, although several had focused their research and instruction on the teaching of language and literature, and others were actively involved in the professional theater. Several faculty were emeriti professors. Faculty contracts were for one summer only, but administrators invited most faculty members to return the following year. Many accepted the offer, often turning down opportunities to earn higher summer salaries elsewhere.

Of the approximately 250 students enrolled in the master's program, about 80 percent were experienced high school teachers, many from rural schools around the country. Most of the other students spent the rest of the year either as doctoral students or editors. About one-fifth of the program's graduates eventually entered doctoral programs. We learned that word of mouth was the program's most effective advertisement and often drew people from across the United States.

A program administrator told us that several of the program's best students were people who had a combination of F's and A's on their college transcripts. He said that, since the program had no set requisites for admission and was designed to "meet individual needs," this was not a problem. As for the quality of students, faculty told us that elsewhere they had worked with more academically prepared and articulate students but had never seen students who were as committed or as much a source of inspiration and ideas.

Program administrators worked hard at finding grants and other sources of financial aid to make it possible for students to attend this relatively expensive program. All of the students in the writing concentration, for example, received tuition grants for at least the first year, while many others received scholarships. In addition, administrators obtained grants to establish a large computer lab and to lend personal computers to students so that they could remain in contact via computer network during the academic year.

The Longmont master's program in English consisted of ten courses, which students were expected to complete during four or five, preferably consecutive, summers. When we interviewed there in 1990, these courses were organized into six categories: writing and the art of teaching, English language and literature through the seventeenth century, English literature since the seventeenth century, American literature, classical and Continental literature, and theater arts. Students were required to select six courses from the four literature categories and another four from the remaining two categories. The program did not require a thesis, internship, or comprehensive examination.

Although the program had undergone few changes since its establishment early in this century, during the past decade administrators initiated a concentration in writing in order to make their program more relevant to teachers, to diversify the student body, and to reverse a decline in enrollment. Supported by external grants, this concentration was designed primarily for rural school teachers from around the country. There was also an initiative to attract teachers from inner-city schools as well, with the result that teachers from public and private schools in both rural and urban settings spent the summer working together. Moreover, we learned that a theater concentration had also been added to infuse an artistic sensibility into the program. The professional actors responsible for this concentration staged regular evening performances, but their most salient contribution occurred in daily classes during which, in the words of one student, "they help us make vital connections between writing, literature, and theater."

Longmont's English faculty and program administrators—and, for that matter, campus administrators—emphasized that making "vital connections" informed their master's program throughout. As they communicated to us, faculty wanted to help students see connections between the ways they were learning in the program and how they could use these approaches in their teaching. As one program administrator put it: "I'm skeptical about patriotism and so forth, but nowhere else do I feel, actually, that I'm as in touch with an entity called 'America' as I do when I'm here. Nor do I feel anywhere else that what I'm doing has as much of a direct impact on the social good as here. I find it an immense privilege to have this position at this time. That's why I come back [every year]." As the following remark made by a faculty member indicates, it was not only program administrators who believed the program should contribute to the well-being of society:

> Students don't just come here to exercise their minds. They want something they can take back with them. They need to have something that's workable. . . . They want to know which theories work, and which ones don't really do anything in terms of enriching a book. There is a healthy skepticism of theory here, in the sense that it is not just taught as theory. One of the reasons that teachers enjoy [Longmont] so much is because we

don't ignore critical social problems because they are so big and difficult. This school is really a place to grapple with those things.

In describing their experiences in the master's program, Longmont interviewees voiced four major themes. First, they emphasized that the program focused on strengthening program participants' commitment to making a difference by drawing upon one another's diverse backgrounds and experiences. Second, they emphasized that the program was designed to provide students with perspectives and skills that were of direct value to them when they returned to their professional positions, usually as teachers. Third, interviewees described, in our terms, the broadly dialogical approach to teaching and learning they experienced both in their courses and outside of class. Fourth, and closely related, Longmont interviewees spoke enthusiastically about the strong sense of community in the program.

Longmont faculty and administrators told us repeatedly that they wanted their master's program to nourish all participants' capacities to make a difference. Elaborating on this point, a program administrator, who was also an alumnus of the program, described what he and others referred to as the "Longmont ripple effect." It begins, he said, with program administrators and faculty who seek to make a difference for their students, whom they see as preparing to go back and, in turn, make a difference to the thousands of students who they then teach. Indeed, many students and alumni told us that the faculty's emphasis on serving society often strengthened their "commitment to secondary school students" and nourished their "desire to contribute something."

During our visit at Longmont, we also came to understand that faculty appreciated the commitment students brought to the program. As a faculty member from England explained: "I like the commitment of the students; they are different than students in England. . . . These students don't see me as a ticket to a career." Another faculty member conveyed this idea with a phrase she had coined: "I call it the 'piranha fish factor,' which means that you say something in class, and they are just into it, because they are all just so anxious to sort things out. It's something to do with their motivation and their sense that they have a very small amount of time to get something very special." Students, too, told us that they greatly appreciated one another's commitment. One alumna put it this way: "You're with teachers who work their butts off ten months of the year. They come here, sacrificing their vacation, to study all summer. The whole attitude is that 'I'm learning these strategies, and I have these people to connect with, and I can take these ideas back with me and can return next year.' And, instead of feeling zapped, you feel energized."

In the context of describing the program's commitment to making a difference, several interviewees emphasized the importance of leadership. One faculty member attributed the successful integration of the socially "relevant" writing and theater concentrations in the traditional literature curriculum to "the vision" of the former director. Faculty stressed that program administrators were "leaders who love their work" and who knew the importance "of choosing great faculty" who were committed to making a difference. Along these same lines, a program administrator described leaders at Longmont College and in the master's program in English as "empowering": "They give power rather than take it. . . . It's a certain way of being in the world: It's [being] a participant in the world." He then explained that the way he and other program leaders "gave power" exemplified the Longmont ripple effect. The program leaders made a difference to the faculty, who, in turn, "didn't just see their twelve or so students but also the hundreds of students behind those teacher-students."

We learned that faculty and administrators, in part to strengthen this commitment, encouraged program participants to share their different perspectives and experiences on schooling, teaching and literature with one another. By way of illustration, one program administrator indicated why they "paired" public school teachers with teachers working at private schools:

> Now if the gap between public and private schools is getting bigger and bigger, as I believe it is, those private school teachers need to know what's happening in the public schools. If they are preparing students who are going to make decisions about all of our lives, and they are, they jolly well better have some experience with the real world. They really team up with each other, live as each other's roommates. I'll have a student from one of the most elite private schools in the country working with somebody from a very poor, isolated rural school. They discover quickly that they have more in common in terms of the questions they have about themselves and what they're teaching and reading than they have differences.

Faculty and program administrators told us that they greatly appreciated the diverse perspectives and experiences students shared with them on literature and teaching. In the words of one program administrator:

> The thing that's most special about this place is the students themselves. You could look at the brochure and say that it's the faculty members that make this place what it is, but they come here *because* of the students. Quite a few of the faculty have told me that—that they would not come if they knew they would find, say, [Ivy League] students here. . . . They're look-ing for the types of people we have here—people from all over the country

who don't necessarily have an academic background. . . . The faculty has come to expect that these students who are nontraditional are the ones who contribute the most valuable insights, who think of things that the professor never has. The professors say it is very refreshing to come to Longmont because of that other view, to see how the rest of the world is reacting to literature.

Students reiterated these faculty views. As one student, whose comments mirrored those of many of his peers, put it:

One of the unique qualities of Longmont is the diversity of the student body. It's part of what higher education is meant to do—to challenge people to enter into a dialogue that creates new perspectives and new ideas and points of view. When you have a student body that comes from traditional East Coast schools and Indian reservations and rural school districts and the odd guy from an urban school [gesturing to a fellow student] who says, "I don't want to have anything to with this stuff," it is tremendously provocative. People who are parts of our classrooms here come from situations that are so alien to the traditional academic environment, and they provide a real challenge to a professor. Students will say, "Hey, that doesn't wash in Nevada." It's a very challenging place to be a professor.

Longmont stakeholders also spoke at length about a second theme: the program's emphasis on helping teachers become more skilled at translating their knowledge of writing and literature into workable understandings for their students. Students and alumni commented that one way faculty did this was by making literature and writing relevant for students. One student, for example, told us: "In my writing class now, what they look for is how to teach English—how to bring English across, how to understand English and teach it, to everyone, not just a small 1 percent of the world or the country. It's not a graduate school where you talk about deconstructionism. Sure, you leave 99 percent of the people behind, and what good is that? It's great that you can talk about that in intellectual circles, but here it's 'English for everyone.'"

Another way Longmont faculty helped students become better teachers was by interweaving literature, writing, and theater throughout the curriculum.[1] An alumna described how she experienced this "interdisciplinarity":

Everybody is finding out how the word can come alive, both in the teaching of writing and in the teaching of literature. It's now a common link. A class with actors is just so magic, it's incredible. Actors have come into my writing classes and talked to us about dramatically reading a story, not a script, a story—having students go into groups, giving them a page or two of text, and having them decide how they are going to divide up the voices in the text. . . . A group will do a presentation of the page, and there will be discussion of why they did it that way. . . . It provides a way of talking about literature from a performance point of view and getting at the intention of the author by having [the students] voice the words.

In effect, this interdisciplinarity encouraged English teachers to draw on three forms of expression, rather than just one, when teaching literature in their own classrooms.

The third major theme faculty, alumni, and students emphasized was that faculty provided students with the opportunity to understand, and practice using, teaching methods that were based largely on dialogical interaction. A professor articulated why she as well as many of her colleagues used a dialogical approach to teaching in the program:

I really believe that what we don't come to know together we won't know very well. . . . If I want to use some jargon, I'd say that we have to construct the knowledge we're going to know together. I think it would be just horrible if I just told the students what I know—to be put in a class with these wonderful experienced teachers. If I were to put on the board the things that I think are important about a text, I would miss what arises from the group, which is much more complicated, complex, important, significant, and goes beyond what I can imagine. But I still think, because I've thought about those texts longer than they have, that I have things to say, and I want my voice to be in there. I'm not going to be quiet and let them have to wonder what my interpretation is, so I get my voice in there.

We [academics] are trained to read as graders and evaluators, so a good bit of our students' imagination and energy goes into trying to understand what we want, what we expect, the conventions—right here at Longmont. So I try hard to figure out a way that will let me read what my students up here write for me and to respond to their texts as if they were valued correspondents of mine. So that we get a chance to think on paper about what we're doing and to learn to really read each other's things. If we can do that, all kinds of barriers break down, and people start struggling to make meaning. And they forget showing off and performing and focusing on conventions and genres, and all their abilities as writers come out. We even get to think a little bit. I want them to go away knowing that so well that they simply can't be just evaluators in their own classrooms. We work hard on this, and naturally they get excited, because some of them have never had anybody, until then, really read what they're thinking, except to assess their understanding or their mastery of conventions and formats.

Many students and alumni enthusiastically described the dialogical interactions they had with faculty. One student, for example, told us: "The professors here are the best. Unbelievable. . . . None are finished learning." Another student added: "Part of what's neat about it is that, while the professors share some similarities in approach, they're all very different. The courses are not dogmatic. The approach is to help get you, as a teacher, to push yourself beyond." An alumna provided a fuller description of this dialogical process:

> What happens [in the classroom] is initially determined by the teacher: they invite the way the class should go. And, overall, the teachers here are far more involved with the students than at other places—willing to give up control and not feel threatened by it. In many other schools, the professor barges ahead because they don't want to be interrupted and questioned. They don't want to lose footing—because a student could run by, pass them by at any moment. There's not a sense here that the faculty feels threatened by you—more that they are inviting you to join them. It's just so different [from other graduate schools]. And, because of what happens in the classroom, it moves out of the classroom. Classes often don't stop. A group will move outside of the class into the grass or out to lunch and keep talking. Different pedagogy is stressed here: students are in groups. You're put in charge of your own learning more here, and [you're] more respected here, than in any other school. And there is this sharing.

The comments of this last alumna point to the fourth theme expressed by Longmont stakeholders: the strong sense of community in the program. A student voiced this theme as follows: "I think the biggest selling point here is community, because what I see here, the professors and the students working the same way—I think most of the education that's done here is done outside of the classroom. It's out on the porch; it's at dinner. If it's not at dinner, it's in the barn. That's where I've found most of the education happens." Another student told us: "The greatest things that go on here don't go on in the classroom. They go on in the theater, in the readings, at dinner."

Interviewees gave several reasons for the strong sense of community in their program. To begin with, many remarked that people did not feel "packaged and commodified." As one faculty member put it: "What it *is* about Longmont is something to do with closeness, in so many ways, and high energy input. . . . I don't know American academic life, but I've heard it's very competitive; it has a star system. Really, knowledge is commodified; what you are is packaged and commodified. . . . But at Longmont that's quelled. I don't think I'm idealizing or romanticizing at all. I genuinely think that this powerful interaction happens." Another reason for the sense of community was the strong respect participants had for one another. "There's great respect for people here," one alumna commented. "The faculty don't seem impressed with themselves." Interviewees also said that this sense of community was related to a "lack of hierarchy within the faculty."

Interviewees emphasized that this sense of community animated the way faculty interacted among themselves and with students. An alumnus noted that the "professors are like peers." A student told us: "The professors—I can't go over this enough—none of them are worried about doing this or that research. They're there to help you all the time. If you wanted to talk with them for half an hour on the porch, they were there."

Other students suggested that professors were not fully peers, only like peers. As one faculty member explained, the faculty are "peers of the students, but at a distance," pointing to the faculty-only table at the center of the dining room as a kind of metaphor for an informal boundary between faculty and students. Another faculty member said: "People also have to remember to keep apart at times too. . . . Teaching can be so intense." An alumnus made this point by observing that the professors are "supersaturated learners," while the students are just "culturally literate." "It's not that the supersaturated learner is the ideal," he said. "It's more give and take, especially now that the canon is opening up and we're not privileging just some voices. But the faculty are more grounded in the knowledge."

In evaluating their overall experiences at Longmont, interviewees made two general observations. First, many indicated that the program exemplified an alternative approach to the traditional model of graduate education. Second, many interviewees emphasized that the critical perspectives and the dialogical teaching approach students learned greatly enhanced their capacities to make a difference in their professional lives, usually as teachers.

In regard to the first observation, interviewees expressed pride that they were participating in a program that was different from the traditional model of graduate education, and, in so doing, interviewees often made comparisons with other programs. An alumna who was working on her doctorate elsewhere told us:

> You walk from this place [Longmont], even each class, thinking that there's so much to life that you can do—as a teacher—and that you can attempt as a human being. Instead of feeling incapable, you feel sort of liberated and challenged. The other part about this place is that it is so charged—magnetic, electric. . . . It stretches you not only intellectually but also socially, culturally, poetically, dramatically.
>
> Here the doors are open. At other places I feel like all the doors are shut. I get zapped during the academic year [in my Ph.D. program] and come

here and get reenergized. There's so much networking here and sharing of ideas and intellectual stimulation. And there's very little of that at other graduate schools I've been at. [There] people are competitive with each other, don't have time to talk . . . not really concerned with anything except the old publish-or-perish thing—all for "number one." But here there's so much sharing of ideas. Every day you're convinced that twenty heads are better than one. There's such a stark difference between the two worlds.

Other students provided similar accounts. One student remarked that he tried to get his master's degree at several other institutions but had always ended up dropping out. Many of those programs, he said, "are such crap—a lot of people getting credits. . . . But this [Longmont] is what a master's education should be about. . . . It is not [just] a means to a slip of paper." Several students, who had "lousy experiences" in other graduate programs, said that, although they initially "dragged themselves" to Longmont, they now "run" there every summer.

It was not the case that Longmont's program was easy and comfortable. To the contrary, many interviewees stressed that it was very intellectually demanding. "People push themselves to do the best possible work," an alumnus informed us, because, in her words:

you respect your teachers very highly, and you want them to respect you. You're invested, and I accomplish things here—and I know others do— that you don't think are physically possible and that are at a very high level of language, of communication, thinking, ideas. You'd think that people would be competitive. But there's no such thing as a bell curve here; you're rewarded for the level of your performance, and, if everybody gets an A, that's fine. You're not really competing with other people, but for quality.

One student told us that Longmont exemplified a "different" approach to graduate education, and he challenged us, as researchers, to contrast Longmont with more traditional master's programs. "What makes Longmont happen," he said,

isn't just the professors, or the quality of the students, or what happens in the classrooms. It's this sense of us as a community, bonded together and tied into this thing that Longmont epitomizes for us. And I guess that's a challenge for other graduate programs to try to create in their own environments, which is going to be very difficult, given what they have to live with. But it's more than the physical space. It's a psychological landscape; it's a sense of identity, of belonging to this project. If you take a more typical university's program, you have day students and evening students, and often it's not a residential program, so you've got people who are pulled in five directions at once. So how do you put them all together and give them a sense of being a community of learners together?

And what I'm suggesting is that not only is it a nice perk when that happens but that it may well be integral to creating the dynamic. It's like a synergy that happens. It's because of this notion that we learn together. I'm not just learning in my class; there is an intensive interaction because of that. It happens at meals; it's just always happening. . . . Intense interactions are typical—never stop around here. That's part of what makes this place work. And it would suggest to me that that's what would energize a graduate community at any university. But it means you have to pay a lot of attention to things outside of the curriculum and the quality of the professors and the academic demands that you make on your students. You have to look at the students as a whole and at their life together. That's what helps create an academic community.

If the point of your project is to understand what's happening with master's programs in this country, I have a sense that Longmont doesn't fit into that category. One thing I'd say is that, as far as its academic rigor, it is one of the most rigorous. And it's clear that all the students that come here are highly motivated and competent, and you're not going to find a nine-to-five teacher on this campus. The students that are here are self-selected. But the niche that Longmont fills in terms of the kind of graduate program that it offers is certainly not normative at all. So your challenge is to figure out what Longmont can tell you about this level of graduate education in more normal environments—because you can't expect this to happen at a typical university.

The second observation stakeholders made when evaluating their master's experiences was that the program helped students learn how to interact more effectively with others, especially their high school students. Employers, in particular, stressed this point. A high school principal remarked that the Longmont alumnus he knew had begun to "allow the kids to discover how things are" by stressing "thinking and problem solving." Another employer said that students in his Longmont alumna's classes "have seen a big change in her": "She used to 'talk at' them and give 'objective' tests, but now all her exams are written essays. She puts great effort into commenting on their writing, and the students are doing things; they're involved, and that means a lot to them. In addition, she has her students do portfolios, following her own Longmont teachers. Her kids come out of her class saying things like 'I want to be in her class again!'" Students and alumni also told us that employers appreciated the "ripple effect" associated with Longmont's program. One alumna, for example, said, "My former principal went through a series of interviews with kids for scholarships—this sounds like I'm bragging—but he came back and said that 'every other one of your students said that they enjoyed your

class the most, because that was the only class they ever got to say anything, and that meant all the world to them—giving them their voice.'"

For their part, students and alumni emphasized that their master's
experiences had a significant impact on their teaching. As one alumnus
told us:

[My professor] taught me how to teach each child's text as if it was a real
text, not just an adolescent text. That was profound for me. I had to
analyze a nine-year-old's story in terms of adult literature. And, ever since
then, I try to look at my students' texts as important texts, whereas other
teachers just look for problems in punctuation. . . . I want to take what I
learned there and look at multiple voicing in texts, at how to treat all texts
in a certain way—without necessarily putting them in a hierarchy. Think
how that impacts the teaching of English.

Another student described how her teaching changed as a result of her
Longmont experience:

I guess the wrong verb would be to say that I "preach" Longmont to those
heathens in North Carolina, but, basically, I do that. You know, [since I
came to Longmont,] I've done a total "180" [-degree turnaround] about
everything that I believe and practice in my classroom. Five years ago I was
that traditional teacher with the straight rows and a totally teacher-
centered classroom, where I was the figure of authority and nobody had
any say in the classroom other than me. But, being acquainted with [a
program administrator in the writing concentration] and [a literature faculty member]—their methods of teaching their classes. . . . I'm not bragging, but, when you go by my classroom, you hear voices—and they are
not mine. Very seldom do you hear me. I initiate things, but my students
take the ball and run with it. . . . And it's all because of what has happened
here.

This alumna's employer corroborated her view: "The faculty bent over
backwards to do things that would help [this alumna] when she went back
to the classroom. . . . The faculty really read and discussed what she
wrote." A program administrator supported this employer's evaluation of
the program. "After one summer here," he told us, "teachers find that,
after they've gone back, their classrooms work in ways that they haven't
before, which accounts for an additional avidity with which they return."

Interestingly, many of the students and alumni we interviewed associated their positive personal outcomes in the program with the place—and
the community. "What is unique about Longmont," one alumna emphasized, "is that it's a community, an island, and everybody is into English.
. . . I want to go and visit. It's like my center. It's where I'm happiest. It's

such a wonderful combination of creativity, curiosity, wit, and humor. There's no place quite like it." Similarly, another graduate of Longmont remarked on the school's appeal: "Suddenly in February, when teaching's tough, you remember the summer." He had recently spoken with a friend from the program, who told him, "I'm feeling Longmont withdrawal!" And a program administrator said: "I've had a number of people come up to me and say, 'I'm graduating this year. That's horrible!' They are already trying to figure out how they are going to come back."

The value of the Longmont master's experience, however, may have been best summarized in the words of a fifth-year student, who said: "The keyword for this program is 'transforming experience.' . . . You are a different person by the time you're a senior. I felt very different even after two or three years, but there is a sense in which Longmont becomes a part of your life." Literally all of the Longmont interviewees confirmed this student's overall assessment of the program, impressing on us that these changes occurred because Longmont faculty dialogically invited, and challenged, students to discuss ideas within a supportive "community of learners" and to link their master's experiences to their everyday teaching practices in their classrooms.

Understanding the Community-centered Idealized Program Type

In our analysis the Longmont master's program in English was broadly representative of the social action, community-centered, character of sixteen other programs we classified as members of the final group of master's programs in our typology. Stakeholders across all seventeen of these community-centered programs made similar choices in three of the five decision-situations featured in part 2. All chose to utilize a dialogical approach to teaching and learning (decision-situation 1) and to provide strong departmental support to their master's programs (decision-situation 3). In all but five of these programs, faculty and program administrators chose a connected program orientation (decision-situation 2). As for the auxiliary decision-situations, institutional administrators provided strong support (decision-situation 4) in slightly more than half of the seventeen cases. Finally, students in nine of the community-centered programs developed synergistic student cultures, and those in the remaining eight cases established participative cultures (decision-situation 5).

All four institutional types were represented in the community-centered program grouping, including ten cases in regional institutions (eight of which were public), four cases in liberal arts institutions (one of which was public), two cases in national institutions (one of which was public), and one case in a specialty institution (which was public). Of the four, the community-centered program type had the lowest proportion of cases at national institutions and the highest proportion at liberal arts institutions. The public-private split was roughly proportionate to that of the entire sample. The programs located at regional institutions were: the nursing programs at Southern State and Peterson; the applied anthropology programs at Southeast State, Southwest State, and City-State; the microbiology programs at Appleby State and Middle State; the English program at Southwest State; the theater program at Helena State; and the education program at Laramie. Four cases were located at liberal arts institutions: the environmental studies programs at Walton State and Vernon; the education program at Lake College; and the English program at Longmont College. Finally, one specialty and two national institutions were also represented in the community-centered program type: the nursing program at Western State Medical Center and the environmental studies programs at Major State and Phelps.

With the exception of engineering and business, all of the disciplines included in our sample were represented in the community-centered grouping. By discipline, these included four of the five environmental studies programs, three each of the nursing and applied anthropology programs, two each of the microbiology, education, and English programs, and one of the theater programs. With respect to the number of degree levels offered by the departments associated with these programs, only three (two nursing departments and the applied anthropology department at Southeast State) granted bachelor's, master's, and doctoral degrees, while five (those associated with three environmental studies programs, the English program at Longmont, and the education program at Laramie) solely conferred the master's degree. The remaining nine departments offered both bachelor's and master's degree programs. (Table 9.1 identifies the seventeen case studies in the community-centered program type by institutional type, field of study, and degree levels offered.)

We develop our portrait of the community-centered idealized program type using the same approach we used in presenting the ancillary, career advancement, and apprenticeship types. First, we describe the overall character of the seventeen community-centered programs and consider the two key program purposes that stakeholders articulated. Second, based on our interviews with stakeholders, we discuss three features characteristic of the community-centered program type: the engagement of program participants in a community of learners; the use of a curricular approach that connects theoretical and applied knowledge through various interdisciplinary and experiential learning activities; and the strong support faculty provided to master's education generally and master's students specifically. In the third and final part of the chapter, we discuss how stakeholders viewed the overall value and quality of their master's experiences.

Table 9.1. **Distribution of Case Studies in the Community-centered Idealized Program Type**

Pseudonym Institution	Field of Study	Degree Levels
Case Studies at Regional Institutions		
Southeast State	Applied anthropology	B.A., M.A., Ph.D.
Southwest State	Applied anthropology	B.A., M.A.
City-State	Applied anthropology	B.A., M.A.
Laramie	Education	M.A.
Southwest State	English	B.A., M.A.
Appleby State	Microbiology	B.S., M.S.
Middle State	Microbiology	B.S., M.S.
Southern State	Nursing	B.S., M.S., Ph.D.
Peterson	Nursing	B.S., M.S.
Helena State	Theater	B.A., M.A.
Case Studies at Liberal Arts Institutions		
Lake	Education	B.A., M.A.
Longmont	English	M.A.
Walton State	Environmental studies	B.S., M.E.S.
Vernon	Environmental studies	M.S.
Case Studies at National Institutions		
Major State	Environmental studies	M.S.
Phelps	Environmental studies	M.E.S.
Case Studies at Specialty Institutions		
Western State	Nursing	B.S., M.S., Ph.D.

Character and Articulated Purposes

We learned that stakeholders in the seventeen cases viewed their master's programs as an experience in which faculty and students, as collegial participants in a learning community, served their professional and broader social environments by generating critically informed understandings and approaches to field-related issues. An administrator in Major State's environmental studies program articulated the community-centered character of these seventeen cases when he told us that faculty and students in this master's program focused on those "outcomes which affect society": "We're interested in being useful to decision-making processes, to the way resources are managed. . . . For this program, usefulness is an important component; there is a certain kind of societal benefit that people involved with this program are trying to produce. . . . They are not just working to garner understanding, knowledge; there *is* an application [for this knowledge]."

The community-centeredness of these master's programs was also expressed by a program administrator at City-State University. Faculty and students in their applied anthropology program, he said, focused on "understanding their region and on coming up with solutions for the region": "It's always been my understanding of what a master's program should be—to get students developing critical thinking ability related to the future of our own region." An alumna of this program elaborated on this point: "The impression you walk away with is that this program is tied back to real things and needs in the city and that the students that come through have had, or have the opportunity, to get involved in hands-on stuff in an urban environment. . . . I really think this program is grounded in serving the community."

We came to understand that the community-centered character of these seventeen cases was shaped, in part, by two program purposes that faculty and program administrators articulated and most other stakeholders embraced. First, faculty and program administrators wanted students to leave their programs as skilled social stewards who were committed to serving their professions and society. Second, these stakeholders felt strongly that students should understand their professional practice as praxis—that is, as critically informed, thoughtful action.[2] This perspective on professional practice was seen as particularly important to many faculty and program administrators because they believed it enhanced students' effectiveness as social stewards.

The first purpose, to develop students as social stewards, was linked to a version of the Longmont ripple effect: most faculty hoped that the perspectives and skills master's students learned would, in turn, ripple out through students' stewardship to benefit other individuals, professional and community groups, and society in general. A Laramie program administrator told us, for example, that faculty in the global education master's program felt strongly "that we need to give students a feeling of efficacy . . . that we are not just talking about involving students in some conceptual way of thinking globally, but also acting locally . . . that there are ways that we can empower them as teachers and they can empower students to actually go out and determine what it is about the United States or about the world that they think could be better. And I think we teach them the skills to do that." A professor at Peterson University similarly remarked that faculty in their nursing program encouraged students to view themselves as "patient-advocates," who served their patients and profession by "influencing and improving the health care delivery system for their clients." And a Phelps environmental studies program administrator said that a primary "goal" of that master's program was "to provide leaders": "Now a leader can be a leader of an organization or of a community. The goal [we have for our graduates] is to take on the mantle of that responsibility and to show some leadership."

Faculty and administrators told us that many students entered their master's programs predisposed to serving society. A Major State environmental studies program administrator, for example, said that the master's students there were "people who are . . . committed to life—fighters—and I don't mean activists carrying placards but, rather, people who see problems, a world that we manage as stewards of the planet, who don't like what we've done." An applied anthropology professor at City-State likewise remarked: "These students have a sense of wanting to help their city. They're [City-State] on the move."

For their part, many students and alumni told us that they had enrolled in their master's program because they wanted to serve their communities. A Phelps environmental studies student, for example, said that she and many of her program peers were "committed to improving the environment": "Believe me, you're not in this field to earn a lot of money." An alumnus of City-State's applied anthropology program told us that his interest in community service led him to earn his master's degree: "[I had this] overriding concern to figure out what's going on in the community . . . this insatiable desire to get out there and do something about it. . . . This [the master's] offered me an outlet to use and understand this gut feeling and to help me do something about it. . . . The ultimate goal [for me] on the applied side [of anthropology] is to seek knowledge to do something with it and to improve the community. The ultimate goal is always not what you know but how you use it."

Throughout our interviews, faculty and program administrators also articulated a second purpose for their master's programs: to help students understand their professional practice as praxis.[3] As we came to understand the concept from interviewees, praxis involves a "dialectic" between theoretical and practical knowledge. In this process individuals critically examine practice in terms of their own experiences as well as their interpretations of established theories and, in so doing, seek to engage in more thoughtfully informed professional practice. In other words, practice requires critical, thoughtful action. An institutional administrator at Lake College explained the concept in these terms:

> For me, the distinction between a training and a professional program would be the fact that one attains the theory and the praxis. You stimulate students to think in those kinds of ways and to see their profession as both practice and theory. They have to learn to question their assumptions about what they're doing. And I think that has to be done to make something genuinely graduate-level work and to genuinely make it professional.

Along these same lines, a professor at Southern State told us that she and her faculty colleagues felt strongly that helping students to develop a more critical perspective on their professional practice was "what master's-level education should be": "We want people to leave the master's prepared to engage in the dialectic—that's critical thinking; it's praxis. It's action with reflection." She added that she expected students to leave their program knowing how to "critique their practice . . . knowing why they did this or that": "I want them [as professionals] to be constantly questioning." A professor in Southwest State's applied anthropology program likewise said that faculty encouraged students to explore how their assumptions about anthropological theory influenced their practice. In his words:

[We] really just want students to understand that basically what anthropological theory is, is the underlying assumptions that you carry into a situation. All we want to do is to get students to be more explicit and systematic about those assumptions. I think that's very important. I think they need to know where they're coming from. . . . We [applied anthropologists] very often end up as cultural brokers, as bridges, between groups. When you are that, you're neither here nor there. This idea of grounding—of knowing what your assumptions are and why you believe them—is very important.

Faculty and program administrators emphasized that praxis involves action as well as the ability to reflect upon, and critically examine, assumptions about practice in the field. As such, many told us that they expected students to become skilled at "translating" their critical understandings of knowledge into action as they worked with others in the field. A Walton State environmental studies program administrator, for example, said that the program's "goal in many ways is producing broadly trained policy specialists . . . [people who] can work with specialists but who are also [developing] some very important translation abilities, integrative abilities." He stressed that faculty encouraged students to examine theory, methods of inquiry, and their own experiences in the profession from a critical standpoint and urged them to act as "bridges" by translating these understandings to specialists with whom they worked in the field. Similarly, an administrator at Lake College noted that faculty in the education program encouraged students to reflect critically on knowledge and practice in their field and to use these understandings to become more active social stewards in their schools: "In this program we are interested in praxis. We are interested in stimulating thoughtful practice. This is our goal. There is a power in this, too. The teacher feels that [the students] have a general understanding of the problems in schools and a conscious sense of being an actor in the school who can become involved in school decision making. It's a sense of empowerment for these students. Once they become sensitized to these issues, they can take reflective action in their schools."

From our perspective, these two articulated purposes were related to the choices community-centered program faculty and program administrators made in the three primary decision-situations discussed in part 2.

To develop their students as social stewards who understood their professional practice as praxis, faculty and program administrators in all seventeen programs chose to utilize a dialogical approach to teaching and learning (decision-situation 1) in which students and faculty, as members of a learning community, mutually examined and generated critical understandings about knowledge and practice. For much the same reason, faculty and program administrators in the majority of these cases also chose a connected orientation (decision-situation 2) for their master's programs, an orientation that emphasized both theoretical and applied knowledge and a range of skills that were valued in both academic and workplace cultures. Finally, since faculty and program administrators were themselves often strongly committed to serving society, they chose to provide strong departmental support (decision-situation 3) in all seventeen master's programs.

Characteristic Features

Upon reviewing our interviews from these seventeen cases, we came to appreciate that three features were broadly representative of the community-centered idealized program type. These features were closely related to the purposes faculty and administrators articulated for their master's programs and the choices they made in the first three decision-situations. They include the emphasis faculty placed on engaging all program participants in a community of learners; the use of a curricular approach that connected theoretical and applied knowledge through a variety of interdisciplinary and experiential learning activities; and the strong support faculty provided to master's education generally and to their master's students specifically.

Community of Learners   Interviewees in the seventeen community-centered programs emphasized that a community of learners formed the basis of their teaching and learning experiences. While they used different terms—such as "communities of trust," "teamwork experiences," "community spirit," and "collegial bonding"—they described a similar experience. In a nutshell, stakeholders viewed these communities as interactive learning experiences in which faculty and students, more or less as colleagues, mutually examined and generated critically informed understandings about knowledge and practice in their fields through a dialogical approach to teaching and learning (decision-situation 1).

We came to understand that their commitment to using a dialogical learning process led faculty and program administrators in the community-centered programs to create an environment that would nurture and support this conception of learning. A professor at Walton State made this point when he remarked that faculty in the environmental studies program there paid attention to "creating an environment that enhanced a kind of collectivist learning." Similarly, a program administrator in Laramie's education program said: "It's a conscious goal on my part to provide an environment which encourages [a sense of community], . . . and I provide the vehicles for doing this, for bonding the group together. I see that as a very important part of our master's experience."

Faculty and program administrators across the seventeen cases often told us that they defined their roles as "teacher" and "learner" in ways that would nurture an interactive community of learners. Many faculty strongly believed that students had important insights and ideas to contribute and that, by taking the role of a respectful "colleague," they could learn from students through mutually supportive dialogue. A Southwest State applied anthropology program administrator said, for example, that faculty in that department had a "shared philosophy that students are very important and they need to be treated as developing professionals, as current and future colleagues." A microbiology professor at Middle State commented that he and his faculty colleagues viewed "students as our partners," while another said of master's students: "We work together like colleagues every day, and we respect each other. They respect me, and I respect them. There is respect for talent and ability both ways." And a professor at Helena State remarked: "Our master's students are treated like junior faculty members here. They are treated like staff, and they have to function like staff. . . . When we're working on productions, for example, there are no division lines of faculty-student. . . . People are expected to produce as equals, regardless of whether they're faculty or students."

We spoke with many faculty in the community-centered programs who were critical of traditional, and hierarchical, views of the faculty-student relationship. Many emphasized that they did not want students to view them as "learned authorities" who transmitted their expert knowledge and advice to them. As a Walton State environmental studies program administrator put it: "We [the faculty] do not take a top-down view of education nor a top-down view of students—that is, the view that we are the disseminators of information and they are the receptacles of information. To a certain extent, that [disseminating information] is a major part of our job, but we definitely see education as a reciprocal process. . . . People [in this program] aren't just allowed to sit and just assimilate ideas. They have an obligation and responsibility to participate." A Lake College education professor expressed a similar view: "In my opinion, the traditional academic model of a teacher pouring information into a student's head does students a disservice. I think a better way to teach is to encourage students to examine their own experiences and make sense of them in a way that is personally valuable for them. This is what we try to do in this program."

Many students and alumni emphasized that faculty treated them as "partners" and "colleagues" who had important insights and ideas to contribute. A Laramie alumnus, for instance, said that faculty in the education program adopted a nonhierarchical approach in their interactions with students: "Very seldom did we meet someone who was such an expert in their attitude that we couldn't talk with them, especially the faculty. There were really good people there who dealt with us as peers, not as superior to inferior." An alumnus of Appleby State's microbiology program told us that there, too, faculty treated students like professional colleagues:

> I like that professional approach. It really gives you a good feeling inside, you know. It's like they [the faculty] believe in you; you're not like a herd of animals, like undergraduates. I remember those undergraduate lecture pits, with the professor standing there and spouting off a certain amount of material, and you just sit there like a sponge and pick it up. In the graduate program, the tables were turned. The groups were very small. We were assumed to be knowledgeable about the material, and each one of us became important. It gave you a better feeling—you want to learn; you wanted to be part of it. That's what it was—it made you want to do things. It made it a pleasure to learn. It really did.

Faculty and program administrators across the seventeen programs told us that they set the tone for collegial and collaborative interactions by inviting students to participate with them, as well as with one another, as full partners within their learning communities. As a student at Middle State put it: "Here [at Middle State] faculty are just so into what they're doing—they're into it so that they pull you into it. It isn't just that 'this is my baby, and I'm teaching you about it, and I'm going to give you this information.' No, here they pull you into it; they care about you, and they really want to help you learn. . . . Faculty are collaborative, not competitive, here." A group of archaeology students in the applied anthropology program at Southwest State said that faculty invited them to participate as colleagues on research projects, and they mentioned how one professor interacted with them. "He was really open to our own explorations," remarked one second-year student. "He allowed us to explore, and he encouraged us to keep going in a direction until a little light bulb went off in our heads." Another second-year student added: "Yeah, he did that, but he also didn't expect us to regurgitate his thoughts. He says to you, 'Here's my perspective; now I'd like to hear yours.' You know, he really wants to know what you think."

Many students and alumni emphasized that the collaborative interactions they had in their learning communities helped them to develop critically informed perspectives on knowledge and practice in their fields. As a Southwest State English student explained:

Here [at Southwest State] the concept of discourse community tends to be very, very strong. People want to hear what other people say. As far as the books, you're going to get basically the same books no matter where you are. You take nineteenth-century literature—you're going to hit some Wordsworth, some Shelley, some George Eliot. You're going to get what the majority of the people know as the great literature, the canon stuff. While that varies, it's fairly consistent. What isn't consistent is the people. And the whole concept of critical study of literature has to revolve around this concept of discourse. People talking about why a certain author is great, what is so good about this, or why they feel someone is horrendous and shouldn't be in the canon. . . . And that has been my experience in all of my education here. I learned far more from talking about these ideas in my classes than I learned from reading Shakespeare by myself.

A Helena State theater alumna offered a similar account: "Faculty forced us to do a great deal of thinking and problem solving and research ourselves. . . . It was nurturing and challenging at the same time. We constantly were saying 'what if, what if, what if?' . . . Faculty expectations were high. They expected that you would be successful; they expected you to pull your own weight; they expected you to question if you had concerns or problems. You didn't just have to regurgitate information to them. They wanted you to think. They stressed thinking and individual growth. I think they pushed me to take risks and to trust myself."

We came to appreciate that the community of learners in these seventeen master's programs was not limited to the collaborative and collegial interactions faculty and students shared. To the contrary, many stakeholders emphasized that they had also developed faculty and student cultures that complemented the overall sense of community. Representing the perspective of many faculty interviewees, a Southwest State applied anthropology professor described this faculty culture: "I think, for the most part, there is a sense of collegiality and cooperation among most of us in the department. I think we have a great deal of respect for each other's work. . . . We often share ideas with one another at lunch; we drop off papers with one another to read; we teach in each other's classes." A member of Helena State's theater faculty said that he and his faculty colleagues "work as a team": "We grow in that way. I've learned so much about music and dance here because I have had colleagues who have shared so freely." A Middle State microbiology professor similarly remarked: "Unlike the biology 'prima donnas' in the department, we [the microbiologists] work as a group. There's lots of interaction here. We go to meetings together, and we're very supportive of one another. They're aren't any prima donnas here."

Students and alumni pointed out to us that they experienced, albeit in varying degrees, a "sense of student community" in their master's programs (decision-situation 5).[4] This was based, in large part, on the eagerness students had to collegially share with, and learn from, one another. A student in City-State's applied anthropology program, for example, told us that students were interested in helping one another learn, not in "cutting each other's throats": "It's not a 'limited good' approach [around here]." Two applied anthropology students at Southwest State elaborated on this point:

> [Student 1:] That was one of the things that surprised me when I started here last year: I would tell somebody about a paper I was working on, and someone would come up to me and say, "Hey, I saw this reference yesterday, and you might want to take a look at it." This happened all the time, and this is wonderful.

> [Student 2:] We are not backstabbing here . . . and, personally, I think that's the way it ought to be. You learn so much more by sharing knowledge than by locking it up and being afraid that someone is going to steal an idea.

Two Vernon College students stressed the sense of student community in their environmental studies program:

> [Student 1:] The program is hard—it's rigorous—but there is a sense of community that holds us together so we can get through it. There is more camaraderie, . . . and this is important. It's not like regular programs where graduate students don't know what the others are doing.

> [Student 2:] The support that you get from the other students helps keep you going. If someone really bogs down and falls behind [we help take care of him or her]. . . . The five or six of us who continued into the second year really worked together.

We came to understand that the collegial, and often collaborative, interactions between faculty and students often formed the basis of, and continuously nurtured, an active community of learners. A Phelps program administrator, for example, described the environmental studies program as a "warm, community-oriented place": "Everybody is interested in everyone else. There is a great sense of community here—it's most unusual. . . . I've worked other places where this was not the case, but here there is just a sense of great warmth." While the intensity of this "communal spirit" varied across the seventeen cases, stakeholders' general experiences did not: most told us that faculty and students interacted with one another as colleagues who mutually engaged in examining and generating critically informed understandings about knowledge and practice in their fields. As a nursing professor at Western State put it: "It's wonderful [here]. We are cooperative; we can discuss diverse ideas and issues and be very constructive. We're all working toward the same goals, and I just love being a part of it." A Longmont faculty member likewise said: "Here I'm in a community. I've a sense that students are my colleagues. I really love this. . . . This place really cultivates good thinking about literature."

Connected Curricula, Connected Learning Experiences Consonant with their emphasis on praxis, we learned that faculty and program administrators across the seventeen cases used a curricular approach that linked theory and practice within the context of a community of learners. This connected approach integrated three kinds of primary learning experiences: interdisciplinary course work (which often included hands-on learning); outside-of-class experiential learning activities (such as laboratory work, clinical placements, performances, and internships); and various "culminating activities" (such as theses, project reports, and capstone seminars).[5]

To illustrate, a program administrator at City-State described the "connected curricular approach" used in the applied anthropology program there. He emphasized that, in addition to having students complete a semester-long practicum and written report, faculty required students to become involved in various hands-on projects while enrolled in their classes. In his words: "Students get involved not just in one practicum but in a series of projects. They go from one to the other, and then they become interactive with you. And then we want them to evaluate, to reflect, to bring that back to a course and say, 'How does this fit in with the literature? What does it mean?'" In much the same way, an environmental studies program administrator at Major State told us that the master's curriculum—with its emphasis on interdisciplinary course work, experiential learning, and interactive seminars—provided students with a connected educational experience that was analogous to a "soufflé": "[It] provides an opportunity for synthesis: you put these ingredients together, and it rises and becomes a new entity. Suddenly everything starts to fit in. You see how things interrelate; you develop a kind of hierarchy of ideas. For the people for whom it works, not only do you connect and link together focused pieces of information, but it all moves up to a different level of conception of how you look at it."

Across the seventeen cases, faculty and program administrators told us that they used this connected curricular approach in their master's programs because they believed that, by providing students with a diversity of perspectives on theory and practice, they would enable students to engage in more thoughtful social stewardship. One Phelps environmental studies professor, for example, spoke to this point when he explained that faculty incorporated interdisciplinary theoretical perspectives into the curriculum "as a matter of philosophy":

> We think that, in order to be effective in the natural resources field, particularly in a management or leadership position, you not only need to know the science of ecology and natural resources, but you also have to understand how society operates as an economic, social, political, and cultural system. In addition to that, you also have to understand some of the humanities aspects; you have to understand the historical context. And you also have to be able to communicate effectively if you're going to be a leader and a manager. . . . And you also have to consider the ethical dimension, which is a very important aspect. For example, what is our ethical responsibility to a healthy and sustainable natural world? What's our ethical responsibility to future generations? These features [the interdisciplinary theoretical perspectives], I think, make us unique [compared] to other natural resources programs in the country.

In all seventeen of the community-centered programs, faculty required students to complete a core set of interdisciplinary, or cognate, courses that were designed to provide students with the opportunity to integrate various perspectives from different disciplines. Environmental studies students at Walton State, for example, linked sociological, geopolitical, managerial, and various natural science perspectives in a nine-credit-hour interdisciplinary course entitled "Population, Energy, and Resources," one of many interdisciplinary courses they completed during their master's studies. Similarly, nursing students at Peterson University completed two interdisciplinary core courses—"Human and Environmental Systems Interaction" and "Health Care Delivery Systems and Social Policy"—which drew heavily on perspectives grounded in psychology, sociology, management, political science, and social work. Most of the other community-centered programs relied primarily on cognate courses to provide students with multidisciplinary learning experiences.

Many of the students we spoke with told us that they often developed new perspectives on issues in their fields through their interdisciplinary and multidisciplinary course work. As an alumnus of Major State's environmental studies program put it: "[The concept of river basin management] pervades this entire program. It's the notion that economists could study water resources management and never understand it, wastewater and flood control engineers could study it and never understand it, fisheries experts could study it and never understand it. [In this program] you learn that you have to integrate all of these fields in order to understand the system." A second-year Phelps student likewise explained how the interdisciplinary course work required in the environmental studies program emphasized the importance of doing environmental policy work "wisely":

Not only is it looking at the managerial aspect of things—it's all very interdisciplinary. So, in an air pollution course, you're not just looking at chemistry; you're looking at regulations and the effects on crops and all that kind of stuff. "Wisely," I think, is a good way to say it because you may not be a technical expert, but you're getting all the aspects of it. [The interdisciplinary course work helps] you know what to question and how to assess things when you don't know the details behind it because you are [just] a manager.

We learned from many stakeholders across the community-centered programs that, while students were studying interdisciplinary theoretical perspectives in their classes, faculty also required them to engage in various experiential learning activities that helped them join theory and practice. Articulating a perspective that was shared by many faculty across the seventeen programs, an applied anthropology professor at City-State told us that he incorporated hands-on research projects within many of his courses: "In the classroom our students are introduced to the basic concepts and methods of anthropology. But, until they get out there and try some of these things, they mean little. I think the research [that students do in the community] reinforces and contradicts what they learn in the classroom." An alumnus of this program illustrated how this intersection of in-class and outside-of-class learning activities helped wed theoretical and applied knowledge together when he addressed real-world problems:

> In a lot of the papers you do, rather than going to the library and doing a theoretical assessment of some anthropological paradigm, you're given the chance instead to test that paradigm out in the real world. And the program is geared to that. In these classes, as you're getting the theory in the classroom, one of the notions about your papers would be: "What's happening in the real world, and where is the appropriate theory that applies to what you can observe in the real world?" And then the next question is: "If you can get that mix, what are some of the things that you would do to recommend change in this situation?" So, in the scheme of things, the theory is important, but the program is definitely designed to be applied.

In our interviews with students and alumni, we came to appreciate that faculty, while not always requiring students to engage in a hands-on project, incorporated various other types of experiential learning in their courses in an attempt to make connections between theoretical and experiential knowledge. A student in Middle State's microbiology program told us that, in her immunology class, for example, the professor "brought in some of the AIDS patients he was working on in the clinic, and they talked to [the students]": "It wasn't just textbook, and it wasn't just 'Here, you have an assignment to do.' It was real. You could talk to these people and see what the disease did to them mentally and physically." Many students in the other community-centered programs shared similar stories, often telling us that theory and practice worked hand in glove in many of their courses.

In addition to their involvement in these interdisciplinary and experientially based learning experiences, students also integrated theory with practice in many outside-of-class laboratory, clinical, workshop, and internship activities.[6] These activities often required students to participate in professional work situations, in which they addressed and solved real-world problems in their respective fields. Students in Peterson's nursing program, for example, completed approximately five hundred hours of clinical practice in local hospitals, where they enhanced their understandings of knowledge and practice in their specific specialty areas (students in Southern State's and Western State's nursing programs also fulfilled major clinical assignments). In the three applied anthropology programs, students engaged in semester-long internships with government agencies, community-based organizations, or health and human services institutions, where they, in the words of a Southwest State program administrator, were "confronted with real-world situations" and learned how to deal with them. In much the same way, faculty in both microbiology programs and in Helena State's theater program told us that students spent considerable time in the laboratory and onstage working through scientific problems and production- or performance-related issues. And students in all four environmental studies programs were required to complete either an internship, workshop, or several field trips through which they, too, gained firsthand experience in addressing and solving pressing environmental problems in their regional communities.

Time and again, stakeholders across the community-centered programs communicated to us that these kinds of intensive, hands-on learning experiences helped students connect the knowledge they had learned in their classes with the practical realities of the workplace. A faculty member in Peterson's nursing program, for example, said that it was when students became "actively involved in their clinical experiences that they learned to put it all together—to see the connections between theory and practice." An alumnus of Middle State's microbiology program provided a similar perspective, explaining that his work in the laboratory provided him with the opportunity to use what he had learned in his undergraduate courses and "do something with it with [his] hands and mind": "I will never forget that lab work we did in my applied micro class. Some of the things we did in these courses were a lot of fun."

Finally, many community-centered administrators and faculty informed us that, in their master's programs, they required students to complete a "culminating experience" of some kind, usually a thesis or project report and, occasionally, a capstone seminar.[7] In almost all of these programs, theses and project reports were based on, and reported findings from, the laboratory, clinical, workshop, or internship experiences students had completed in the program. The primary difference between theses and project reports was that the former tended to be written in a more scholarly format and primarily for a university audience, while the latter were written as professional documents for clients in nonuniversity workplace settings (such as high school curricula for teachers, policy reports for government agencies, and staff development proposals for hospitals). In a handful of programs, students were required to complete a final seminar in conjunction with the writing of their theses or project reports. These seminars provided students with the opportunity to share and learn from one another's experiences "in the field."

Interviewees stressed that often it was through these culminating experiences that students brought together what they had learned both in and outside of class to develop more reflexive views of their professional practices. A program administrator in Southwest State's applied anthropology program, for example, told us:

> In the postinternship seminar, students are put in a situation where they have to think about what is the impact of the internship: here's the theory you learned; now integrate it into your postinternship experience. We want them to integrate that because they usually have kept theory and practice separate to this point. We want them to ask: "What happened to me, as an individual? What kinds of changes have I seen in myself?" This is really important because this is a program where the major instrument for change is an individual, and that individual changes as they cause change. So we want them to think about who they are and what they did and what they got out of it.

An alumna of this program told us that her postinternship experience helped her to understand more fully, and to make the link between, the theoretical concept of "cultural brokering" and her internship experiences as an applied anthropologist in an unfamiliar setting:

> It was in the postinternship where things started making sense to me. This is where everything came together—where I assimilated all of my experiences and figured out what was what and why. I learned how to distance myself from the individuals in the situation and to separate my culture from another culture and to look at myself within my own culture. . . . What I learned was that I had trouble communicating with people at the

clinic because that was a very different culture from my experience. And I didn't get that until postinternship, and I could have never gotten that without a program like this.

Students and alumni in other community-centered programs likewise remarked that these culminating curricular experiences, in the words of one Western State nursing alumna, helped them to "pull together" theoretical and applied knowledge and to develop a more integrated view of their professional practice. An alumna from Appleby State's microbiology program provided an anecdote about how her thesis experience provided her with that "missing piece":

> This is the piece you need that makes all of this other information fit together. It was the piece I needed that applied to so many things that I had just been blocked from knowing before. It just fit things together. . . . That piece would be different for everybody, but, in my case, it was how the structure of molecules is put together on a different level than in chemical interactions. It was the experience of realizing that most everything is held together by very weak hydrophobic interactions and hydrogen bonds—van der Waal's forces—and that those are the weakest link. . . . It was at that point when I realized that all of biology is based on the weakest link, and this is it. And I teach this now; I teach biology based on the weakest link.

She added that she may have never grasped this point if she had not participated in this culminating experience: "It's like I suddenly saw it from the ground up, you know. . . . This wouldn't have happened had I not simultaneously been assembling research and doing things in the lab and trying to figure out why one degree of temperature matters. If you are never forced to do that, I don't know if you can still put it in perspective. It's a struggle. I mean, I didn't *want* to learn about van der Waal's forces."

Faculty Commitment to Serving Students and Society   In our interviews with stakeholders, we learned of one other feature that characterized the community-centered programs: the strong commitment faculty and program administrators had to serving master's students and to serving others in their broader social communities. Largely on this basis, faculty and administrators provided strong department-level support (decision-situation 3). They expressed their commitment to, and demonstrated support for, the service-oriented mission of their master's programs through strong program-level leadership, individualized attention to master's students, and active involvement in various community-related activities. Indeed, the commitment of faculty and program administrators to this service-oriented mission was so strong that many chose to support their master's program even when institutional administrators did not. Of the seventeen community-centered programs, eight received weak institutional support from campus administrators (decision-situation 4).[8]

Time and again, faculty and program administrators told us that they became involved in their master's programs because they strongly felt that they could make a difference to their students and to others through their teaching and research. As one administrator in Laramie's education program explained to us, he became involved in instructing teachers about global education because he was "always looking for some philosophical way to make a difference in the world": "I think that global education offers me that opportunity and that my way of doing that is the multiplier effect [teaching teachers who then share their understandings of global education with their students]. . . . So, for me, this is not just a job. I have a personal philosophical investment in who I am and what I project into this program and what this program projects." An Appleby State microbiology professor voiced a similar perspective: "I feel like if I stay up-to-date [with my research] and do my teaching, that's my mission and the mission of this institution. That's what I hang onto, and that's where I think I can make my impact, where I can make a difference."

Faculty and program administrators also told us that, while their individual and collective commitments to social stewardship strongly influenced their choice to provide strong support to their master's program, it was not the only factor. In most of the seventeen cases, they indicated that they also supported their master's programs because they enhanced their department's resource base and reputation. In all but two of these cases, faculty and program administrators said that their master's programs either generated adequate revenues to meet their operating costs or actually contributed additional dollars to their departments' budgets. In addition, faculty, program administrators, students, alumni, and employers emphasized that their master's programs enhanced the reputations of their departments—and frequently their institutions as well—with nonuniversity employers and others in their local, state, and regional communities.

Many faculty in the community-centered programs told us that their commitment to social stewardship was often supported by one or more visible leaders. These individuals were enthusiastic advocates for the particular program, who clearly articulated its service-oriented mission to others, both within and outside of the program. Several interviewees in City-State's applied anthropology program, for example, mentioned that their department chair was particularly effective in recruiting faculty who had an interest in serving the university's local and regional communities. When we, in turn, asked this department chair to tell us about his leadership, he provided a response that reflected the community-centered character of this master's program:

I don't want this program to get locked into intellectual triviality. If it did, we'd lose the most important force [in this program], which is, "What is this region all about? Why is it the way it is? How come it's still a racist society here? Why is it that we still want to have a few rule for the good of all, or a plantation mentality?" That's the job of the department—to raise these questions and then to put what the student is involved with into that context.

In much the same way, stakeholders in Major State's environmental studies program said that their director was a strong advocate for the program, constantly nudging institutional administrators to reconsider the importance of interdisciplinary, service-oriented master's programs in the university. This administrator said that he frequently told campus administrators:

You have to decide on the front end that you're going to commit to this kind of educational realm, not as the only thing that a great university does but as a *legitimate* thing that a university does. You don't go around apologizing for it. . . . If you look at our [graduates] some years out, they still have that synoptic point of view and set of interests; we're training people with great capability, with a critical level of thoughts.

"The plea I make [to campus administrators]," he said, "is that we're not lesser or better; we're different. It's a legitimate and important kind of academic activity."

We spoke with many interviewees across these seventeen cases who informed us that their leaders not only were skilled at articulating the missions of their respective programs and garnering support for them but that their enthusiasm for serving students and other constituents often further animated faculty commitment in these areas as well. A program administrator in Helena State's fine arts department, for example, told us that the director of the theater program inspired "a lot of excitement among faculty and students": "They're always delving into unusual things that kind of set us apart [from other institutions]. The impetus for all of that comes from the faculty and, in particular, from [the director of the program]. He's a ball of energy, and he lives and breathes theater."

We learned that, with support from program leaders, one way community-centered faculty were committed to the service-oriented mission of their master's programs was by taking seriously the individualized needs of students within their learning communities. Time and again, interviewees across these seventeen cases told us that faculty embraced a "student-centered" philosophy, dedicating significant amounts of their time and energy to working with students. A program administrator in Peterson's nursing program expressed this philosophy, or mission, when she said, "I believe that the most important thing in our master's program is the faculty's commitment to making a program that meets an individual's needs—that helps [students] meet their professional and personal goals." A professor in the same program elaborated on this point, noting that faculty members "really try to get [to] know each student, sort of in the same way we would like them to get to know each of their patients." He added, "This is a very individualized, student-centered program." Similarly, a professor in Lake College's education program remarked that he and his colleagues encouraged the "education of the whole person" and were "just as concerned about developing people as . . . about developing knowledge."

In many instances, faculty pointed out to us that their top priorities were teaching and learning with their students. As a Middle State microbiology professor told us: "Let me be frank with you. I don't care about making myself look good. I mean, that's not a big deal [to me] at all. But what I want to see is students learn and really do well. That's where I get my kicks. These students are my junior colleagues. I really want to see them do well." An Appleby State microbiology professor likewise said: "If I felt like I wasn't helping these students, I'd get out of the field. I'd go wash dishes or something. But I do feel like I'm making a difference. I hope so, anyway. I hear the feedback, and I think we are doing the right thing—helping these people to reach their own potential, develop themselves, and helping to facilitate them to a better life. But [it isn't the contribution by faculty as much as that] they're doing it themselves; they have to have the basic talent and the desire, and they have to do the work, but we can sure help them channel it."

In line with their focus on the students, faculty in the community-centered programs often provided them with individualized attention. A professor in City-State's applied anthropology program, for example, told us that she and her faculty colleagues "put a tremendous amount of energy into nurturing interactions between faculty and graduate students": "This is a very labor-intensive program in terms of advising and supervising education outside the classroom in terms of tutorials, individually directed readings, taking students out for lunch, and simply being open to drop-by chats." A Helena State professor noted similarly that faculty in the school's theater program believed in providing individualized instruction within the context of a nurturing, supportive learning community: "You don't let people think that they're where they need to be if they're not. You level with them, and then you help them move beyond. We are a very individualized program. There is a family quality about what we do here. I guess that's what we mean by 'nurturing.'"

Indeed, students and alumni we spoke with emphasized, frequently with great enthusiasm, that faculty in these seventeen community-centered programs were involved with students both in philosophy and in action. As one Lake College student put it: "Faculty are very concerned about students—first, for the person and, second, with their performance. I've heard this from every prof I've ever had at [Lake College]. . . . They have a 'put people first' philosophy. They want to help teachers become better teachers. This is a very humane place to go to school. The faculty really care about you here." A Middle State microbiology alumnus remarked, along the same lines, that "faculty really care about students [there]": "They really want students to succeed. Most are willing to go out of their way to see this happen. They really work with you."

This "caring," we came to understand, was often experienced most intensely by students in the one-on-one collegial interactions they had with faculty. An applied anthropology student at Southeast State, for example, told us that it was "heartening" for him to "just be able to work four or five hours with [his] advisor and then to go out for a beer or salad [with him]": "That's heartening for [me] that's he's that accessible and we're able to talk about what he's doing and what I want to do. There's no distancing, no hierarchical structure. Some professors can make you feel like you aren't equal to them, and I've seen that in other departments, but there's none of that here." A student in Middle State's microbiology program described the individualized instruction she was receiving from faculty within this master's program by comparing it to her undergraduate experience:

> Instructors [at Middle State] walk down the hall and know you by name because they're so into what you're doing. I like this, in contrast to the professors I had at my undergraduate institution. . . . There were great minds up there. And that's fine, but, if those minds aren't willing to let some of that stuff filter out to other students, what good are they? If you have an instructor that could teach you lots of stuff but they don't have time for you, what good are they? At [Middle State] it's different. The one-on-one between the faculty and the students and the students and the students is great here.

Faculty and program administrators were committed to the service-oriented mission of their master's programs in another way: they actively served their professional and broader social communities. A program administrator in Southern State's nursing program made it clear to us that a substantial part of its mission was public service: "We try to do a lot of community-based research—solving problems—that's part of our mission here." A professor in the same program, elaborating on this point, noted that she and her faculty colleagues were devoted to serving the "highly diverse, multicultural population" surrounding the school: "We serve a unique purpose and a unique need here in the city. . . . We serve the needs of health care workers in our city."

Faculty and program administrators in all three applied anthropology programs also told us that they served the needs of their local and regional communities. As a City-State faculty member put it: "We try to make a difference in the community here. We're advocates for our community. . . . We often speak for people who don't speak up for themselves." Another professor in the same program said: "There is a tremendous appreciation in the local community for applied anthropology. We have really commanded the respect of the city in areas where we have interfaced with them. We have done a lot for city and county government and for some of the local health care centers in the community." And, articulating a perspective shared by many faculty and program administrators in the four community-centered environmental studies cases, the director of Major State's program told us that its faculty were actively involved with local and state government agencies in solving regional environmental problems: "I'm thinking about this [faculty involvement in the community] in the tradition of the mission of our university, as a university working hand in hand with the community to help that community solve real-world problems."

Employers emphasized that faculty in the community-centered programs served their communities in a variety of ways. One employer associated with Appleby State's microbiology program, for example, remarked that faculty were "very open and friendly to industry's needs," while another said that faculty "unselfishly" served their region's local community colleges. An employer told us that faculty at City-State served their community by "establishing critical ties between business and education" which benefited people in the community "by opening up lines of communication that were nonexistent, by bringing together groups of people who before believed they had no common interests": "[They have] taught people in our community that they are not isolated and that they do have recourse—that they do have channels for action." And, finally, an employer at a state environmental agency noted his appreciation for the ideas and "workable" suggestions Major State's environmental studies faculty gave to their joint research and policy projects: "We learn a lot from [Major State faculty] because they bring some high-powered ideas to [the problem at hand]. . . . Our work with them has yielded rather workable products."

Overall Stakeholder Evaluations of Community-centered Program Experiences

We learned that, broadly speaking, faculty and students in these seventeen cases experienced their master's programs as participants engaged in serving their professional and larger communities by generating critically informed understandings and approaches to issues in their respective fields. For the most part, stakeholders were very positive about their master's experiences. Many students and alumni told us that these experiences, in the words of a Peterson nursing alumnus, had a "transforming" effect both on how they thought about and engaged in their professional practices. Moreover, interviewees, including many employers, indicated that students often graduated from these programs as skilled social stewards who were able to translate their knowledge into action when working with others. Additionally, most faculty and program administrators valued their involvement in master's education, and many felt their work with students revitalized them both personally and professionally. On the negative side, stakeholders in about half of these cases expressed serious concern about weak institution-level commitment to the service-oriented mission of their master's programs. We discuss these broad evaluative themes below.

Transformative Experience for Students   Stakeholders often used the words *changed* and *transformed* when they evaluated the overall learning experiences of students and alumni. As we came to understand, this "transformation" referred to how students became more enthusiastic and thoughtful "self-starters," who developed fundamentally different ways of thinking about their professional practices because of their master's experiences.

Many students and alumni spoke about being transformed by their master's studies. A Peterson nursing alumnus, for example, told us that his master's experience had changed him: "I know who I am. I know who I want to be. I feel proud about the fact that I learned what I learned. I now function at a much higher level. I'm focused. I have established relationships with people I feel comfortable with, professional peer relationships, which I didn't have three or four years ago. So I was transformed. It's like night and day." A second-year student in Middle State's microbiology program said that, since enrolling in her master's program, she had begun to "think differently about things": "I approach problems differently; I realize there's not always one right answer. I now question more. I see how things relate. I realize that everything isn't just black and white. . . . There's a big difference in me. There's a lot of personal fulfillment in this." And, reflecting on how she had changed during her master's experience, a Southern State nursing alumna remarked: "Before [my master's studies] I was just a robot. . . . I was a good staff nurse. But it wasn't like anything I can do now. Everything now has to be questioned. At that time [during her master's] I began looking through a different lens. It made things very difficult, but I enjoyed it. I found it very refreshing and very valuable."

Many faculty and program administrators underscored that students changed during their master's experiences. A professor at Western State, for example, commented: "These students have more confidence; they have a clearer sense of what they want to do. Sometimes they even go back and create new jobs—and they couldn't have done that before. . . . They just have a better feel about who they are. . . . I have students who come in here [to her office] and say to me that they were just going to take courses, and now their whole life has been turned upside down—that they can't go back to their jobs and be the same way they were before." Similarly, a program administrator in the education program at Lake College said that many students told her that they had changed: "I've known some students who come in, and they are really moved by the courses. . . . These students really do get inspired. They leave this program with the sense that they're professionals."

We learned that these changes were related to the critical, reflexive, and holistic ways of thinking students developed while enrolled in their master's programs. Illustrating this point, a Peterson program administrator said: "I think the students that leave this program do change. . . . They begin to think on a theoretical basis; they begin to see things in a bigger perspective. . . . And I think that's what students get in this program—a framework for seeing more and more of the world. They can conceptualize now; they begin to think theoretically and critically." Likewise, an administrator in Middle State's microbiology program suggested that a "whole new world opens up" for students during their master's studies because they "learn to see new and different kinds of ideas": "That impacts on how they see the world. As they gain more and more confidence, they're more willing to go out there and experience more of the world."

Students and alumni emphasized too that they developed broader and more reflexive ways of thinking during their master's experiences. As a second-year student in Walden State's environmental studies program put it: "I've learned that I have to be able to synthesize everything, from how much memory a computer uses to how we look at how we write and how we regulate what we put into the waters. I've been taught to think critically, to think broadly, and to draw connections that I have never seen before." In discussing the critical and reflexive "kind of thinking" she learned in her applied anthropology program, a Southwest State alumna said:

> It was in my master's where I started to get this different kind of thinking. . . . I learned how to step out of my own value system—and that's really hard. That takes time. I remember I started to get so mad at everyone around me because I kept seeing how locked in they were by their own assumptions. . . . You would think you'd get this thinking process in your bachelor's, but you don't. . . . It's a whole different experience at the

master's level. You learn how to look at yourself and different cultures in a more critical way. You just don't go along with the flow; you just don't accept everything that everyone says and does anymore. You really get critical. You really begin to question.

We learned from interviewees that the critical, reflexive, and holistic ways of thinking that students developed in these master's programs often had a transforming effect on their professional practices. A Southern State nursing alumna illustrated this point when she said that her master's experience helped her think in new ways:

> OK, if I look at this from the medical model perspective, I would say "What's the pathology? What's the treatment?" And that's how I looked at things in my bachelor's program. Having a master's degree, I now look and say "How well is this person doing? What is this person's strengths? What is it that they need? What is their social support? How can I interface what I know into their lives to help improve their lives?" It's not just pathology [anymore]. . . . My focus is: how can I help this person? How can I educate them? Support them? It's a much more holistic approach.

Many employers of community-centered program alumni told us that they greatly valued the "different kinds of thinking" that these individuals brought to their professional practices. An employer associated with City-State's applied anthropology program said that she hired its graduates because "they have a different way of looking at the world": "That's what they bring, and that's why I hire them. . . . I think they will be able to think holistically, that they will be able to look at the parts and put them together, that they will be able to see systems, that they will be able to pull things together. . . . It has obviously been worth it to me to get that piece. . . . They bring a worldview that's really helpful." In much the same vein, an employer with a local public works utility remarked that she "valued" the Walton State environmental studies alumni who worked for her because "they have the broader perspective and understanding of the system and the world and the context for their technical work": "I think they have that understanding of the big picture and how the pieces fit together and how the system works."

Many employers associated with community-centered programs emphasized that these different ways of thinking, as well as the self-confident professionalism that program graduates brought to the workplace, were hallmarks of the overall value of these programs. As an employer associated with Western State's nursing program put it:

> I see these students as they go through [the program], and I would say that, four years down the line, [these students] would say that this was a significant thing in their lives, if they had to list significant changes. Be-

cause, in my experience [working with them], these people are significantly different because of their master's at [Western State]. . . . They are different in the way they think. It happens during that period of time, as an employer watching it. . . . [At our hospital] we need people who can help all of us think globally and inclusively and work with different disciplines in a way that is equitable and assertive and with a strong knowledge base. And I have to say that the master's-prepared people I get from [Western State] can do that. They have that way of thinking.

Another employer, who had hired several nursing graduates from Peterson University, told us that she so strongly valued the changes in these individuals that she would like to "clone them": "They're just a different kind of person. . . . They seem to be more well-rounded, enthusiastic, self-starter types."

Skilled and Committed Social Stewards In reflecting on the overall quality and value of their programs, many students, alumni, and employers communicated that students left these community-centered programs as skilled and committed social stewards. Students and alumni said that they developed the necessary skills, confidence, and enhanced sense of commitment while involved in their master's work, and many employers indicated that they respected these students' professional capabilities and also stressed that the students made important contributions to their professions and society.

Students and alumni emphasized that one of the most valuable skills they learned during their master's experiences was how to translate their knowledge into action that benefited others. As a Vernon environmental studies student observed, this translating skill helped him to "bridge the gaps among people in arriving at workable solutions [to environmental problems]": "We're supposed to be the people in the middle. . . . Good solutions can't be developed unless people understand several perspectives. You can't have people standing and yelling from different sides of the fence. . . . Because environmental problems are man-made, you have to solve them in a man-made way. I'm learning how to do that [in this program]." Many students and alumni told similar stories, ranging from that of a Southwest State archaeology student who said that she was "trying to give archaeology back to the public" by converting "academic jargon" into more comprehensive prose to a Longmont student who remarked that she was using new methods in her classes to "teach English to everyone."

We learned from many students and alumni that their ability to translate knowledge and information to others—in concert with the critical, reflexive, and holistic ways of thinking they had developed—gave them the confidence they needed to be successful social stewards. An alumna of City-State's applied anthropology program, who now serves as the director of a local metropolitan community center, said her "master's [education] was a real confidence builder. [I developed] confidence in my ability to adapt and to do just about anything I needed to do. It helped me in my ability to relate [information]. . . . It let me know that I could relate to everyday commonsense issues and have an impact." An alumna of Lake College's education program told us that she had learned to "understand the whole complexity of the field [of education]": "I'm now on a task force—the parochial schools in the town are studying if they should consolidate and all that. I volunteered for the task force because I really feel like I have a lot to contribute, because I know [the field of] education now. I don't think I would have had the confidence [to have joined the task force before getting my master's degree]."

Other students and alumni emphasized that their master's experiences affirmed and inspired their interests in serving their communities. A City-State applied anthropology alumnus told us that, during his master's work, he began to feel "a real dedication to give something back [to the surrounding community]": "That became more focused for me during my master's [studies]. . . . The master's [program] taught me how to become actively involved, and I learned how to play this out. Before maybe I was just a good neighbor, as opposed to being a community servant." A Southern State nursing alumna said that it was during her master's program that she began to "think that [nurses] help the community through education, support, listening to families and patients, and nobody else is going to do that. Nurses are the leaders in community health support."

Many employers made it clear to us that they valued the stewardship skills many of these master's graduates brought to their schools, government agencies, businesses, and health care centers. An employer associated with Walton State's environmental studies program, for example, said she was very pleased that the master's graduates she employed could effectively translate their own and others' knowledge into action: "In this organization we do a lot of teamwork across departments, and we do a lot of work with citizens. The whole nature of public sector decision making in the environmental arena means that you have to have an understanding of different values and perspectives and you need to be able to work with people of different disciplines and technical expertise and understand them, . . . and this program does prepare people to do that. People come out of there, and they know how to sit down in meetings and work with other people." In much the same way, an elementary school principal emphasized that the "broadened perspective" and "sense of self-confidence" teachers developed in Lake College's education master's program enhanced their ability to interact effectively with parents and students. As she explained: "These teachers have an improved interpersonal, professional approach with parents. They can sift through information and move it into a larger perspective and then use this information constructively in working with parents and students." This employer later added that Lake College graduates enriched their local community not only by "significantly improving these teachers' teaching skills" but also by "helping parents to feel like their teachers are well educated . . . to increase their faith in [the quality of] teachers."

Revitalizing Experience for Faculty and Program Administrators   Faculty and program administrators in community-centered programs told us that they often felt revitalized by their involvement in master's education for three reasons. First, they found it fulfilling to work with students. Second, many found it rewarding to be associated with a program that prepared students who successfully assumed stewardship roles in their various communities. Third, many faculty and administrators felt invigorated by the opportunities these programs provided for them to engage in community-related work with their faculty colleagues.

We learned that most faculty and program administrators in community-centered programs enjoyed their interactions with master's students, and they continued to participate in master's education because they greatly valued learning from students. As a microbiology professor at Middle State put it: "I stay at [Middle State] because the greatest self-satisfaction I get is from working with these students. The value of this program to me is the students. I really enjoy the students. I get a tremendous amount from them. The kids are great. They help me. I would never give this up." A program administrator in Peterson's nursing program voiced a similar perspective. "These students keep me humble," she explained. "As much as I have to offer them, they offer an incredible amount to me. . . . A lot of these people are out in the real world on a daily basis. These students constantly remind me of what's happening out there; they keep me up-to-date. These students change me as much as I have helped them to change."

Many faculty and program administrators also told us that they valued their involvement in master's education because they found it satisfying to watch students develop their potential. A program administrator in Southwest State's applied anthropology program, for example, said that this part of his master's experience was just "flat out fun": "It's exciting to work with students and see them change and grow. That's a real positive benefit that you can't put dollars and cents on." An Appleby State microbiology professor remarked how enjoyable it was for her to teach students: "I've enjoyed that immensely. I've really enjoyed working with these exceptionally bright students and watching them grow." A Peterson nursing professor likewise noted: "On a very personal level, I really love what I do; I really, really like adult students and watching them develop. And I like being a part of that." And a Lake College professor, whose comments reflected the view of many faculty and program administrators in these community-centered programs, told us that it was "reenergizing" for him to "walk away from an experience feeling like [he'd] enabled growth for people": "That's reenergizing for me. That's my mission in life."

Faculty and program administrators in the community-centered programs stressed that they found it personally and professionally fulfilling to assist master's students in becoming more effective social stewards. As a City-State applied anthropology professor put it, the program was "really fulfilling" for her:

> It works. I don't know how else to put it. We set some goals, and we set certain standards, and we stick by them. It's been mutually beneficial for students and faculty alike. The program really works here. . . . We turn average citizens into anthropologists, and then they go out there in the real world and proselytize by changing things in an anthropological way. . . . This program is really fulfilling for me because I don't feel like I'm leading people down a primrose path. . . . The community grabs up our students.

We learned that almost all of these programs boasted strong placement rates for their graduates. Faculty in the three nursing programs, for example, said that many of their master's-prepared graduates moved into leadership positions in the field of health care. Program administrators in both microbiology programs pointed out that they had impressive placement records: Appleby State placed 100 percent of its graduates, and a Middle State faculty member told us that, "for the most part, placing our students is usually only a phone call away." Faculty in three of the four environmental studies programs offered similar assessments. Even in the applied anthropology and theater programs, areas in which job market demand was relatively weak, faculty said that their graduates often found employment in their fields. A Southwest State program administrator remarked that their students were "gobbled up by employers," and a Helena State alumna commented that many peers in her graduating class had "thriving" careers, both in the professional theater and as secondary and postsecondary drama teachers.

Finally, many community-centered program administrators and faculty told us that these programs revitalized them because they provided opportunities to interact with faculty colleagues who shared a similar commitment to serving society. As a Southwest State program administrator put it: "There is a really interesting group of faculty [here], and we actively do things. I get to learn things all the time from them that I didn't know.

And that's important to me. . . . On top of that, we have the opportunity to go out and make a difference—to deal with societal issues—in our research. And we can act as a role models for our students that way; we can actually be applied anthropologists in this way." A Major State faculty member illustrated the revitalizing effects his involvement in the environmental studies master's program had on his life when he remarked: "I have met marvelous people [in this program]. This sharing with faculty from different disciplines is very rewarding. I wouldn't have met some of these close friends of mine if I hadn't been involved in [this program]. We share the conviction that this really is the way that this [solving environmental problems] has to be done. It is not just an engineering problem or just a political problem; it is all of it together."

Weak Institutional Commitment Notwithstanding these positive assessments, stakeholders in eight of the seventeen community-centered programs expressed concern over the weak institution-level commitment to the service orientation of their master's program.[9] Institutional administrators in this subset of cases were generally committed to basic research or undergraduate teaching, and they advocated and supported institutional reward structures that primarily reflected those interests. Some community-centered program administrators and faculty informed us that such reward structures undermined the efficacy of their programs by failing to recognize, and appropriately reward, faculty involvement in community-service, applied research and teaching activities benefiting students as well as external constituencies.

To begin with, interviewees in several community-centered programs made it clear that, even though institutional administrators publicly stated that service was an important part of their campus mission, their commitment to, and support for, service-related activities was weak at best. A Major State environmental studies professor told us that, while "service to the state" was considered an abiding commitment of the university, most campus administrators gave "lip service" to master's programs that sought to actualize this mission. He found this particularly troublesome because administrators seldom provided their master's program with the recognition or resources needed to sustain its service-centered emphasis: "The university doesn't give anything more than lip service to this program. So there are no rewards; when new space becomes available, this program doesn't get it. The program hasn't been recognized by the chancellor or given rewards or highlights of any sort, to my knowledge. And it's so silly because the university is always looking for ways to show that it has been useful to the state. And this is sitting here, ready-made. . . . So you have some potential benefits to the university that are not being milked." Similarly, a Southern State nursing professor remarked that, while serving the "urban community" was an integral part of the institution's mission, the university's new president was "not supporting that at all": "He has focused on developing a national reputation for [Southern State] at the expense of providing a rich educational experience for the city's larger urban community."

Interviewees in other programs, particularly at those national and regional universities where the doctorate was conferred, often supported these interpretations, emphasizing that the service orientation of their master's programs often went unsupported by institutional administrators. As one Western State faculty member put it: "Our master's is a very undernourished program. . . . We're a stepchild to [Western State's] medical school." Similarly, a Phelps environmental studies professor told us: "Most universities like [Phelps] are, at the graduate level, very doctoral oriented. And they don't have professional master's programs. . . . It's [professional master's education] still an anomaly at this university. We're like an outer moon of Pluto in a large constellation; we routinely disappear from sight."

We learned from faculty and program administrators in these eight programs that institutional reward structures, including promotion and tenure policies, seldom recognized their involvement in community-service or applied (and, frequently, collaborative) research. In particular, reward structures minimized the value of the professional contributions faculty made when working with practitioners (either directly in the field or in an advisory capacity on external boards and committees). A Phelps professor told us, for example, that faculty publications in nonuniversity professional magazines and service on community and professional committees often went unaccounted for in the university's tenure review process:

> During my tenure review process, I had what I thought were just a bunch of publications in professional newspapers and journals that didn't count for anything. And I had lots of appointments on prestigious outside [environmental policy] boards. But then I was told that this wasn't going to help me get tenure; I needed to get more peer-reviewed journal articles. So, for about four years, all I did was "pump out" peer-reviewed publications. It worked for me, but I can think of one person who didn't do this, and he didn't get tenure. And he did great service to the university. He sacrificed himself to this place, and, in the end, it wasn't good enough because he didn't have the publications.

A faculty member in Appleby State's microbiology program also expressed frustration and concern over the lack of recognition provided to service-related activities in tenure and promotion decisions at her institution. "When I went through tenure," she remarked, "people didn't have this propensity for adding up numbers—how many publications you had. . . . Now, I think, the young people coming in will not have the luxuries I had. . . . They will be forced to give up some of the things that we [the older faculty] got to do, like service. Service to the department, service to the institution, service to the community. That's downgraded now. [The message is:] 'Don't spend your time on that [service] because you don't get any credit for that in P & T (promotion and tenure decisions) and merit. That wasn't true when I went through the process." In fact, a high-ranking administrator at Appleby State made it very clear to us that faculty service to "running a good master's program" had little to no effect on promotion or tenure decisions at this traditionally undergraduate institution.

Faculty and program administrators throughout this subset of community-centered programs likewise communicated to us that applied research was seldom recognized in their institution's reward structure. To wit, many noted that campus administrators often dismissed the value of applied research activities because they failed to "advance" knowledge (and thus contribute to the institution's reputation) to the same degree that basic, or pure, research did. An environmental studies program administrator at Major State made this point:

Many [institutional administrators] recognize the quality, rigor, and value of these applied projects, but many do not. It depends on whether the person has had any exposure to this kind of [applied] work. Frankly, many do not know what goes into a project like this; they don't know what quality is. They have a prejudice against group, team efforts—how do you identify who did what? is it integrative work or simply disciplinary pieces poorly done and stapled together with no integration? . . . So there has been a real feeling that this is not basic knowledge, not serious stuff, not adding to the corpus of knowledge that will advance human understanding and human activity. I'm not downgrading basic research at all. It's all [basic and applied research] very critical; I believe it all advances human welfare and understanding [but many institutional administrators disagree].

In varying degrees, institutional emphases on "basic" over "applied" research had significant implications for the awarding of tenure in many of the community-centered programs. A professor in Southern State's nursing program told us that their president's emphasis on "pure, bench-type research" in tenure decisions was leading many faculty to abandon the applied research studies they conducted on community health care issues. At Southeast State a program administrator similarly explained that campus administrators were moving away from their traditional emphasis on applied research in tenure and promotion decisions. In turn, untenured faculty were producing fewer technical reports and other documents for nonuniversity professionals, focusing their energies instead on basic research for publication in peer-reviewed journals. And a Major State environmental studies professor remarked that he advised junior faculty members to establish themselves as "basic researchers" before branching out into more action-oriented research projects in the community: "The institutional attitude is that, once you have a focused [basic] research record, have built up your credentials, you gain elbow room, [that's when you can] feel emancipated."

Faculty and program administrators identified one other indicator of the relatively weak commitment campus administrators demonstrated toward this subset of community-centered programs: the lack of recognition and rewards provided for teaching in master's programs. Many interviewees—including those at Western State, Phelps, Major State, Southern State, and Southeast State—told us that teaching often accounted for relatively little in their institution's tenure and promotion decisions. At primarily undergraduate institutions like Appleby State and Vernon, faculty said that teaching master's students came "out of their hides" since merit reviews seldom recognized their involvement with master's education. As one Appleby State faculty member put it, "I write down all of the teaching and advising I've done in the master's program on my merit reviews, but it never does any good; it's the journal articles that matter."

Despite the lack of recognition and rewards provided to faculty and program administrators in this subset of programs, many of these individuals remained strongly committed to community service, applied research, and teaching-related activities associated with their master's programs. They told us, however, that the experience they offered students, and the quality of services they provided to their nonuniversity constituents, was not at the level it would be if their program received stronger support from campus administrators.

By way of comparison, we spoke with several interviewees in the other nine community-centered programs who suggested that they were able to provide a high-quality master's because institutional administrators valued, and rewarded, master's-related activities. We learned, for example, that institutional administrators at four of these nine institutions had developed institutional policies that supported applied, community-centered research activities and placed a high priority on teaching in tenure and merit review decisions. Many interviewees in these programs impressed on us that university administrators supported master's education largely because they, too, were devoted to university service in their communities, through both research and teaching-related activities. A City-State institutional administrator represented the views of many stakeholders in these community-centered programs when he remarked: "I think the master's degree affords the best opportunity to educate beyond the baccalaureate the largest proportion of people and to advance them professionally, culturally, philosophically. I think the master's provides our society with the best opportunity to enhance individuals in all of these ways." He later added that he "strongly encouraged" and recognized departments in which faculty "broadened their understandings" of applied master's programs and "took master's students seriously."

While some faculty and program administrators told us that the quality of their master's program would have been enhanced if institutional administrators were more fully committed to service-oriented activities, most stakeholders in the community-centered programs nonetheless expressed a high degree of satisfaction with the overall quality and value of their master's programs. Many student and alumni interviewees said that their master's experiences had transformed them into confident social stewards who conceived of, and approached, their professional practices from more critical, reflexive, and holistic standpoints. A Peterson nursing alumna aptly summarized the overall character and value of the community-centered experiences students had in their master's programs:

> After twenty-one years of nursing, I am very enthusiastic about nursing. You would think, with everything that I've been through in my career, I would have said, "To hell with this. I don't have to deal with this." But I think that's what the program does. [It generates an enthusiam for serving others and the profession.] I'm a different person than what I was when I entered the program, not just because of the theory I learned or how to apply it but also because of what I learned about myself, about nurses, about the nursing profession, and what I learned about working with other people—all of that is really what makes the program special for me. As far as I'm concerned, a home study course could teach the book knowledge. But this program was a lot more than that for me because of the people—the faculty, the students, the clinical supervisors. . . . This program gave me the confidence to listen to myself and to trust myself.

## PART FOUR

REINFORCING VITALITY
IN MASTER'S EDUCATION

We have thus far viewed master's education at two levels: the individual-case level, as represented in vignettes and case studies, and the cross-case level, as represented in decision-situations and program types. In part 4 we extend our cross-case analysis by generalizing across the entire sample of forty-seven master's programs.

In chapter 10 we address the quality of master's programs by examining a single question: What characteristics, or "attributes," of master's programs did stakeholders believe contributed most to enhancing the quality of master's experiences? To address this question, we define "attributes of high-quality master's experiences" as those program characteristics and conditions that substantially strengthened stakeholders' experiences and had positive, long-term effects on participants in master's education.

We chose this approach as the last passageway through our interview material for three reasons. First, in describing their master's experiences, almost all interviewees told us how their program enhanced their own learning and development as well as the growth and long-term development of other program participants. Second, because many of our readers are in positions (administrative, faculty, student, policymaker, employer) to influence master's education, we presume that they will be especially interested in what we learned about the conditions and factors that contribute to high-quality master's experiences. Third, and closely related, we assume that this approach will be useful as a "thinking device" as stakeholders plan, develop, and evaluate master's programs.

In developing attributes of high-quality master's experiences, we build upon the analyses and findings presented in parts 2 and 3. This notwithstanding, our approach is different in two ways. First, we analyzed our interview material across all forty-seven cases without partitioning the cases. Second, we focused exclusively on a single dimension related to stakeholders' experiences: attributes of high-quality master's experiences. (In the concluding section of each of the four chapters presenting an idealized program type, we presented stakeholder evaluations of the quality and value of their overall experiences. In these sections we examined interviewees' evaluations of their overall experiences, not attributes of high-quality master's experiences.)

To identify these attributes, we used two criteria: (1) each had to be communicated by interviewees in more than one stakeholder group (institutional and program administrators, faculty, students, alumni, and employers), and (2) each had to be viewed as important by a substantial number of interviewees. All of the program attributes we identified were present in a small number of cases in our sample, and many of them were exhibited in most of the other programs. Programs we classified in the apprenticeship and community-centered idealized program types exhibited more of these attributes than did programs included in the ancillary and career advancement program types.

Chapter 10 is divided into two sections. In the first section, we present the attributes that emerged from our analysis, grouping them into four broad clusters: culture, planned learning experiences, resources, and leadership and the human dimension. We discuss why stakeholders considered each attribute important, and occasionally we draw from our case study material. In the second section, we revisit traditional perspectives on the attributes of graduate program quality in light of our findings.

In the final chapter, chapter 11, we develop our overall conclusions and offer some suggestions for reinforcing vitality in master's education in the United States. In the first of two sections, we discuss stakeholder views of their experiences as well as their assessments of the individual and social benefits of master's education. We learned that, despite often being relegated to second-class status within academe, master's education is far more successful than the literature and the conventional wisdom suggest, and it provides a critically important bridge between colleges and universities and the professional workplace. We conclude that master's education is a "silent success," especially for students, degree holders, employers, and society at large.

In light of our findings, we conclude the chapter, and the book, with a series of considerations that we hope will help reinforce this already vital element of higher education. We raise considerations, including the overall suggestion that master's education should be viewed as a separate and legitimate degree activity worthy of strong support, for each of the following groups involved with master's education: policymakers, professional and accrediting associations, employers, institutional administrators, faculty and program administrators, and students.

10

Attributes of High-Quality Master's Experiences

Throughout our nearly eight hundred interviews, we found most stake-holders eager to discuss the ways in which their master's experiences contributed to their own and others' learning and development. Notwith-standing overall variation across the forty-seven programs in our sample in terms of stakeholder experiences (as well as in terms of program purposes and other contextual factors such as student characteristics and instruc-tional delivery), we learned that there were certain attributes that cut across programs which substantially strengthened stakeholders' master's experi-ences and had positive, long-term effects on participants.

In this chapter we present our findings about attributes of high-quality master's experiences. First, we discuss specific attributes of master's pro-grams within each of four broad clusters: culture, planned learning experi-ences, resources, and leadership and the human dimension. We describe each attribute, discuss why stakeholders felt it contributed to the quality of their master's experiences, and consider supporting conditions. In the concluding section, we revisit the literature on attributes of program quali-ty in light of our findings.

We introduce three caveats to inform the reading of this chapter. First, we emphasize that the attributes we identify were often expressed differ-ently across the programs in our sample. For the most part, we collapse these differences in order to describe common themes. Second, we stress that it is the combination among many, not necessarily all, of these at-tributes within any given master's program which contributed to the quali-ty of stakeholders' experiences. Third, we urge readers not to embrace uncritically the attributes described in this chapter as a "cookbook" for planning and evaluating master's programs: our intent is for readers to use these attributes, along with the decision-situations and program types

295

presented earlier, as thinking devices to facilitate continuing dialogue aimed at reinforcing the vitality of master's education.

Culture

Unity of Purpose among Program Participants

We learned that high-quality master's experiences were associated with master's programs in which there was a unity of purpose among faculty, administrators, students, and, occasionally, employers. This unity was centered around stakeholders' common understandings of, and support for, a single purpose, or set of purposes, for their master's program.

Interviewees made it clear that unity of purpose was important for three major reasons. First, faculty, administrator, and student agreement on program purposes helped to develop a collective ownership in, and commitment to, the specific program. Second, because stakeholders shared mutual understandings about program purposes, their behaviors and activities could be informally coordinated without the need for elaborate rules and procedures, which can stultify a program. Third, when participants were unified about purpose, they sent a clear and unambiguous message to their internal and external audiences about what was important and valued in their programs. Such a message, we learned, was especially important in building effective relationships with institutional administrators and employers as well as in recruiting students and faculty who shared similar interests and commitments.

To illustrate, interviewees from all stakeholder groups at Parks-Beecher University repeatedly articulated one overarching purpose for their business master's program: to provide African Americans with the knowledge and skills to secure and be successful in advanced-level positions, mostly in Fortune 500 corporations. Interviewees told us that unity of purpose engendered a strong sense of commitment among all participants and helped focused their energies. Students, for instance, developed numerous outside-of-class learning activities targeted at increasing their skills as business professionals, and faculty, in addition to their own teaching responsibilities, took the initiative to invite corporate professionals into the classroom to share their expertise with students.

Two underlying conditions, in particular, helped to facilitate unity of purpose among participants in master's programs. First, and perhaps most important, there was a leader (or leaders) who actively listened to program participants and communicated a shared direction for the program. Second, faculty and administrators invited students (both full- and part-time), alumni, and employers to serve on program committees and advisory boards in order to foster purposes that would be mutually understood and shared by all participants.

Supportive Learning Environment

We also learned that high-quality master's experiences were nurtured in learning environments in which an ethic of cooperative support and rigorous intellectual challenge were at one and the same time embraced by program participants. When this ethic informed and infused the culture of master's programs, it substantially enriched the experiences of both faculty and students.

Interviewees emphasized that they greatly valued a program environment that encouraged cooperative learning among faculty, administrators, and students. In many programs this was manifested in animated classroom discussions, small-group activities, and laboratory experiments. Cooperative learning carried over into outside-of-class learning interactions and activities as well, with students and faculty interacting with one another during "brown-bag" lunches, faculty dinners, student-sponsored gatherings, joint research activities, and informal discussions. An Appleby State microbiology alumnus, for example, recalled the cooperative interactions he had in his master's program:

> The instructors that I had were really interested in what they were doing, and it almost seemed like . . . everybody was getting together and doing this learning. I still remember the day when we made DNA, when we actually wound this material out on a glass rod—and how many years ago that was! It was something we all worked together on. We were like colleagues, and it kind of gave you a good feeling, and you learn so much from it. I like that professional approach.

Effective master's programs also emphasized rigor and challenge by weaving high expectations and risk taking into the fabric of the master's experience. Not only did faculty and program administrators hold high expectations for themselves, but they also assumed that students would challenge them, and one another. Likewise, students assumed that they would learn a great deal from one another, and they expected to share their experiences, insights, and knowledge with other students and faculty alike.

Similarly, we learned that rigor and challenge were supported when participants were encouraged to take risks in their learning. Faculty laid the foundation for risk taking in two major ways. First, they developed a trusting learning environment in which students felt "safe to fail." Second, faculty took risks themselves, serving as models to show students that they too were constantly learning, including learning from their mistakes.

A Helena State theater alumna, for example, told us that faculty encouraged risk taking by leading the students and actually doing the exercises with them and by building an "environment that was nonthreatening": "The faculty allowed students to be vulnerable but at the same time safe within that vulnerability so that they [students] felt trusted. They built a trusting environment, a trust among students and their advisor. Taking those risks was important." Within the context of the trust that developed between students and faculty in these supportive, and demanding, learning environments, participants challenged orthodoxies, considered alternative perspectives on issues, and often engaged in learning activities that were new to them.

Mutually shared expectations for intellectual rigor and challenge, when emphasized within a supportive and cooperative learning environment, were important because they encouraged faculty and students to take risks that pressed the boundaries of their potentials and helped them to grow in unanticipated ways. As a Phelps theater alumnus put it: "I was able to stretch myself in incredible ways [in my master's program]. I may have possibly done the best work of my life there. I did things there that I may never have the opportunity to do again. . . . I feel a lot more powerful and self-assured as an actor now than I did before I entered the program."

Planned Learning Experiences

Core Course Work

Many stakeholders highlighted core course work as an important attribute associated with high-quality master's experiences. These core learning experiences were constructed around an integrated set of disciplinary, multidisciplinary, and, occasionally, interdisciplinary courses. They were offered on a regular basis and were classified as master's courses; they were not advanced baccalaureate-level courses in which students obtained graduate credit by writing an additional class paper, as was sometimes the case in master's studies.

To illustrate, in most of the business programs in our sample, students completed core courses within each of four functional areas in the discipline (marketing, finance, management, and accounting) then enrolled in a business policy course, which integrated the knowledge and practices from these functional areas in a capstone learning experience. In most of the environmental studies programs, the core learning experience consisted of a collection of interdisciplinary courses. In several of the nursing, applied anthropology, and education programs, both disciplinary and cognate courses comprised core requirements.

Interviewees emphasized that core course work contributed to the quality of students' master's experiences because it provided them with a broad understanding of the theoretical underpinnings and practices of their disciplines. To again borrow a phrase from a Prestige State engineering professor, these courses "put more tools" in a student's "toolbox" by teaching them the fundamental knowledge and skills of their fields.

We came to appreciate that there were two underlying conditions that supported core learning experiences in master's programs. First, faculty and program administrators shared clearly defined understandings of the knowledge, skills, and practices they expected master's students to learn. Accordingly, they constructed core course work requirements that, as one part of the overall curriculum, satisfied their own, and also student and employer, expectations for what a master's-educated graduate in their field should know. Second, effective core learning experiences were dependent upon a "critical mass" of faculty to teach core courses as well as an adequate number of students to ensure that these courses were offered, primarily for graduate students, on a regular basis.

Immersion

We learned that high-quality master's experiences involved students and faculty in intense, immersion-type learning situations in which they became deeply engaged in their education, often to the point of being completely absorbed in their work. These immersion experiences took many different forms in the master's programs we studied.

In programs serving a part-time student population, faculty and administrators provided an immersion-type experience for themselves and their students by offering nontraditional, intensive courses that met for extended time periods over a series of weekends during the academic year or a number of weeks in the summer. These immersion experiences not only allowed part-time students and faculty to explore issues in depth without the constraints of traditional shorter class sessions but also provided faculty and students with the opportunity to work closely with one another, which often contributed to building a strong sense of camaraderie among program participants. In programs that served a full-time student population, immersion-type experiences were nurtured by the creation of an environment in which faculty and students were continually interacting with one another. At best, these interactions permeated an entire program—in classroom discussions, in hallways, over lunch or coffee, in the laboratory or field, and at student- and faculty-sponsored gatherings.

Based on our interviews, the importance of immersion experiences in cultivating high-quality master's experiences cannot be overstated. For faculty, these learning experiences helped to engender a strong sense of dedication to master's students and to their master's programs. For students, they afforded the opportunity to know faculty and other students on a more intimate basis, strengthened their commitment to a given program and field, helped them develop a sense of professional identity, and provided a forum for the development of student cohort groups. Overall, immersion experiences provided faculty, students, and administrators with a powerful vehicle for helping to build a cooperative, collegial, and challenging learning environment in their master's programs.

Doing-centered Learning

Another attribute of high-quality master's experiences was that students "worked the interface between the workplace and academe" by engaging in what we label doing-centered learning—activities such as laboratory or field research, internships in local health care or social service agencies, consultancies for government or nonprofit agencies, practica in schools, and participation in professional arts performances. Students were given sufficient responsibility in these situations such that their on-the-job performances entailed economic, personal, and policy consequences. While encouraging students to be independent and responsible for their work, faculty and site supervisors also recognized that students occasionally needed guidance and hence arranged periodic meetings to provide feedback.

Interviewees told us that the doing that was the centerpiece of these learning experiences was particularly important to students because it helped them to connect the principles and theories they learned in their courses to the kinds of "messy" problems they faced in the real world. Indeed, since students often experienced real consequences associated with the work they completed in doing-centered activities—and were provided supportive guidance from faculty, site supervisors, and work colleagues—they learned how to work more effectively as professionals in their fields, how to test and revise their assumptions, and why some approaches and theories were more workable in addressing or solving issues than others. As part of this process, students developed a critical awareness of their respective fields within a larger context, questioning assumptions about the changing nature of a given field, seeing practical problems in terms of alternative solutions, and understanding real-world problems and situations in various shades of gray.

To illustrate, a microbiology student at Middle State described the value of doing in this way: "The real learning for me takes place when I can go into the lab and apply it. Then I go back again and read the text. Then I go back to the lab and manipulate the parameters. The more practical experience I have, the better off I am. The experience [in the lab] helps to drive home the ideas they [the professors] are trying to get across." Along these same lines, a City-State applied anthropology alumnus told us why he valued his practicum experience:

The practicum, to me, was the strongest piece because you're out there in the real world. You act in a real-world setting. That's critical. . . . You're only getting half the story sitting here [at the university] learning about whatever it is you're learning about—because implementing it in the real world is a whole other ball game. There's not a textbook out there about what to do about the feud between the social workers and the planners. There's not a textbook about why the grants come down the way they do, how to handle competition, how to become competitive in your grants writing. To learn about competition, personalities, state and local government, institutions, who the players are—all those things are things you can only learn when you're in the practicum.

There are two key underlying conditions that promoted and fostered effective doing-centered learning experiences in master's programs. First, faculty themselves often took part in these activities, usually as researchers, consultants, or nonuniversity workplace professionals. Because of their involvement, faculty modeled their own doing to students while also encouraging, and frequently requiring, students to participate in laboratory, performance, internship, clinical, or practica experiences. Second, faculty and administrators who valued the importance of doing-centered learning in their master's programs maintained strong ties with employers and alumni. These ties often helped faculty locate sites at which students could practice doing within a real-world setting.

Individualization

To ensure that students had personally fulfilling learning experiences that encouraged their growth, faculty associated with high-quality master's experiences provided all students (full- and part-time alike) with sustained individualized attention. In effective master's programs, there was at least one person who was highly attentive to each student's personal and professional needs. In some programs, individual student needs were addressed by a faculty advisor (or, occasionally, a committee of faculty members) who worked closely with the student to develop his or her course of study in a conscientious manner and spent a meaningful amount of time with the student. In others, postdoctoral students and advanced doctoral candidates assumed this role, and sometimes this individualization was fostered by program administrators or faculty who took special interest in a student.

Interviewees emphasized that, regardless of the means by which it was offered, giving personal attention to students was important for two major reasons. First, it dignified each student and helped ensure that his or her individual learning needs were addressed. Second, when students worked with faculty who took an active interest in them as individuals, it not only helped them to understand that they could make valuable contributions to the learning process, but it also provided that "little bit of extra attention" they often needed to develop into competent and confident professionals.

Devoting individualized time and attention to students is a time-intensive task that requires the commitment of faculty and program administrators to master's students. This underlying condition, more than any other, infused and informed individualized learning experiences. Needless to say, individualization was best facilitated and sustained in master's programs when institutional and departmental reward structures and policies recognized and supported faculty for engaging in teaching, advising, and collaborative research with students.

Tangible Product (Thesis or Project/Report)

We learned that another attribute of high-quality master's experiences was that students produced a tangible product—whether a thesis, project report, or internship report—which was of some value to the field as well as to them personally. Students presented their product orally to a faculty committee and, in some instances, an extradepartmental audience.

The activities involved in producing a document that presents a student's research or practicum results were important because they encouraged students to integrate perspectives developed both in core course work and in doing-centered learning experiences and to use and further develop their analytical and written communication skills. Further, since the completion of a tangible product required a significant amount of time, individual effort, and mental endurance, students often became more self-confident in their abilities to make valuable contributions to their field.

By way of illustration, an alumnus of Appleby State's microbiology program told us that, while her course work provided her with greater understanding, it was not until she began writing the thesis that she moved beyond "simply acquiring" knowledge. As she put it:

> You have to do both—have to have the knowledge and apply it, and you have to be able to communicate it, in writing and verbally. . . . The process requires lots of red pens, lots of frustration. It requires a certain amount of struggle. If you're only doing what came easy before it, then what is the point? It requires that personal struggle. It's different for each person. Some people can't write, others aren't well organized, others can't communicate verbally, but, in finishing a master's thesis, you have to do all of these things. You are forced to do it.

Many interviewees emphasized that the single most important condition underlying effective "tangible-product" learning experiences was faculty commitment to master's students. This commitment was expressed when faculty spent time guiding students through the research process, discussing problems as they arose in the lab or the field, and critically reviewing and providing constructive feedback on drafts of student theses and reports.

Outside-of-Class Activities

Taking a cue from a Southern State nursing professor—who described the curriculum as "everything that happens to students, . . . not just the courses and the content . . . [but] the whole context of their educational experience"—we came to appreciate that outside-of-class activities significantly contributed to high-quality master's experiences. These activities included orientation programs, brown-bag seminars, journal clubs, faculty-student social hours, and end-of-semester parties and picnics.

Outside-of-class activities were an important attribute of quality master's experiences for several reasons. To begin with, they provided faculty and students with forums for keeping abreast of emerging developments in their fields. A Major State sociology student told us, for example, that the brown-bag seminars she attends "are a valuable part of being in this program because you really see what people are doing in their research": "In the class analysis specialization, they bring in guest lecturers [from universities all across the United States], and they stay on campus for three weeks, and they give two brown-bag seminars a week. They're great." Several stakeholders also said that activities such as journal clubs, laboratory meetings, and performance rehearsals offered valuable opportunities for faculty and students to learn from one another in relaxed, informal settings. As a microbiology student at Major State put it:

> In this program, we have group lab meetings where we'll just get together and talk about what we're doing in the lab at the current time. They're real casual and informal, but some of the students and faculty who are in the other labs will get up and say, "I think you're doing that wrong; maybe you should try this or that." I know my department and my lab, in particular, really try to get involved with other laboratories because they think that interaction is very important. I think the more interactions you have in journal clubs and in lab meetings, the better off you are. You learn so much from other students and faculty [in those meetings].

Still other interviewees suggested that outside-of-class activities were important because they helped to cultivate a sense of camaraderie among program participants. In Pierpont's business program, for instance, students and faculty said that the program's emphasis on outside-of-class study groups—as well as numerous faculty- and student-sponsored social and sporting events—contributed to the development of a Pierpont "spirit" that stressed cooperation and teamwork among students.

In the master's programs in our sample, outside-of-class learning experiences were nurtured and sustained when faculty and administrators recognized and supported, financially and otherwise, the important contributions that these activities made to the master's experiences of program participants. In addition, when students became actively involved in developing and sponsoring colloquia, speaker series, and assorted social events, their efforts significantly added to the overall quality of outside-of-class activities in master's programs.

Resources

Institutional Support

We came to appreciate that institutional support was another important attribute of high-quality master's experiences. With few exceptions, campus and departmental administrators as well as faculty and students underscored the supporting role that adequate institutional and program facilities, equipment, and funding played in enhancing the overall effectiveness of master's programs. In addition, interviewees emphasized that supportive institutional promotion and tenure policies were critical in fostering faculty involvement in master's education.

Sufficient institutional resources provided an important part of the basic infrastructure upon which quality master's experiences were initially developed. When programs had adequate facilities and equipment—such as laboratories, theaters, computers, library resources, and essential field-related equipment and supplies—faculty and students were able to focus their full attention on teaching and learning, rather than being distracted by the absence of the "basic tools" needed to perform their tasks. As many science, engineering, and theater students pointed out to us, when scientific equipment was so outdated that it broke down or theater facilities were so limited that certain kinds of productions could not be mounted, it was difficult to learn. In much the same way, when institutional administrators provided adequate funding to ensure adequate faculty and students in master's programs (such as through additional faculty lines and student assistance dollars), they provided the foundation upon which a supportive learning environment could be built. As an Appleby State institutional administrator put it, when faculty and students do not have peers with whom they may share their ideas or collaborate on joint research projects, they feel isolated and miss out on the opportunity to participate in an "exciting graduate-level atmosphere": "Education is not only in the classroom—it's also in contact with your colleagues. Critical mass is important to developing this camaraderie."

We learned that institutional administrators in effective master's programs went one step beyond providing financial support for facilities, equipment, faculty lines, and student assistantships: they also provided visible symbolic support to master's education. Not only did these individuals recognize the role that master's education played in developing highly skilled professionals for university and nonuniversity workplaces; they also acknowledged disciplinary differences and recognized faculty involvement in master's education in institutional promotion and tenure policies. An institutional administrator at Helena State explained, for example, that he encouraged faculty involvement in master's education by crafting supportive promotion and tenure policies "that have an understanding of the varied nature of scholarship": "You have to understand what a show would mean to an artist. You have to understand what kinds of things master's students in theater do." He said that Helena State's institutional reward structure recognized juried exhibits and dramatic performances by "crediting them in the same way as research and publication" and also rewarded faculty generously for their involvement in teaching master's students, both in class and in university-related productions. Across many cases in our sample, program administrators and faculty told us that pecuniary and nonpecuniary institutional support contributed substantially to the effectiveness of their master's programs.

Departmental Support

Interviewees also emphasized that strong departmental support greatly enhanced stakeholders' experiences in master's programs. In particular, we learned that sufficient allocations of departmental financial resources to master's programs, faculty commitment to master's education, and faculty assistance in placing master's students were closely associated with effective master's programs.

To begin with, when departments allocated sufficient financial resources to their master's programs, both in terms of dollars for general instructional support and for student assistantships, faculty and students received the basic resource support necessary to fully participate in the learning process. Contrariwise, when departmental financial support for master's education was lacking, faculty and students frequently were forced to divert time and energy away from master's-related activities as they scrambled to find sufficient funds for equipment, supplies, student stipends, or part-time employment for students. Moreover, in departments in which faculty and administrators shared a general commitment to master's education—and developed merit review policies that supported faculty for their involvement—faculty and students generally had higher-quality master's experiences.

In effective master's programs, there was one other expression of departmental support: faculty assisted master's students, upon graduation, in advancing their professional careers (either as doctoral students or as practitioners in the nonuniversity workplace). As one Appleby State administrator told us, faculty and administrators who take master's education seriously provide this kind of support because, "when you take on master's students, you also take on an obligation that they will be employed or will go on for a Ph.D.": "Master's programs that are successful are the ones that have adopted that attitude—that students entrust us with another two or three years of their life and that we have an obligation to them that goes beyond the classroom." To this end, faculty maintained active alumni networks in their programs, utilized their informal contacts with colleagues, invited employers to campus to share information with students, cosponsored employer fairs, and allocated time to meet with students to discuss their questions about a specific field as well as strategies that might benefit them in realizing their professional goals.

Leadership and the Human Dimension

Faculty Involvement

We learned that high-quality master's experiences were also distinguished by another attribute: program faculty were both actively involved in their respective fields and strongly committed to master's education. Faculty not only contributed to their fields through various combinations of research, publication, performance, and community-related activities; they also devoted significant time and energy to master's students, largely out of their conviction that master's education served an important role in developing students as competent and confident professionals.

In many of the science and engineering programs in our study, for example, faculty told us that they combined their interests in research and master's education by involving master's students in joint research projects and, occasionally, by publishing and presenting papers with them. In other programs, faculty preferred to make individual contributions to their given field but assisted master's students by investing significant amounts of time discussing professional projects and research-related activities with them.

Interviewees emphasized that faculty who were jointly involved in field- and master's-related activities enhanced the quality of students' master's experiences in three ways. First, faculty who remained active learners in their fields often instilled a kind of cutting-edge excitement in master's students. As one Major State electrical engineering alumnus put it: "Being at the cutting edge . . . that was valuable for me [during my master's]. I knew I was working with professors who were at the edge of what was being done in the area, and it was fun. It was a lot of fun being at the edge."

Second, faculty who shared their research, theatrical performance, or service-related experiences with master's students often provided students with valuable insights into perspectives and practices that shape their field.

Perhaps most important, faculty who took an active interest in master's students—by involving them in joint research activities, discussing problems or issues with them which arose during their internship or clinical experiences, or simply meeting with them outside of class to explore their research interests and professional goals—often instilled a passion for learning in their students. As a student from Middle State's microbiology program told us: "The faculty really care about you in this program. And you'd be surprised—they have their own families and their own problems, but somebody takes time out for you. And you're willing to do the effort, and you can see how much you can do. . . . When you have an instructor and you have a question and you can talk about it, then you're willing to go and find out even more about it on your own." Indeed, we learned that, even when faculty were "scholars of the first magnitude," this alone did not guarantee enriching master's experiences for students. As many students and alumni emphasized, faculty, regardless of their scholarly reputations, who were not committed to sharing their knowledge or taking time to meet with and assist students did not markedly enhance the overall quality of students' master's experiences.

Supportive institutional and departmental reward structures that recognized faculty for being involved in their fields—both as scholars and as teachers committed to developing master's-prepared professionals—were important conditions that contributed to faculty involvement with master's education and master's students. Additionally, when faculty and program administrators came together as a group and agreed on the purpose and role of master's programs in their departments, they were better able to integrate the time and effort they devoted to their field-related interests and to master's education.

Faculty with Nonuniversity Workplace Experience

We also learned that faculty with professional nonuniversity workplace experience often contributed important insights and understandings that enhanced stakeholders' master's experiences. Administrators in effective master's programs (particularly in established and emerging professional fields) incorporated these perspectives into their programs by employing part-time adjunct professors who worked full-time as professionals in the nonuniversity workplace as well as full-time faculty who had spent part of their professional careers in nonuniversity work settings.

We were told that faculty who had professional experience in settings outside of academe enhanced students' learning experiences in three ways. First, these individuals provided students with firsthand knowledge of how theories and practices "work" in the real world, information that enabled students to become more effective at translating theory into practice in their professional work situations. Second, such faculty were more aware of the competencies and skills that students needed to perform successfully on the job, and they often were very effective at teaching these skills because they understood their applicability in nonuniversity workplace settings. Third, students often trusted and more easily related to faculty who "had been there," who themselves had experienced how difficult it is to integrate knowledge learned in a range of classes and textbooks and then use it effectively in messy, real-life situations. According to many students and employers, such faculty were important in helping students successfully learn how to "work the interface between the workplace and academe."

Faculty and administrators in effective master's programs developed recruitment strategies for hiring full- and part-time faculty who had diverse work experiences and who displayed a commitment to helping students successfully negotiate the transition from academe to the nonuniversity workplace. In addition, faculty and administrators also developed and supported departmental reward structures that recognized faculty for being involved in applied research, developing and monitoring internship and clinical student placements, and working with nonuniversity professionals on assorted committees. These activities often enriched faculty understandings of the nonuniversity workplace and, particularly in established and emerging professional fields, further enhanced their teaching effectiveness.

Committed Students with Diverse Backgrounds and Experiences

In accordance with the conventional wisdom, we learned that "good" students were critical to nurturing and sustaining high-quality master's experiences for both faculty and students. Yet, in effective master's programs, good students were defined less in terms of conventional indicators—such as high student test scores and undergraduate grade point average (G.P.A.)—than in terms of three other attributes: commitment, diversity, and experience. We came to appreciate that students who were strongly committed to learning and who had diverse backgrounds—in terms of race, ethnicity, gender, and class as well as work, educational, and life experiences—significantly enhanced the intellectual and social milieu of master's programs, regardless of field of study.

Students and faculty alike gained in knowledge and insight when students brought a variety of cultural and work experiences to master's programs. As one Longmont student told us, students who had diverse backgrounds and experiences often acted as "living libraries" for their peers and professors. Indeed, we spoke with many students and alumni who indicated that listening to, and learning from, their peers' varied professional and life experiences proved to be one of the most valuable aspects of their master's experiences.

Student commitment to learning, both in interaction with their peers and in terms of their individual studies, likewise was an important characteristic of good master's students. One Longmont professor described this as the "piranha fish factor": faculty would raise an issue in class, and students, because they were strongly motivated to learn, immediately "sank their teeth" into exploring and discussing the issue in depth. According to many of the faculty members we interviewed, this kind of student commitment (regardless of full- or part-time student attendance) significantly enhanced faculty and students' learning experiences. A Major State microbiology faculty made this point when he said that the "best" students he worked with were "absolutely motivated": "I don't give a damn if they're a 2.2 [G.P.A.] student if they're motivated. . . . [Motivated students] walk in the lab, find what they want, and then all of sudden they become a 3.9 student because they know what they want. . . . I like to see students who are intense. I don't want somebody who tells me I am right. I want a student who will prove me wrong, then I know they're motivated—that they have an inquiring mind. That's when I know they'll be successful."

Administrators and faculty in effective master's programs established admissions criteria that not only included conventional measures of student quality but also placed considerable emphasis on attracting motivated, diverse students with a wide range of work and life experiences. Moreover, because they were interested in attracting, and retaining, full- and part-time students who were committed to their studies, administrators and faculty also reviewed carefully the stated goals and expectations students described on their applications for admission. This strategy helped faculty to determine if there was a "good fit" between student goals, program purposes, and faculty interests.

Leadership

Interviewees emphasized one final attribute of high-quality master's experiences: strong program leadership. As we came to understand, individuals who assumed leadership roles in effective master's programs emphasized a management approach that values listening to disparate stakeholder voices, recognizing similarities and differences among them, and working cooperatively with constituents in developing a clearly articulated and mutually shared direction for the program. In addition, the program leader (or leaders) was also savvy about how to make the program work. He or she acted as a strong advocate for the program to campus administrators, knew how to creatively make the most of resources, was adept at recruiting faculty committed to the program's focus, and was skilled at creating an environment in which faculty felt appreciated for devoting thoughtful and sustained effort to teaching and learning.

In some programs in our study, leadership was assumed by the department head or program director, while, in others, a full-time faculty member or a small group of faculty took on this responsibility. A professor at Southeast State, for example, described the way in which faculty worked cooperatively to develop their applied anthropology master's program:

> The faculty came together as a group, talked over their options, talked over what was happening in the field of anthropology, what kind of master's degree would really make sense. There were a number of people who were already doing applied anthropology and a number who did more traditional stuff. As a body, they agreed they would write a grant, reorient their own personal research programs, and develop a master's program that was integrative, comprehensive, and focused on this particular specialization. I was impressed.

Whether expressed by individuals who did or did not have positional power, leaders in effective master's programs capitalized on opportunities to nurture emergent leadership among program participants. They did so by developing a program culture that encouraged participants to express their views, develop new ideas, and exercise leadership in both small and large ways. In this respect, leaders not only listened to their diverse constituents, but they also invited them to share responsibility for building and sustaining an active learning environment in their master's programs. As a Longmont administrator put it, such an approach is "empowering—it gives power rather than takes it." Viewed in this way, leadership can be seen as a linchpin that connects the various components of a master's program and provides the essential glue that enables participants to cultivate an enriching master's experience for everyone involved.

Revisiting Traditional Perspectives on the Attributes of Program Quality

As we described in chapter 1, administrators and faculty in higher education have long voiced concern about the quality of master's education. Many administrators and scholars (as well as various representatives of colleges and universities, higher education agencies, and professional associations) have suggested criteria and indicators for evaluating and strengthening graduate programs in general and master's programs in particular. In effect, these criteria and indicators have been viewed as attributes of high-quality master's programs and, as such, provide a reference point against which to compare our findings.

As Conrad and Blackburn noted in their review of the literature on program quality in higher education and found in their quantitative studies of program quality at the master's level, there is no universal agreement on a single definition of *quality* in the literature (1985b, 1985a, 1986). Yet, as they and others have noted, there is nonetheless fairly widespread agreement on the general characteristics or attributes of quality master's programs. Only a few individuals have raised strong objection to these attributes (see Clark 1979; Millard 1984).

For the most part, those embracing traditional perspectives on program quality at the master's level have emphasized program characteristics that concern the "input" features of programs. These include attributes related to faculty, students, and resources (Ames 1979; Andrews 1979; Carr 1979; Conrad and Eagan 1990; Downey 1979). The quality of program faculty has received the most emphasis, with faculty quality defined largely in terms of their training, academic experience, and scholarly productivity. The quality of students has also been stressed, including their academic backgrounds, abilities, and willingness to commit to full-time study. Moreover, program resources (including facilities, services, financial aid, and library and computer support) have been underscored repeatedly.

Turning to program requirements, stakeholders who have embraced traditional perspectives—including many university presidents, graduate deans, and scholars—generally have emphasized four attributes of high-quality programs. First, they have stressed the importance of comprehensive examinations. Second, they have advocated a thesis requirement for all graduates of master's programs. Third, they have highlighted the importance of residency requirements. And fourth, they have underscored the salience of rigorous admissions requirements.

What have we learned in relation to these traditional views of the attributes of high-quality programs? To begin with, many of the faculty and administrators we interviewed believed that most, if not all, of these traditional attributes were important. They often placed considerable emphasis, for example, on the quality of students, faculty, and resources as traditionally defined. Further, some stressed the importance of comprehensive examinations, a thesis requirement, and the desirability of a full-time student population. Likewise, some students, alumni, and employers also valued these attributes.

Yet, while we found support for traditional attributes, especially among faculty and administrators, most were viewed as less important than other characteristics of master's programs. We learned, for instance, that the culture of master's programs, which has scarcely been discussed in the literature, was one of the most important overall dimensions of effective master's experiences. In particular, a unity of purpose among program stakeholders and a rich learning environment—one that stresses cooperation and support among program participants while they engage in rigorous, challenging learning experiences—were important attributes that significantly enhanced the vitality of master's education for all stakeholders.

In terms of program requirements, we learned that planned learning experiences such as core courses, immersion opportunities, doing-centered learning, individualization, and the completion of a tangible product (a thesis, project, or major report) were curricular attributes that substantially enriched the quality of stakeholders' experiences in master's programs. These requirements, with the exceptions of core courses and a thesis, rarely have been mentioned in the literature. Moreover, outside-of-class activities also added a significant quality dimension to master's education for students, faculty, and administrators.

Turning to program resources, we came to appreciate that institutional and departmental support were necessary, but not sufficient, conditions that contributed to high-quality master's experiences for program participants. Indeed, adequate financial support, equipment, facilities, and institutional and departmental reward structures provided the basic infrastructure that informed effective master's programs. Our findings suggest, however, that it was only when such resources were coupled with other program attributes that quality master's experiences were realized.

Finally, we came to understand the importance of leadership and the human dimension in master's education. To wit, full- and part-time faculty who were passionately invested both in their fields and in master's education—and who frequently also had nonuniversity workplace experience—significantly enhanced master's programs. Indeed, faculty who shared the belief that training at the master's level was an important endeavor and chose to invest themselves accordingly played a critical role in strengthening the vitality of master's education for all program participants. Similarly, committed students who had diverse backgrounds and work experiences, regardless of whether they pursued their studies on a full- or part-time basis, substantially enriched the master's experiences of faculty and students alike. Moreover, program leaders who nurtured a sense of shared ownership among program participants also contributed to the development and maintenance of high-quality learning experiences in master's programs.

In light of our findings concerning program attributes, we believe that everyone concerned about master's education should reexamine traditional assumptions and beliefs about quality in master's education. In suggesting this, we readily grant that program quality is an elusive concept that is easy to reify, and we do not advance the claim that our findings should be accepted without further consideration. Nevertheless, we hope that the understandings we developed—by listening to the diverse voices of nearly eight hundred stakeholders who expressed their views about attributes of program quality in relation to the different kinds of experiences they had in master's programs—will provide a useful thinking device for those involved in enhancing, evaluating, and studying the experiences of participants in master's education.

11

A Silent Success
Master's Education in the United States

Having listened to stakeholders' accounts of their master's experiences and analyzed their perspectives, we conclude by presenting our overall conclusions concerning the present and future of master's education in the United States. In the first of two sections, we develop our interpretations in relation to traditional views of master's education and propose that master's education has been far more successful than either the conventional wisdom or literature suggest. In the second section, we introduce some considerations intended to reinforce the vitality of master's education in the United States. As in the remainder of the book, the conclusions and interpretations in this chapter solely represent those of the three authors.

A Silent Success

Throughout the twentieth century, the literature conveyed widespread concern about the purposes, meaning, and quality of master's education. Policymakers and authors of numerous national reports, studies, and scholarly papers sharply criticized master's programs in the arts and sciences as well as in professional fields of study. Repeatedly, master's degrees were assigned second-class and consolation prize status, mostly by individuals associated with colleges and universities. As one recent observer put it: "The master's degree remains the weakest collegiate degree in America. . . . If there is a skeleton in higher education's closet, surely it is the poor quality of master's degrees that have been consistently neglected over the years" (Barak 1987, 32).

This conventional perspective on master's education persisted in the literature despite what we have labeled the "transformation" of master's education during the 1970s and 1980s. Spencer (1986), who referred to the "new face of the master's degree," and Glazer (1986), among many others, described how master's education had slowly been transformed with the rise of many new fields of study and the increased emphasis on interdisciplinarity, professionalization, career development, nontraditional delivery systems, new instructional technology, and a part-time student clientele. Interestingly, most people making substantive, field-specific contributions to the literature on master's programs during these two decades viewed master's education as a separate and legitimate degree activity. At the same time, however, many policymakers and observers questioned the quality and "integrity" of master's programs.

In recording the perspectives of those directly involved in master's education—including students, alumni, and employers as well as faculty and administrators—we came to understand that the experiences these individuals had with master's education were, for the most part, very positive and inconsistent with the largely negative views of master's education portrayed in the literature. Despite being relegated by some of the educators we interviewed to second-class status, we conclude that master's education in the United States has been a silent success—for degree holders, employers, and society in general.

Significantly, stakeholder esteem for master's programs, as well as variation in stakeholders' experiences, was not highly associated with any of the program and contextual features that we had incorporated into our sampling design, except that institutional administrators, and program faculty and administrators associated with departments in which the Ph.D. was offered, were generally less positive about master's education than were other stakeholders. For the most part, then, our conclusions are independent of factors such as type of control, geographic location, traditional or nontraditional delivery system, program prestige, and full-time or part-time student attendance. Instead, we came to understand that the experiences of the wide range of stakeholders we interviewed could be best understood in terms of five decision-situations, four program types, and selected attributes of high-quality master's experiences.

Throughout the study, we were often impressed—sometimes even astonished—by the extent to which students, program alumni, and faculty valued their master's experiences. Students and alumni particularly appreciated learning about diverse points of view and new developments in their fields, having the opportunity to pursue independent projects, and working with faculty who took an active interest in their learning. They highlighted the excitement of engaging in doing-centered learning and of successfully completing a major project or thesis. They took pride in becoming more knowledgeable and skilled contributors to their chosen professions. Moreover, many faculty and program administrators told us that they greatly enjoyed working with master's students and with one another in master's programs. In some instances they remarked that these interactions revitalized their personal commitment to teaching and learning.

More broadly, interviewees repeatedly emphasized the individual and social benefits of master's education. Most students and alumni told us that, at the individual level, their master's degrees were a valuable credential in the workplace and a boon to advancing their professional careers. Most graduates who pursued their doctorate similarly remarked that the master's prepared them well for more specialized study. Faculty, administrators, and employers generally concurred with these observations.

Equally important, we learned that there are important social benefits associated with master's education—benefits that have been largely invisible in the literature and to many people in higher education. As regards this larger social significance of master's education, we learned that those master's programs that prepared students to return directly to the workplace had immediate value to society because most master's-educated graduates make meaningful and sustained contributions to their professions and communities. Many students and alumni told us that their master's education greatly enhanced their knowledge and understanding, sharpened their ability to connect theory and professional practice, developed a big-picture perspective, refined their analytical ability, made them more critical questioners of knowledge, and honed their communication and professional practice skills. Many faculty and program administrators echoed these views, sometimes telling us that, for many students, master's education was a "rite of passage" in which the professions and society were major beneficiaries. Employers emphasized that most graduates of master's programs were far more competent and confident professionals—and, in some instances, were even transformed by their master's experiences. They returned to the workplace as more productive employees, who brought fresh perspectives and insights to their work. Indeed, many employers described master's graduates as the "movers and shakers" and "leaders" within their respective professions.

In addition, many stakeholders, especially employers and program graduates, told us that they greatly benefited from the multidisciplinary and interdisciplinary character of master's programs. They observed that, because master's programs were more directly responsive to society than traditional discipline-based doctoral programs, they often included cross-disciplinary experiences that bridged the gap between academe and the nonuniversity workplace. As a consequence, graduates were better able to integrate and apply knowledge and perspectives from several disciplines to real-world problems.

We also learned that master's education has larger societal benefits as well. During the past several decades, changes in the nature of knowledge, work, and the economy have often required practicing professionals to return to colleges and universities for postbaccalaureate education. Master's education, more than any level of education, has most directly responded to these changes by providing a wide range of master's programs and alternative delivery systems that serve the needs of professionals and employers in a knowledge-centered society. No less important, master's education significantly promotes greater equity in the academic and non-university workplace by preparing people—including many from diverse ethnic, racial, gender, and socioeconomic backgrounds—to assume key leadership positions in the larger society.

Paradoxically, despite the success stories most interviewees relayed about their own and others' experiences, we also learned that some of these interviewees did not fully appreciate the value of master's education. On the one hand, most students, alumni, and employers—along with many faculty and administrators—placed great personal and social value on master's education. On the other hand, some institutional administrators, program administrators, and faculty continued to view master's education as a mixed blessing, as reflected in the weak institutional and program support provided to many of the programs included in our study. Needless to say, we were strongly persuaded that the master's experiences of most stakeholders were so affirmative that the skepticism of these latter stakeholders can be questioned. We believe it is time for all of us, whether directly or indirectly involved, to view master's education as distinct from baccalaureate and doctoral education—as a separate and legitimate degree activity worthy of strong support. In line with this shift in perspective, we should invest in master's education at levels consistent with the important individual and societal benefits it provides in its own right.

Enhancing the Visibility and Vitality of Master's Education

In light of our findings and conclusions, and consonant with our emphasis throughout on providing a "thinking device" for people concerned about master's education, we conclude by raising considerations that may help to frame the continuing discourse about master's education in the United States. These considerations are targeted at each of the audiences for whom this book was written: policymakers, professional and accrediting associations, employers, institutional administrators, faculty and program administrators, and students.

Policymakers

At both the federal and state levels, master's education seems to have been largely ignored, save for recent statewide initiatives to evaluate master's programs for "quality control" purposes. Given our conclusion that master's education significantly enhances the nation's professional work force and provides much of the leadership that informs public life, we strongly encourage public officials and policymakers to treat master's education as a distinct activity separate from doctoral and baccalaureate education and worthy of strong support on its own merits. Perhaps more than any level of education, master's education is directly serving important societal needs and, in so doing, significantly enhancing overall relations between higher education and society.

At the federal and state levels, consideration should be given to providing greater financial support to master's students, especially in such public-service fields as nursing, education, and environmental studies in which the social benefits seem to at least equal the personal benefits enjoyed by degree recipients and for which there is strong consumer demand. At the state level, in particular, policymakers might give further attention to providing stronger financial and symbolic support for innovative master's programs seeking to assist the part-time and place-bound working adults who comprise the majority of master's students. Our research indicates that nontraditional degree formats—from distance delivery using telecommunications technology to extended degree programs offered in intensive weekend and summer sessions—can provide learning experiences that are no less rigorous and effective than those offered in traditional formats and, at the same time, better serve place-bound and part-time students than traditional formats can. We believe state higher education boards and agencies would reap great benefits for their states by supporting master's programs that incorporate nontraditional approaches in order to serve professionals working in both rural and urban settings.

Professional and Accrediting Associations

We learned that in some professional fields—such as nursing, engineering, and applied anthropology—professional and accrediting associations have strongly supported and nourished ongoing discussions about master's education and that these dialogues have stimulated administrators, faculty, and students to reconsider their master's programs. In contrast, we were told that professional associations in other fields focused primarily on doctoral or baccalaureate education and that accrediting agencies were less a force for revitalizing master's education than an external force to be accommodated.

We suggest that all professional associations and accrediting agencies follow the lead of professional associations such as the Society for Applied Anthropology and the National League of Nursing by creatively reconsidering the extent and nature of their involvement in master's education. Far from diminishing their efforts to enhance reputation and maintain standards, such endeavors would serve the interests of professional associations. By actively providing public forums and sponsoring publications on teaching and learning, curriculum content, and the role of master's study in their respective fields, we believe these organizations would be far more likely to have salutary effects on master's education than by their focusing primarily on "quality assurance."

Employers

Most employers we interviewed were enthusiastic about master's education, yet they differed widely in their support for master's students and master's education. On the one hand, some employers provided strong incentives—including tuition reimbursement and other financial support, flexible work schedules, and temporary leaves of absence—for employees to secure their master's degrees. Yet others, particularly those in hospitals, schools, social service agencies, theaters, government, and business and industry, sought to assist employees who were master's students by providing supportive learning environments. Some employers, for example, provided special facilities and services, including in-house libraries and support staff, which benefited everyone involved. On the other hand, other employers, including many who encouraged employees to earn master's degrees, provided little support of any kind for employees to continue their education.

Given the significant social and economic benefits associated with master's education in many fields—including the leadership exercised by master's-educated professionals in such fields as business, engineering, nursing, and education—we urge employers to review their policies and practices concerning master's education. Among other things, they might provide stronger financial and in-house support, establish flexible and supportive leave policies, and encourage employees to share their professional knowledge and experience as guest lecturers in colleges and universities. We believe that such policies would greatly enhance employee and organizational creativity, productivity, and effectiveness.

Institutional Administrators

Of all interviewees, college and university administrators were often the most critical of master's education. Many told us that they viewed master's education as subordinate to doctoral education—as a steppingstone to the doctorate and a consolation prize for students who did not pursue the doctorate. Many university administrators also stated in no uncertain terms that they viewed doctoral education and research as the wellsprings of institutional advancement, prestige, and external funding and, therefore, assigned master's education second- or third-class status in their institutions.

For two reasons, we strongly encourage such administrators to treat master's education more equitably. The first reason is that master's education has significant benefits for degree holders, employers, and society in general. As such, the success of master's education provides college and university administrators with an excellent opportunity for building and strengthening bridges between their institutions and current and prospective students, employers, and society. The second is that the overwhelming majority of graduate students, including many in the arts and sciences, do not intend to earn the doctorate but, rather, seek the master's degree as a terminal credential. As we have repeatedly emphasized, most students enter master's programs intending to earn a terminal degree that will facilitate their professional careers as applied anthropologists, teachers, research and development scientists, and government officials.

Because ancillary programs often diminish the identity and integrity of master's education, institutional administrators might give special attention to master's programs that faculty and program administrators view primarily as a steppingstone or consolation prize. In our view, master's degree programs, both in professional fields and in the arts and sciences, should be treated as separate and legitimate degree programs, capable of standing alone as bona fide advanced degree programs and not simply as appendages to Ph.D. programs offering "second-class" degrees. We believe universities should eliminate degrees that are chiefly consolation prizes and offer bona fide terminal degrees that adequately address the needs of students and employers.

Institutional administrators might also be more receptive to master's programs that do not conform with traditional conceptions of graduate education. Many program administrators and faculty told us that their efforts to respond to new student and societal needs by introducing reforms and innovations such as off-campus programs and nontraditional instructional delivery systems were often met with institutional indifference and resistance. Our findings suggest that campus administrators would better serve their institutions by considering such proposals as potentially rich opportunities rather than as inappropriate deviations from traditional academic norms and practices.

Finally, we suggest that institutional administrators give further thought to developing institutional support and reward structures that support master's education. Many interviewees told us that master's students were ineligible for student financial assistance because they were enrolled part-time or were unlikely to receive awards because doctoral or baccalaureate students had higher priority. Further, many faculty and program administrators explained that their institutional reward structures were unsupportive of their involvement with master's education and master's students. In particular, many people emphasized that institutional promotion and tenure policies ignored the contributions of faculty and program administrators to master's education. These rewards, in our view, are not commensurate with the benefits most master's programs provide to individuals, departments, and society at large.

Faculty and Program Administrators

For the most part, we were impressed by faculty and program administrators' commitment to master's education and master's students. In many cases this entailed considerable financial and personal sacrifice. We spoke, however, with a number of faculty and program administrators, especially those in ancillary master's programs, who suggested that there were no compelling reasons for them to invest in master's education and master's students. We invite faculty and program administrators who hold this perspective to reexamine their views of master's education in light of the decision-situations, types of master's programs, and attributes of high-quality master's experiences presented in this book. If they are not committed to master's education, we suggest that they divest themselves of their involvement in master's programs and invest their energies instead in baccalaureate or doctoral education.

We strongly urge administrators and faculty to ensure that their master's programs have clear and compelling rationales that are independent of the missions of their Ph.D. programs (if they have a Ph.D. program). While a master's program can effectively serve both as a steppingstone and a terminal degree, it is easy for the steppingstone emphasis to become superordinate to the terminal one. Therefore, we urge program administrators and faculty committed to providing a steppingstone experience to make sure that the terminal master's is offered alongside it as a legitimate, not a second-class, degree. We suggest that those departments offering only a period of graduate work which leads to a consolation prize master's degree (for those who do not pursue a doctorate) label the degree symbolizing the completion of this period not a master's degree but, rather, a graduate degree in course. This distinction would allow students and employers to differentiate graduate programs that treat the master's as an authentic terminal experience from postbaccalaureate experiences that serve primarily as steppingstones to the doctorate.

Students

We learned that the majority of students and program graduates were positive about their master's experiences. Still, we emphasize the importance of a good "fit" between student expectations and master's program characteristics and experiences and urge students to consider this matter carefully when choosing between programs. Moreover, given that students also can shape, often in dramatic ways, their master's experiences, we encourage students to become more active in influencing their student culture and the larger environments of their program by taking responsibility for sponsoring social events, joining student organizations, organizing colloquia and other profession-related activities, and nurturing collegial and collaborative learning experiences among themselves and faculty.

This book represents the perspectives of nearly eight hundred people, all of whom share a vital stake in master's education. In listening to these diverse voices, we developed a fuller appreciation and understanding of master's education and its significance within American society. We hope that our inquiry will not only help to enhance the visibility of master's education but will also stimulate discussion among stakeholders in master's education. We invite you to join us in continuing the conversation and to use this book as a stimulus for reflecting and acting on your involvement in master's education.

Technical Appendix
Philosophical Underpinnings of Positioned Subject Approach

Barwise and Perry's (1983) relation theory of meaning provided the philosophical underpinnings of our positioned subject approach to research, both at the level of individuals in specific settings and across programs. Starting with the old question "What and where is meaning?" Barwise and Perry pinpointed problems with Descartes's answer: in one's own thoughts. According to Descartes, ideas are intrinsically meaningful and hence do not depend on what is actually the case in a given person's time and place. From such a perspective, the world is secondary: ideas are merely represented by words that, in turn, merely stand for objects in the world. Among other problems, Barwise and Perry noted that "eternal sentences"—which do not depend on actual points of view, times, or places—have long served as the paradigm of meaningful expressions in linguistics, and yet such sentences are only possible in pure mathematics. Barwise and Perry maintained that Descartes's approach cannot explain how meaning inheres in expressions that do not refer to objects and yet are clearly related to events in the world: "If expressions were not systematically linked with kinds of events, on the one hand, and states of mind, on the other, their utterance would convey no information; they would be just noises or scribbles, without any meaning at all" (3). Barwise and Perry felt certain that there were important clues to this problem in the work of Ecological Realists, such as the psychologist J. J. Gibson. These researchers "found much more meaning and information in the world and less in the head than the traditional view of meaning assumed" (x).

Dissatisfied with existing philosophical and linguistic approaches to the question "What and where is meaning?" Barwise and Perry searched for a more adequate answer by focusing on "situations":

> Reality consists of situations—individuals having properties and standing in relations at various spatiotemporal locations. We are always in situations; we see them, cause them to come about, and have attitudes toward

them. The Theory of Situations is an abstract theory for talking about situations. We begin by pulling out of real situations the basic building blocks of the theory; individuals, properties and relations, and locations. These are conceived of as invariants, or as we shall call them, uniformities across real situations; the same individuals and properties appear again and again in different locations. (7–8)

Barwise and Perry explained that, in order to survive, all organisms (humans, animals, and so forth) must be "attuned to" uniformities—similarities across situations—and to relations between uniformities. As Barwise and Perry put it, "It is by categorizing situations in terms of some of the uniformities that are present, and by being attuned to appropriate relations that obtain between different types of situations, that the organism manages to cope with the new situations that continually arise" (10).

In developing their theory of meaning, Barwise and Perry emphasized that different organisms are attuned to quite different uniformities across situations. They explained that the uniformities that are of primary importance to a dog, for example, may go entirely unnoticed by a human. As they put it: "Different organisms can rip the same reality apart in different ways, ways that are appropriate to their own needs, their own perceptual abilities and their own capacities for action. This interdependence between the structure its environment displays to an organism and the structure of the organism with respect to its environment is extremely important. For while reality is there, independent of the organism's individuative activity, the structure it displays to an organism reflects properties of the organism itself" (11).

We chose to ground our research approach, at the philosophical level, in Barwise and Perry's theory of meaning because we believed it would provide a useful way to understand that the meaning of situations—master's programs, in our case—is present in the very "uniformities" to which individuals in specific environments are attuned and to which they act. Because it would direct our attention to the different ways people "rip reality apart," we assumed it also would enable us to make sense of the different meanings that master's programs have for individuals within specific programs; in other words, the meaning of a program could vary depending on the uniformities individuals within these situations perceived. Likewise, it would help us understand the different meanings that programs have for the groups of people associated with them; depending on the uniformities to which individuals in these programs are attuned, their interpretations of master's programs would be different.

As Barwise and Perry made clear, however, it is necessary to recognize that the uniformities to which people respond, while always abstractions, are nevertheless always constrained by actual phenomena. As they further

explicated their theory: "Constraints give rise to meaning; [but] attune-
ment to constraints makes life possible" (94). (In other words, if anything
were possible, there could be no meaning.) Thus, while not *anything* is
possible (that is, "constraints give rise to meaning"), constraints do not
necessarily *determine* the meaning of situations: it is often the case that
more than one thing is possible, depending on which uniformities and
relations among uniformities are selected as important and "real."

In philosophically grounding our research in Barwise and Perry's theory of meaning, we became aware that people often tend to confuse
uniformities—which are abstractions *about* actual situations—with the actual situation. As Barwise and Perry put this with respect to science in
particular: "It sometimes happens in science that the vocabulary of a particular theory becomes so ingrained that the scientist starts confusing the
empirical data with its theory-laden description. If the categories of the
theory cut across the grain of actual phenomena, then artificial problems
are created, problems whose solutions cannot be given until a new framework is adopted. One is simply missing the properties of things and relations between things that really matter" (xi). Often it is only by seeing
others using a contrasting theory to make sense of a similar situation that
we become aware that we have confused our theory (a "sense-making"
uniformity across situations) with actual phenomena. As we embarked on
the analysis of our research, we hoped that Barwise and Perry's theory
would help us perceive uniformities, and relations among uniformities,
that are important to master's education stakeholders. In addition, we
hoped their theory would help us become aware when we and other
master's education stakeholders had become so attached to certain uniformities that we were prevented from seeing other uniformities that might
make better sense of the situation and, moreover, "really matter."

We note that Barwise and Perry's relation theory of meaning, with its
fundamental organism/environment interdependence, contrasts with the
Cartesian model, which postulates that the human mind is fundamentally
separate from the environment, which it apprehends in terms of timeless
objective principles that lay under the immediacy of everyday life (see
Bardo 1987). Barwise and Perry's theory also contrasts with a radical rela-
tivist or subjectivist approach, which doubts the validity of any universal
principles underlying the perceived world and postulates that meaning is
only what people make of it, as members of society and, ultimately, as
individuals. Distinct from either of these approaches, Barwise and Perry's
theory treats human mental states, on the one hand, and the natural and
human environments in which humans are situated, on the other, as constantly interdependent. Neither is privileged as prior to, or more real, than
the other. Both are necessary for the other to be known (see Palmer 1983).

Notes

Chapter 1: Historic and Contemporary Perspectives on Master's Education

1. Conrad and Eagan (1990) recently completed an extensive review of the literature on master's programs. In various places throughout the chapter, we have adapted material, both directly and indirectly, from this publication. Interested readers may find the Conrad and Eagan publication a useful companion to this chapter. In addition, we recommend Glazer 1986.

2. The acronym NCES refers to the National Center for Education Statistics, which is housed in the Office of Educational Research and Improvement (OERI) in the U.S. Department of Education. Throughout this chapter "NCES" refers to reports and data provided to us by NCES.

3. In 1948 the graduate deans within the Association of American Universities (AAU) established the Association of Graduate Schools (AGS) under the umbrella of the AAU. In essence, the AAU became the organization for AAU university presidents, and the AGS became the organization for AAU graduate deans.

4. NCES provided us with these data. We recommend the following source: NCES 1991.

5. Given space limitations, our review of the literature on change and innovation is necessarily selective. Glazer's (1986) review focused on trends and innovations in twelve professional fields at the master's level. She provided considerable detail in the fields of business and management, teacher education, and engineering, lesser detail in nursing, health services administration, fine and performing arts, international education, journalism, law, library science, public administration, and social work. Conrad and Eagan (1990) reviewed reports and studies on innovation in master's education across many fields, especially in those fields (business, nursing, and education) that received the most attention in the literature.

6. New instructional technologies also were introduced in master's programs in social work and nursing, both on and off campus. Petracchi and Morgenbesser (1989) described efforts at the University of Wisconsin–Madison to broadcast master's social work courses over the Wisconsin public television network, and Skaggs (1983) described the implementation of an interactive computer-video system in nursing at the University of Texas–Austin. And many scholars, representing a wide range of professional fields, published material describing widespread use of computers and other technological aids in classroom instruction at the master's level (American Nurses Association 1987; Conklin 1983).

7. With respect to the introduction of external degree programs in the field of nursing, Reilly (1980) and Kelley and Flowers (1985) described experimental external master's programs developed at Wayne State University and the University of Alabama–Birmingham, respectively. Both of these programs were created to address critical statewide needs for master's-trained nurses by providing postbaccalaureate education to individuals employed full-time. Forni's (1987) survey of 105 nursing schools found that over one-third offered nontraditional options and one-fifth offered off-campus classes or outreach programs.

8. According to Conrad and Eagan (1990), the literature on experiential learning can be classified into two main categories: descriptions of specific programs and cross-program comparisons. Most of the program-specific studies were in professional and technical fields. Wolfe and Byrne (1980), for example, described an experiential master's of business administration program at Southern Methodist University which required extensive project-based experience. Jacobs (1982) reviewed seven master's-level graduate and professional programs and discussed the diverse ways in which these programs integrated "experiential components" (such as project courses and fieldwork). Similarly, Radar (1982) described a variety of innovative experiential master's programs, including several offered through Antioch College which required supervised, field-based internships in a range of disciplines.

Chapter 2: A Positioned Subject Approach to Inquiry

1. The concept implicit in our use of the term *positioned subject* has long been used by anthropologists to describe a particular interpretive approach to research (Geertz 1974, 1983; Rosaldo 1989). More recently, scholars in other disciplines also have discussed very similar approaches to inquiry. See, for example, the work on "standpoint epistemologies" by a philosopher (Harding 1986, 1991) and a sociologist (Smith 1990).

2. Barwise and Perry's (1983) relation theory of meaning provided the philosophical underpinnings of our positioned subject approach to research, both at the level of individuals in specific settings and across programs. For a brief review of this theory, see technical appendix.

3. Like any research design, ours implies ahead of time the general shape of the explanations that will result from the study and also places constraints on the research design and methods that can be used fruitfully. As Lincoln put it, "any model or paradigm for research can entertain some questions with great facility and power, and cannot entertain other questions—perhaps equally significant—well or at all" (1991, 22).

4. We emphasize that we did not utilize the kind of statistically representative sampling method often employed in experimental and survey research studies where the intent is to "generalize about relationships between variables" (Greene and David 1981, 15). Rather, our "substantively representative" sample was informed both by broad statistical considerations (in regard to field of study, institutional type, and type of control) along with other potential theoretically relevant criteria (e.g., geographic location).

5. The heterogeneity of our sample is partially limited by our decision to exclude bachelor's/master's combination degree programs and master's degrees awarded by correspondence schools.

6. Our original sample included five programs in each of eleven fields. After

completing intensive case studies of master's programs in ten of these fields at a national university between September 1989 and January 1990, we reconsidered the necessity of including two traditional arts and sciences fields—sociology and computer science—in our study. Since only 15 percent of the master's degrees annually conferred are granted in these fields (including professional fields in the arts and sciences) and we had representation in several emerging professional fields in the arts and sciences (applied anthropology and environmental studies), we decided to reduce our representation from the traditional liberal arts and sciences by eliminating sociology. Moreover, since stakeholders interviewed in the computer science program suggested that their program was similar to a master's in engineering, we decided to drop computer science. With these adjustments, our sample was reduced to forty-seven case studies: five programs in each of nine fields plus one sociology and one computer science program.

7. Because we believe that the Carnegie Classification inadequately distinguishes between universities serving national audiences and those serving regional audiences, we use an institutional classification scheme that differs from the Carnegie Classification insofar as it incorporates the criterion of "audience served." For our purposes, "national" universities are institutions that are heavily committed to research and graduate education and serve national and international audiences. "Regional" universities are institutions that are involved in research and graduate education and, in some instances, offer doctoral as well as master's programs. But, in contrast to national universities, regional institutions are oriented largely to serving regional audiences through both their faculty research and program offerings. "Liberal arts" colleges are institutions that place a major emphasis on undergraduate education in the liberal arts and sciences, although many offer master's programs in a limited number of fields. Liberal arts institutions, for the most part, tend to serve regional or local audiences, though a relatively small number attract students from throughout the nation. Finally, "specialized" institutions are those that offer degree programs ranging from the bachelor's to the doctorate, with at least one-half of all degrees awarded in a single field. These institutions often serve a national or a regional audience through their faculty research and program offerings.

8. Our selections were guided, in part, by data for 1985–86 provided by the National Center for Education Statistics. (NCES does not use the institutional classification scheme developed by the Carnegie Foundation for the Advancement of Teaching (1987), the most widely used institutional classification scheme in higher education in the United States. Somewhat to our surprise, we could not locate national data on the number of master's degrees awarded by Carnegie Classification type and type of control.) These data indicated approximately 85 percent of all master's degrees in recent years were granted by "doctoral" and "comprehensive" institutions, with the remaining 15 percent awarded by "general baccalaureate" and "specialty" institutions. Thirty-nine (83 percent) of the forty-seven case studies we selected are located at national universities and regional colleges and universities and the remaining eight (17 percent) are located in liberal arts colleges and speciality institutions.

9. Our case studies were distributed within each type of institution as follows: of the seven national universities, one program at five institutions, three at one institution and ten at one institution; of the sixteen regional colleges and universities, one program at thirteen institutions, two at two institutions, and four at one institution; of the five liberal arts colleges, one program at each of five institutions; and of

the three specialty institutions, one program at each of three institutions.

10. According to estimates by the National Center for Education Statistics, slightly more than three-fifths of all master's degrees have been awarded by public institutions in recent years.

11. To provide for broad geographic representation, we distributed the forty-seven cases in our sample across four geographic sectors. We selected eleven cases in the eastern United States, including the Mid-Atlantic, Tri-State, and New England areas. In the West we chose fourteen cases spread across the Western coastline, Rocky Mountain, and desert Southwest states. We chose nine cases from the South and thirteen cases from the Midwest. Nineteen states were represented in our forty-seven-case sample.

To provide for representativeness in terms of student attendance patterns, we included twenty-four (mostly) full-time, nineteen (mostly) part-time, and four "mixed" student enrollment cases. For the same reason, we included some cases in our sample in which the master's was the only degree offered in the department (seven cases) and other cases in which the master's degree was offered either with the bachelor's degree (twenty-two cases) or with both the bachelor's and doctoral degrees (eighteen cases).

In light of the rapid growth of innovative, nontraditional instructional delivery systems in master's education, we included nine programs that offered nontraditional delivery systems. We chose, for example, seven cases in which the master's degree could be completed by either taking a combination of intensive evening, weekend and summer courses (two cases in business and three cases in education) or in which the master's program was offered only during intensive summer sessions and required a three- to five-year summer residency for completion of the degree (one case each in English and environmental studies). Additionally, we chose two cases in engineering in which satellite-based instructional technology was extensively utilized to deliver master's programs to students at off-campus locations.

We also included cases in our sample which varied in terms of their "prestige" within their respective fields of study. We used field-specific reputational rankings to help us identify these programs. (With the exceptions of business and engineering, only reputational rankings on "graduate programs"—not master's programs— were published in the literature. In the other nine fields, we used rankings of graduate programs to identify "high-prestige" programs.) Across the eleven fields included in the study, we selected at least one "top five"–ranked program in each field for inclusion in our sample; there were a total of twelve high-prestige cases in our sample.

12. Depending on a researcher's approach, *stakeholders* might be defined in different ways (1989a, 1989b). Critical theorists (Giroux 1988; McLaren 1989; Tierney 1989a, 1989b; Weis 1985) are particularly attuned, for example, to "oppressed" and "privileged" stakeholders. Recently, scholars using more traditional approaches— who, for the most part, have relied heavily upon the perspectives of administrators and faculty at national universities and in national professional organizations—also have included a broader range of stakeholder perspectives in their work (Chaffee and Tierney 1988; Clark 1987; Conrad 1989, Kuh, Schuh, and Witt 1991). Our assumption was that, if a person—whether "powerful" and in the cultural, political, and economic mainstream or not—had a vital stake in master's education, we would consider him or her a stakeholder.

13. For each case study, we spoke with an average of sixteen stakeholders, with a low of twelve interviewees and a high of twenty-four.

14. The conventional terms for the people interviewed during a social scientific study—*informant, interviewee,* and *subject*—do not adequately convey the character of the interactions that occurred during our interviews. We use the word *interviewee* because it is the least problematic of these three terms. For variety, we also use the term *stakeholder* as a substitute for *interviewee.*

15. In addition to asking each program liaison to arrange interviews with individuals in each of the six stakeholder groups, we also requested that they select males and females who represented diverse racial and ethnic backgrounds within each stakeholder group. In addition, we specified other types of diversity which we hoped would be represented. In the faculty stakeholder group, for instance, we sought interviews with both senior and junior, tenured and nontenured, and "research-oriented" and "practitioner-oriented" faculty. In terms of students, we asked to speak with individuals who differed in terms of part- and full-time status, level of financial support for graduate study, years of professional experience, and time in the program (from beginning to nearing completion of the degree). Within the alumni group, we requested interviews with alumni who were employed professionals in the nonuniversity workplace as well as those who had pursued doctoral study and asked to interview alumni who were at various stages in their careers. For employers of alumni, we asked to speak with individuals who represented both the public and private sectors and who represented a diversity of employment opportunities for program graduates.

16. While we acknowledge that our sample is positively biased, we have no basis for believing, as one reviewer of an early draft of our work suggested, that department chairs went so far as to instruct interviewees about what to say.

17. As it turned out, we occasionally interviewed one or two people in a program who had not been selected in advance. When interviewees canceled or did not show up, either we or the program liaison found substitutes. In our analysis, the responses of last-minute substitutes were no more negative or positive than those of other interviewees.

18. In her ethnography *Crafting Selves: Power, Gender, and Discourses of Identity in a Japanese Workplace* (1990), Kondo provides an illustration of a researcher self-consciously working as what we refer to as a positioned subject. "My informants," she writes,

> were hardly inert objects available for the free play of the ethnographer's desire. They themselves were, in the act of being, actively interpreting and trying to make meaning for the ethnographer. In so doing, the people I knew asserted their power to act upon the anthropologist. This was their means for preserving their own identities. Understanding, in this context, is multiple, open-ended, positioned—although that positioning can shift dramatically, as I have argued—and pervaded by relations of power. These power-imbued attempts to capture, recast, and rewrite each other were for us productive of understandings and were, existentially, alternately wrenching and fulfilling. (17)

19. Our idea of the "interview as conversation" is very similar to ideas of "education as conservation" developed by Oakeshott (1962) and Bruffee (1991), among others.

20. Most of our interviews lasted about one and one-half hours. Some, however

(when an interviewee was able to take the time and was particularly involved in the dialogue), lasted two or more hours. A small number of our interviews were also conducted over the telephone. These interviews were usually conducted with employers and, in a few instances, alumni who were not available at our research sites. Telephone interviews were usually tape-recorded.

21. The use of tape recorders enabled us to concentrate on the dialogue when it moved too fast to take notes.

22. Typically, three of the four interviewers worked together on a program, though, in some cases, either two or four people conducted the interviews.

23. While reviewing and analyzing the perspectives of these multipositioned stakeholders, we sometimes noted one or two interviewees associated with a particular program whose experiences were clearly idiosyncratic compared with those of the other interviewees. We used these "outlier" perspectives in our analysis with great caution.

24. We noticed, for example, that on occasion one of us had an inappropriately negative reaction to master's programs at "elite" universities, that one of us was predisposed to master's programs in liberal arts colleges, and that one of us was predisposed to master's programs at leading national universities. On each of these occasions, we tried to make one another aware of these biases.

25. Ideally, we would have included a longitudinal dimension in our study design such that we returned to each program and reinterviewed many of the same people a year later, comparing their initial remarks with more recent ones. This was simply not possible given time and funding constraints.

26. The differences in our biographies frequently forced us to confront and thereby understand our working assumptions. And every one of these reflexive episodes allowed us to listen to our interviewees with more discerning ears and to make analytical distinctions that, up to that time, we had taken for granted.

Chapter 3: Primary Decision-Situations

1. These dualistic terms were not, for the most part, used by faculty in these programs. Indeed, we found it was much easier to explain this "action-focused" orientation by referring to what it was not than by utilizing more conventional understandings of different "types" of knowledge. Interviewees in these programs often explained this action-focused perspective on knowledge by suggesting to us that they understood knowledge in terms of a dynamic relationship between the "theoretical in the applied and the applied in the theoretical."

2. Each faculty member had a "tenure home" in his or her department, and almost all had earned tenure before joining the MWR program. As one faculty member explained it,

> We are very careful when we involve untenured people from departments that just tolerate [activities like MWR]. . . . It is so wide open here—so full of intellectual stimulation—that a new faculty person can easily lose their way. This place is full of things like MWR—so that there's a danger for untenured faculty to become too diffuse [and thus not get tenured]. Those of us who have been around have to take a mentor's attitude and try to keep these people on track while they build their credentials in their own discipline. . . . The institutional attitude is that once you have a focused record, have built your credentials, you gain elbow room, feel emancipated.

3. Students normally took all fifteen of these credits in one department. The brochure listed twenty-two departments—such as agricultural economics, geography, water chemistry, rural sociology—in which students commonly specialize.

4. In most cases, the administrative unit that provided support to a master's program was a department. In those cases in which a master's program was not located within a departmental structure, the administrative unit supporting the program usually was a school, college, center, or institute. For convenience, we use the term *department* to refer to any administrative unit responsible for a program.

Chapter 5: Decision-Situations and Program Types

1. Another way of expressing this is to say that, prior to completing our analysis, we saw only forty-seven idiosyncratic programs, whereas afterward the shared character of various programs was evident. It was not until we began to organize the case studies into the four groupings that these themes within master's programs, as opposed to others, became evident as the ones that "really mattered" across programs.

2. To sort the forty-seven programs by the five decision-situation criteria, we used an electronic spreadsheet, treating each program as a record and the five decision-situations as data elements in each record.

Chapter 6: Ancillary Programs

1. In addition to the M.A. in English (Literature), the Department of English offered a master's degree in applied English linguistics. This figure includes enrollment in both programs.

2. Since our visit, the M.B.A. program at Major State has been considerably modified, and the new program places much less emphasis on scholarly training.

3. Although we have chosen not to discuss them in this chapter, there are two other characteristic features of the ancillary programs which deserve mention. First, we learned that faculty in most of the ancillary programs placed a considerable emphasis on evaluating students, both for purposes of screening students for the Ph.D. and ensuring that students had acquired the "theoretical knowledge" that faculty deemed important. While the ancillary programs differed somewhat in terms of the specific approaches used to evaluate students, all used at least three of the following four mechanisms: (1) course grades, (2) comprehensive or oral exam, (3) thesis, and (4) informal faculty evaluation. For example, the two liberal arts and science programs at Major State (English and sociology)—both of which placed heavy emphasis on faculty evaluation of students in order to screen students for the Ph.D. program—emphasized different evaluative mechanisms: the English faculty relied heavily on the comprehensive examination, while the sociology faculty emphasized the master's thesis. As a professor in sociology told us: "The thesis is supposed to be a demonstration that students are capable of going on in the Ph.D. program and doing independent research. The model for the master's thesis is a paper that's publishable. It shows the potential for doing publishable work." Interestingly, we also learned that seven of the ten ancillary programs required a comprehensive or oral examination and that, in all but two of the programs, faculty informally evaluated students to determine if they should be allowed to pursue the Ph.D.

Second, except in education at Major State and microbiology at Mountain State, peer relations among students tended to be either competitive or isolated in nature in the ancillary programs.

4. Faculty in the three liberal arts cases (English at Major State and Phelps and sociology at Major State) did not incorporate workplace-related knowledge and experiences into their master's programs.

Chapter 7: Career Advancement Programs

1. Although faculty and administrators in Land-Grant's applied anthropology program and United Tech's engineering program did not have a formal core course requirement, students were expected to complete a nine- to twelve-credit "breadth" requirement consisting of courses that were determined by the student in consultation with his or her advisor. Consistent with the other cases in this grouping, both programs required students to complete eighteen to twenty-one credits in their given specialization areas. Particularly in Land-Grant's case, where there were few courses offered within each specialty track, students completed a core of required courses by default.

2. Chester College did not have any formal specialization course requirements, but students were expected to complete a highly prescribed course of study (all but three of the program's eleven courses were required) which concentrated exclusively on teaching theories, practices, and methods.

3. Interviewees at Trafalgar College and Urban State did not indicate if they utilized adjunct practitioner faculty in their master's programs. United Tech relied entirely on the services of full-time faculty members at more than thirty different colleges and universities across the United States to teach classes in its master's program. Although not real-world practitioners, per se, these individuals technically were adjunct faculty in the program.

4. The business programs at Pierpont and Parks-Beecher and the applied anthropology program at Atlantic State utilized traditional, day-only instructional formats that served an almost exclusively full-time student population. The applied anthropology and theater programs at Land-Grant and Trafalgar offered both day and evening courses for their mixed full- and part-time student populations.

5. These services were emphasized by interviewees in just over one-half of the cases in the career advancement grouping.

6. Institutional administrators associated with the Parks-Beecher, Peterson, Pierpont, Chester, and United Tech master's programs communicated to us that they provided institutional financial and symbolic support to these programs, in part because it significantly enhanced the overall reputation of their institutions. University administrators at Land-Grant and Southwest State likewise expressed approval of the increased visibility these master's programs brought to their institutions. According to faculty in these two cases, however, institutional administrators seldom provided adequate financial support to their master's programs. In each of the preceding seven cases, these programs also contributed to the institution's resource base and advanced its mission. Finally, institutional administrators at Atlantic State, Trafalgar College, St. Joan's, and Urban State chose not to provide adequate financial or symbolic support. With the exception of St. Joan's program—which increased the professional, but not the liberal arts, reputation of its sponsoring institution—administrators told us that these programs seldom enhanced the overall reputations and visibility of their campuses (decision-situation 4).

Chapter 8: Apprenticeship Programs

1. An exception to this was the Major State computer science program, which did not formally require master's students to produce a culminating paper. Stakeholders indicated that many students nevertheless did produce such papers, simply because they became very involved in a particular problem.

2. Students in the microbiology, computer science, and engineering programs at Major State University and the environmental studies program at Carver A&M developed what we have referred to as "participative" student cultures. The interactions among students in the engineering programs at Prestige State and Moore A&T, the theater programs at Phelps and NCC, and the microbiology program at Southwest State were more interdependent and communal, and, as such, we suggest that these students constructed "synergistic" student cultures in these five programs.

3. The microbiology, computer science, and engineering programs at Major State University, along with the environmental studies program at Carver A&M and the electrical engineering program at Prestige State, received "weak" financial and symbolic support from institutional administrators. With the exception of Carver A&M, the remaining programs were housed in national universities where doctoral education was highly valued by institutional administrators. Campus administrators at Carver A&M, a regional institution, tended to reward faculty for their involvement in baccalaureate education and, increasingly in recent years, in doctoral education as well.

4. Stakeholders in the engineering programs at Moore A&T and Prestige State, along with those in Major State's computer science program and Phelps' theater program, did not voice this concern. Rather, most noted that their institutions provided them with generally satisfactory financial and space allocations to maintain adequate instructional laboratories and equipment.

5. Stakeholders in the theater program at NCC, the engineering program at Moore A&T, and the microbiology program at Southwest State told us that they were generally pleased with their institutions' reward structures.

Chapter 9: Community-centered Programs

1. Other students, however, noted that, while "the 'lit' people are becoming more aware of the need to talk about teaching," the literature courses were "more strictly academic and less well integrated."

2. Although only a selected number of faculty and program administrators actually used the term *praxis*, in our interpretation many interviewees articulated this conception of professional practice.

3. Freire has written extensively on the concept of praxis and its implications for teaching and learning. In his book *The Politics of Education: Culture, Power, and Liberation*, Freire defines *praxis* as an "act of knowing" which "involves a dialectical movement that goes from action to reflection and from reflection upon action to a new action" (1985, 50).

4. Students developed participative student cultures in eight of the seventeen community-centered programs. Of these, student attendance patterns were distributed as follows: three programs (English and applied anthropology at Southwest State and environmental studies at Major State) enrolled almost exclusively full-time student populations. Students generally enrolled on a part-time basis in

four of these programs (nursing at Peterson, Southern State, and Western State as well as applied anthropology at City-State). The environmental studies program at Walton State had a mix of full- and part-time students. Students in the remaining nine programs chose to develop synergistic student cultures. Distributed by student attendance patterns, students were enrolled on a full-time basis in five programs (microbiology at Middle State and Appleby State, environmental studies at Phelps, theater at Helena State, and applied anthropology at Southeast State). The remaining four programs had part-time student populations (education at Laramie and Lake College, environmental studies at Vernon, and English at Longmont).

5. From our perspective, this curricular approach emphasized that students make "connections" both within each of these activities as well as across them.

6. The English programs at Longmont and Southwest State, as well as Lake College's education program, did not require students to complete a formal laboratory, clinical, workshop, or practicum experience.

7. Exceptions to this included the English programs at Longmont and Southwest State and the nursing program at Western State Medical Center.

8. These eight programs included three located at national universities (environmental studies at Major State and Phelps as well as nursing at Western State); four at regional universities (applied anthropology at Southeast State, education at Laramie, microbiology at Appleby State, and nursing at Southern State); and one at a liberal arts institution (environmental studies at Vernon).

9. These cases included the environmental studies programs at Major State, Vernon, and Phelps; the nursing programs at Southern State and Western State; the microbiology program at Appleby State; the applied anthropology program at Southeast State; and the education program at Laramie University.

References

Albrecht, Paul A. 1984. "Special Factors in the Design of New Programs for Practicing Professionals." In *Graduate Education: Courses and Programs for Practicing Professionals*, by Council of Graduate Schools. Washington, D.C.

American Nurses' Association. 1987. *Computers in Nursing Education*. Kansas City, Mo.: American Nurses' Association.

Ames, Russell. 1979. "Issues in the Development and Use of Appropriate Measuring Devices." In *Proceedings on the Conference on the Assessment of Quality of Master's Programs*, by Council of Graduate Schools. College Park: University of Maryland.

Andrews, Grover J. 1979. "Traditional vs. Nontraditional Master's Programs and Their Relationship to Quality Standards." In *Proceedings on the Conference on the Assessment of Quality of Master's Programs*, by Council of Graduate Schools. College Park: University of Maryland.

Association of American Universities (AAU). 1935. "Problems of the Master's Degree: Committee on Problems Relating to the Master's Degree." *Journal of Proceedings and Addresses of the Thirty-seventh Annual Conference of the Association of American Universities* 37:32–37.

———. 1945. "The Master's Degree: Report of the Committee on Graduate Work." *Journal of Proceedings and Addresses of the Forty-sixth Annual Conference of the Association of American Universities* 46:111–25.

Barak, Robert J. 1987. "A Skeleton in the Closet." In *The Master's Degree: Jack of All Trades*, edited by Joslyn Green. Denver: State Higher Education Executive Officers.

Bardo, Susan R. 1987. *The Flight to Objectivity: Essays on Cartesianism and Culture*. Albany: State University of New York Press.

Barwise, Jon, and John Perry. 1983. *Situations and Attitudes*. Cambridge: Massachusetts Institute of Technology Press.

Berelson, Bernard. 1960. *Graduate Education in the United States*. New York: McGraw-Hill.

Blegen, Theodore. 1959. "How Can Graduate Schools Increase the Supply of Teachers?" *Journal of Higher Education* 30:127–33.

Boddy, Francis M. 1970. "The Master's in the Social Sciences and Humanities." In *Reassessment: Proceedings of the Tenth Annual Meeting of the Council of Graduate*

Schools, edited by James Eshelman. Washington, D.C.: Council of Graduate Schools.

Broderius, Bruce W., and Mary L. Carder. 1983. "Delivering a Non-Resident Master's Degree: Qualitative and Quantitative Measures of Effectiveness." *Alternative Higher Education* 7:116–27.

Brubacher, John S., and Willis Rudy. 1976. *Higher Education in Transition: A History of American Colleges and Universities, 1636–1976.* New York: Harper & Row.

Bruffee, Kenneth. 1991. "Collaborative Learning and the 'Conversation of Mankind.'" In *A Sourcebook on Collaborative Learning in Postsecondary Education,* edited by Anne Goodsell, Michelle Maher, and Vincent Tinto. University Park: National Center on Postsecondary Teaching, Learning and Assessment (Pennsylvania State University).

Burke, Kenneth. 1957. *The Philosophy of Literary Form.* New York: Vintage Books.

Butts, R. Freeman. 1939. *The College Charts Its Course.* New York: McGraw-Hill.

Carmichael, Oliver C. 1960. "A Three-year Master's Degree: Beginning with the Junior Year in College." *Journal of Higher Education* 31:127–32.

———. 1961. *Graduate Education: A Critique and a Program.* New York: Harper & Brothers.

Carnegie Foundation for the Advancement of Teaching. 1987. *A Classification of Institutions of Higher Education.* Princeton, N.J.: Carnegie Foundation for the Advancement of Teaching.

Carr, Edward F. 1979. "Standards of Quality and the State Accreditation Process." In *Proceedings on the Conference on the Assessment of Quality of Master's Programs,* by Council of Graduate Schools. College Park: University of Maryland.

Carroll, Mary Ann. 1982. "Innovations in Education/Cooperative Education/Continuing Education." In *Recent Developments in Graduate Programs,* by Council of Graduate Schools. Washington, D.C.: Council of Graduate Schools and the Graduate Record Examinations Board.

Chaffee, Ellen E., and William G. Tierney. 1988. *Collegiate Culture and Leadership Strategies.* New York: American Council on Education and Macmillan.

Clark, Burton R. 1987. *The Academic Life: Small Worlds, Different Worlds.* Princeton, N.J.: Carnegie Foundation for the Advancement of Teaching.

Clark, Kenneth E. 1979. "The Issue of Quality in Master's Degree Programs." In *Proceedings on the Conference on the Assessment of Quality of Master's Programs,* by Council of Graduate Schools. College Park: University of Maryland.

Conklin, Dorothy N. 1983. "A Study of Computer-assisted Instruction in Nursing Education." *Journal of Computer-based Instruction* 9:98–107.

Conrad, Clifton F. 1989. "Meditations on the Ideology of Inquiry in Higher Education: Exposition, Critique, and Conjecture." *Review of Higher Education* 12:199–220.

Conrad, Clifton F., and Robert T. Blackburn. 1985a. "Correlates of Departmental Quality in Regional Colleges and Universities." *American Educational Research Journal* 22:279–95.

———. 1985b. "Research on Program Quality: A Review and Critique of the Literature." In *Higher Education: Handbook of Theory and Research,* edited by John C. Smart, vol. 1. New York: Agathon Press.

———. 1986. "Current Views of Departmental Quality: An Empirical Examination." *Review of Higher Education* 9:249–65.

Conrad, Clifton F., and David J. Eagan. 1990. "Master's Degree Programs in American Higher Education." In *Higher Education: Handbook of Theory and Research*, edited by John C. Smart, vol. 6. New York: Agathon Press.

Council of Graduate Schools in the United States (CGS). 1966. *Proceedings of the Sixth Annual Meeting*. Washington, D.C.: Council of Graduate Schools.

———. 1972. *Proceedings of the Twelfth Annual Meeting*. Washington, D.C.: Council of Graduate Schools.

———. 1977. *Proceedings of the Seventeenth Annual Meeting*. Washington, D.C.: Council of Graduate Schools.

Downey, Bernard J. 1979. "What Is the Assessment of Quality?" In *Proceedings on the Conference on the Assessment of Quality of Master's Programs*, by Council of Graduate Schools. College Park: University of Maryland.

Doyle, Richard J. 1979. "The Results of Graduate External Degree Programs: Some Emerging Patterns." *Alternative Higher Education* 4:48–60.

Eells, Walter C. 1963. *Degrees in Higher Education*. Washington, D.C.: Center for Applied Research in Education.

Eells, Walter C., and Harold A. Haswell. 1960. *Academic Degrees: Earned and Honorary Degrees Conferred by Institutions of Higher Education in the United States*, no. 28. Washington, D.C.: U.S. Office of Education.

Elder, J. P. 1959. "Reviving the Master's Degree for the Prospective College Teacher." *Journal of Higher Education* 30:133–36.

Eurich, Nell P. 1985. *Corporate Classrooms: The Learning Business*. Princeton, N.J.: Carnegie Foundation for the Advancement of Teaching.

Fisher, James L. 1979. "Establishing Quality Criteria in Master's Programs." In *Proceedings on the Conference on the Assessment of Quality of Master's Programs*, by Council of Graduate Schools. College Park: University of Maryland.

Forni, Patricia. 1987. "Nursing's Diverse Master's Programs: The State of the Art." *Nursing and Health Care* 8:71–75.

Freire, Paulo. 1985. *The Politics of Education: Culture, Power, and Liberation*. South Hadley, Mass.: Bergin and Garvey.

Geertz, Clifford. 1974. *The Interpretation of Cultures*. New York: Basic Books.

———. 1983. *Local Knowledge: Further Essays in Interpretive Anthropology*. New York: Basic Books.

Geiger, Roger L. 1986. *To Advance Knowledge: The Growth of American Research Universities, 1900–1940*. New York: Oxford University Press.

Giroux, Henry. 1988. *Schooling and the Struggle for Public Life*. Minneapolis: University of Minnesota Press.

Glazer, Judith S. 1986. *The Master's Degree: Tradition, Diversity, Innovation* (ASHE-Eric Higher Education Research Report no. 6). Washington, D.C.: Association for the Study of Higher Education.

Glazer, Nathan. 1980. "The Disciplinary and the Professional in Graduate School Education in the Social Sciences." In *The Philosophy and Future of Graduate Education*, edited by William K. Frankena. Ann Arbor: University of Michigan Press.

Grant, W. V., and Thomas D. Snyder, eds. 1983. *Digest of Educational Statistics, 1983–1984*. Washington, D.C.: Center for Education Statistics, U.S. Department of Education.

Green, Joslyn L., ed. 1987. *The Master's Degree: Jack of All Trades*. Denver, Colo.: State Higher Education Executive Officers.

Greene, David, and Jane L. David. 1981. "A Research Design for Generalizing from Multiple Case Studies." Palo Alto, Calif.: Bay Area Research Group.

Harding, Sandra. 1986. *The Science Question in Feminism.* Ithaca, N.Y.: Cornell University Press.

———. 1991. *Whose Science, Whose Knowledge: Thinking from Women's Lives.* Ithaca, N.Y.: Cornell University Press.

Hatala, Robert J. 1982. "A Problem-Solving Model of Graduate Education." In *Expanding the Missions of Graduate and Professional Education* (New Directions for Experiential Learning no. 15), edited by Frederic Jacobs and Richard J. Allen. San Francisco: Jossey-Bass.

Jacobs, Frederic. 1982. "Experiential Programs in Practice: Lessons to Be Learned." In *Expanding the Missions of Graduate and Professional Education* (New Directions for Experiential Learning no. 15), edited by Frederic Jacobs and Richard J. Allen. San Francisco: Jossey-Bass.

Jones, Howard Mumford. 1959. *One Great Society: Humane Learning in the United States.* New York: Harcourt Brace.

Kelley, Jean A., and Juanzetta Flowers. 1985. "Reaching Out: An Innovative Approach to Graduate Education in Nursing." *Journal of Professional Nursing* 1:235–43.

Kirkwood, Robert. 1985. "The Quest for Quality in Graduate Education." *Educational Record* 66:5–8.

Kondo, Dorrine. 1990. *Crafting Selves: Power, Gender, and Discourses of Identity in a Japanese Workplace.* Chicago: University of Chicago Press.

Kuh, George, John H. Schuh, and Elizabeth J. Whitt. 1991. *Involving Colleges: Successful Approaches to Fostering Student Learning and Development Outside the Classroom.* San Francisco: Jossey-Bass.

LaPidus, Jules B. 1987. "The Future of the Master's Degree in Public Master's Only Institutions." Paper presented at the Conference on Graduate Programs and Research in Public Master's-Only Institutions, Western Washington University.

Leys, Wayne A. R. 1956. "The Terminal Master's Degree." *Harvard Educational Review* 26:233–40.

Lincoln, Yvonna S. 1991. "Advancing a Critical Agenda." In *Culture and Ideology in Higher Education: Advancing a Critical Agenda,* edited by William G. Tierney. New York: Praeger.

Matchett, W. H. 1980. "Master's Degree Program in Computer Science under Contract to a Large Electronics Firm." In *Industry/University Cooperative Programs,* by Council of Graduate Schools/National Science Foundation. Washington, D.C.: Council of Graduate Schools.

Mayhew, Lewis B., and Patrick J. Ford. 1974. *Reform in Graduate and Professional Education.* San Francisco: Jossey-Bass.

Mayville, William V. 1972. *A Matter of Degree: The Setting for Contemporary Master's Programs* (AAHE-ERIC Higher Education Research Report no. 9). Washington, D.C.: American Association for Higher Education.

McCarty, Donald J. 1979. "Issues in Quality Education and the Evaluation of Nontraditional Graduate Programs." *Alternative Higher Education* 4:61–69.

McLaren, Peter. 1989. *Life in Schools: An Introduction to Critical Pedagogy in the Foundations of Education.* White Plains, N.Y.: Longman.

Millard, Richard. 1984. "Assessing the Quality of Innovative Graduate Programs." In *Keeping Graduate Programs Responsive to National Needs* (New Directions for Higher Education no. 46), edited by Michael J. Pelczar, Jr., and Lewis C. Solmon. San Francisco: Jossey-Bass.

Miller, John P. 1966. "The Master of Philosophy: A New Degree Is Born." *Journal of Higher Education* 37:377–81.

Mitroff, I. I., and R. H. Kilmann. 1978. *Methodological Approaches to Social Science.* San Francisco: Jossey-Bass.

Morrison, Samuel, E., ed. 1930. *Development of Harvard University, 1869–1929.* Cambridge: Harvard University Press.

Nash, Nancy S., and Elizabeth M. Hawthorne. 1987. *Formal Recognition of Employer-Sponsored Instruction* (ASHE-ERIC Higher Education Research Report no. 3). Washington, D.C.: Association for the Study of Higher Education.

National Center for Education Statistics (NCES). U.S. Department of Education. 1991. *The Condition of Education, 1991,* vol. 2: *Postsecondary Education.* Washington, D.C.

Neumann, Anna, and Estela M. Bensimon. 1990. "Constructing the Presidency: College Presidents' Images of Their Leadership Roles: A Comparative Study." *Journal of Higher Education* 61:678–701.

Ness, Frederic W., and Benjamin D. James. 1962. *Graduate Study in the Liberal Arts College.* Washington, D.C.: Association of American Colleges.

Nicholson, Morris. 1982. "The Association of Media-based Continuing Education for Engineers." In *Recent Developments in Graduate Programs,* by Council of Graduate Schools. Washington, D.C.: Council of Graduate Schools and the Graduate Record Examinations Board.

Oakeshott, Michael. 1962. *Rationalism in Politics.* New York: Basic Books.

Palmer, Parker J. 1983. *To Know as We Are Known.* San Francisco: Harper Collins.

Pelczar, Michael J., Jr. 1979. "Deliberations of the Council of Graduate Schools of the United States on the Master's Degree." In *Proceedings on the Conference on the Assessment of Quality of Master's Programs,* by Council of Graduate Schools, College Park: University of Maryland.

Pelczar, Michael J., Jr., and Carol Frances. 1984. "Graduate Education: Past Performance and Future Direction." In *Keeping Graduate Programs Responsive to National Needs* (New Directions for Higher Education no. 46), edited by Michael J. Pelczar, Jr., and Lewis C. Solmon. San Francisco: Jossey-Bass.

Petracchi, Helen E., and Melvin Morgenbesser. 1989. "The 'VCR Semester': An Innovative Approach to Social Work Education." Paper presented at the Thirty-fifth Annual Meeting of the Council of Social Work Education, Chicago.

Radar, Frank J. 1982. *Innovative Graduate Programs Directory.* Saratoga, N.Y.: Empire State College.

Rashdall, Hastings. 1895. *The Universities of Europe in the Middle Ages.* 3 vols. Oxford: Oxford University Press.

Reilly, Dorothy E. 1980. *One Approach to Master's Education in Nursing* (Publication ser. 80, no. 1). Washington, D.C.: American Association of Colleges of Nursing.

Rosaldo, Renato. 1989. *Culture and Truth: The Remaking of Social Analysis.* Boston: Beacon Press.

Rudolph, Frederick. 1962. *The American College and University: A History.* New York: Vintage Books.

Skaggs, Betty. 1983. "Computer-Video Interactive Systems: Role in Nursing Education." In *Nursing in the Year 2000* (Proceedings of a Symposium at West Virginia University), edited by Joan S. Bilitski and Margaret C. Z. Taylor. Morgantown: West Virginia University Press.

Slichter, Charles S. 1927. " 'Debunking' the Master's Degree." *Journal of Proceedings* and *Addresses of the Twenty-ninth Annual Conference of the Association of American Universities* 29:107–11.

Smith, Dorothy E. 1990. *The Conceptual Practices of Power: A Feminist Sociology of Knowledge.* Boston: Northeastern University Press.

Snell, John L. 1965. "The Master's Degree." In *Graduate Education Today,* edited by Everett Walters. Washington, D.C.: American Council on Education.

Spencer, Donald S. 1986. "The Master's Degree in Transition." *Communicator* 19:1–3, 10, 12.

Spurr, Stephen H. 1970. *Academic Degree Structures: Innovative Approaches.* New York: McGraw-Hill.

Stewart, David W., and Henry A. Spille. 1988. *Diploma Mills: Degrees of Fraud.* New York: American Council on Education and Macmillan.

Storr, Richard J. 1953. *The Beginnings of Graduate Education in America.* Chicago: University of Chicago Press.

———. 1973. *The Beginning of the Future: A Historical Approach to Graduate Education in the Arts and Sciences.* New York: McGraw-Hill.

Thomas, Calvin. 1910. "The Degree of Master of Arts." *Journal of Proceedings and Addresses of the Twelfth Annual Conference of the Association of American Universities* 12:34–50.

Tierney, William G. 1989a. "Cultural Politics and the Curriculum in Postsecondary Education." *Journal of Education* 1:72–88.

———. 1989b. *Curricular Landscapes, Democratic Vistas: Transformative Leadership in Higher Education.* New York: Praeger.

Toombs, William. 1973. "Radical Surgery on the Master's Degree." *Educational Record* 54:147–53.

Veysey, Laurence R. 1965. *The Emergence of the American University.* Chicago: University of Chicago Press.

Walters, Everett. 1965. "The Rise of Graduate Education." In *Graduate Education Today,* edited by Everett Walters. Washington, D.C.: American Council on Education.

Weber, Max. 1947. *The Theory of Social and Economic Organization.* New York: Oxford University Press.

Weis, Lois. 1985. *Between Two Worlds: Black Students in an Urban Community College.* Boston: Routledge and Kegan Paul.

Wertsch, James U. 1991. *Voices of the Mind: A Sociocultural Approach to Mediated Action.* Cambridge: Harvard University Press.

Whaley, W. G. 1966. "American Academic Degrees." *Educational Record* 47:525–37.

Wolfe, Douglas E., and Eugene T. Byrne. 1980. "An Experiential M.B.A. Program: Results of an Experiment." In *Developing Experiential Learning Programs for Professional Education* (New Directions for Experiential Learning no. 8), edited by Eugene T. Byrne and Douglas E. Wolfe. San Francisco: Jossey-Bass.

Zumeta, William, and Lewis C. Solmon. 1982. "Professions Education." In *Encyclopedia of Educational Research,* 5th ed., edited by Harold E. Mitzel. New York: Free Press.